REAL ESTATE
Market Analysis

A CASE STUDY
APPROACH

Adrienne Schmitz

Deborah L. Brett

**Urban Land
Institute**

About ULI—the Urban Land Institute

ULI—the Urban Land Institute is a nonprofit education and research institute that is supported by its members. Its mission is to provide responsible leadership in the use of land in order to enhance the total environment.

ULI sponsors education programs and forums to encourage an open international exchange of ideas and sharing of experiences; initiates research that anticipates emerging land use trends and issues and proposes creative solutions based on that research; provides advisory services; and publishes a wide variety of materials to disseminate information on land use and development. Established in 1936, the Institute today has more than 16,000 members and associates from more than 50 countries representing the entire spectrum of the land use and development disciplines.

Richard M. Rosan
President

ULI Project Staff

Rachelle L. Levitt
Senior Vice President, Policy and Practice
Publisher

Gayle Berens
Vice President, Real Estate Development Practice

Adrienne Schmitz
Director, Residential Community Development
Project Director

Nancy H. Stewart
Director, Book Program

Laura Glassman
Publications Professionals LLC
Copy Editor

Betsy VanBuskirk
Art Director
Cover Design

Jeanne Berger Design
Book Design/Layout

Diann Stanley-Austin
Director, Publishing Operations

Joan E. Campbell
Information Center Manager

Cover photograph: Christian Hoehn/STONE

Recommended bibliographic listing:
Schmitz, Adrienne, and Deborah L. Brett. *Real Estate Market Analysis: A Case Study Approach.* Washington, D.C.: ULI–the Urban Land Institute, 2001.

ULI Catalog Number: M28
International Standard Book Number: 0-87420-868-8
Library of Congress Card Number: 2001090212

© Copyright 2001 by ULI—the Urban Land Institute
1025 Thomas Jefferson Street, N.W.
Suite 500 West
Washington, D.C. 20007-5201

Third Printing, 2004

About the Authors

Adrienne Schmitz

Adrienne Schmitz is director of residential community development at ULI—the Urban Land Institute. She is responsible for developing programs and publications relating to urban and suburban community development and the new urbanism. Schmitz was the primary author of the *Multifamily Housing Development Handbook*, editor and a contributing author of *Trends and Innovations in Master-Planned Communities*, and project director for *Density by Design*. She is currently working on the second edition of the *Residential Development Handbook*. Schmitz was the editor in chief of *Multifamily Trends*, a quarterly magazine for the multifamily housing industry. Before joining ULI, Schmitz was a market research consultant to real estate developers and home builders. She holds a master's degree in urban planning from the University of Virginia.

Deborah L. Brett

Deborah Brett has been a real estate consultant since 1973. She conducts feasibility studies, prepares market analyses, and analyzes economic and demographic trends for residential and commercial properties throughout the United States. Brett formed an independent consulting practice (Deborah L. Brett & Associates) in 1992. The firm is located in the Princeton, New Jersey, area. Previously, she served as senior vice president and national consulting director of Real Estate Research Corporation in Chicago.

Brett has been widely published in professional journals and real estate business periodicals. She is also a regular contributor to books published by ULI, of which she has been a member since 1979. Brett holds the AICP designation of the American Institute of Certified Planners, and was elected to Ely Chapter of Lambda Alpha, the real estate and land economics honorary society in 1990. She holds a master's degree in urban and regional planning from the University of Illinois at Urbana—Champaign.

Case Study Authors

Multifamily Housing: Colinas Gateway
G. Ronald Witten
Witten Advisors
Dallas, Texas

For-Sale Subdivision Housing: The McCall Tract
Adrienne Schmitz
ULI–the Urban Institute
Washington, D.C.

A Master-Planned Community: Silver Knolls
John A. Walker
Legg Mason Real Estate Services
Bethesda, Maryland

Downtown Housing: Old Town Square
Janet Smith-Heimer
Bay Area Economics
Berkeley, California

Office Building Purchase: Suburban Chicago
Tsilah Burman
CB Richard Ellis Investors
Los Angeles, California

Warehouse Property: Valwood
Marvin Christensen, with
    Asieh Mansour
RREEF Funds
San Francisco, California

Flex/R&D Property: Peachtree Industrial Park
Steve Laposa
PricewaterhouseCoopers
Denver, Colorado

A Value-Retailing Center: La Cantera
Mark E. Kissel
Kissel Consulting Group
Rockville, Maryland

Street Retail: Granby Street District, Downtown Norfolk
H. Blount Hunter
H. Blount Hunter Retail & Real
    Estate Research Company
Norfolk, Virginia

Retail Entertainment Center: The Lake at Riverdale
Jill Bensley
JB Research Company
Ojai, California

Town Center: Wilanow, Warsaw, Poland
Anne B. Frej
ULI–the Urban Land Institute
Washington, D.C.

A New Hotel: Downtown Austin
John M. Keeling
PKF Consulting
Houston, Texas

Mixed-Use Development: El Toro Military Base Reuse
Emma Tyaransen
The Concord Group
Newport Beach, California

Other Contributors and Reviewers

Other Contributors

Smiti Kumar
Consultant
Atlanta, Georgia

Richard Ward
Development Strategies
St. Louis, Missouri

Reviewers

William Becker
The William E. Becker
  Organization
Teaneck, New Jersey

Lewis Bolan
Bolan Smart Associates, Inc.
Washington, D.C.

Richard Gollis
The Concord Group
Newport Beach, California

Valerie Kretchmer
Valerie S. Kretchmer Associates,
  Inc.
Evanston, Illinois

Robert Lefenfeld
Real Property Research Group, Inc.
Columbia, Maryland

Preface

"If you build it they will come." Many real estate projects have relied on this familiar Hollywood axiom. But in the real world of bricks and mortar, the economic success of any real estate development hinges on its market potential. Developers must fully understand who their tenants or buyers are, and how to satisfy them with the right product at the right location and for the right price. It is the market analyst's job to identify and analyze all of the factors relating to the market so that educated decisions can be made by the developer.

Real Estate Market Analysis was conceived as a practical guide for analyzing the market potential of real estate development. Other textbooks on this topic have emphasized economic theory and mathematical formulas, but many instructors and practitioners have expressed interest in a different kind of book—with a more hands-on approach.

The Urban Land Institute often relies on case studies as instructional tools, and we believed that case studies would indeed provide a good basis for teaching market analysis. We assembled a group of 13 practitioners who provided sample case studies representing a range of real estate product types and situations, such as developing a new apartment complex, purchasing an existing office building, revitalizing an urban retail core, and preparing a flex/R & D building for resale. The case studies also depict a range of methods for analyzing real estate markets, including the most straightforward analysis of demand and supply data, as well as more qualitative

techniques such as focus group analysis. From these examples, students should learn a wide variety of methods and their applications.

This book is organized around real estate product types. Chapter 1, Understanding Real Estate Market Analysis, introduces the topic, discussing who uses market analysis and how they use it, as well as how it fits into the feasibility and development process. Chapter 2, Basic Approach to Real Estate Market Analysis, explains the nuts and bolts of how to collect and organize data and analyze demand and supply.

Chapter 3, Residential Development, begins the more specific discussions based on product types. The chapter deals with rental and for-sale residential products. Chapter 4, Office and Industrial Development, discusses the continuum of office and industrial, flex, and research and development product types. Chapter 5 covers retail development, and Chapter 6 covers hotels and resorts. Chapter 7, Mixed-Use Development, looks at the synergies and complexities of mixing uses in a project. Finally, a list of sources and a glossary are included in the appendix.

Please note that the case studies included in each of the chapters have been condensed from their original versions to provide as much instructive material as possible within the framework of a textbook. Actual market analysis reports may be considerably more detailed and lengthy than the summaries provided here. In some cases, however, market analyses may be quite short, depending on the requirements of the client, the stage of the development process, and the size and value of the project.

This book is intended for university students in schools of planning, architecture, real estate, and business. It is also a useful tool for individuals starting out in real estate development or shifting to a different discipline within the real estate development field.

Many people were involved in the production of this textbook. We are most indebted to the authors of the case studies, who rewrote their market studies to fit the format of this book. Their work forms the nucleus of the material. We also want to thank the contributors who wrote parts of chapters, and the reviewers, who provided valuable comments on the early manuscript. Finally, ULI staff members deserve recognition. Thanks to Gayle Berens, Nancy Stewart, Betsy Van Buskirk, Diann Stanley-Austin, and Joan Campbell for their efforts in seeing this book through to publication.

Adrienne Schmitz
Deborah Brett

Table of Contents

REAL ESTATE
Market Analysis
A CASE STUDY APPROACH

Winthrop Square, a mixed-use development in Cambridge, Massachusetts.

Chapter 1

Understanding Real Estate Market Analysis

Real estate market analysis provides guidance for the many decision makers—both private and public sector—involved in real estate development. It is an ongoing process that provides information during the predevelopment, acquisition, development, marketing, and disposition of property. Large fortunes have been made and lost in real estate development, and the goal of market analysis is to minimize the risks and maximize opportunity to developers and investors by providing analysis that is as timely and accurate as possible.

Private sector real estate developers have a public sector partner in every deal. Government, particularly at the local level, regulates the development process and has a vested interest in the product. The public sector's goals are to ensure that new developments are appropriate for the community and that they meet the needs of the public. Market analysis can provide some of the tools to help meet those goals. Often, however, public officials become involved with issues of density, design, and traffic, and fail to consider whether a proposed development has the market potential to succeed.

Equally important, the developer can use a market study to determine what project types will gain the support of public participants. The market analyst should investigate both regulatory requirements and the attitudes of neighbors and public officials. Market research not only indicates ways for the developer to win public approvals and entitlements, but also it guides the project's size and design.

Beyond convincing lenders and investors that a project is feasible, market research is useful in planning and designing a project. When the target market for the proposed project has been accurately identified, the development can be shaped to meet the needs of that market. Location, design, quality, pricing, and marketing strategy can all be programmed in accordance with the market's demands.

What Is Real Estate Market Analysis?

Regardless of the type of development being examined, every market study addresses three basic questions:

1. Will there be users to rent or buy the proposed project?
2. How quickly, and at what rent or price, will the proposed project be absorbed in the market?
3. How might the project be planned or marketed to make it more competitive in its market?

Real estate market analysis is the identification and study of demand and supply, usually for a particular product. On the demand side are the users: the buyers or renters of real estate. The supply side is made up of competitors: both existing properties and those that are expected to enter the market before or during the same period as the subject project. Market analysis is the synthesis of supply and demand analyses as they relate to the decision-making process. A critical flaw of many market analyses is that they present data without analysis.

Because real estate exists at a fixed location, supply and demand are location specific, most often in

Successful retail development depends on finding the appropriate tenant mix to serve the market area demographics.

an area surrounding the subject property. The "market area" is the geographical region from which the majority of demand comes and in which the majority of competitors are located. In some cases, the two are similar or even identical, but many exceptions exist.

The word "market" can be used in a variety of ways. Business people usually use the word to refer

to different ways of grouping customers, including geographic location (the Pacific Northwest, the Midwest), demographic profiles (urban professionals, empty nesters), and product types (family restaurants, high-fashion apparel). Economists refer to both buyers and sellers when describing markets in terms of supply and demand, whereas marketing professionals (the people who try to convince us to buy a Buick instead of a Lexus) consider the sellers as the industry and the buyers as the market.

In real estate, product refers to property type (e.g., apartment buildings, offices, or warehouses), which is further distinguished by size or configuration, quality, and services. "Quality" relates to the project's architecture, construction, layout, and finishes. "Services" represent the developer's commitment to ongoing property management, such as providing security and janitorial services, or, in the case of residential development, it might mean a master-planned community with maintenance services and planned activities.

Real estate markets are categorized by property types: office, retail, residential, hotel, and industrial, among others. Each property type can be further segmented into smaller markets based on categories within each type, locational factors, and price ranges. Market segmentation is the process of identifying and analyzing submarkets of a larger group of property markets. For example, hotels can be subdivided into luxury resort properties, downtown conference hotels, roadside motels, and so on. Retail markets can include regional malls, strip centers, outlets, and urban street retail. Residential can be segmented into single family, attached, and multifamily as well as for-sale or rental properties. Narrowly defining the market segment helps to fine-tune the analysis.

Most real estate market analyses examine both the market potential and the marketability, or competitiveness, of the proposed project. The market potential analysis examines aggregate demand and supply data, which assist the developer in understanding the effective demand for and supply of space by user group. Demand is, by far, the more difficult half of the equation. Projecting how much demand exists, where it comes from, and how to satisfy it requires a mix of research, experience, and intuition. Demand analysis considers the following data:

- Population, households, and demographic characteristics;
- Income, affordability, and purchasing power;
- Employment, by industry or occupation;
- Migration and commuting patterns;
- Other factors, depending on the type of real estate development being studied.

Analysis of the supply of competing projects takes into consideration the following factors:

- Inventory of existing space or units;
- Vacancy rates and characteristics of vacant stock;
- Recent absorption of space, including types of tenants or buyers;
- Projects under construction and proposed;
- Market rents or sale prices and how they differ across locations and by quality of product;
- Features, functions, and advantages of existing and proposed projects;
- Lease or sale terms and concessions (free rent, bonus features, tenant improvement allowances, etc.).

The marketability portion of the analysis usually assesses the property's demand attributes. Thus, the developer can adapt the real estate product, price, and merchandising appeal to better fit the market and to attract a group of users with particular preferences. Marketability analysis usually includes profiles of the user to be served by the development; the product's features, amenities, and services; and the pricing strategy.

The marketability analysis usually goes beyond establishing the demand for the type of product being considered and determines whether the proposed project will be able to capture the desired share of the market. Will it be competitive within its market in terms of value and quality? The analysis may study whether the proposed development responds to demand for a particular type of product that existing facilities in the area have failed to meet. In a retail market, for example, demand unsatisfied by local facilities either leaks or flows to retailers located outside the immediate market, remains pent up, or is diverted to other purposes. Or the analysis may indicate that the project under consideration is not responding to market demand because local demand is already being met or will be met by projects in the pipeline, or because the proposed project is not properly targeted to meet the specific needs of the local market.

Market analysis forms the basis for decisions regarding location and site, size, design and quality, features, target audience, pricing strategies, and so on. The most detailed type of market analysis is usually performed as part of an overall feasibility study. The price and absorption data that result from real estate market analysis form the basis for the cash flow portion of the feasibility analysis, which can answer many of the following questions: How many square feet should be built? For what rents can it be leased? How many houses can be sold over what period of time? How can an office building be repositioned to become more competitive? What is a viable selling price for a parcel of raw land? What cities should be included in a chain store's expansion?

Although the market analysis examines statistical trends and projections of sales, rents, vacancies, and absorption in the market area, nonquantitative analysis is becoming increasingly important. Qualitative characteristics, such as how certain market segments perceive a themed retail center, or what design features appeal to homebuyers in certain communities, are increasingly being examined through surveys, psychographic research, focus groups, and cluster-group analysis. As real estate markets become more and more segmented and specialized, traditional statistical models and formulas, which rely on large data pools, do not work; therefore, it becomes necessary to rely on more qualitative analysis.

When developers enter a new market where they have little or no experience, they obviously assume added risk. To limit risk, developers must pay special attention to assessing their position in the marketplace as well as to the realism of their goals and objectives. Solid market analysis helps the developer illuminate the unknowns of a new market and identify a project's potential for success.

A strong overall market does not necessarily equate with a good opportunity for development. Neither does a weak market mean that a good idea cannot be implemented. In-depth market analysis can reveal opportunities that may not be readily apparent. Understanding the market is a necessary prerequisite to generating ideas. Poor implementation can undermine the most promising opportunities in any market, but flawless implementation cannot redeem a bad idea.

Generation of Ideas

To keep abreast of short- and long-term aspects of the market, real estate professionals must keep up with national and regional market trends and forecasts and talk to people familiar with the national and local economies. The further into the future an analyst must project, the less reliable the projections and the greater the probability of error because of changing macroeconomics. Because real estate development is a relatively slow process, market analysis must continue throughout the entire process, monitoring changes as they occur.

Knowledge about both supply and demand is necessary background for the generation of ideas, which is the initial stage of the development process. Knowledge should begin with a broad, national picture, because financing is national (and increasingly international), some tenants are national, and some developers are national. Knowledge should also include a regional, a local, and, depending on the nature of the project, a neighborhood picture of current conditions. At the local level, developers need to know how comparable properties are performing and what trends are emerging. In most instances, local market and economic conditions are a more important part of the market analysis than macro trends.

Different from Toothpaste

Classic marketing theory helps bring greater structure and discipline to real estate development. The real estate product, however, differs substantially from standard mass-produced and nationally advertised products. Four major differences predominate.

- The real estate product is highly differentiated. It serves several needs of different space users and is produced in more variable styles and price ranges than most common household products. Above all, the real estate product is distinguished by the importance of location. Unlike all other products, people cannot take real estate home. Instead, the customer must move to the product, which offers a location that is unique to the specific product.
- Constraints on supply are far more variable. Unlike mass manufacturing, the local vagaries of site availability and political entitlements often control the volume of competing supply and direct the developer's opportunities. Supply is further constrained by the sheer time and expense involved in its production.
- Market data are much less certain in the case of real estate. Developers lack the finely structured data banks of corporate America, although recent years have seen significant improvements in data sources. Nevertheless, the uniqueness of different locations and market niches, combined with the volatility of local economies and construction cycles, implies that developers must work hard to know their markets.
- Most projects must be custom tailored and cannot be mass produced or mass marketed. Without the economies of scale of a Procter & Gamble or a Ford Motor Company, developers cannot create their products as efficiently as corporate giants.

Who Uses Market Analysis?

Developers can no longer rely on instinct to decide what to build or to assure prospective lenders that the project will be successful. A rigorous market study early in the process stimulates development ideas, improves initial concepts, and serves to control risk. Reexamining the market in greater depth helps to refine concepts as the development plan begins to take shape. Developers are not the only players who benefit from market analysis. Research may be undertaken for the benefit of the investor, the lender, or the community whose well-being will be affected by the proposed project.

- **Developers and builders:** Market analysis is used by the developer of a project to determine whether a location is suitable for development and what product best meets the demands of the market. The market analysis is usually part of the package submitted to the lender(s) to provide documentation that the project is financially feasible. A developer might also use market analysis later in the process to fine-tune the product or to find out what went wrong—why the product is not selling or leasing as expected.
- **Investors and lenders:** Funding sources rely on market analysis to assess the project's financial viability, ensuring a sound basis for a loan or investment. Federally backed lenders require that a market study be performed as part of due diligence.
- **Designers:** Architects, planners, interior designers, and others involved in design must understand the target market for a development so that the project's styling, amenities, features, unit sizes, and so on, will be suitable for that market. For example, an office building designed to appeal to startup high-tech firms might look entirely different from one designed for large, well-established law firms.
- **Marketing managers:** Like designers, marketers must formulate their sales strategies, advertising campaigns, interior merchandising, public relations, and other promotional efforts to reach the target market.
- **Local governments**: A market analysis might help determine whether a proposed project will be accepted by the public and will serve the public's needs. In jurisdictions where fiscal impact analysis (a method that determines how much financial benefit or deficit a development will bring to the jurisdiction) is conducted, the market analysis provides key information for the analysis. Such information might also help to determine development impact fees that are sometimes assessed.
- **Tenants and occupants:** The companies that lease or purchase retail, office, or other commercial space might have a type of market analysis prepared as part of their site-selection process. The analysis might be at the macro level, to determine which cities the tenant should consider, or at the micro level, to examine suitability of specific properties for leasing.
- **Sellers, purchasers, and landowners:** Generally, transactions are backed by an appraisal, but sometimes a market analysis report is completed either as part of the appraisal or instead of one. Market research can identify an appropriate selling price for a completed project or a parcel of land. The value of raw land is determined by constructing a market analysis of a likely completed project, then extrapolating the value of the land based on the value of the completed project.
- **Property managers:** Managers use market analysis to gain the necessary insights and information for repositioning an existing property. Repositioning might involve a complete renovation or minor upgrades, depending in part on what the market dictates.

How Does Market Analysis Fit into the Development Process?

Market analysis is a crucial part of the initial feasibility study for a real estate project, but it does not end there. Market research continues to play an important role in shaping the project throughout its development and management phases. Market analysts are commonly consulted for repositioning strategies after a project is up and running and the developer realizes that absorption does not meet projections. As many types of market analysis exist as variations in development projects, stages of development, and interests being served.

At the earliest stages of development, an analyst might be asked to study one or several metropolitan areas for development potential (sometimes called "market screening"). Then the analyst will focus in on a submarket and finally seek out a site that is most appropriate for the proposed development concept. But given the limited availability of developable land today, it is more common for a developer to have a specific site in mind and to ask that the site be studied.

If the site proves viable, the market analyst might provide a basis for determining the value of the site so that a purchase price can be negotiated. Or this valuation might be performed by an appraiser. Sometimes the analyst investigates the development climate of the jurisdiction. That is, will the proposed project likely meet with public acceptance and gain the necessary approvals in a timely manner? Are utilities readily available? Might other difficulties slow

Figure 1-1
Market Studies: Clients and Their Objectives

Purpose or Objective	Developer	Equity Investor/ Partner	Buyer	Seller	Lender	Redevelopment Agency	Housing Finance or Economic Development Authority	Tenant/Owner	Realtor/Broker
Market overview for use in brochures and publications	X					X	X		X
Input for corporate location/relocation/expansion decisions								X	
Devising/revising real estate investment strategies	X	X							
Product planning, design, pricing, phasing	X								
Obtaining zoning or other government approvals	X					X			X
Input/assumptions for cash flow analysis	X	X	X		X				
Loan application support	X				X				
As part of a sales offering package				X		X			X
Acquisition due diligence		X						X	
Lender due diligence					X	X	X		
In ongoing asset management		X						X	

or hinder the development process? Some market analysts prefer not to get involved in such nonmarket research, leaving it to planners, engineers, or others.

Further refining of the analyses would reveal specifics about potential users (tenants or buyers) and their demands in terms of product niche and pricing. After the project is developed, a market analyst might be asked to assess the project's sales or rental performance. Is retail space renting as quickly as the market allows? Are the office rents in line with the market? Should the homebuilder add a higher-priced product type? Why is a nearby competitor selling faster, or for higher prices, than the subject project?

Savvy developers not only beat the bushes for new customers to stimulate demand, but also manage demand—its level, timing, and composition—to achieve a company's objectives. The market analyst needs to stay abreast of emerging land planning and design trends to recommend the most competitive and appropriate product type.

For example, sometimes developers can effectively create a market for a new product type. The reality is that they are not creating a new market, but exploiting an existing one that has not been satisfied in other ways. Dissatisfaction with existing space occurs whenever new needs are discovered or, more simply, whenever standards are raised. The most typical example occurs when the design of a more prestigious development—with all the latest features and finishing details—is unveiled. The notion of what constitutes the most desirable office space, shopping center, or housing can change overnight, forcing owners and managers of existing projects to upgrade their own buildings or lower their price points. For example, a Class A office building that does not meet the most current standards will fall to Class B, which means less-prestigious tenants and lower rents.

In the 1970s, shopping centers had low ceilings and dark, earth-tone finishes. By the 1980s, that look had given way to light, airy atriums. As a result, older centers either lost status and prestige retailers or had to be renovated to compete with newer standards. Residential development cycles through trends at a faster pace than other types of development. A new style or feature can quickly render existing units obsolete in the minds of homebuyers or renters, thus creating an instant market for new, more stylish units.

Market research provides the input for analyzing marketing opportunities and selecting target markets. Ideally, the development team never stops gathering market intelligence, continually using new information to reposition the project as change occurs.

The Feasibility Study

The results of the market analysis lead to the core assumptions used in the financial feasibility analysis for a real estate project. A developer must be able to defend cash flow projections with a rational system of analysis and data inputs to legitimize the project's feasibility, demonstrating that there will be tenants or buyers, that rental rates or sale prices will return a sufficient cash flow, and that the type of product proposed is what the market desires.

The feasibility study is the formal demonstration that a proposed project is viable. A typical feasibility study includes an executive summary, a market analysis, preliminary drawings, cost estimates, information about terms and sources of financing, government considerations, environmental assessments, and a determination of the financial feasibility of the project.

The key components of the feasibility study follow. Together they provide the documentation for determining whether the project is financially feasible.

- Concept and target market for the project, from the big picture down to an absorption schedule for the particular market niche—progressing from region to city to neighborhood to site;
- A careful enumeration of the target market—number of people, their preferences, their income—tied to the specific idea;
- Identification of appropriate comparable properties (the competition) along with the major features, functions, and advantages of each;
- The economic performance of comparables;
- The foregoing information tied into a discounted cash flow model;
- A sensitivity analysis to move from feasible to optimal, with an individual evaluation of each component of the plan;

- A review of risks in the realistic configuration, with appropriate risk-control techniques;
- Confirmation that the project is feasible for each participant.

Depending on the size and complexity of the development, the feasibility study can vary dramatically in length, scope, and cost. At one extreme, if the project is a small neighborhood shopping center in an established area and is to use architectural drawings from a previously built project using the same contractor and lender, then the feasibility analysis is a simple activity that involves applying the market information for the new submarket to a proven course of action. In other words, new market data are used to project rent and absorption, with most other factors refined from previous developments. In such a simple case, developers often choose to perform the feasibility study with in-house staff at limited cost.

This simple case contrasts sharply with a 5,000-acre planned community that includes a full array of housing types, retail town centers, and an office park. Such a community requires extensive infrastructure as well as aboveground construction. Because the project is likely to take many years to complete, and upfront costs are considerable, the risks are considerably higher and the recognition of long-term trends is more important than for a simple project—even for designing the first stage of the project.

A concept for a complex, expensive, long-term project often results in a complex, expensive feasibility study that involves a team of outside professionals, such as architects, land planners, soils engineers, hazardous-waste experts, public relations consultants, marketers, and so on. The developer must coordinate all the professionals and ensure that they are all talking about precisely the same project so that collectively they can determine its feasibility. Likewise, the market analysis for such a project is more complex. Multiple land uses and types of occupants must be considered, a longer time frame must be projected, and a wider array of product types, with synergies and spillovers of demand, come into play.

The market study is a crucial item in a feasibility analysis. It analyzes all the economic trends that were initially identified during refinement of the idea. These trends are now formally brought to bear on the existing local situation as the analyst projects an absorption schedule for the project, with which the market study usually concludes. How many units at what price over what time period will the target market be likely to absorb? It is necessary to segment the market carefully by defining all the features, functions, and benefits of comparable projects to be able to predict the overall absorption rate for the market segment. The developer can then attach value to the distinctive features of the subject property and compare it with the market to estimate the proposed development's capture rate and expected rents. The data culled from the market analysis provide the assumptions for the cash flow analysis.

Because various state and federal regulatory agencies oversee the lenders who bear a portion of the risk in major developments, financial institutions usually require feasibility studies when they underwrite a loan. An outside feasibility study prepared by a well-respected firm meets this requirement. Some lenders prefer to prepare their own analysis, either as backup, or instead of an outside study.

Although the government hoped to end by regulation the unsubstantiated assertions of financial feasibility and property values that led to many financial disasters during the 1980s, lenders now bear much of the burden in evaluating the accuracy of feasibility reports. Regulators no longer spell out what lenders must demand of appraisers and market analysts. Rather, lenders are required to demand whatever analyses are necessary in a particular situation, shifting the burden of proof to the lender. If they do not require thorough research by an independent party and a loan subsequently goes into default, then the government regulators will fault the lender for not performing sufficiently detailed due diligence.

The New Demographics and the Need for Qualitative Research

Not so long ago, it was commonly assumed that market segments could be defined by age and income brackets and that, within those brackets, everyone was fairly homogeneous. It was assumed that people looked and acted the same and were attracted to the same product types. Middle-income shoppers always shopped at suburban malls, seniors always moved to Sunbelt golf resort communities, and law firms always leased Class A downtown office space. Of course these assumptions were never true, but today they are less true than ever. So segmented is today's demographic pie, that extensive research is required to fully understand who the market is and what it wants. Consumers are increasingly sophisticated and demanding; they will not settle for what they do not want.

According to U.S. Census Bureau projections, the American population is aging and becoming increasingly multicultural. For years, the baby boom has had

a profound effect on every kind of market, including real estate. This influence will continue as the baby boom ages into retirement and beyond. In 2000, those aged 65 and older accounted for 13 percent of the population. In 2030, they will increase to 20 percent of the population. At the same time, those aged 18 to 64 will have declined from 62 percent to 56 percent of the population. (See Table 1-1.)

Along with aging, a concurrent trend is the increasing cultural diversity of the population. (See Table 1-2.) In 2000, the non-Hispanic white population accounted for 71 percent of Americans. In 2030, that group will decline to 60 percent and, by 2050, to 53 percent of the population. Hispanic Americans in 2000 were 12 percent of the population, and that percentage is expected to grow to 19 percent by 2030 and to 24 percent by 2050. Because of increasing diversity, the 2000 census reported on an expanded number of categories of race and ethnicity. For the first time, respondents were allowed to check more than one race to indicate their racial identity, for a total of 63 possible combinations. In addition to ethnic diversity, the household unit is changing. No longer is the stereotypical family with two parents and two children the norm. In 1970, the largest household segment was such fami-

Table 1-1

The Aging of America (Percentage of Population)

Age	2000	2030
Under 18	26	24
18–64	62	56
65 and Over	13	20

Source: U.S. Census Bureau.

Table 1-2

America's Increasing Diversity (Percentage of Population)

Race	2000	2030	2050
Non-Hispanic White	71	60	53
African American	13	14	15
Hispanic	12	19	24
Asian/Pacific Islander	4	7	9

Source: U.S. Census Bureau.

lies, constituting about 45 percent of households. By 2010, this segment will shrink to about 29 percent, while people living alone will make up an equal share of households—28 percent, up from about 18 percent in 1970.[1] (See Table 1-3.)

Population shifts will be geographic as well. The western states will gain a larger share of population, whereas the population living in the Northeast and Midwest will decline. These significant shifts all need to be considered and understood by those who provide homes and places of work, play, and commerce.

Psychographics: The Search for Segmentation

Developers seek to identify market segments—whether defined socially, spatially, or behaviorally. Historically, real estate development has been a spatially segmented industry: most developers worked in only a few locations and constructed only one or two product types. Since the 1950s, however, developers' geographic scope and product mix have increased with the size of their companies. The proliferation of REITs in the 1990s further broadened the scope of both developers and their real estate portfolios. Now, in addition to serving a variety of geographically and functionally segmented markets, developers search for important socioeconomic and behavioral distinctions among potential customers. Research into these different factors identifies target market segments that usually consist of a distinctive combination of people, lifestyles, purchasing power, and place. Identifying new markets or niches within established markets is a crucial application of marketing research to real estate development.

Sometimes called "psychographics," this branch of market research studies lifestyles and other psychological characteristics of demographic cohorts.

Understanding psychographics allows for fine-tuning of product niches to meet narrow and specialized market segments. Chapter 2 explains focus groups and surveys as ways to understand psychographics.

Political Homework: Marketing for Entitlements

Understanding the market for a real estate product takes time and careful analysis. But satisfying the market carries the developer only so far. It is useless to determine the demand for a product if the developer cannot gain approval for such a product from the surrounding residents and the local government. A market analyst should understand the development climate in a jurisdiction. Developers must satisfy at least some of the needs of neighbors and regulators and should consider government their partner. A community will ultimately alter the development approval rules to the detriment of the project owner if a project does not serve the community well. However, few developers want such information included in the analyst's report because they do not want community issues to be identified in writing.

Developers need to make certain that their projects respond to government's overall plans for the community, including plans developed by numerous community, county, regional, and state agencies. The most relevant plans are land use plans and zoning ordinances, but others that may be equally important in particular development situations include transportation, economic development, and environmental plans and policies. Local political approval is generally binding, although plans issued by higher-level agencies can be influential and should not be disregarded.

How well does the proposed project support the intent, if not the letter, of the community's general plan or of regional comprehensive plans? It is important to recognize that the plans developed by various agencies often conflict with one another and express a variety of opposing objectives. For example, local land use plans may not accommodate the economic goal of creating jobs, or the land use map may not have been updated to reflect new transportation corridors, or environmental protection may be served better by the proposed project than by alternatives in other locations. In addition, skilled developers know that the members of decision-making

---

Table 1-3

Household Types in 2010

30%	married couples without children
29%	with children under 18 (8% single parents)
28%	singles living alone
7%	other family types
5%	roommates

Source: U.S. Census Bureau.

bodies are often not of a single mind and that even individual decision makers subscribe to a variety of goals and objectives that are at times internally inconsistent.

Recognizing that the entitlement authorities represent customers to be sold on a project, experienced developers have learned that it is useful to address local authorities' needs and desires from the beginning of project design. A series of negotiations often transpires as developers seek to tailor their projects to regulators' expectations. Public relations experts recommend that developers organize their project's marketing along the lines of a political campaign to ensure neighbors' and officials' acceptance of the project. Careful research into public opinion is essential in the effort to gain such acceptance.[2] It is far better to identify and address community concerns early during the project's approval process than to face an angry audience in a public hearing before the responsible authorities. Elected officials are much more comfortable issuing approvals when the electorate supports a project.

Why Hasn't Anyone Else Thought of This?

Successful development responds to the needs of space users and, to a lesser extent, to the requirements of government and citizens or neighbors. Products, places, people, and capital add up to many areas of inquiry.

When the developers believe that they have arrived at a good choice for a proposed project, they must still ask one nagging question: Why has no other developer stumbled across this fine opportunity? Is something wrong with the idea? Why do we see the opportunity more clearly than others? Asking such a skeptical question brings added discipline to the process of market analysis. The question is especially important for developers working in a new locale; they may be less knowledgeable about local politics and local market trends even if they are more sophisticated about development in general.

As part of their research, developers must identify and recognize the competition so they can position their own product competitively to reach the target market. Better price, quality, and location are obvious attributes of competing real estate products. Only slightly less important are reputation, expertise, and financial depth.

Simply discovering a development opportunity is not enough. For the development firm to prevail, it may also need to secure the best site, to come up with the best design, to arrange the earliest loan commitment, to obtain needed entitlements, to secure the key anchor tenant, to develop the best marketing plan before other developers come up with the same idea. Most often, the successful developer integrates several key advantages and builds all decisions around a total marketing concept. When a developer follows a systematic marketing approach, an objective evaluation will likely reveal if the developer has a competitive edge and is thus well advised to proceed.

Summary

Market analysis is the investigation into needs and wants (demand) and into products that compete to satisfy those needs and wants (supply) and the synthesis and understanding of the two. Although usually thought of as formal, focused, and systematic, market analysis for generating development ideas involves a large informal component made up of experience, observation, reading, conversation, and interdisciplinary analysis. The discipline has incorporated many technological advances, but nothing takes the place of old-fashioned shoe leather fieldwork for understanding the project and its competitors. Analysts must integrate objective data and instinct born of experience. Successful developers are able to unite the rational with the intuitive. Formal knowledge of marketing principles and market research enhances the use of both faculties.

The importance of market analysis in the real estate development process, particularly in unfamiliar or highly competitive markets, cannot be overemphasized. Market analysis begins at the project's inception, when an idea first emerges to acquire a property or to develop a site, and continues through the development and eventual disposition of the project. All development projects should start with the demands of customers and satisfy those demands competitively.

Book Outline

This chapter has defined market analysis and discussed its uses and users. It has shown how market analysis fits into the development process as a way to improve decision making at each stage. Useful research can be both broad (including global, national, and regional economies and product trends) and highly focused (for example, fine-tuning the features to be included in kitchens of an apartment complex).

Subsequent chapters explain how to perform market analysis. Chapter 2 lays out the broad concepts, including delineating a market area, studying demand and supply, assessing marketability, collecting reliable data, and understanding qualitative research. Chapters 3 through 7 describe how to tailor the process to each specific product type, including how market areas differ for the various product types, what methods of analyzing supply and demand are unique to specific product types, and what kinds of data are most useful for each product type. Each of these chapters includes condensed case studies that illustrate the concepts explained in the chapter. An appendix identifies some of the public agencies and private companies that provide data for real estate market analysts.

Notes

[1]National Projection Program, Population Division, U.S. Census Bureau; Washington, D.C., www.census.gov/population/www/projections.

[2]See Debra Stein, "Taking the Guesswork out of Winning Community Support," *Urban Land,* vol. 50, no. 10 (October 1991): pp. 2–5; Debra Stein, *Winning Community Support for Land Use Projects* (Washington, D.C.: ULI–the Urban Land Institute, 1992); Debra Stein, *Making Community Meetings Work* (Washington, D.C.: ULI–the Urban Land Institute, 1996); and David Godschalk et al., *Pulling Together: A Planning and Development Consensus-Building Manual* (Washington, D.C.: ULI–the Urban Land Institute, 1994).

Pennsylvania Convention Center, Philadelphia, Pennsylvania.

Chapter 2

Basic Approach to Real Estate Market Studies

This chapter outlines a general approach to real estate market analysis, setting forth the basic tasks to be done and identifying the types of information needed to reach supportable conclusions. Details for analyzing specific property types are presented in Chapters 3 through 7, and data sources are cited in the appendix.

Defining the Market Area

One of the initial challenges facing the market analyst is to define the boundaries of the property's market area (also referred to as the "trade area"). In reality, residential and retail properties often have two market areas: one from which the majority of potential tenants or buyers will be drawn, and another in which the key competitors are located.

Trade areas for residential and retail properties are usually defined as a combination of census tracts, zip codes, transportation corridors, municipalities, or counties from which the vast majority of customers (homebuyers, apartment renters, shoppers) will be drawn. The analyst should recognize that census tracts and zip codes often do not conform to municipal boundaries, nor do they necessarily reflect neighborhood residents' sense of turf.

Preliminary studies may define the trade area based on municipal or county boundaries or may use three-, five-, or ten-mile rings to determine if the population meets a minimum threshold size. (The ring includes the area within the stated number of miles from the subject site, without taking access or natural barriers into consideration.) With demographic data

for user-specified areas readily available from private vendors (described subsequently), analysts can easily, and inexpensively, obtain information for rings. Such simple trade area definitions are useful for initial review of a market's population size or expenditure potential, but they will not accurately portray a site's likely trade area and should not be used as the market area for more in-depth studies.

The most precise trade area definition will not be a uniform size or shape, nor will it extend equally in all directions. Yet, the analyst needs to take data availability and the cost of information collection into account when drawing a study area. Also, devising an accurate market area definition will usually require visiting the site of a proposed development or acquisition.

Although analysts have traditionally been forced to approximate market areas by using census tracts, zip codes, or county boundaries because of data limitations, emerging geographic information systems (GIS) technology, or electronic mapping, is liberating real estate decision makers from relying on arbitrary boundaries. GIS is a combination of data, software, and geographic analysis that allows the creation of maps and sophisticated analysis; it has tremendous potential for real estate. Examples of GIS data include county property assessment files, geodemographic information, traffic volume counts, and projections of absorption rates. Property assessment files include all of a property's characteristics used by property tax assessors to arrive at assessed values, as well as latitude and longitude coordinates of the property. Geodemographic information includes hundreds of census-year demographic measurements, such as income, education, race, and family composition, as well as projections for present and future years.

Traffic volume count is a key data input for making judgments about commercial real estate. The most important data available are U.S. road networks in digital format. First digitized in 1990, TIGER/Line data is available from the U.S. Census Bureau. TIGER/Line data, when combined with appropriate software, allow the assignment of latitude and longitude coordinates based on a property's address. GIS software has often been referred to as a "spatial spreadsheet." Today's commercial software is user-friendly, available from a variety of sources, and relatively inexpensive.

Whether analysts are armed with elementary analysis tools or sophisticated electronic-mapping technologies, their knowledge of the market's vehicular and mass-transit patterns, natural barriers, competitive projects, and economic and demographic profiles is of critical importance in defining market areas. Key factors affecting the size and shape of the market area include the following:

- Natural features: In some cases, lakes, rivers, or mountains cannot be easily traversed. Roads might be narrow or winding, or bridges might be few and far between. Traffic congestion may be a factor. In other cases, natural features act as psychological or social barriers. ("Nobody from around here would drive halfway around the lake just to go to the supermarket.")
- Constructed barriers, such as interstate highways or railroad tracks: Infrastructure that restricts access to the site from nearby neighborhoods will limit the size of the trade area. At the same time, these improvements can expand the catchment area if they improve accessibility or shorten commutes.
- Population density: A shopping center proposed for a densely developed city neighborhood will have a much smaller market area than one proposed for a small town in a rural county.
- Political boundaries between cities and suburbs, or between school districts: Properties located in communities with low crime rates and good schools will (all other things being equal) draw from a larger trade area. This factor is more important in residential market analysis than for retail or commercial properties. However, political boundaries also determine real estate tax rates for all types of development. Tax rates can vary dramatically among municipalities in the same general area.

- Neighborhood boundaries and demographics: Household income, family composition, racial mix, and ethnicity all play a role in defining market areas for both residential and commercial properties. Community identity and insularity influence where people are willing to live, shop, or commute from.
- Type and scope of development: A large regional shopping mall or a large master-planned community draws from larger market areas than a neighborhood shopping center or a small infill residential subdivision.
- Location of competitive projects: Sometimes a market area is realigned to include certain competitive projects.

For office buildings or industrial properties, the local market area depends less on the geographic location of potential tenants than on the location of competitive buildings. Industrial and office tenants frequently move from outside the immediate community or the metropolitan area. Hotel, resort, and second-home properties also target consumers who live well beyond a metropolitan area. Demand is more dependent on transportation access (easy interstate highway or air connections) and conditions in the general economy (growth in tourism; participation in sports such as golf, tennis, or boating; increasing affluence) than on local demographics.

Primary and Secondary Trade Areas

More sophisticated residential and retail market studies define both a "primary market area" (from which 60 to 80 percent of residential or retail patronage will be captured) and "secondary market areas" that will generate the balance of demand. (In emerging markets at the fringe of development or beyond, the reverse is true.) A portion of demand will also be allocated to "inflow"—retail purchases made by tourists and other visitors who do not reside in either the primary or secondary market. This methodology is most common for regional shopping center or outlet malls, but it is also used for retirement housing.

The market study report should include a map that defines the boundaries of the primary and secondary trade areas, showing the location of the subject site, nearby interstate highways, and key arterials. (See Figure 2-1.) If the trade area includes multiple political jurisdictions, they should also be noted. Many computer mapping programs are now available that allow the user to specify boundaries, place-names, roads, and natural features.

Figure 2-1

Shopping Center Trade Areas

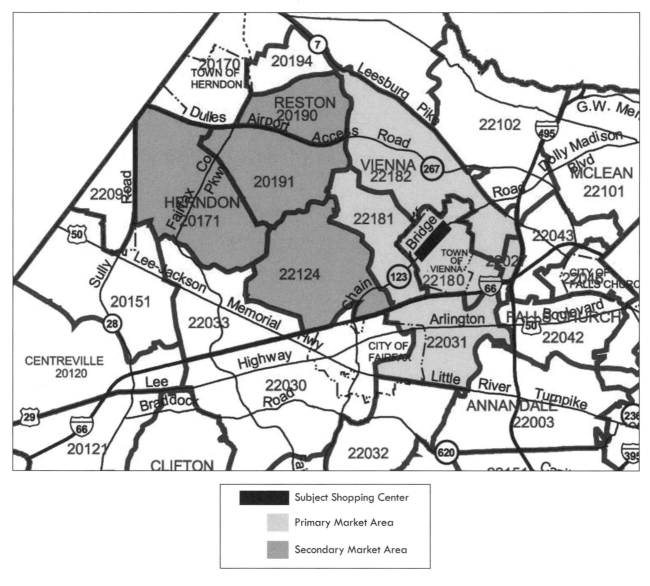

■	Subject Shopping Center
▨	Primary Market Area
▨	Secondary Market Area

Source: Fairfax County GIS and Mapping Services.

Competitive Clusters

Office and industrial land uses tend to cluster along transportation routes, at highway interchanges, or around activity centers such as airports, universities, or regional malls. For building tenants, access—to labor force, clients, customers, and suppliers—is paramount. Availability and cost of land and utilities, along with zoning and supportive local government policies, are also important factors in attracting new development. The precise number of nearby residents and their household characteristics are less important for hotel, office, and industrial projects than whether the community is stable or growing and has a good reputation in the real estate community.

Metropolitan areas have multiple office clusters, both in the central business district and at key suburban nodes. Industrial and warehouse buildings can also congregate in multiple locations—near a port or an airport, along freight rail lines, or at the junction of two interstate highways. The marketability of a proposed new office or industrial development (or the economic potential of an existing property being considered for acquisition) is examined in light of both the regional economic conditions and the performance of similar properties within the cluster or submarket. Comparative analysis of the clusters is also relevant for positioning and capture analysis across a region.

Analyzing Demand

National, regional, and local economic conditions all affect property demand, but the most important factors are local, and the study of local economics and demographics should be the major focus of the market study. Macroeconomic conditions (interest rates, inflation, job security, industrial productivity, and stability in the stock market) shape consumer confidence and business investment activity. The strength of the national economy influences whether businesses expand their space, retailers seek more store locations, families move up the housing ladder, and travelers book more hotel room nights. Even if the written report does not include detailed charts and tables, the analyst should be aware of current and future macroeconomic factors when drawing conclusions about the advisability of starting a new project or investing in an existing building.

Local economic conditions may not precisely mirror national trends. Not every metropolitan area benefits from strong growth in population and employment during an economic boom. And some communities will survive a national recession relatively unscathed. As a result, real estate market studies usually give greater weight to regional and local economic indicators than to nationwide statistics. For example, employment growth at trade area businesses that use office space (banking, insurance, legal services, business services, consulting) will be the key demand determinant for new Class A office space. The need for additional hotel rooms will, to a large extent, depend on continued growth in local tourist, convention, and business visitation.

Local market dynamics are the most important factors used for identifying sources of housing demand. Consumer demographics (population growth, household formation, age and family char-

acteristics, income, and myriad lifestyle choices) are all critical in determining how much to build, which product types will sell or rent quickly, what unit sizes to build, and which asking prices or rents are appropriate. In turn, demand for retail space is highly dependent on the location of new residential construction because households prefer to buy food and other day-to-day necessities without traveling far from home. As suburban sprawl turns farmland into subdivisions, real demand for new retail stores is generated in these newly developing areas, even if the overall metropolitan area has little or no population growth. At the same time, the need for store space declines in neighborhoods experiencing net population losses.

Economic Indicators

A review of the local economy should highlight indicators most relevant to the particular land use or property type being studied. Real estate developers and their financial partners need to understand the drivers of economic growth—the mix of industries, the area's largest employers, and the nature of new and expanding businesses. Investors must have confidence in the market's continued economic vibrancy, so they look for evidence of a growing labor force and new job creation. They will want to see an economy that can generate work for a growing labor force without increasing the unemployment rate.

A region's "location quotient" can show which employment sectors are most significant. The location quotient is derived by calculating the percentages of the workforce employed in each major industry locally and dividing them by the percentages of the workforce employed in the industry groups nationally. If the value of the location quotient is greater than 1.0, the industry is considered to be one that drives the local economy.

Market analysts must consider whether the local economy is diverse or focused on a small number of industries. An area that is dependent on a few large employers or a single industry (such as automobile manufacturing and parts) will be more vulnerable to recession. This factor will affect absorption of new space and continued strong occupancy in existing buildings.

Also, the mix of industries found in the metro area will determine the strength of demand for different types of properties, as in the following examples:

- A community dominated by large, corporate-owned manufacturing facilities will need fewer multitenant office buildings than one dominated by small, high-tech business services or financial services firms.

- Tourist destinations (such as Honolulu, New Orleans, or Orlando) will need far more hotel rooms than their resident populations would suggest.
- A city located at the confluence of three interstate highways is often a center for warehousing and distribution uses. Deepwater ports, major rail switching yards, and international air cargo terminals also create above-average demand for warehouse space.

Using Employment Statistics

Real estate investors are interested in both the composition of the job base and how it has changed over time. Market studies should include current statistics on a metropolitan area's total employment by industry, using one- or two-digit standard industrial classification (SIC) codes, as shown in Table 2-1. Comparisons with state and national norms will be helpful in highlighting those industries that are underrepresented or overrepresented in the metropolitan job mix. The U.S. Census Bureau is replacing the existing SIC system with the North American Industry Classification System (NAICS). NAICS makes substantial structural improvements and identifies more than 350 new industries. In many respects, NAICS reporting categories will more closely reflect the number of business establishments that use different types of real estate. The transition from SIC to NAICS began in 1997 for national and state data; however, substate data will not be available for a number of years and there will

be limited conversion of historic data, making trends difficult to discern and historical comparisons difficult to perform.

For office and industrial market studies, analyzing employment at the two-digit SIC level zeros in more precisely on job growth at potential tenant businesses. A closer examination of the diverse types of businesses constituting the service sector tells why. Demand for multitenant office space is generated by job growth in business and legal services (SICs 73 and 81) but not in repair shops (SICs 75 and 76), movie theaters and video rentals (SIC 78), or amusements and recreation (SIC 79).

The economic overview should include data on total job growth over the last five to ten years, and on the distribution by industry of these jobs. In large metropolitan areas, at-place employment data may be presented for both the metropolitan area (CMSA, PMSA, or MSA as designated by the Census Bureau or by a state's department of labor) and submarkets (such as individual counties or large cities). Employment growth rates for the local market area should be compared with state and federal statistics by SIC or sector. Annual averages can be used when available. If monthly data series are used, the analyst should use the same month for every year shown.[1]

State labor departments (and their Web sites) are the best sources of monthly employment data. Annual averages for metropolitan areas can be found in the January issue of the U.S. Bureau of Labor Statistics' publication *Employment and Earnings*.

Key Employers and New Industries

Noting the top ten- or 20-largest employers is also helpful in portraying the area's economic base. Not surprisingly, supermarket chains, discount department stores, universities, countywide school districts, and teaching hospitals are typically found in the top 20. Federal, state, and county government may also be important to the economic base, especially in state capitals or areas with military installations.

It is useful to focus extra attention on the area's largest private sector businesses, noting if their payrolls have grown over the last five years, or if they are outsourcing work to smaller local firms. Conversations with local economic development officials (from the chamber of commerce, power companies, or public agencies) can help clarify which segments of the economy are generating direct demand for space, bringing in new workers, and so on. If well-known Fortune 500 companies are expanding or relocating into the area, their plans should be noted. Similarly, if a key employer is contracting its opera-

Table 2-1

Standard Industrial Classifications

Codes	Industry
01–02, 08–09	Agriculture, Forestry, and Fisheries
10–14	Mining
15–17	Construction
20–39	Manufacturing
40–42, 44–49	Transportation, Communications, and Utilities
50–51	Wholesale Trade
52–59	Retail Trade
60–65, 67	Finance, Insurance, and Real Estate
07, 70–87, 89, 90	Services
No SIC	Government

tions and layoffs are anticipated, this fact should also be noted.

Local chambers of commerce, economic development agencies, and business magazines or newspapers are the best sources of information on major employers and their future plans. Printed materials, telephone or in-person interviews, and agency Web sites can provide statistics to use in the market study report.

Labor-Force Profile

Labor-force availability and skills are important to employers and are carefully considered when businesses make location decisions. At a minimum, market studies should provide information on growth in the resident labor force and the local unemployment rate during each of the last five years. The market analyst should then provide a brief interpretation of the data and their implications, if any, for the subject property.

An economically healthy county will be able to maintain or reduce its unemployment rate even as the number of potential workers grows. In most situations, low unemployment is a positive indicator for real estate: it boosts demand for homes and household services, and sustains retail sales. However, if the supply of available workers is too small, labor costs increase and businesses may look elsewhere for space as they expand.

If potential tenants will need highly trained or well-educated workers, the market analysis report should also provide background information on local area resources (such as education attainment of the resident population, community college training programs, and university enrollment).

State labor departments compile monthly labor-force estimates and unemployment rate statistics for metropolitan areas, counties, and larger cities. Metrowide statistics are also available each month in press releases available from the U.S. Bureau of Labor Statistics. Unlike at-place employment data from the U.S. Census Bureau's Employment and Wages Reports, which are based on filings for unemployment insurance, labor force and unemployment rates are sample-derived information. Such changes in methodologies can have a dramatic effect on the presentation of labor-force data. Thus, analysts must be careful that patterns in time series of labor-force statistics are based on economic changes rather than on methodological changes.

Visitor Profiles and Tourism Trends

Visitor statistics are important in determining potential demand not only for hotels and resorts but also for entertainment, amusement, and cultural facilities that derive a significant source of patronage from out-of-towners. These data are obtained through a variety of methods, including consumer surveys, and are not necessarily consistent from city to city.

Tourist information (usually collected by hotel associations, convention and visitors bureaus, or government tourism promotion agencies) can include the following statistics:

- Estimates of total visitation (based on data collected at airports, train and bus stations, museums, or other attractions);
- Breakdowns of visitors by type (convention attendees, business travelers, and pleasure visitors);
- Trends in occupied hotel room nights and average daily room rates.

Agencies responsible for tourism promotion also collect data on local spending by tourists at restaurants, stores, and entertainment venues. In locations where tourists constitute a significant share of store patronage, these data should be included in the market study if they are available.

Consumer Demographics

Housing and retail market studies require considerable detail on trade area demographics. At a minimum, the market study should include the most recent U.S. census counts and any reliable current estimates (from a local government or economic development agency) of the population and number of households, median or average household income, and household income distribution for the trade area. Information on age characteristics, household size, and housing tenure will also shape the analyst's conclusions and recommendations for any proposed project that is targeting specific population subgroups (such as senior citizens, homeowners, or families with young children). Projections are important, especially for larger projects that will be built and marketed over a period of years.

With the growing importance of niche marketing, sophisticated clients often demand more detailed population profiles that offer insight into lifestyle choices, racial and ethnic characteristics, educational attainment, and occupation and employment patterns. Aside from conducting in-depth surveys or focus groups, an analyst can turn to one of the data vendors that provide lifestyle cluster analysis. (See appendix.)

Clearly formatted tables help the reader understand the characteristics of the population, and how they have changed over time. Comparisons with growth rates and population profiles statewide, in the metropolitan area, or in the county where the property is located demonstrate how the trade area differs from the larger community. Key indicators should be highlighted in text discussion, with any unusual patterns or trends explained. The type of project being studied and the characteristics of the trade area will dictate that some demographic indicators receive greater attention than others in the written report.

Depending on the amount of time and money available for market research, the analyst can prepare his or her own estimates of short-term future space needs, obtain forecasts from local or state planning agencies, or purchase projections prepared by economic or real estate consulting firms. It is important to remember that judgment based on local knowledge and experience can be as important as sophisticated modeling in generating an accurate forecast of future demand.

Population Trends

Demand demographics begin with the number of people in the primary and secondary trade areas from the most recent census and often the one before that as well. The most recent year for which reliable estimates are available should also be included. In some cases, adding data from an even earlier census may also be helpful—especially in older city neighborhoods where population levels have fluctuated over time.

Many state and regional planning agencies prepare population projections for counties and larger municipalities. (See Figure 2-2.) The forecast period can be five, ten, or even 20 years into the future. Reports can often be obtained free of charge, either in printed form or through a government agency's Internet site. Population projections for small areas (such as combinations of zip codes or census tracts) must typically be purchased from private data vendors such as Claritas or CACI. When locally generated estimates are available, they can be more accurate than others because they usually reflect local knowledge regarding zonings and building trends that influence where and how much growth will be accommodated.

Population growth indicates that the trade area is attracting new residents and shoppers, generating demand for additional housing or store space. Such growth is usually, but not always, associated with new housing construction or conversion of nonresidential properties to apartments or condominiums (typically found in urban neighborhoods where older factories or warehouses are converted to loft apartments).

However, it is possible for a trade area to show population growth without any homebuilding. Older residents may be moving out, only to be replaced by young households with children. Or the neighborhood could be attracting recent immigrants or new ethnic groups with larger-than-average family sizes. Conversations with knowledgeable local sources, such as real estate agents or community planners, or school district growth estimates can provide insights that help explain unusual population growth patterns.

Households and Their Characteristics

A trade area with little or no population growth may nevertheless need additional housing units. Neighborhoods that once served larger families with children who have since moved away could register a drop in population, but they could still be attractive for empty nesters or seniors' households with evolving shelter needs. Similarly, demand from singles or young couples could be growing, even if the total number of residents has dropped.

Current estimates of the total number of households and average household size are often available from private data vendors, as cited previously. However, market analysts must rely on the decennial Census for local information on other household characteristics, such as marital status and presence of children.[2]

Age Characteristics

Private data vendors and some local planning offices estimate the number of households by age of householder and provide population estimates by five-year age cohorts. A trade area's age profile will influence both housing and retail markets. An area with a high percentage of young adults will be attractive to developers of rental apartments and condominiums. Opportunities for building seniors' housing and assisted living facilities may also become evident after a review of trade area demographic trends. Shopping center developers look for communities with a high incidence of preteens and teenagers because so many successful chain stores cater to those age groups.

Race and Ethnicity

Overall population growth and household income are more important predictors of housing demand and retail expenditure potential than race or ethnicity. Nevertheless, developers and investors may want to know about the racial and ethnic composition of a trade area. Government agencies often require such information as part of the market studies for low- and moderate-income housing. If data from the decennial

Figure 2-2

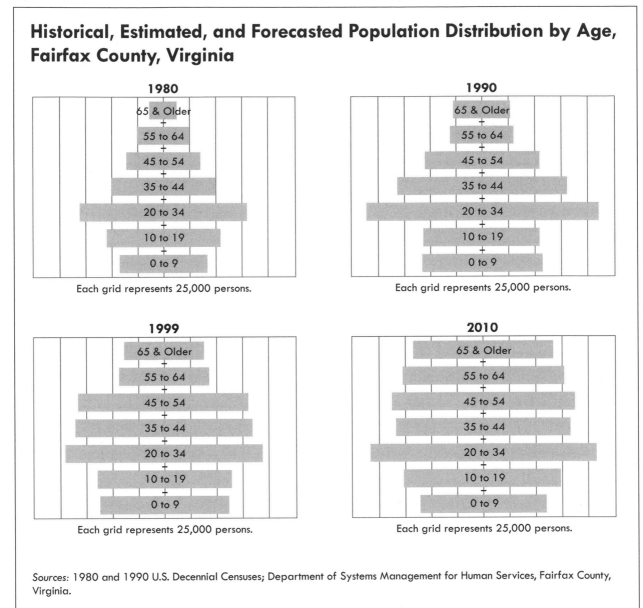

Historical, Estimated, and Forecasted Population Distribution by Age, Fairfax County, Virginia

1980

65 & Older
+
55 to 64
+
45 to 54
+
35 to 44
+
20 to 34
+
10 to 19
+
0 to 9

Each grid represents 25,000 persons.

1990

65 & Older
+
55 to 64
+
45 to 54
+
35 to 44
+
20 to 34
+
10 to 19
+
0 to 9

Each grid represents 25,000 persons.

1999

65 & Older
+
55 to 64
+
45 to 54
+
35 to 44
+
20 to 34
+
10 to 19
+
0 to 9

Each grid represents 25,000 persons.

2010

65 & Older
+
55 to 64
+
45 to 54
+
35 to 44
+
20 to 34
+
10 to 19
+
0 to 9

Each grid represents 25,000 persons.

Sources: 1980 and 1990 U.S. Decennial Censuses; Department of Systems Management for Human Services, Fairfax County, Virginia.

census or other sources suggest dramatic shifts, the market analyst should consult local sources about the reasons for such change.

Household Income

Demonstrating that trade area residents have sufficient income to buy or rent in a proposed new housing development is very important in deciding whether to build and what type of product should be offered. Retail market studies use aggregate household income estimates for the trade area to calculate expenditure potential for a proposed shopping center or a particular store type.

A market report should provide a breakdown of the estimated number of households by income bracket. It will also indicate the median and average household income in the area.[3] Household income statistics include single people living alone and unrelated people living together. Average and median household incomes tend to be lower than for families (which consist of two or more related people living together). In some reports, the analyst will provide similar estimates and projections of family income. Measuring family income may be useful for residential subdivisions because family households tend to make the majority of purchases. This pattern does not always hold true, however.

U.S. Census Bureau income statistics are based on sample surveys of money income. The census relies on the willingness of respondents to fully and accurately report what they earn. Not all households are fully forthcoming. Moreover, census income surveys do not include noncash payments (such as housing subsidies or food stamps), nor do they consider investment income. Consequently, census numbers provide an understated estimate of households' ability to pay for housing, or their retail expenditure potential. This understatement is especially problematic in low-income neighborhoods where government transfer payments and subsidies are a key source of purchasing power, as are unreported and "underground" income sources.

Understanding household assets is also important when analyzing the marketability of move-up housing and especially seniors' housing. Money income of senior citizens tends to be below the overall average, but many retirees have substantial savings and investment assets, with little debt. Counting a portion of assets (especially equity in owner-occupied housing) is important in determining whether trade area seniors can afford monthly payments for new housing.

Information on household wealth in particular communities or zip codes is far more difficult to obtain than income data. The U.S. Census Bureau does not measure wealth. Some private data vendors provide their own estimates of household wealth (assets minus liabilities), but methodologies vary and accuracy can be questionable, even for larger areas.

Housing Tenure

Tenure describes whether a household owns or rents its home. Although not a population indicator per se, the extent to which trade area households own or rent their homes is important not only for housing market studies but also for retailers. Home-improvement centers; lawn and garden shops; home decor, flooring, and furniture stores prefer to be located in areas with a high degree of homeownership. In contrast, mini-warehouses tend to be located in areas with a high percentage of apartment dwellers because renters often need additional storage space and are more transient. Precise tenure estimates are difficult to obtain in noncensus years. Building permits can be helpful indicators of the types of units constructed since the

last census, but the analyst must recognize that multifamily permits cover condominium units as well as rental apartments.

Demographic Data Sources

As indicated previously, the U.S. Census Bureau's decennial counts form the basis for most demographic estimates and projections. Because conditions can change dramatically between census years, market analysts must use more current demographic estimates. To fill the gap between decennial censuses, the Census Bureau is implementing the American Community Survey. Beginning in 2003, the annual survey will be implemented in every county, and will collect demographic, housing, social, and economic data that was formerly collected only in the one in six sample of the decennial census.

The U.S. Census Bureau prepares state and county population estimates every year. Estimates for metropolitan areas and large cities are issued bi-annually. Annual breakdowns by age, sex, and race or ethnicity for states and counties can also be obtained from the U.S. Census Bureau's Web site. However, the bureau prepares population projections only for the nation as a whole and for states. They are updated every two years, but are of little value (except in comparisons) when studying a local market.

Not surprisingly, private data vendors have stepped in to fill the void. Firms selling demographic estimates and projections include the following:

■ Economic consultants, which use proprietary models to describe national, regional, and local economic conditions, and then estimate and project population, households, income, and, in some cases, housing demand. Some of these firms provide customized research and consulting services in addition to selling standardized economic analyses and projections. Clients can subscribe to reports for the nation as a whole, for regions, or for one or more metropolitan areas. Regular updates are available in print, on tape, disk or CD-ROM, or online, either by subscription or as a one-time purchase. A list of such firms is included in the appendix at the end of this book. Such sources are useful for market analyses for commercial and industrial properties because they can provide detailed employment projections by industry.

■ Demographic data vendors that focus on consumer demographics rather than economic modeling. These firms provide more detail on population and household characteristics. They also provide estimates and projections of retail expenditure potential by type of store or by type of merchandise. As a result, they are widely used in housing and retail market studies. These vendors usually provide clients with local trade area estimates based on distance from a particular site, for a combination of zip codes or census tracts, or for specific latitude and longitude coordinates. They also offer five-year forecasts of key demographic indicators. Their data are available by subscription or on a per report basis.

Woods & Poole Economics and NPA Data Services sell historic trend data, current estimates, and long-range (25-year) projections, but only for states, counties, and metropolitan areas. Some vendors, such as Demographics USA, provide current estimates and color mapping for key demographic indicators but do not offer future projections. Still other firms specialize in consumer information needed for product marketing, advertising, or store location planning.

Psychographics: Portraying Household Lifestyles

Information on age, income, ethnicity, and housing tenure may not fully portray important differences in trade area populations. Education, occupation, the presence or absence of young children, hobbies, recreational pursuits, and community involvement can vary widely among residents in a given age or income bracket, thereby influencing their shopping habits and housing preferences. As a result, today's market studies often include information on trade area psychographics. Analysts can purchase trade area lifestyle profiles from private data vendors in much the same way they obtain current population and household counts or income estimates and projections.

Psychographic data providers use information from a variety of sources—television and radio ratings services, newspaper and magazine circulation bureaus, store frequent-buyer programs, and so on—to assign trade area households to one of numerous lifestyle clusters. Residents of most local trade areas (consisting of a combination of communities, census tracts, or zip codes) will be divided into at least two clusters. A large area will contain households in multiple lifestyle groups. Data vendors assign colorful names to each socioeconomic cluster: for example, "Blueblood Estates," "Bohemian Mix," and "Pools and Patios" are three of 62 clusters used by

Claritas. Case study 5.3 includes an example of lifestyle cluster data.

Lifestyle cluster analysis helps retail developers determine the types of stores that would be best suited for a new shopping center. They are widely used by retail chains to see if the trade area surrounding a proposed location fits the profile of the existing customer base, as in the following examples:

- A bookstore chain would seek locations with high concentrations of well-educated, upscale patrons.
- A supermarket specializing in prepared gourmet foods will target a trade area with young singles or two-worker families.
- Toy stores need to see large numbers of households with children under age ten.
- Consumer preferences for home lot sizes, interior amenities, community rooms, exercise facilities, privacy, and open space become more obvious when residential developers use lifestyle data.

Using Consumer Surveys

Survey research can play a vital role in real estate market analysis. It provides the developer, property owner, or investor with direct information on customers' perspectives. In the real estate industry, "customer" can refer to either consumers or business-to-business targets, depending on the type of property. For instance, a shopping center developer may be interested in the perceptions of current or prospective retail tenants, or in what shoppers think.

Using surveys, focus groups, or both improves the accuracy of real estate market studies. Researching the customer's perspective allows the market analyst and the client to explore existing or prospective customers' perceptions of a variety of issues. Survey research can

- Identify the strengths and weaknesses of individual project features or of the entire property;
- Help determine how a property is positioned in the marketplace and what its advantages or disadvantages are when compared to its competition;
- Gauge customer interest in new concepts or features not previously seen in the market;
- Reveal which factors (location, price or rent, amenities) are most important in customer decision making;
- Suggest how much tenants or buyers will be willing to pay for space in a proposed project;
- Tell ownership how tenants feel about property management and maintenance.

It is not uncommon for marketers to ignore the need for research or consciously to decide against conducting customer research, either for budgetary or timing reasons. Real estate developers know their products well; they are very familiar with their competition, their market, and their industry, so they are tempted to assume that they know their customers' needs and preferences. This misconception is common, but potentially serious.

The most obvious time for conducting research is before developing or building a new project. This timing provides the best opportunity for using the research results to influence design, amenities, and pricing. Investors can also use survey research before purchasing an existing property or starting renovations or expansion. Owners of existing shopping centers, office buildings, or hotels benefit from surveying their tenants or patrons when new competition enters the market. They need to stay informed regarding customer satisfaction.

Two primary types of customer research exist: quantitative and qualitative. Quantitative research is statistically projectable, meaning it allows the marketer to learn that a specific percentage of customers have particular demographic characteristics or will behave in a certain way. Qualitative research is not statistically projectable, but it allows for more detailed exploration into customer perceptions of the product, the competition, the market, the industry, their shopping habits, their housing preferences, and so on.

Consumer surveying, though it employs scientific methods, is not an exact science and has limitations. Changing market conditions, such as the economy and competition, cause research results to be very time-sensitive and require that studies be updated periodically. For example, large shopping centers usually survey shoppers every year or two to learn which stores they are patronizing, what they are buying, and where they live. Research results provide an educated guide for developing a property and its marketing program and for keeping it competitive. However, survey research cannot guarantee success. Rather, it minimizes the risk of making wrong decisions and maximizes the possibility for success.

Regardless of which type of research will be conducted, the first thing that must be done is to identify the characteristics of the people who should be asked to participate in the study. These characteristics can be either demographic or psychographic. They are used to select the area from which survey respondents will be drawn and to screen survey participants, as in the following examples:

- A developer of retirement housing may want to focus his or her survey on persons aged 60 and older living within ten miles of the proposed site.
- An office developer will want to focus on tenants in the trade area whose leases will be expiring within the next 36 months.
- People who visited a shopping center at least once in the previous month could be the focus of a study used to evaluate the center's expansion plans.
- A hotel will ask its frequent guests if it should add a spa.
- Trade area manufacturers and retail stores will be asked about their need for additional warehouse space and their interest in a proposed multitenant facility.

Using Quantitative Research

Quantitative research is conducted when it is necessary to be able to predict the target group's behavior with statistical accuracy. An example of what can be learned is the potential percentage of people who are likely to shop at a certain store or shopping center or who react positively to a proposed apartment development. Quantitative research (statistically valid and projectable) usually requires a relatively large sample size. Frequently, 150 or more completed surveys will be needed; requirements could be higher if the client needs to know about the characteristics and perceptions of particular subgroups.

Quantitative surveys can be performed by mail (using a printed questionnaire with a postage-paid return envelope), on the telephone, through the Internet, or in person. In all cases, the survey instrument must be designed for easy computer data entry and analysis. Questions must be simply worded and easy to answer. Each survey method has its own strengths and weaknesses. Consistent administration, cost, and timing are the most important considerations. Market researchers must select the methodology that most appropriately fits their needs and budget.

Mail Surveys

Mail surveys are fairly inexpensive to administer. After the target respondents have been identified, a list of potential recipients is obtained and a sample selected for mailing. Sources include current customer or tenant lists, address directories, membership rosters, or commercially available lists purchased from reputable marketing companies. The mailing is then prepared and sent out, often with a nominal incentive to encourage participation (such as a dollar bill or a card that enters the respondent in a drawing).

Denver Pavilions is an entertainment retail complex in downtown Denver, Colorado.

When the completed responses are returned, they are tabulated and the results are analyzed.

Response rates for mail surveys are usually low (1 to 2 percent is typical for a random list, 10 to 20 percent for a qualified list). A short survey may draw more responses than a lengthy questionnaire. A key drawback with mail surveys is that respondents may not be representative of the population at large. Older respondents are more likely to participate than young adults. Those with strong opinions (pro or con) will send back their questionnaires; those who are uninformed or apathetic will not. Another concern may be length of time needed to obtain the required number of responses. Follow-up postcards may be necessary.

Telephone Surveys
Telephone surveys are more expensive to administer than mail questionnaires because qualified interviewers must be hired. Response rates are usually higher than in mail surveys, but responses are still relatively low. Potential respondents can be reached using ran-

dom-digit dialing within particular exchanges or by purchasing phone lists. Although telephone surveys can be completed more quickly than waiting for mail-ins, the process will still take a few weeks. Survey staff may have to phone respondents multiple times before the interview is completed, and noncompliance rates are high. Some of the sampled phone numbers will not be usable. And in multiethnic trade areas, bilingual interviewers will need to be hired to ensure that a representative group of households is reached. Despite their high cost, telephone surveys are often preferable to mail surveys because they generate more valid, representative results.

Internet Surveys
Internet surveys are relatively inexpensive and fast to administer and can easily be revised and readministered, but the audience is limited to customers who are online. The survey can be put onto an appropriate Web site where respondents will see it and have the opportunity to respond or, as in the case of written and telephone surveys, after the target respondents

have been identified, specific groups can receive the questionnaire by E-mail. Although it is easy to put out a consumer survey on the Internet, the results suffer from the same limitations as mail questionnaires—responses may not be representative of the target market as a whole.

Intercept Surveys

In-person intercept surveys are conducted at high-traffic locations, such as shopping malls. Surveyors stop potential respondents at a shopping mall or on the street and ask a series of questions, or they have shoppers fill out a printed survey form.

Intercepts are inexpensive but more costly than mail or Internet surveys. They are relatively easy to administer, but less reliable than telephone studies because it is almost impossible to ensure that each respondent meets specific demographic or psychographic characteristics. Also, intercept surveys must be shorter than a questionnaire completed at home or on the telephone. Despite their limitations, intercepts can provide a reasonable portrait of shopping center patrons and their purchasing habits. The key is to structure the survey properly.

Qualitative Research

Qualitative research is usually conducted with a small number of respondents. Although not statistically projectable, this type of research allows perceptions to be probed in depth. Some examples of qualitative research methods include focus groups, one-on-one interviews, and intercept interviews. As with quantitative issues, the client's objectives and the available budget will determine the method used.

As with quantitative methods, it is first necessary to identify target respondents by their geographic, demographic, and/or psychographic characteristics. Then, a topic outline must be developed for the interviewer or moderator to follow.

The focus group is the most common type of qualitative research because it provides a good balance between accuracy and cost. Respondents are prescreened to meet specific demographic and psychographic criteria. Groups are usually made up of ten to 12 participants. Multiple focus groups can be used to see variation in the perceptions or reactions of different targets. A professionally trained facilitator is usually hired to conduct the discussion. A facilitator with specific real estate experience is preferred.

Clients can be present or they can listen to audio and video tapes of the proceedings. After all the focus group sessions have been conducted, the moderator reviews the tapes or transcripts and provides a written analysis.

One-on-one interviews are the most expensive type of qualitative research to conduct because they are very time consuming to administer. However, personal interviews allow control over respondent targeting and provide the most time to probe issues in depth. After potential respondents have been identified by demographic and psychographic criteria, a professional firm should be hired to recruit the respondents. A moderator conducts each interview. After all the interviews are completed, the responses must be analyzed. Case study 3.4 illustrates the use of focus groups when quantitative studies do not provide adequate information.

Intercept interviews, which, like intercept surveys, are conducted at high-traffic locations, such as shopping malls, are the least expensive form of qualitative research. However, as with intercept surveys, they allow little control over targeting and selecting respondents, and they must be shorter than focus groups. Interviewers stop potential respondents at a shopping mall or on the street and ask them to sit down for an informal discussion using the topic outline. To speed up the process, more than one interviewer might be hired, which presents a risk of inconsistency because the method of questioning is conversational in nature.

Some examples of how qualitative research can be applied to specific real estate projects follow:

- A residential builder can conduct focus groups with consumers who are potential buyers or renters.
- A retail developer can conduct intercept interviews with consumers (shoppers) and one-on-one interviews with potential tenants (retailers).
- An office and industrial leasing firm might use focus groups with potential tenants.
- A hotel or motel can use focus groups with both business and pleasure travelers and then conduct one-on-one interviews with business travel managers regarding corporate accounts.
- A developer of a master-planned community can make use of focus groups with both retail and office tenants, one-on-one interviews with builders, and intercept interviews with consumers as they leave the sales center.

It is important to remember that any survey research, whether quantitative or qualitative, is a single component of a comprehensive market study and cannot replace the vital information that is gathered through the other market analysis techniques.

Analyzing Supply

Market analysts must devote considerable attention to supply factors that affect development feasibility. Typically, supply-side analysis considers (1) macro-market conditions (measuring metrowide or county-wide absorption, vacancy trends, and rent or price growth); (2) local trade area market indicators and construction activity; and (3) characteristics and performance of competitive buildings, both existing and proposed. Brokers, economic consultants, real estate market analysis firms, and appraisers are the usual sources of information on metrowide and submarket conditions, both current and historical. Understanding the physical character, tenancy, and performance of key competitors requires field visits and personal or telephone interviews with building owners or managers.

Supply Overview

Key indicators are the size of the current inventory (number of housing units, or square feet of commercial or industrial space), its growth over time, and anticipated near-term new construction. Also important are current vacancy rates and sales prices or rent levels over time.

Historic Trends and Current Conditions

Supply analysis begins with a profile of the current inventory by property class. For homes and apartments, data tables should indicate the total number of housing units by tenure, current vacancy rates, and the age of units (by year built). Apartment market studies will also provide information by property class (A, B, or C)[4] if data are available. For office and industrial buildings, statistics are usually grouped by type of property (single tenant versus multitenant; manufacturing, warehouse, laboratory or research and development, or flex) as well as by class.

Current rents and prices are also part of the market overview.

- Apartment rents should be portrayed as the average rent (total and per square foot), on either a monthly or an annual basis depending on local custom. In some markets these data are available by unit configuration (studio, one, two, or three bedroom) or unit size (square feet of living space).
- Average and median sales price for both new and existing homes sold during the previous year should be provided. Prices for condominiums and townhouses should be displayed separately from those for single-family homes. Note whether new-home prices include the value of buyer upgrades as well as base price per square foot. In most cases the emphasis is on new-home sales, which are more competitive with a proposed development. But existing home prices are useful for analyzing the character of the neighborhood and for determining whether current residents have the equity to afford the proposed new housing. Also, in assessing the market for a low- or moderate-income project, existing home prices indicate whether the proposed prices will compete favorably with existing market-rate housing.
- Commercial and industrial rents are expressed in dollars per square foot of leasable area, either annually or monthly depending on local custom. Measurable space varies by type of property. Office rents are typically calculated based on net rentable area, whereas shopping centers report gross leasable area.

Historic trends in the size of the inventory, average rents, and average vacancy rates should also be presented. The narrative should discuss the changes in rents and vacancies over time, average annual additions to the inventory, leasing activity (number of units or space leased each year), and annual net absorption (change in number of occupied units or amount of leased commercial space).

To the extent possible, trends in the trade area should be contrasted with the larger citywide or metropolitan market. Steady absorption, rising rents, and lower vacancies can occur in a hot submarket (a cluster, neighborhood, or sector within the region) even when areawide indicators are negative. The opposite can also be true. An underperforming market could be the victim of localized overbuilding, or it may be affected by the relocation of one or more important tenants. The analyst must explain the reasons for any significant deviation from areawide norms.

Using Apartment Directories, Inventories, and Vacancy Surveys

Apartment directories (published by local housing advocacy groups, chambers of commerce, and advertising companies) are designed to assist prospective tenants in locating available rentals, but they can also be useful to the market analyst. These sources list the name, phone number, and location of apartment complexes, and they may provide information on the types of units offered, featured amenities, and even rents. Directories can identify competitive projects prior to field visits. Advertisements in the real estate section of local newspapers can serve the same purpose.

Consulting firms frequently sell more detailed project-by-project inventories, providing rental rates, square footage, unit mix, and occupancy rates, as well as listing project amenities. Reports may also contain metrowide and submarket occupancy and rent averages, along with commentary on market trends.

Office, Industrial, and Retail Surveys

Local real estate brokerages, consultants, and appraisal firms are the traditional sources of commercial property inventory, vacancy, and rent data. These firms are very familiar with individual properties as well as marketwide conditions. However, relying solely on local firms poses problems for those market analysts who must prepare reports for properties located in numerous metropolitan areas. Property class definitions are often inconsistent among sources and across markets. Some sources count single-tenant office and warehouse buildings in their inventories if they are not owner-occupied. Others count only multitenant buildings or focus on structures larger than a certain minimum size. As a result, they may undercount the supply.

National firms have stepped in to provide a measure of consistency across markets. Market and submarket overviews (with both data and commentary) are often available from local affiliates of larger commercial real estate brokerages. Some firms provide free copies of their quarterly or annual market reports; others sell them for a fee.

Also, many national real estate research and consulting firms sell detailed trend information and projections for a fee. These consultants cover the largest office markets in the United States (usually no more than 75 metro areas), providing historic background and projections. Increasingly, such sources are able to provide information on individual competitive buildings. The data are updated semi-annually or quarterly, depending on the source, and are provided in print, online, or on CD-ROM.

Subscribing to individual market reports can be costly and may be justified only when the researcher completes more than one report in a given market area each year. In smaller markets, local business magazines, newspapers, or commercial real estate brokerages often prepare building inventories or summary statistics.

It is important to note whether quoted commercial rents are gross or net. Gross rents include some or all utilities, real estate taxes, and other operating expenses. Most newer commercial space leases use triple net rents—utilities and taxes are billed separately, based on either metered usage or a pro rata share of total building expenses. Tenants in enclosed malls typically pay a common area maintenance (CAM) charge, and often must pay a percentage of their sales in addition to their base rent.

The Importance of Fieldwork

Although the quantity and quality of statistical information on competitive supply improves each year, even the best inventory reports and consultants' projections cannot substitute for field observations. Seeing the subject site (or building) and its competition results in a more precise definition of the trade area. Preparing a thorough market analysis also requires "kicking the bricks"—determining how a competitor's location, image, design, amenities, and operations compare with the subject property.

A competitor's "curb appeal"—architecture, building materials, landscaping, exterior signage and surrounding uses—draws potential tenants into the leasing office. Lobby appearance, interior signage, lighting, elevator systems, security, and other design elements also influence whether an older building can effectively compete with a new project. Whenever possible, the analyst should visit model apartments or vacant commercial spaces to observe room layouts, natural light, quality of built-ins, and storage space. Older competitors may not have floor plans or measurements readily available. Looking at the bedrooms in an older apartment complex tells the analyst if prospective tenants will be able to fit their furniture or find enough electric outlets. In a shopping center, frontage visibility from the street, parking lot, or internal corridors is an important consideration.

The market analyst should look at the tenant directory in an office building, shopping center, or business park to determine whether the property is leased by a few large space users or by numerous small businesses. The directory provides insight into occupancy in those situations where data are unavailable. Note the types of tenants present—are they national chain retailers or Fortune 500 businesses, or is the space occupied by individual entrepreneurs? Where questions persist, follow-up telephone calls to key buildings should be considered.

Interviewing Building Managers and Leasing Agents

Interviews with building managers or leasing staff can be very helpful in understanding market dynamics, especially in areas where published data are too

Fieldwork is essential to gain a full understanding of the subject site, surrounding areas, and competitive projects.

expensive or unavailable. These conversations yield insight into what types of households are attracted to an apartment complex (young singles and couples versus empty nesters and seniors, or a mix of both), whether children are present, and what attracts tenants to the complex. Such knowledge helps in accurately determining a reasonable capture rate for a new apartment community.[5]

Similarly, commercial real estate agents and building managers know about the types of tenants that are looking for office or industrial space and their space preferences, technical requirements, and parking needs. Analysts will not be able to interview every building manager in the field. Time and budget constraints may intervene, and building staff will not always cooperate. Some building owners refuse to permit their personnel to divulge project-specific information to market analysts, especially if they represent potential competitors. Vacancy rate and lease expiration information is especially sensitive, although asking rents will usually be shared. Sometimes an offer to share survey results brings cooperation.

Documenting Historic and Future Construction Activity

Accurately gauging demand and supply balance requires careful consideration of the future construction pipeline and how it will differ from the recent past.

For housing market reports, the average annual number of single-family and multifamily building permits issued over at least the last five to ten years should be tabulated. Discuss any dramatic shifts in construction levels or the mix of unit types. In most instances, these shifts will result from national economic cycles and changing consumer preferences. However, local zoning, land availability, and price or rent trends can also influence the type of housing being built. The local trade area's capture of county or metrowide housing development activity should be highlighted.

Commercial and industrial properties already under construction will be among the most important competitors for a proposed development that has yet to line up financing and break ground. In areas with many visible construction projects, it is important to determine the size of these competitors at full buildout, and how much of the space has been preleased or presold. Asking rents for space still to be leased should also be included in the supply analysis.

Some local governments periodically update lists of projects that have received planning approvals but have not yet been started. Where no such reports exist, conversations with planning officials are needed to clarify the size of the development pipeline and when planned projects will begin construction. Where a trade area covers more than one municipality, planning officials for all jurisdictions should be contacted.

For both residential and commercial projects, the analyst should consider the amount of well-located, properly zoned, but as yet undeveloped land that could be competitive with the subject development in the future. A new project located in a built-up community with little or no vacant land will face less competitive pressure than one surrounded by sites where similar or identical buildings might be constructed within two or three years. Redevelopment of underused or obsolete properties should also be considered as potential competition.

Building Permits and Construction Reports

Local government agencies and the U.S. Commerce Department publish monthly and annual reports covering residential building permit issuance, providing data on both the number of units permitted by size of building and the estimated value of the construction.[6] Builders take out permits shortly before construction begins. However, permits provide no indication of when construction will be completed.

Local permit-issuing agencies are less reliable sources of data for tracking commercial and industrial construction. Nonresidential building permits provide little detail regarding the type of development or its timing. Real estate magazines, newspaper supplements, and economic development agencies often track construction announcements and feature new building or project openings. Data can also be purchased from the F. W. Dodge Company, which monitors construction activity in jurisdictions across the United States. These data include projects of all sizes, both single user and multitenant. Dodge reports are usually more costly than data published by local brokers or consulting firms.

Mapping the Competition

Market studies are more easily understood when accompanied by a map that shows the location of the subject property and its key competitors. The map should include buildings under construction and proposed as well as those already completed, keyed to tables or text with detailed information on project characteristics. Such maps can be compiled by hand or by using GIS mapping software.

Marketability Analysis

Market analysis is as much an art as a science; it requires judgment and vision as well as facts. After the analyst has completed fieldwork, collected data,

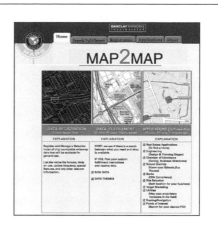

MAP2MAP

A privately sponsored Internet GIS clearinghouse referred to as MAP2MAP enables users to query online www.map2map.net for available digital map data by state, county or city, and local government data type. Participants can preview the data online by layer, review the price, request immediate delivery by media, project, and software platform. Fully geographic information systems (GIS)—ready spatial data themes, made up of combinations of feature types (layers), cover parcels linked to assessor records, land use, zoning, general plans, environmental issues, school/service districts, and street centerlines.

A number of cities and counties currently participate in MAP2MAP's public domain spatial data (PDSD) distribution program. Under a public/private agreement, Hayward, California—based Barclay Mapworks, a map publishing company, publicizes, markets, fulfills, and supports the use of mapping data, freeing up local governments to develop, maintain, and improve public databases, including GIS. This combined effort enables participants to use PDSD to help lower the cost and improve the quality of planning, design, and investment.

Roughly 85 percent of all counties with a population of more than 450,000 are maintaining jurisdiction-wide, GIS-ready parcel maps, as well as many other completed map overlays. Affiliate jurisdictions can register and update descriptions of their available data at MAP2MAP's registration center. Each custom fulfillment request is processed, a fee is collected, and the revenue is shared with local governments. More sales mean more revenue for government to improve data quality. And improved data can mean a spiraling cycle of wider use, greater revenue, better quality, and lower price.

Source: Dennis Klein, "Map2Map," *Urban Land,* vol. 59, no. 5 (May 2000): p. 27.

and prepared maps and tables, he or she must then synthesize the findings and reach conclusions regarding a proposed project's marketability or the future performance of an existing property. A summary should be presented at the front of the market report, along with a brief statement covering the scope of work, sources consulted, when fieldwork was completed, and any limitations or caveats.

Assessing the Site's Advantages and Disadvantages

If the subject site is unimproved, the report should discuss its size, shape, visibility, dimensions, access, and proximity to services. Topography and vegetation should be noted briefly, along with the presence of streams, ponds, or wetlands. The analyst should mention both positive and negative aspects of the property and its location. Site advantages might include location in a historic district, attractive views of the downtown skyline, or mature trees that will remain after construction. Incompatible neighboring uses, deteriorating nearby buildings, or noise from highways, rail lines, or airports are examples of negative factors—especially for proposed residential development. Any problems with access or visibility should be noted, and the analyst should indicate if these disadvantages could hamper marketability. If any changes are planned (a new commuter rail station, highway construction, road widening, intersection improvements, traffic signalization), their timing should be indicated.

Certain site attributes can be viewed either positively or negatively, depending on the land use being studied. Proximity to a major airport would benefit absorption of hotel rooms or warehouse space, but it would be less than ideal for an upscale residential subdivision. High traffic counts will not draw seniors to a retirement community but are welcomed by shopping center developers and their tenants.

The property's zoning and permitted uses should be discussed, noting if rezoning is necessary prior to development. Beyond the site and its immediate environs, the analyst must also consider factors such as community character and reputation. Crime rates as well as proximity to shopping, libraries, places of worship, and health care could also be important. For residential projects targeted to young families, the reputation and performance of the local school district, the availability of nearby daycare, and community parks and recreation programs should be mentioned. Residential real estate brokers and apartment community managers will be useful sources of information and insights.

Comparing the Subject with Its Competition

The analyst should highlight how the subject property compares with its competition in terms of the following factors:

- Location and linkage (access, convenience, visibility, prestige);
- Rent or purchase price, condominium or home-owner association fees;
- Unit sizes and mix by number of bedrooms and baths or by lot sizes for single-family homes;
- Occupancy costs (estimated monthly cost of utilities, property taxes, common area charges for shopping centers);
- Parking ratios and availability of garage spaces versus open lots;
- Building or project amenities such as exercise facilities, on-site daycare, concierge services, clubhouses, pool;
- Ability to support current and future technologies;
- Security;
- Maintenance of building and grounds.

Not all of these factors will be equally important for every property type. Building and grounds maintenance take a back seat to visibility and occupancy costs for retail space. Community prestige is very important for residential developers. Parking availability and electrical or mechanical capacities are critical to office tenants, and warehouses need to be close to major highways.

Of course, competitive rents or prices are critical to all land uses. When the analyst looks at new construction, it is important that he or she compare asking rents in current dollars, even though a new building could take two or more years to complete.

Some clients will ask the market analyst to recommend changes to the building or site development plans that would improve its competitive position. This function is one of the most valuable that a market analysis can perform. Such recommendations might include the following:

- Shifting the mix of units in a proposed apartment project to include more (or fewer) two-bedroom units;
- Offering an amenity or service for tenants that was not originally envisioned (such as a drop-off dry cleaning service);
- Reducing rents or sales prices to be more in line with what the competition is offering—or raising rents or prices if data indicate such a move to be prudent;
- Modifying the mix of large and small shop space in a proposed shopping center.

Will Demand Be Sufficiently Strong?

Developers and investors in residential and retail space look for population growth, new household formation, or both. Housing developers may also want to see growth in particular types of households (families with children, seniors, young singles), depending on the product they are marketing. A discount department store will want to see working households with middle incomes; it will not be drawn to an area where consumers are not budget conscious.

Housing market analysts will factor in demand for replacement of deteriorated or abandoned units. Similarly, commercial market studies will not count Class C buildings as truly competitive if their locations or physical characteristics are unsuitable for expanding businesses.

If demand analysis is based on employment growth, "space per worker" estimates will be used to translate jobs into supportable space. These ratios vary dramatically by industry. Law firms use more space per worker than data processing firms do. Private sector offices are usually more spacious than government buildings. Moreover, space standards change periodically, as warehouses become more automated, executive offices are downsized, or more space is required for high-tech equipment. Real estate journals, trade associations, and design professionals are good sources of information on how to translate job growth into space demand.

In some cases, real demand exists that cannot be demonstrated on the basis of household growth or income gains. An underserved city neighborhood—long neglected by retailers, entertainment venues, or restaurants—may already have sufficient purchasing power to support a proposed development, even though its household count is static. The same neighborhood may have what is called pent-up demand—that is, an ability to support new construction based on improvements that have occurred to the existing housing stock or retail inventory.

Supportable demand for shopping center space can exist even in trade areas that appear to be saturated. For example:

■ A trade area has a number of grocery stores with sufficient total space to serve the market, but the stores are undersized, poorly capitalized, or competitively weak. A new chain could successfully enter the market and challenge the existing competitors.

■ A strong anchor tenant, new to the market, commits to a significant share of a proposed center's space, thereby creating demand from smaller tenants that will benefit from proximity to the anchor.

Under such circumstances, the market analyst may find sufficient support for the new development, even though older properties may suffer as a result.

Capture Rates

Growth in target market groups needs to be sufficiently strong so that a new project will not swamp the market. As a result, market analysts look at "capture rates," or "penetration rates," which reflect the share of projected demand growth a project must attract in order to fill its rentable space or to sell its lots or homes.[7]

Determining whether a projected capture rate is reasonable or excessive requires judgment based on experience. There are no hard and fast rules. A well-conceived project in a dynamic market (with a growing number of income-qualified households or a surge in high-tech jobs) might succeed even with a high capture rate. Just how high depends on the amount of competitive space coming on line at the same time. In contrast, a niche product serving a select group of potential customers will, under the best of circumstances, attract only a small share of demand, and should be assigned a lower capture rate. Consider the following examples:

■ If a proposed seniors' housing development has to capture one-third of all the age- and income-eligible households in the trade area in order to fill its units, development will be risky and absorption will be slow. This project probably is too big for the local trade area. Relatively few seniors move in any given year; some will move outside the area, and many are simply not attracted to age-segregated living. Ownership would have to spend heavily on advertising outside the trade area in order to attract tenants.

■ A developer is considering construction of an 800,000-square-foot downtown office building that will take three years to complete. Employment in office-prone industries rose strongly over the last five years, vacancy rates dropped, rents escalated, and two other new multitenant structures have been started in response to positive market conditions. With the economy slowing, much of the space already under construction has yet to be leased. Because the other new competitors will not be completed for 18 months, the proposed building should not be expected to capture all of the projected demand. Vacant space may remain available long after the building is completed.

Determining Supply/Demand Balance

Analysts should be on the lookout for the following warning signs of an imbalanced or overbuilt market:

- Construction activity levels that dramatically exceed new demand, as indicated by household or employment projections. Note, however, that some excess is tolerable (and even desirable). A market with very low vacancy levels will experience rent increases that will eventually force out price-sensitive tenants. Also, obsolete or abandoned buildings must be replaced.
- Escalating vacancy rates that cannot be readily explained by the movement of a single large tenant.
- Negative net absorption, with more space being vacated than new leases signed.
- Declining real (inflation-adjusted) rents.

Absorption Rates

Developers and investors will look for the analyst's estimated absorption rate—the pace at which the proposed project will be able to lease or sell space. Depending on the property type, the absorption rate could be expressed in the following ways:

- The number of apartments that will be leased or the number of homes sold each month;
- The length of time it will take to sell off building sites in an industrial park;
- The number of months until an office building or shopping center is fully leased.

Absorption rates are important inputs in financial feasibility models, determining how long investors will have to carry the property before it starts generating positive cash flow. Many analysts express absorption rates as a range, 12 to 16 apartment units leased per month or 20,000 to 30,000 square feet of retail space leased per quarter. Preleasing (space rented before construction is completed) must also be factored into the absorption rate.

To a large extent, the analyst will rely on the absorption experience of recently completed competitive projects, especially those that are still actively being marketed. He or she will consider the competitive strengths and weaknesses of the subject relative to these competitors, as well as changes in economic conditions and the property market generally, when estimating absorption.

Calculating how fast a project will lease up or sell out is much more difficult in a location where no similar new construction has occurred in years. If demand trends are positive and the project is appropriately priced, a new apartment complex should absorb 20 to 30 units per month initially, but the pace will slow as the most desirable unit types or floors are fully leased. The same is true of shopping center space. A 200,000-square-foot center might have 50 percent of its gross leasable area (GLA) committed to two anchor tenants before construction starts, and another 20 percent of the total GLA leased by the time the center opens. Less desirable storefronts (with odd configurations or reduced visibility) will take much longer to lease; the center might not be 95 percent committed until a year after opening.

This chapter has described the general process for conducting real estate market analysis. The methods and data sources vary somewhat depending on the product type. Chapters 3 through 7 give more specific instruction and information on how to conduct market analysis for various product types and include case studies that illustrate the methods described.

Notes

[1] Monthly employment data are available with and without seasonal adjustments. Adjusted data present a more accurate picture of economic growth. Annual averages take seasonal variations into account and do not require adjustments.

[2] In areas with neighborhood school attendance areas, the analyst could supplement demographic information with local school enrollment statistics covering the previous five years. Such data would not be useful, however, in trade areas where a high percentage of children go to school outside the neighborhood or attend private or parochial schools.

[3] Average income is the total reported income from all sources for the entire trade area divided by the number of households. Median income is the point at which half the households are earning less and half are earning more.

[4] Class A apartments typically are less than ten years old or, if older, built to luxury standards and periodically renovated. They have modern kitchens, expansive closet space, efficient HVAC systems, ample parking, and security features. Class B projects are older but well maintained; the units may be smaller and lack certain unit or project amenities. Class C apartments tend to be more than 30 years old, including small walkup buildings that lack air conditioning and off-street parking.

[5] Analysts should be aware that fair housing laws limit how much information apartment leasing staff or home sales agents will share about residents. Visual observations (toys, bicycles, playground use) will indicate the presence of children.

[6] Construction value information is not useful to the market analyst because it does not reflect the market value of the property in question. Rather, it is the cost of construction exclusively.

[7] As a practical matter, capture rate calculations assume that a portion of space (usually 5 to 7 percent) will remain vacant, and that some share of demand will come from outside the trade area (new firms relocating from other regions, corporate transferees buying or renting housing, etc.).

The Townhomes on Capitol Hill, Washington, D.C.

Chapter 3

Residential Development

Analyzing the residential development market requires an understanding of location preferences, community types, building styles and materials, floor plans, amenities, and pricing trends. The housing market encompasses a wide range of product types and communities, including the following:

- Single-family detached houses, townhouses, multifamily units;
- For-sale and rental properties;
- Fee simple, condominium, and cooperative ownership;
- Stick-built, modular, and manufactured (factory-built) construction;
- Mobile homes;
- Year-round residences and seasonal or second homes;
- Master-planned communities, new towns, infill subdivisions, age-restricted communities, and seniors' communities.

Each of these housing types can be found in a variety of sizes, floor plans, elevations, and price or rent ranges. Despite the wide array of housing types, the vast majority of units are single-family detached houses and mostly owner-occupied. From 1990 through 1999, about 78 percent of all housing completed was single-family detached units. This percentage represents an increase over the 1970s and 1980s, when about 65 percent of all new units were single family. Trends appear to be reversing. For example, during 1999 and 2000, the share of homes that were single family once again averaged about 65 percent.[1]

Development Types

In many parts of the United States, master-planned communities are a popular development type. Such communities usually include a range of housing types along with recreational amenities, supporting retail, and other commercial development. Some master-planned communities may encompass several thousand acres and may include schools, libraries, and other public facilities, as well as a substantial amount of office and retail development—enough that they eventually become recognized as cities in their own right. Irvine, California, and Reston, Virginia, are two such examples.

A development type that is growing in popularity is the new urbanist community, which is modeled after the cities and towns developed prior to World War II. New urbanist communities are pedestrian oriented, rather than dominated by automobiles. Tree-shaded sidewalks connect all parts of the development. Streets are usually narrow and arranged in grids with short blocks containing a mix of housing types and supporting commercial uses in street-facing buildings.

Increasingly, as prime developable land has become scarce, developers are turning to infill sites for new developments. These sites have a number of market advantages, including fewer competitors, existing transportation and other community services and facilities, and a preexisting market—the residents of the surrounding community. Infill sites are typically much smaller than suburban greenfields, and developers are often challenged by one or more constraints on development, such as steep slopes, environmental hazards, or the expense of removing existing structures. Nevertheless, many developers are finding that the rewards outweigh the difficulties.

People's lifestyles are changing and so must the communities in which they live. So-called nontraditional households now form a larger portion of households than do married couples with children. Women have entered the workforce in vast numbers, and increasing numbers of people work out of their homes. These trends are just a few that will affect the kinds of neighborhoods people will choose in the coming decades. For example, people who work at home will most likely require the kinds of amenities and services—copy centers, meeting space, coffee bars—that are usually available to those working in offices. At the same time, child-focused amenities like playgrounds and ballfields may decline in value in some communities.

Characteristics of Single-Family Homes

Building styles and materials tend to reflect regional preferences. In the Northeast and the Midwest, vinyl siding dominates: more than 60 percent of new homes use it. But in the South, brick is slightly more popular than siding. In the West, stucco is used on 54 percent of new homes, a reflection of the popularity of southwestern architectural styles. Basements (full or partial) are very common in new homes built in the Northeast (86 percent) and the Midwest (76 percent). They provide insulation from cold winter temperatures and valuable floor space for homes built on small lots. Basements are rare in the South, where 82 percent of units are built on a slab or crawl space.

Home size is one of the major determinants of price. When comparing competitive projects, the market analyst examines not only the base sales price (plus extra charges for upgrades and options) but also the price per square foot. Homes have been getting bigger. Figure 3-1 shows trends in the median size of new single-family homes built since 1975.

While homes are getting larger, lot sizes are getting smaller. According to the U.S. Census Bureau, the median lot size for homes completed in 1999 was 8,750 square feet, down from 10,000 square feet in 1990.[2] The high cost of land in desirable locations is the key factor. Keeping homes affordable means reducing lot sizes when possible. At the same time, however, many fast-growing communities use their

Figure 3-1

Median Size of New Single-Family Homes

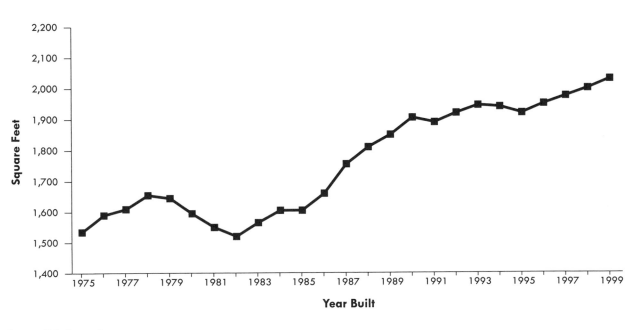

Year Built

Source: U.S. Census Bureau.

zoning ordinances to limit residential development by requiring larger lots.

Amenities once considered the preserve of upscale or custom homes (central air conditioning, two-car garages, a minimum of 2.5 baths) are now found in a majority of new single-family homes built by developers (Table 3-1). More than 60 percent of new homes have fireplaces. In the Northeast, nearly 80 percent of all new homes have two or more stories; in other parts of the country, the mix is more evenly split between single-story ranch styles and multistory construction. The split-level home, very popular in the 1960s, accounts for just 3 percent of units built today.

Table 3-1

Characteristics of New Single-Family Homes

	1975	1980	1985	1990	1998
			(Percent)		
Central Air Conditioning	46	63	70	76	83
Fireplace	52	56	59	66	61
4+ Bedrooms	21	20	18	29	33
2+ Car Garage	53	56	55	72	80
2.5 Baths+	20	25	29	45	52
2,400+ Square Feet	11	15	17	29	30

Source: U.S. Census Bureau.

Characteristics of Multifamily Homes

Multifamily homes have increased in size. The median new multifamily unit completed in 1999 had 1,105 square feet of space, up from 882 square feet in 1985. (See Figure 3-2.) Note that census statistics include an allocation for common areas such as hallways and lobbies whereas apartment developers and leasing staff typically base their calculations only on in-unit living space. Typical sizes for new suburban garden units for rent are 600 to 800 square feet for one-bedroom, one-bath apartments and 875 to 1,100 square feet for two-bedroom, two-bath units. For several years, high-rise multifamily buildings were not considered a viable product, but that has changed. Urban lifestyles have

Figure 3-2

Median Size of New Multifamily Units Built

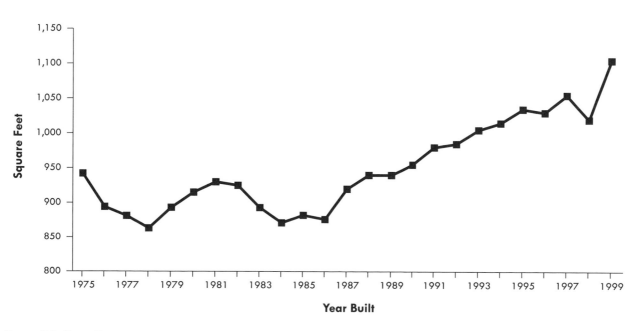

Source: U.S. Census Bureau.

gained in popularity since the late 1990s and along with that trend has come a resurgence in high-rise apartment and condominium building. Many high rises are built as luxury housing and include a wealth of building amenities and unit features.

Today's suburban garden-apartment complex typically consists of six or more two-story walkup buildings (some may be three stories), each with at least 12 to 16 units.[3] More than 80 percent of new multifamily units have air conditioning. The mix of unit types consists of 50 percent two bedrooms and 35 percent one bedrooms, with the remaining units primarily having three or more bedrooms. Efficiency apartments (also known as studios) account for only 2 percent of new units built during the late 1990s; they are much more common in high-rent downtown markets than in the suburbs.

An outdoor swimming pool and a clubhouse (often including an exercise room, a library, a party room) are typical of the newest suburban rental complexes. In more upscale apartment communities, covered parking (single-car garages tucked under the units or freestanding) or carports are frequently provided at an additional cost to the tenant. Additional cars are parked in unreserved outdoor spaces, usually free of charge. An overall parking ratio of 1.5 to two spaces per unit is desirable in a typical suburban setting, whereas a ratio of one space per unit—or less—may be acceptable for more urban settings.

Traditional suburban garden apartments still account for a majority of new multifamily development. However, luxury mid-rise and high-rise buildings constructed on infill sites in downtowns and older suburbs are increasingly popular.

In urban areas, where denser development is the norm, mid-rise and high-rise apartment and condominium buildings are common. Some buildings include commercial space on the lower floors. Parking may be in separate structures or underground garages. In very dense cities like New York, no parking at all may be provided, even in very high-end buildings. Amenities may include a gym, a rooftop or indoor pool, concierge services, and business and conference facilities. Views can be a primary consideration in pricing and planning the units. An outstanding view can add large premiums to the rents or sale prices of units.

Table 3-2

Characteristics of New Multifamily Units

	1985	1990	1999
		(Percent)	
< 600 Square Feet	11	5	4
1,200+ Square Feet	14	20	28
With 2+ Bathrooms	37	44	54
With 3+ Bedrooms	7	11	19

Source: U.S. Census Bureau.

Table 3-3

Innovative Features Found in New Multifamily Communities

Community Amenities
- On-site daycare and activities for latchkey children
- Community gardens
- Indoor basketball courts, sand volleyball
- Media rooms
- Billiard rooms
- Business centers, conference facilities
- Car wash and car-detailing facilities
- Concierge services, including plant watering, dog walking, dry cleaning pickup and delivery, and grocery shopping

Technology Amenities
- In-unit alarm systems with closed-circuit TV monitoring
- In-wall speaker systems with theater-quality sound
- Units prewired for multiple telephone lines
- Units wired for integrated telephone, cable, and Internet service
- Computer workstations with high-speed Internet service
- Video libraries and video-on-demand service
- Coinless laundry rooms, vending machines, and business centers using smart-card systems

Unit Features
- Private entries
- Direct-entry garage parking
- Nine-foot ceilings with crown moldings
- Bay windows and skylights
- Double-sided gas fireplaces
- Better soundproofing
- Two-level units in multifamily buildings
- Gourmet kitchens and deluxe master baths
- Full-sized laundry facilities, larger water heaters
- Keyless entry systems

Source: National Multi Housing Council.

Residential Market Analysis

Analysis of residential demand includes demographic and economic characteristics of households in the determined market area. Analysis of supply examines trends in prices and absorption and—perhaps most important—surveys of competitive projects currently being marketed and those likely to be marketed during the same time as the subject property. A residential market analysis should seek answers to several questions, including the following:

- Who is the target market?
- What is the appropriate price or rent range for the target market?
- What types and sizes of homes are suitable for the target market?
- What amenities and features should be provided to appeal to this market?
- What are absorption or lease-up and market capture rates?

Much of the analysis for residential development must rely on a qualitative understanding of the market and its dynamics. Both the product and the consumer must be understood in terms of choices people make, evolving lifestyles, personal tastes, and many other considerations that cannot be quantified. Focus groups, buyer surveys, and other qualitative techniques augment the hard data of the market study. Understanding the lifestyles and other qualitative characteristics of consumers can help to appropriately define a residential product. The analysis for rental apartments is different that for single-family for-sale houses. In fact, some analysts specialize only in one or the other. Single-family residential market analysis usually places more emphasis on the nonquantitative factors and focuses on what individual homebuyers want.

In multifamily development all design decisions must be made up front, 12 to 24 months prior to the time when actual marketing to residents is initiated. By comparison, builders and developers in other property segments can often refine their product offering as market response dictates. Single-family homebuilders have the opportunity to adjust their product based on which models are selling best and which features or amenity upgrades are purchased most often.

Identifying the Market Area

As with other real estate product types, a residential market study generally begins with an examination of the regional setting where the proposed development will occur, including population and household trends, recent or anticipated changes in the economic base, and employment patterns. The focus then narrows to the county or municipality for more specific information. Analysts collect data about population, households, employment, housing needs and development activity, regulatory issues, transportation patterns, local schools, and other services.

Most residential development draws a good portion of its market from the existing local community. A rule of thumb is that between 50 and 75 percent of the buyers or renters in a new development come from the local community, but there are many exceptions to that rule. A project in a rapidly growing metropolitan area might draw a much higher portion of its residents from outside the region. An infill project that offers move-up housing might attract nearly all of its residents from the immediate neighborhood. A second-home community draws most of its residents from outside the local area.

The market area for a primary-home residential project usually centers on a major employment node, a transportation corridor, or a desirable locational amenity. Physical barriers, either natural or constructed, or political considerations, such as a county line or school district, usually determine the borders. Employed consumers often focus their housing search on the basis of commuting times and distances.

The size of the market area varies, depending on the project proposed and the community. For example, in a densely populated large city, a market area for a typical medium-priced high-rise condominium project might encompass only a single neighborhood. In a sparsely populated, semirural community with few competitive projects, the market area could comprise the entire county or even several adjacent counties. The market area for a large master-planned community on the outskirts of a rapidly expanding metropolitan area might encompass the entire metro area and even out-of-state areas. Further, a distinctive project with little or no competition will draw from a larger market area than a more standard project that has a large pool of similar competitive projects. Relatively standard projects of moderate size usually have a market area of no more than a four- or five-mile radius.

In many cases, the market areas for supply and demand are identical, although competitive projects can exist outside the target market area. In some instances, the two market areas are regions apart, as in the case of second-home resort developments. Most market areas for primary shelter, however, are within a reasonable commute of major employment centers or other key destinations. Some factors to consider in delineating the market area include the following:

- Travel time from major employment centers. By identifying major employment centers and making assumptions regarding acceptable commuting time, market analysts can define a target market area. A new wrinkle in weighting this factor is the growing number of telecommuters and other home-based workers, creating new opportunities for housing those who can live anywhere.
- Mass-transportation facilities and highway links. Commuting patterns and times are based largely on ease of access; thus, the target market's geographic size is influenced by the availability of mass transit, the location of transportation corridors, and the speed at which they operate during peak travel times.
- Existing and anticipated patterns of development. Most urban settings contain areas of both growth and decline. Growth areas might be distinguished by certain desirable attributes, such as proximity to employment, housing affordability, physical attractiveness, and outstanding community facilities. A large master-planned community with attractive amenities can create its own desirability.
- Socioeconomic composition. An area's income, age, household characteristics, and other demographic characteristics influence housing choice and location and thus target market areas (but note that it is illegal in the United States to target housing-market segments based on race, religion, or ethnicity).
- Political subdivisions. Municipal boundaries can be especially important when adjoining jurisdictions differ markedly in political climate, tax policies, or status, or when different attitudes about growth exist. School-district boundaries can be critical if households with school-age children represent a major market segment.

Competitive analyses of for-sale products usually include only new developments and proposed projects that are expected to be selling during the marketing period because such projects are the most comparable to new development and the most suitable for assessing absorption trends. For rental projects only the newest projects in the market should be included, generally not more than ten years old. Projects that have undergone recent renovations are also included.

Competitive projects should be of similar product type(s) to those proposed for the subject project. Ideally, the market area consists of sufficient competitive projects to allow the survey to exclude any others. If the proposed project is a high-rise rental apartment building, only other elevator rental buildings should be included in the inventory. Similarly, an amenitized master-planned community relies only on that type of project for its competitive survey. Small subdivisions without similar features would not be competitive. On the other hand, in a market area with few competitive projects, the prospective consumer has limited choices and so does the market analyst. In such an area, it might be necessary to widen the definition of "competitive," possibly including all projects within a certain price range. Or it might be necessary to widen the geographic net, enlarging the market area to include more zip codes, more jurisdictions, or a larger radius.

Demand Factors

Demographic trends and projections form the basis for determining the demand for housing. Several demographic factors are of primary importance in analyzing the market potential for a project: employment, population and households, and household income.

- Employment usually drives population and household growth. If an area has an increasing employment base, new workers will likely take up residence in the local area.
- People form households. Households are the unit of measure most relevant for assessing the housing market because it is households that buy or rent a unit of housing.
- Household income is key to determining the pricing structure for the proposed development. Some analysts rely on standards such as the rule of thumb used by mortgage lenders that housing should not cost more than 30 percent of the borrower's income. Although these rules may be useful to keep in mind, they usually do not translate directly into affordability or marketability of housing.
- Other demographic statistics may be relevant for evaluating the project's potential, such as household size, ages of householders, family versus nonfamily or single-person households.

Employment

Demographers use projections of employment growth as one of the bases for determining population growth. Some analysts—especially those studying multifamily housing—prefer to base demand scenarios on employment rather than household projections because in most metropolitan areas, demand for new housing is closely tied to workers moving into an area. (See Case Study 3.1, Multifamily: Colinas Gateway.)

Housing competes for customers within the context of a regional market. In general, the growth of a regional economy determines how many new households are seeking shelter at a given time because job availability and the opportunity for career advancement are the magnets that draw newcomers, both transferees and young job-seekers just entering the market. The total housing pie is then divided, as existing residents and new arrivals alike decide whether to buy homes or to rent. Thus, a model that can forecast both total housing demand and the share of demand likely to be captured by rental apartments is critical to understanding aggregate housing demand at the metro level.

Because employment throughout a region determines population growth, metrowide employment statistics should be gathered. Some of the data to examine include historical growth trends, total employment projections, and comparisons of local unemployment figures with metropolitan, state, and national unemployment rates. These figures give some indication of the area's general economic health. A survey of major employers in the area, including expansion plans, reductions in force, relocations, and any new employers entering the region should be part of the information presented. A major new industry moving into an area will most likely affect housing demand. Other factors, such as the breakdown of employment by industry and occupational classifications, are sometimes included as part of a more comprehensive market study.

Population and Households

Population and household projections provide the number and characteristics of current and future households and thus the forecast of demand for new housing in the market area. An analysis of in-migration and out-migration also offers insight into present and future demand for housing in the market area.

A population trends analysis should begin with the population count from at least the last decennial census. Next, the analyst looks at the population for the current year, or sometimes the midpoint between the last census and the next, depending on the availability of data. For a large project, the more important, but unfortunately more elusive, data are the population projections for the next ten to 20 years.

Of greater significance in determining housing demand and market potential are the number and type of households that contain a given population. Growing populations signal a corresponding, but not proportional, increase in the number of households. In many areas of the country increases in the number of households are more a function of decreasing household size (fewer children, more singles) and immigration than of natural population growth.

Over the last few decades, national trends have pointed to smaller households. In 1950, the average household contained 3.37 persons. By 1970, it had declined to 3.14 persons, and in 1990, the average household contained only 2.63 persons.[4] Household size appears to have leveled off at around that number. In the mid-twentieth century, households consisted mainly of a married couple and their children. This type of household is now a minority and its share continues to shrink. Today's household mix includes a broad array of nontraditional family and nonfamily household formations: unmarried couples, single or divorced parents, childless couples, singles at all stages of life, unrelated roommates, and others. Each household type has specific housing needs, providing opportunities in a variety of market niches. Studying local trends in household size and type can help determine the concept and design of the community and housing units. However, it would be incorrect to conclude that smaller households typically prefer smaller housing. In fact, as household size has declined, home size has increased.

Income

An analysis of household incomes in the target market area indicates the region's economic vitality and provides valuable insight into the scope and magnitude of available purchasing power (not counting a household's equity and appreciation). This part of the analysis involves tracking historic changes and projections in median or average household income for the target market area, secondary market area, and region, including the rate at which incomes rise and the number of households in each income bracket. Such information is invaluable in determining price ranges that a significant portion of the population can afford. Income alone, however, cannot be used as an exact indicator of housing affordability. Because the affordability of housing is tied to a household's wealth (that is, the household's assets less its liabilities) not just its income, it is not possible to construct precise predictors of affordability. Broad correlations can be drawn between recent sales

Table 3-4

Different Generations, Different Tastes

How generational characteristics translate into homeowner priorities.

1 = not important   2 = important   3 = extremely important

| Age | Characteristics | Technology | Security | Housing Implications | | | | |
				Privacy	Equity	Community	Prestige	Health
<24	"Echo Boom." Will benefit from present-day insistence on quality education and cleaning up the budgetary crunch.	3	1	1	1	2	1	3
24–35	Generation X. Takes pride in pragmatic approach. Savers, adult children living at home. Future burden of being caregivers.	3	2	1	3	2	1	2
36–55	Baby Boomers. Take enormous pride in generational distinctions. Drive the market. Politically active.	2	3	2	1	2	3	3
56–69	Empty-nesters. Ambivalent response to societal confrontation. "Sandwich generation," strong work orientation.	2	3	3	2	1	2	3
70 +	Retirees. Depression-era roots and values. Firm belief in public harmony and cooperative social discipline.	1	2	1	3	3	1	3

Except for retirees, all consumer groups want their homes to be equipped for the technological age. Also important across nearly all groups are health and community.

Source: The Concord Group.

prices and income levels. Conversations with sales agents and mortgage brokers are also useful for gauging home prices.

Market Segmentation

In today's competitive environment, understanding the local market and targeting specific segments can help set a development apart from the competition. After defining the market segment, the analyst must be careful not to overgeneralize with regard to the target customers' needs. Not all young families want a suburban backyard, and not all retirees want to play golf. Within age or income cohorts, markets can be quite diverse, and to reach potential consumers, their preferences must be understood. Techniques for learning about preferences include focus groups, surveys of local residents, and surveys of current shoppers for homes. Market research can yield a wealth of information on the potential residents of a new project. But market research can also be flawed if the wrong questions are posed or the data are not

interpreted correctly. It is important to be aware of the potential for incorrect assumptions.

Supply Factors

The current and projected housing stock in the competitive market area forms the supply side of the market analysis equation. Supply factors include the total number of housing units by unit type, price range, and absorption. These factors enable analysts to translate data about employment, population, households, and income into estimates of potential demand for a specific new development. The present housing stock is determined through an extensive survey of comparable, currently selling developments in the competitive market area. The future housing market must be estimated by an analysis of the proposed projects, which can be identified through preliminary and final plan approvals and relevant rezonings. The market analyst may need to contact planning departments of multiple jurisdictions to obtain the necessary information.

Counting the entire housing inventory of a market area allows the analyst to consider household growth trends. This scale of analysis can use the number of units as published in the most recent census, with additions from building permit data.

Analyzing the Competition

In most housing market studies, the analysis of existing competitive projects is the most detailed part of the report. The existing project inventory provides a wealth of information about successful and not-so-successful projects being marketed at the current time in the specific market area. The competitive inventory analysis usually includes the number of units sold or leased and the number still on the market, prices or rents, square footage, and tabulations of price per square foot. Tables might also summarize standard features, available options, project amenities, and buyer/renter profiles.

To identify competitive projects, there is no substitute for getting out and visiting each project in the competitive area and talking with a sales manager or other representative from each project. It is the only way to determine whether a project is truly competitive with the planned development. Discussions with staff at projects underway are the most effective way to learn who constitutes the market, where buyers come from, what they like (or don't like) about current offerings, and what the most desirable products are for this specific group of consumers. Products and consumers are constantly evolving and it is important to discern any trends.

Market area averages and totals indicate how specific projects compare with the average and show overall leasing pace, absorption, units remaining on the market, average prices, and average square footage. Data also show which projects are selling better than the market average and allow analysis in terms of size and price per square foot. The market area's average price and absorption rate can help gauge how quickly competitive products are selling. Arranging the data in a spreadsheet or plotting a simple regression reveals the gaps in the market that offer development opportunities and shows where the market is saturated. Case studies 3.1 and 3.2 include an example of projects plotted on a regression diagram.

The simplest way to allow for variances in price and unit size in a project is by computing the average price per square foot for all units in the project, even though consumers do not think in such terms. Communities with the lowest average prices or the lowest average prices per square foot should report the highest absorption rates, assuming all other factors are equal.

If the analyst finds that consumers are not responding consistently to value, then all things are *not* equal and other, less tangible, factors must be examined. For example, features that are standard in one project may be upgrades in another. Locations can have small differences that matter a great deal to buyers. A particular builder's reputation may add perceived value. No two projects are totally comparable in every way.

For rental projects, vacancy rates in a market area give an indication of its strength. A high overall vacancy rate should be seen as a sign of limited potential in this market. A 5 percent or lower vacancy rate can indicate a strong market for this type of product. It is important to view vacancy rates qualitatively. Older rental projects that lack modern amenities may skew the market's vacancy rate upward and not accurately represent demand for a new project. Moreover, projects in the initial lease-up phase should be separated before tabulating the vacancy rate for the market area, because they have an artificially high percentage of vacancies. These projects do need to be counted in the absorption analysis. It is important to quantify the total leasing activity in the market.

The analyst also evaluates nonquantifiable characteristics of competitive projects. Factors such as location, design, and image must be considered. The quality of management, recreational amenities, or site advantages sometimes makes the difference between a top performer and a less successful project. These intangibles can often be ascertained only through discussions with sales agents or surveys of home shoppers. Of course, the analyst's own judgment is crucial in these evaluations.

Projects in the development pipeline must be identified, and relevant data, similar to that for existing projects, should be provided: the project name, the developer and/or builders, location, timing, number of units planned, and, if known, the type of units planned, estimates of price ranges, and expected opening dates. Some data may be unavailable for projects in the early planning stages. Occasionally, a developer may be unwilling to reveal plans for a proposed development. Some planned projects may never actually get off the ground. Although the inventory of proposed projects usually fails to identify some developments and includes others that never become reality, it does provide a good overall indication of future plans for local building activity.

Identifying Product Types and Niche Market Opportunities

Location, site, and market potential are the factors that determine the appropriate product to be developed. An urban locale demands a different type of residential development from a suburban one. The typically higher price of urban land requires higher densities. The identified market segment should suggest a special type of development. If the target market is young, first-time buyers, a moderately priced townhouse development with few amenities and maximum unit space for the dollar might fit the bill. If the research detects strong demand from young families with small children, then the project should be planned with this market segment in mind and the greatest percentage of homes should be of the size and type that appeal to such households in the local area. A growing elderly population might suggest a need for an active-adult or retirement community and elder-care facilities. Amenities, features, design, and unit size should reflect residents' needs and should be determined through market consumer research.

Although it is easy to continue developing and marketing products that have sold well in the past, it can be rewarding, both financially and in terms of serving a public need, to develop a new type of product. Comparable residential projects might not currently exist in the immediate market area, but if the demand analysis shows a need, the analyst should explore the possibilities. In an overbuilt market, thinking in terms of less typical types of development may lead to better opportunities but will require looking beyond the immediate market area for examples of analogous projects that were successful in other locations.

Calculating Capture and Absorption Rates

Housing demand includes newly formed households, households moving into the market, and households moving within the market. In high-value real estate markets, a factor for demolition of older, functionally obsolete units may be required. In low-income neighborhoods, dilapidated units are also lost to demolition or fire.

Analysts must estimate shares of total demand that major housing types will attract—single family versus multifamily and for-sale units versus rental units. These allocations should be based on historic trends in the local market and projected on the basis of economic and demographic changes. For example, as an area becomes more urbanized, a larger percentage of its households tend to reside in higher-density housing types. Census data provide breakdowns of households by unit type, unit size (number of bedrooms), and tenure (renter versus owner).

After these data are refined, analysts can identify all components of the basic equation for demand

(total demand minus total absorption by competitive products equals residual demand). Total absorption is projected based on the absorption performance of existing communities as well as projections of the expected performance of proposed communities that will be competitive during the marketing period of the subject project. The residual demand yields the number of units that can be absorbed by additional projects, including the subject property.

After residual demand is known, the analyst must determine what share of that demand the subject project is likely to capture. Determining this capture rate is highly subjective and must take into account all the project's advantages and disadvantages in relation to all others that will be on the market. Factors to consider include location, site, features, amenities, design appeal, and value. The capture rate should not be overestimated. Projects currently being marketed provide a reasonable model for the potential capture rate of the subject development. Capture rates vary based on trade area size, the number of competing units, the supply of land, desirability of the project, and many other factors.

Although a market study is one of the first elements in the development process, market research and analysis does not end with a project's completion: it often continues after the project begins selling, to fine-tune prices and even to change designs, features, and options. In a rental project, such research is part of an ongoing effort during leasing and management to keep tabs on competitors' vacancies, rents, and incentive programs.

Sources of Data

Numerous reference sources are available to assist the market analyst in learning about housing product, amenities, sales, and pricing. The U.S. Census Bureau tabulates data, both nationally and regionally, on residential construction activity through each key stage in the building process: permits, starts, completions, sales (for homes and condominiums), and absorption (for apartments). Data on selected structural elements, physical characteristics, amenities, and prices or rents are collected as well. Some information is tabulated monthly, while other items are available in annual statistical series. The National Association of Home Builders (NAHB) is an excellent source of background and trend information on single-family homes; the Manufactured Housing Institute covers mobile homes. Trade publications (*Builder, Professional Builder*) and organizations such as the National Multi

Housing Council and the American Seniors Housing Association are also helpful.

Although these sources are useful in helping to understand broad market and product trends, they are of little help to the market analyst looking at a specific property or development proposal in a local market.

- The Census Bureau's building permit tabulations[5] are the only uniform nationwide source of construction pipeline information for individual counties or municipalities. They offer data on the number of units permitted (broken out by number of units per building). However, the Census Bureau's building permit statistics do not indicate whether multifamily units are intended for sale or for rent. No information on unit mix, size, or pricing is provided.
- The Census Bureau also tabulates housing starts and unit completions but not at the municipal or county level. Numbers for the larger metropolitan areas are published quarterly and annually. National and regional data are useful, however, in estimating the share of permitted units that are actually completed. Reports on apartment completions distinguish between rental and condominiums or cooperative units and provide benchmarks for gauging absorption rates in new buildings.
- Annual vacancy rate estimates for the nation's largest metropolitan areas are also available from the Census Bureau, but they do not provide detail on occupancy in individual counties, municipalities, or submarkets.
- In certain major markets, data on comparables are published by private firms. The appendix lists some of these data providers.

Some local governments maintain databases of rental apartments. Trade groups (such as local affiliates of the NAHB), local apartment building owners' associations, and private consultants compile information on new projects planned, under construction, or in initial marketing. Fees are often charged for these reports, but they can save time. Larger metropolitan areas often have apartment guides that provide basic information and contacts for both new and existing complexes. The Sunday real estate sections of local newspapers contain both advertising and features on new homes. Even the *Yellow Pages* can be a starting point. However, use of secondary sources cannot substitute for field visits and conversations with sales and leasing managers regarding the types of product being marketed. Contacts with municipal planning and building staffs will also be needed to determine the number of units that are planned and approved for future development.

Special Niches

Some types of housing fall outside the standard methods of market analysis. Very high end custom-home communities cater to such small, well-defined markets that general demographic trends are of limited use. Analysis of the potential for these developments requires a clear understanding of target households and their preferences. Determining the market's size can be difficult because census and other demographic data do not provide the fine detail required. Low-income housing generally has more demand than can be met and market studies must address issues dictated by government funding sources. Second-home markets depend on discretionary buyers. Markets can be national or even international in scope. Identifying the sources of demand for second homes, as well as the comparables, can be a daunting task.

Low- and Moderate-Income Housing

The demand for affordable rental housing using low-income housing tax credits is very strong in most regions, especially for housing suitable for families. The market analysis is often conducted for the housing finance agency as a way to determine the most viable and worthy projects to be funded. Recent federal legislation mandates market studies that are conducted by disinterested third parties for all tax-credit projects.

Subsidized housing programs have income limits that vary by household size, but each program has its own specific requirements. State housing finance agencies have rigid requirements for funding projects. They are particularly concerned with oversaturation of neighborhoods and smaller towns with too much low-income housing, which would negatively affect the stability of the neighborhood. They might also be concerned with oversaturating the housing supply for a narrow income band while not meeting the need in others. Another consideration for the market analyst is whether the existing nonsubsidized housing in a community might already satisfy some or all demand for affordable housing as well as a proposed subsidized project would. This situation occurs sometimes in smaller cities or towns, particularly in the Midwest, where housing values are low.

Independent Living Seniors' Rental Housing

Made popular by the availability of low-income housing tax credits, affordable rental communities for independent seniors target healthier seniors. These communities offer units and optional services. Units generally offer one or two bedrooms and full kitchens; buildings include lounges, libraries, activity rooms, and sometimes a room for visiting doctors to use on an occasional basis. Services range from transportation, social, and recreational activities to wellness programs and sometimes meals. However, monthly payment covers rent, and possibly utilities, exclusively. Any other services offered would be optional on a separate fee basis. This product has traditionally focused on moderate-income households of seniors with incomes at 60 percent of median income or less. However, mixed-income or market-rate rental communities for independent seniors are now being developed, offering the same building and optional service package at rates addressing more affluent households.

Seniors' Housing

Market studies for housing targeted to active adults and retirees require an understanding of the hierarchy of housing types for these households. Many of the generalizations about where seniors live and how they live are not true. The vast majority of seniors—especially "younger" seniors—do not relocate to age-targeted housing, but remain in place. Only 4 to 5 percent of seniors move each year, compared to 16 percent of the general population. Demand projections based solely on age and income cohorts will result in overbuilding. Not all seniors who can afford to relocate to an age-restricted community will want to spend their dollars on shelter, and some simply do not want that kind of lifestyle.

Projects designed for and marketed to retirees are a growing share of multifamily construction activity. Some facilities require upfront entrance fees (or endowments) as well as monthly service charges; others are strictly rental.

Independent living/congregate housing complexes can include detached homes as well as apartments. The typical project has 70 to 250 units with kitchens; the residents furnish their own apartments. Amenities include a dining room serving at least one meal per day, lounge, library, activity rooms, and beauty salon/barber shop. Some projects also have convenience stores. Scheduled transportation, social and recreational activities, on-call medical professionals,

and wellness programs make these projects attractive to retirees. Rentals are most typical, but condominium or cooperative tenure (with monthly service fees) is also possible. Services such as meals, linens, laundry, and housekeeping can be included in the rent or service charge, or billed separately. The typical resident of congregate housing is a single female, over the age of 80, who is generally in good health and able to live independently.

Assisted living residences are smaller buildings (typically fewer than 100 units), offering 24-hour supervision and assistance for frailer seniors who need help with bathing, dressing, medication administration, mobility, or other activities of daily living. Single-occupancy or shared rooms may come furnished or unfurnished. Most rooms are rented on a daily or monthly basis, with charges based on the extent of personal assistance needed by the resident. Three meals daily are usually included, along with housekeeping services and activities. Assisted living is proving to be an acceptable alternative to nursing homes for seniors who do not need skilled nursing. Increasingly, assisted living facilities offer specialized floors or wings for persons with Alzheimer's disease or similar illnesses.

Continuing care retirement communities (CCRCs) offer a range of living arrangements and services that support seniors at various stages in their lives, allowing them to age in place. Independent living, assisted living, and skilled nursing are available in a campus setting. CCRCs usually require payment of an entrance fee or endowment, as well as monthly charges. Some facilities provide "life care" commitments; others provide only a guarantee of admission to buildings or units offering more intensive care as the need arises. Today, most entrance fees are partially or fully refundable based on length of residence. CCRCs appeal to both couples and singles who are still in good health, but who are concerned about their future needs. Retirement facilities may or may not be affiliated with local hospitals and nursing facilities. Churches or not-for-profit fraternal organizations are frequent sponsors.

The American Seniors Housing Association (ASHA) found 320 market-rate senior housing properties comprising more than 35,000 units under construction in 2000. Of these, 51 percent were assisted living communities.[6] California, Texas, New Jersey, Pennsylvania, and New York led the country in the number of new seniors' housing construction activity in 2000.

Absorption periods for retirement housing tend to be longer than for conventional new apartment complexes. The seniors' market serves a much narrower

The Hierarchy of Seniors' Housing

Five distinct types of housing fall under the term seniors' housing. Generally speaking, seniors' housing refers to housing that is restricted to those aged 55 and older; the different types of housing are distinguished by the increasing levels of service and care provided to the residents. The five types include

- *Active adult*—houses or apartments are targeted to people 55 years and older and may formally prohibit rentals to younger people. The communities offer residents complete independence, and few, if any, services are aimed specifically to residents' age or health. Homes may include such universal design features as grab bars and doorways that allow wheelchair access. These communities often have a recreational focus, such as golf, and services are typically offered on a pay-per-use basis. Active adult communities tend to attract seniors at the younger end of the spectrum. Very little special regulation applies to this category, and the size of projects varies widely, from 20 to more than 1,000 units.

- *Congregate care, or independent living housing*—is targeted to residents in their late 70s and older. In addition to housing, such projects usually provide limited additional amenities such as transportation, assistance with or provision of meals, and assistance with household tasks. Units are normally rented on a monthly basis with additional fees for specific services used. These types of development are not heavily regulated. The average size of a project is 70 to 250 units.

- *Assisted living*—housing is directed at the more frail elderly and is often mixed with congregate care housing. Assisted living projects offer higher levels of service, such as daily assistance with personal and household tasks. Typical residents are older than 80 years and are usually women. Some recent projects focus on the needs of residents with Alzheimer's disease or other forms of dementia. Residents are usually provided with three meals daily. Skilled nursing facilities may be available in limited cases. These types of projects are subject to increasing licensing and regulation and may also be eligible for financial assistance from government sources. Average projects range from 50 to 75 units.

- *Nursing homes*—offer a distinctly different environment from the projects in the previous categories because they provide full-time nursing care for residents, many of whom have serious medical problems. Nursing homes are subject to the heaviest regulation. They have increased dramatically in number, partly because of a trend toward shorter hospital stays. Nursing homes that provide skilled nursing care should be thought of as more like a medical or institutional facility; they are mentioned here only to provide readers with a complete picture of the range of housing available for seniors. Skilled nursing facilities may be combined with other types of seniors' housing.

- *Continuing care retirement communities (CCRCs)*—also occupy a special category of seniors' housing. They typically offer two or more of the housing types listed above in the same project. The guiding concept behind CCRCs is that they attempt to provide a variety of housing units and services to meet residents' changing needs and preferences over time so that residents are not forced to relocate as they age. These projects average more than 200 units and can be found in a wide variety of configurations and densities, depending on the project's location. They offer amenities comparable to other kinds of housing along with services and features designed to facilitate "aging in place." In CCRCs, residents pay an entrance fee and monthly service charges, or they rent units on a monthly basis.

Sources: Douglas R. Porter et al., *Housing for Seniors: Developing Successful Projects* (Washington, D.C.: ULI–the Urban Land Institute, 1995); and Bonnie Solomon et al., "Retirement Communities: Designing for the Aging Rental Market," presentation at the 1998 Multi Housing World Info Expo, April 17, 1998.

age range. For younger seniors in good health, moving to a retirement community is a lifestyle choice, not a necessity, and often is a difficult decision. Although some seniors cannot afford market-rate housing without assistance from relatives, others who can are simply unwilling to move until they have to. Studies have shown that seniors make far more visits to retirement buildings before making a decision to rent or buy than does a typical apartment tenant or condominium buyer.

Determining effective demand for seniors' housing requires looking not only at the number of seniors in

I'On, in Mount Pleasant, South Carolina, consists of 762 residential units, 30,000 square feet of commercial space, and six civic sites for churches or community centers.

©1998 Steve Hinds

Stone Manor Apartments, in Dallas, Texas.

the market area and their current incomes, but also at their assets and the value of the homes they would sell before moving. Most important, their health and need for assistance determine whether they will move and what level of housing and care they will need. The diversity of products, services provided, and pricing plans also poses challenges when examining the strengths and weaknesses of competitive properties in a given area. For example, per square foot rents must be adjusted to account for variations in meal plans; some facilities include maid service in the rent and others do not.

Second-Home Markets

Market analysis for a residential development in a metropolitan area oriented to primary-home residences involves a fairly straightforward market analysis process. Demand is driven by local employment, population, household income, and other key variables. For a resort community, however, several different components of housing demand might exist, including second-home investment and second-, preretirement-, retirement-, and primary-home use, each of which is explained below.

Although second homes can be found in nearly every state in the United States, the top states, in order of preference, are Florida, California, Colorado, North Carolina, Texas, and Arizona. Beach property, followed by lake settings and the mountains are the most common locations for second homes. Other locales—such as the tropics, golf course areas, attraction areas, ski areas, and the desert—are significantly less common.[7]

Although appropriate market research is important in planning any real estate project, it is particularly important for second-home developments because of both demand-timing issues (the decision to take a vacation or purchase a second home is discretionary and can be postponed or accelerated) and location issues (vacationers and second-home buyers can choose any area across the country or around the world).

Given that second homes are not necessities, estimating demand does not rely solely on population or household growth, but requires a closer examination of the quality of potential demand. The analyst must determine from where demand is likely to emanate: from the immediate state, a multistate area, completely different sections of the country, or international locations. The task can be very difficult, requiring interviews with realtors and others who have experience in the subject area and who know where buyers have traditionally come from.

Projections should reflect the feeder market's economy. For example, California is a primary feeder market for resorts in Hawaii, Baja Mexico, the desert Southwest, and the Pacific Northwest. Therefore, the demand for resort properties in those locations is in part a function of the strength of California's economy.

Most resort communities compete over a much wider geographic area than traditional primary-home residential communities. Resorts in Hawaii draw from the entire United States as well as from Japan, Europe, and South America—essentially the entire globe. Even regional resorts may draw from a relatively broad geographic market. The second-home market is typically made up of households whose heads are in their 40s and early 50s with incomes in the top 10 percent of all households. Typically, they are drawn from large metropolitan areas where the stress of everyday life is an additional motivation to own property in a completely different environment. Of those people who meet these criteria, only a small portion actually do buy second homes.

Although the type of product preferred differs among communities, the market generally favors condominiums or small cabins or cottages, with exterior maintenance managed by a condominium regime or homeowners' association. In general, units that rent best to transient guests are in greatest demand because of their investment potential. For example, in areas dominated by conference guests, a one-bedroom condominium may rent well and therefore have strong buyer appeal; in areas dominated by family vacationers, two- and three-bedroom cottages may be the preferred product.

Second-Home Users

Second-home users or owners are differentiated from second-home investors principally by their financial independence. Because second-home buyers by definition do not rent their property to others and instead maintain their units for personal and business use, access to the property is a major influencing factor. At the high end of the market, access by air and even the proximity to small airports serving private planes are important considerations. For most of the market, however, driving time from the owner's primary residence is a pivotal consideration.

Although some second-home buyers choose a multifamily product, most prefer a detached cottage or cabin. In addition, a portion of this market buys a lot in anticipation of building a second home sometime in the future. Some lot buyers are attracted by the quality of a golf course and associated club facilities or other amenities in a private community and purchase property primarily to secure access to private club facilities. Many of these buyers never build.

Preretirement- and Retirement-Home Buyers

The preretiree purchases property with the intent of eventually using it as a retirement home. Typically, the buyer is five to seven years away from retirement. The preretiree may use the property as a second home until retirement, thus making it difficult to distinguish the preretiree purchaser from the second-home purchaser. Even after retirement, many buyers think of their property as a second home if they continue to maintain a home in their place of origin. The mindset of a preretiree, however, differs significantly from that of other market segments.

Preretirees are attracted by a community's recreational amenities but are also concerned about its social fabric. Privacy and security issues assume greater importance in view of the likelihood of buyers' establishing permanent residence in the community. As a result, preretirees are more likely than other segments to buy property in a private community. In addition, while preretirees are more likely to buy in a less established community, they are still interested in climate, the quality of the area's medical facilities, convenience shopping and services, cultural opportunities, the cost of living, and learning opportunities. Some recreational communities position themselves as adult communities and partially target to the preretirement market.

Retiree households are looking for a place for immediate occupancy. Although they may buy a lot and build a custom home, they are typically concerned about the ultimate cost of the home and are drawn to built-for-sale single-family detached homes, model-home products, and resale single-family homes.

Primary-Home Buyers

Primary-home buyers are distinguished from other market segments in that they are either currently employed in the area or planning a move to the area. Most of these households include school-age children and therefore prefer to buy single-family detached homes. Primary-home buyers often make up a large percentage of the buyers in communities targeted to second-home buyers.

Although resort-home markets generally track closely with the economic cycle, their swings are often more severe, creating significant hazards for the resort homebuilder. Careful consumer research is required. Particularly on the demand side, a market study for a resort or retirement development differs significantly from a traditional market study.

Overview of Case Studies

Four case studies are presented, representing a variety of residential development types and using a variety of methods to analyze the potential markets.

Case study 3.1 is for a multifamily rental project. It illustrates a somewhat different approach to market analysis. The market penetration factor (MPF) method examines the share of demand captured by the local submarket in recent years and applies a factor to projected growth. Unlike other methods, it relies on employment rather than population projections. The overall increase of population, important in some sectors, can be an inaccurate predictor of housing demand—particularly for the multifamily sector, in which most households are childless. Net migration is the component of population growth more important to household formation, and net migration follows patterns in employment growth for all but a handful of cities (mostly resorts or retirement havens).

Case study 3.2, a suburban subdivision, illustrates the simplest type of analysis. In this case, the analysis is used to narrow down a product type and recommend a price range for development of a specific site.

Case study 3.3 illustrates the market analysis for a large master-planned community that includes an age-restricted component. It analyzes each product type separately and explores synergies among the various components. Key factors are identified, including commuting patterns, local taxes, the aging of the targeted population, and the quality of the public schools.

Case study 3.4, a pioneering downtown condominium project, demonstrates the value of focus groups and surveys when no new projects or buyer profiles exist. Around the United States, in major cities and smaller towns, planners and developers have been promoting downtown residential living as a way to bring vitality to urban areas. Some housing markets would appear perfect for new downtown housing, and almost all community leaders think it is a good idea in principle. Indeed, success stories exist. However, in many cities, on-the-ground experience for this product type is nonexistent, creating the classic problem of perceived risk for a pioneering project until proven otherwise.

In such circumstances, market analysis is a critical tool for demonstrating that an innovative concept can actually work and be profitable. Yet, if the product is pioneering, there are no comparables or tenant/buyer profiles to analyze. Market analysis for in-town pioneering projects must go beyond traditional methods to test consumer acceptance; primary research, such as surveys and focus groups, becomes a critical component of these market studies.

Notes

[1] U.S. Census Bureau, "New Privately Owned Housing Units Completed, 1968–1999," annual data prepared by the Census Bureau (Washington, D.C., 2000).

[2] NAHB data on lot sizes are for homes constructed on builder-owned lots. Such data do not include custom homes built on lots previously purchased by the homeowner, which tend to be larger than average. Over the previous 20 years, median builder lot sizes have been as small as 8,200 square feet and as large as 10,125 square feet.

[3] The National Multi Housing Council (NMHC) reports that 22 percent of the nation's existing apartments are found in complexes with 200 or more units.

[4] U.S. Census Bureau, Historical Time Series HH6, Average Population per Household and Family: 1940 to Present (Washington, D.C., December 1998).

[5] U.S. Census Bureau, Construction Reports Series C40, published monthly (Washington, D.C.). The December issue contains year-to-date statistics.

[6] American Seniors Housing Association, *The Seniors Housing Construction Report, 2000* (Washington, D.C.: ASHA, 2000).

[7] Ragatz Associates, Inc., *The American Recreational Property Survey: 1995* (Washington, D.C.: International Timeshare Foundation, 1995).

Multifamily Housing:
Colinas Gateway (1998)

G. Ronald Witten

A nationwide developer of luxury rental apartments controls a 12-acre tract of land zoned for multifamily housing in the Las Colinas neighborhood of Irving, Texas, a suburban community located northwest of Dallas and adjacent to Dallas/Fort Worth International Airport. Apartment demand in Las Colinas is supported by the area's desirable, upscale character and its large employment base. Direct access to the airport helps Las Colinas attract major corporate employers, and the workforce at office centers and industrial parks in the city of Irving exceeds 100,000 persons. Another 35,000 to 40,000 persons work at Dallas/Fort Worth International Airport.

The subject site is at the eastern edge of Las Colinas, which is not only convenient to the large job centers in Irving but also an easy commute into downtown Dallas. Surrounding development is mostly commercial in nature, including restaurants, entertainment centers (a multiscreen movie theater, several nightclubs), and small office buildings. The market's existing luxury apartments are concentrated in areas three to five miles west and northwest of the subject site.

Among the developer's concerns about the proposed development's outlook, two questions are paramount. First, what is the overall outlook for the Las Colinas apartment market given a sharp acceleration in new construction in metropolitan Dallas that includes a large block of new apartments just underway in Las Colinas? Second, what do prospective renters think about upscale apartments in the subject site's as yet untested immediate neighborhood?

Analyzing Market Demand:
Metropolitan/Regional Level

For metropolitan Dallas, multivariate analysis indicates that the best predictors of total housing demand are (1) employment growth in both the current year and the previous year, and (2) apartment availability, including both vacant existing product and new units just coming online. Those factors explain approximately 83 percent of the year-to-year variations in total housing demand in Dallas from the mid-1980s through the late 1990s. This model predicts demand for about 12,000 apartments annually in the Dallas metropolitan area during

the 1998–1999 time frame, rising to just over 14,000 units in 2000.

Supply/Demand: Future Market Support for New Development

The geographic area in which the Colinas Gateway project would expect to compete will be defined primarily by its residents. Where else would a prospective resident of this new development seriously consider living? Most often, this answer is shaped by ease of access to job centers within easy commuting distance of the subject site. That is, job centers are often (but not always) the defining central issue for a market area. Other factors, such as how the school district is perceived and whether the location is on the "right side of town" or has access to retail and other services, may come into play. The competitive market area for Colinas Gateway is defined as the city of Irving's Las Colinas neighborhood.

Next, what share of Dallas's apartment demand will Las Colinas capture? How this metropolitan level of apartment demand is divided depends on a variety of influences, such as locations of new job centers, availability of support services like shopping and restaurants/entertainment, perceived desirability of neighborhoods (based on prestige, safety/crime issues, school system reputation, and so on), and accessibility and traffic flow. One quantitative measure that can be used to reflect these various influences on neighborhood selection is the concept of a market penetration factor (MPF). This statistic calculates the proven ability of a given market area to capture its fair share of absorption across the metropolitan area.

Las Colinas posted an average MPF of 2.2 for 1989 through 1997, meaning the market area's 11.1 percent share of metropolitan Dallas's apartment demand was 2.2 times its 4.9 percent share of available apartments (Table 3.1-1). From 1989 through 1997, then, Las Colinas drew a disproportionately large share of metropolitan Dallas renters, whether because of superior job growth locally, accessibility to other growing job centers, prestige, neighborhood services, or some combination of those factors.

The market area's proven desirability can be used to forecast its future share of metropolitan demand and, thus,

Table 3.1-1
Apartment Supply/Demand Trends in the Market Area

Year	Units Absorbed		New Supply		Available Supply[1]		Market Penetration Factor[2]
	No.	Percent of Metro	No.	Percent of Metro	No.	Percent of Metro	
1989	345	3.2	0	0.0	802	2.0	1.6
1990	52	1.6	0	0.0	457	1.6	1.0
1991	1,052	39.9	1,758	41.0	2,307	8.2	4.8
1992	866	16.0	286	11.2	1,541	4.8	3.4
1993	144	2.8	358	13.9	1,033	3.6	0.8
1994	301	5.8	319	8.9	1,208	4.6	1.3
1995	953	12.5	536	8.7	1,443	5.4	2.3
1996	1,270	11.8	1,709	14.1	2,199	7.1	1.7
1997	1,859	17.1	1,508	15.2	2,437	8.2	2.1
1989–1997 Annual Average	**760**	**11.1**	**719**	**15.2**	**1,492**	**4.9**	**2.2**
1998	670	6.4	514	3.6	1,067	3.4	1.9
1999	1,480	13.1	2,364	12.5	2,761	6.9	1.9
2000	1,490	11.3	1,588	8.2	2,869	5.9	1.9

[1]Vacant existing units at the beginning of the year plus new supply to be completed that year.
[2]The market area's share of absorption divided by its share of available supply.
Source: M/PF Research, Inc.

actual apartment absorption. In this case, however, Las Colinas's future MPF was expected to dip slightly from the average seen from 1989 through 1997, reflecting that the total pool of apartment demand across metropolitan Dallas would be divided among a greater number of neighborhoods, including some areas that were under-supplied in the previous few years. In 1998, Las Colinas is forecast to account for just over 3 percent of available apartments in metropolitan Dallas, with an MPF of 1.9 pointing to a share of demand reaching just over 6 percent. Market area absorption thus is forecast near 670 units in 1998. Continuing that methodology, expected demand will climb to almost 1,500 units annually in the 1999–2000 period.

From these demand and supply forecasts, the market area's occupancy outlook can be calculated. Anticipated occupancy in Las Colinas reaches a peak of 97.6 percent in 1998 before easing to 93.3 to 93.4 percent in 1999–2000 (Table 3.1-2). By the time the proposed apartments come online in 2000, overall market conditions are expected to be somewhat more competitive than

Table 3.1-2
Apartment Market Outlook in the Market Area

Year-End		
1997	Existing Units	16,279
	Occupied Units	15,726
	Occupancy	96.6%
1998	New Supply	514
	Existing Units	16,793
	Absorption	670
	Occupied Units	16,396
	Occupancy	97.6%
1999	New Supply	2,364
	Existing Units	19,157
	Absorption	1480
	Occupied Units	17,876
	Occupancy	93.3%
2000	New Supply	1,588
	Existing Units	20,745
	Absorption	1,490
	Occupied Units	19,366
	Occupancy	93.4%

Source: M/PF Research, Inc.

in 1998, but the outlook still is healthy enough to merit planning the development of Colinas Gateway.

Competing Project Analysis: Performance of Similar Product

One of the most valuable barometers of the market support that may be available for a new development is the experience of similar properties already operating in the market area. The leasing efforts of these properties have, in effect, tested the market demand for the kind of product to be offered by the subject development.

Selecting the most relevant comparisons requires taking on the prospective resident's point of view: If I were seeking exactly the product that the subject development will offer, where else would I look, and what properties would

I consider? Restated, what would I substitute until the subject development opens (even though that substitute may not be a perfect match for the subject)?

Data on the performance of competing properties are most often assembled through detailed interviews with on-site leasing and management personnel and with the developers or owners of the project. The information from the Colinas Gateway market analysis is shown in Table 3.1-3. Although no apartments exist in the subject's immediate neighborhood, a sizable selection of new communities is found within a three- to five-mile radius. Within this cluster of competitors, projects most similar to the proposed development in overall quality achieve strong occupancy, an average of 97 percent. Rental rates average 98.9 cents per square foot for a mix of units with a typical size of 935 square feet.

Table 3.1-3
Competitive Apartment Communities in the Market Area

Community Name	Date Compl.	Occu.	Total Units	Unit Size Range/ Average Size	Average Total Rent	Total Rent/ Sq. Ft.	Base Rent/ Sq. Ft.[1]	Bedroom-Bath Mix 1-1	2-1 or 1+den	2-2	3-2
Bluff View	1997	98%	503	386–1,750 804	$877	$1.090	$1.011	327 65%	107 21%	68 14%	1 0%
Colinas Ranch	1994	95%	319	743–1,363 1,018	938	0.921	0.908	80 25%	24 8%	174 55%	41 13%
Concord	1997	98%	258	710–1,135 913	818	0.895	0.878	116 45%	40 16%	102 4%	—
Crossroads	1997	98%	440	778–1,391 1,007	983	0.976	0.881	268 61%	25 6%	147 33%	—
Eastside	1991	98%	476	707–1,240 966	894	0.925	0.879	160 34%	68 14%	204 43%	44 9%
Meadow Oaks	1993	96%	358	631–1,384 918	971	1.058	0.944	198 55%	30 8%	102 28%	28 8%
Mission Creek	1998	99%	514	710–1,390 938	937	0.999	0.957	264 51%	10 2%	218 42%	22 4%
Vista Ranch	1997	97%	308	651–1,271 946	957	1.012	1.007	144 47%	—	140 45%	24 8%
Total/Average		**97%**	**3,176**	**386–1,750 935**	**$923**	**$0.988**	**$0.935**	**1,557 49%**	**304 10%**	**1,155 36%**	**160 5%**

[1] Base rent reflects the starting price for the most basic unit (i.e., one without custom features such as garages, views, fireplaces, or other features that may be available only in select apartments).
Source: M/PF Research, Inc.

To allow meaningful conclusions to be drawn for the subject, the rental rate performance of each competing property is "scrubbed" by adjusting for age of the property and for amenity and feature differences. The goal is to arrive at base rents that reflect, as closely as possible, a common level of product offering. Further, these rents must be related to the corresponding size of the apartments in the property, recognizing that smaller apartments typically produce higher rents per square foot than do more spacious units. Table 3.1-4 illustrates this process.

Maximizing Absorption and Potential Income

Strategies for achieving maximum absorption and rental income may vary by developer type. For example, many publicly traded real estate investment trusts (REITs) that are directly involved in apartment development focus on speeding lease-up at the expense of achieving peak rents. In that fashion, two REIT goals are realized: earnings flow is accelerated, and some rent upside remains to show earnings growth in future periods. In contrast, merchant builders may focus on maximizing rents (even with the use of free rent at move-in) because the property will be sold when stabilization is reached, and the sales price is based in part on the rents in place at that time.

Underserved Niches

Whether the developer expects to be a short-term or long-term owner of the property, two strategies are immediately relevant from a market-research perspective. First, the property will perform best if its product taps specific resident demand segments not fully served by competitors. Second, the economics of new, upscale development characteristic of construction in recent years hinge heavily on the ability to provide amenities that residents value sufficiently to pay added rent. Features previously found only in single-family homes—for example, private garages, marble entries, side-by-side refrigerators with built-in ice and water dispensers, other top-grade kitchen appliances, and oversized oval bathtubs—today contribute significantly to the initial investment yield of new apartment development.

Understanding the Target Market

Critical to identifying the product niches to seek out in a given site location is a basic understanding of the residents who most likely will be drawn to new apartments at the subject site.

■ Who will walk through the leasing office door on opening day? Singles? Professional couples? Young families? Empty nesters? Retirees? How many of each? What product will they seek, and what can they afford?

■ The answers to these and other questions can come only from primary survey research. Although generic demographic data is available, including information on owners as well as renters, the key issue is coupling the apartment residents' demographic characteristics with their locations and product preferences for apartment living.

Resident Survey Research

To plan for leasing at the subject property, one assumption is made: occupants of the apartment properties most similar to the subject are representative of the prospective residents who will want to live at the subject property. Although not all of the subject's future residents will move directly from these existing properties, competitors' residents do represent a cross section of the prospects who deem rental housing like the subject an attractive option in this general market area.

Mail-survey techniques are most appropriate for statistically valid results on a wide range of detailed product questions. (After this detailed market analysis reveals a product concept that can be developed by the project's architect, focus groups with a small number of renter prospects may help refine the product designed.) The sample design for any resident survey must take into consideration response rates, which can vary from 5 percent to 50 percent depending on survey incentive, length of questionnaire, and other survey logistics. Cautious questionnaire design is obviously critical to successfully eliciting a meaningful survey response.

In the case of Colinas Gateway, 2,000 questionnaires were mailed to a stratified sample of residents in the

Table 3.1-4

Comparable Property Rent Adjustment Model for the Market Area

	Colinas Ranch	Crossroads	Concord	Meadow Oaks	Vista Ranch	Eastside	Bluff View	Mission Creek
Year Opened	1994	1997	1997	1993	1997	1991	1997	1998
Age (years)	4	1	1	5	1	7	1	0
Age Factor (per year)	0.5%	0.5%	0.5%	0.5%	0.5%	0.5%	0.5%	0.5%
Total Rent Adjustment	$18	$4	$4	$22	$5	$30	$4	$0
Age-Adjusted Rent	$942	$893	$806	$888	$957	$879	$817	$898
Low Monthly Rent (minus parking)	$924	$888	$898	$867	$952	$849	$813	$893
Average Unit Size	1,018	1,007	913	918	946	966	804	933
Total Base Rent/Sq. Ft.	$0.908	$0.881	$0.878	$0.944	$1.006	$0.879	$1.011	$0.957
Amenity Deductions[1]								
Nine-foot Ceilings ($10)	$10	$10	$5	$10	$10	$10	$10	$10
Bay Windows ($5)		2			1		1	
Bookshelves/Desks ($3)			1	1	2	0	3	5
Breakfast Area ($10)						1		
Ceiling Fan ($5)		5	5	5	5	5	5	5
Ceramic Tile Entry ($3)		5	5	5			5	5
Crown Molding ($5)		5	5	5	5	5		5
Double-Sink Vanity ($5)	1			1		1		
Double-Sided Fireplace ($30)							9	
Fireplace ($25)	16	25	14	20	21	25	6	
Fireplace Custom Mantle/Tile ($5)	3	5		4				
Intrusion Alarm ($5)	5	5	5	5	5	5		5
Kitchen Island ($20)						3	5	
Kitchen TV ($10)	10							
Microwave ($3)	3	3	3	3		3	3	3
Mirror Walls/Doors ($5)				5		5	3	
Multiple Phone Lines ($5)		5						5
Oval Tubs ($5)						2	3	
Townhome-style								
One-Bedroom Unit ($75)	2						3	
Two-, Three-Bedroom Unit ($150)	16				9		1	
Under-Cabinet Lighting ($5)						5		
Utility Room ($10)	1	3			1			
Total Interior Amenities	$67	$71	$45	$64	$59	$70	$55	$43
Business Center ($5)	5				5			5
Car Wash ($5)	5							
Jacuzzi ($3)	3	3				3		
Picnic Area ($3)		3		3				3
Sauna ($3)		3		3		3		
Sport Court ($10)	10	10						
Total Common Area Amenities	$23	$19	$0	$6	$5	$6	$0	$8
Total Amenity Deductions	$90	$90	$45	$70	$64	$76	$55	$51
Age- and Amenity-Adjusted Monthly Rent	$852	$803	$761	$818	$893	$803	$762	$847
Age- and Amenity-Adjusted Rent/Sq. Ft.	$0.84	$0.80	$0.83	$0.89	$0.94	$0.83	$0.95	$0.90

[1]Deductions are based proportionally on the percentage of units having an amenity.
Source: M/PF Research, Inc.

properties viewed as primary and secondary competition to the subject. At the conclusion of a two-week response period, 340 completed survey forms had been returned, which gives a response rate of 17 percent.

For each site, a "target market" is defined to help focus product planning. The target market for a given property is the resident group that (1) is favorably predisposed to the subject's location, and (2) earns income adequate to afford at least the lowest-priced floor plan in the property. The target market for Colinas Gateway is dominated by very affluent single people and childless couples, many of whom are newcomers to metropolitan Dallas. Figures 3.1-1 through 3.1-4 and Tables 3.1-5 and 3.1-6 illustrate the findings produced by survey research.

Through survey results, prospective residents expressed strong interest in a luxury product and a willingness to pay the extra rent required to provide upgraded features. Among the interior amenities that at least half the target

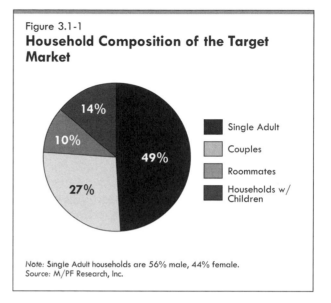

Figure 3.1-1
Household Composition of the Target Market

Single Adult
Couples
Roommates
Households w/ Children

Note: Single Adult households are 56% male, 44% female.
Source: M/PF Research, Inc.

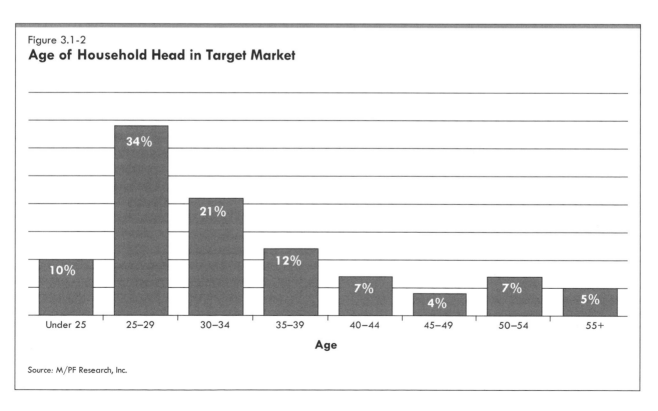

Figure 3.1-2
Age of Household Head in Target Market

Source: M/PF Research, Inc.

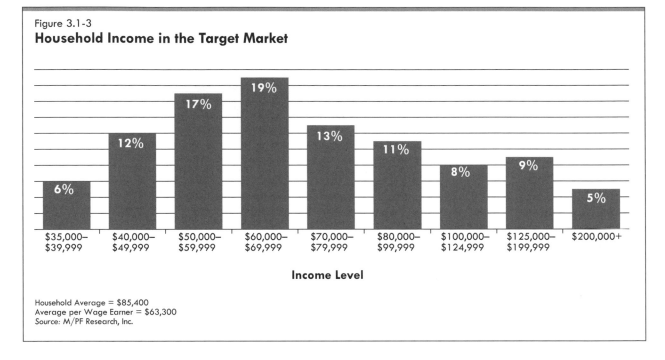

Figure 3.1-3
Household Income in the Target Market

Income Level

Household Average = $85,400
Average per Wage Earner = $63,300
Source: M/PF Research, Inc.

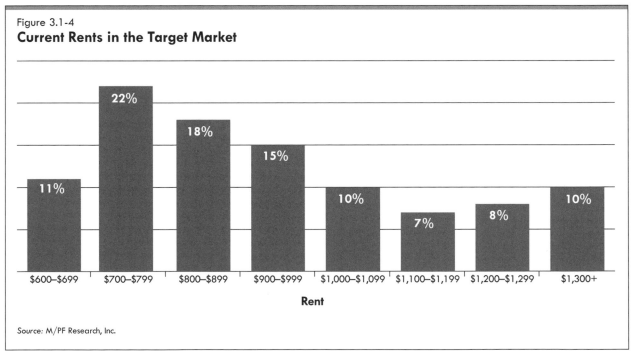

Figure 3.1-4
Current Rents in the Target Market

Rent

Source: M/PF Research, Inc.

Table 3.1-5

Location of Employment in Target Market

Area	Percent
DFW Airport or West/Northwest Dallas Suburbs	36
Downtown to Northwest Highway	30
Northwest Highway to LBJ Freeway	10

Source: M/PF Research, Inc.

Table 3.1-6

Rental Rate/Income Levels in Target Market

Annual Household Income	Average Monthly Rent	Rent as a Percentage of Income
$35,000–$ 39,999	$ 838	27
40,000– 49,999	847	23
50,000– 59,999	861	19
60,000– 69,999	904	17
70,000– 79,999	963	15
80,000– 89,999	1,015	14
90,000– 99,999	1,055	13
100,000– 124,999	1,049	11
125,000– 199,999	1,183	9
200,000+	1,355	8

Source: M/PF Research, Inc.

market rated worth the cost were attached storage closets, Berber carpeting, utility rooms, built-in bookshelves, kitchen pantries, water filter systems, microwave ovens, side-by-side refrigerators, and double-sink vanities (Table 3.1-7). Tested in separate questions, fireplaces held considerable appeal. Common-area amenities that ranked high included a top-notch fitness center, a resort-style pool area, a jogging trail, and a car wash, plus controlled access into the property.

Of course, the expressed support for upgraded product must be cross-checked with the residents' ability to afford their wish list of product features. In an upscale development charging new-apartment rents, how many prospective renters can afford the floor plan they prefer? To answer this vital question, the recommended rental rates are translated into a minimum income level (based on the target market's actual spending patterns—not on the maximum management policy of, for example, 33 percent of income devoted to rent). Next, actual income levels are compared to required incomes to determine what share of prospective residents could afford their preferred apartments. In the case of Colinas Gateway, affordability is not a challenge; more than 96 percent of the target market households can afford to lease their floor plan of choice (Table 3.1-8).

Profiling Future Competition

After documenting the nature and depth of demand in the competitive market area, the next step is carefully to assemble as comprehensive a profile as possible of planned new developments. Factors important to the supply/demand analysis discussed above include not only the overall quantity of new competition but also the nature of the product to be offered. What floor plan types and sizes will be available? What common area amenities and parking options will be provided? How will the locations of competitors compare to the subject's location?

Research for Colinas Gateway reveals that near-term deliveries will offer units in about the same floor plan mix already seen in the marketplace, but that unit sizes in the two-bedroom and three-bedroom sectors are increasing notably. Also, premium parking (either private garages or carports) will be a standard feature for all units in the next round of completions.

Developing Product Design Recommendations

Business sense would lead a developer to position a new project to avoid the bulk of competition that will be leasing during the subject's lease-up period. That approach is sound, as long as avoiding competitors' product does not push the subject into a niche lacking adequate demand. Sometimes, what appears to be a void in the market

Table 3.1-7
Preferred Interior Amenities of the Target Market

	Extra Monthly Cost	Interest Level
General Features		
Unit-attached storage	$5	70%
Upgraded Berber carpet	5	52
Separate utility room	10	51
Washer/dryer in unit	35	44
Monitored security alarm	25	43
8' x 10' storage space separate from apartment	30	35
Arched doorways	5	28
Built-in computer desk	25	27
Upgraded entry foyer with travertine floor	3	21
Living/Dining Room		
Bookshelves	3	75
10' ceiling	10	47
Track lighting	3	43
Mirrored accent wall in dining room	5	43
Vaulted ceiling	20	33
Art niche	3	29
Kitchen		
Kitchen pantry	5	77
Water filter	3	54
Large microwave oven	3	52
Side-by-side refrigerator with ice maker and water dispenser in door	50	50
Hardwood floor in kitchen	10	46
Gourmet kitchen island with pot rack above	25	41
Master Bedroom/Bath		
Double-sink vanity	5	56

Source: M/PF Research, Inc.

turns out to be a black hole: no product serves that niche because no demand exists.

To define the optimum unit mix for Colinas Gateway, resident demand is contrasted with current performances are with future supply profiles. In this case, performances were strong across every general floor plan type, and near-term supply does not appear likely to notably overstock or underserve any option. Thus, the target market's income-qualified demand preferences (excluding the handful of households who could not afford the unit type desired) provide a direct guide to the subject's appropriate floor plan mix, which is recommended at 50 percent one-bedroom/one-bath units, 14 percent one-bedroom/den/one-bath or two-bedroom/one-bath units, 32 percent two-bedroom/two-bath units, and 4 percent three-bedroom/two-bath units (Table 3.1-9).

Appropriate unit sizes and unit mix within each general floor plan type are determined for Colinas Gateway by examining (1) performances at existing properties, (2) new supply scheduled for delivery in the immediate future, and (3) the size preferences expressed in the renter survey. This information for one-bedroom apartments is arrayed in Table 3.1-10. The large stock of existing available product covers a broad spectrum of unit sizes, and occupancy is healthy in every sector. Future supply also is expected to be ample and diverse, though projects under construction include only a few units in the already popular category of 750 to 799 square feet. Renter prospects voice support for a variety of options, with the largest demand registered for mid-sized apartments. Similar analysis is performed to recommend Colinas Gateway's appropriate amenity package by unit type.

Pricing the Units Recommended
The optimum monthly rent level for each recommended floor plan can be identified by a statistical array of the rents achieved by competing floor plans in the market area. After adjustments are made for major amenities specific to each floor plan (e.g., fireplaces, direct-entry garages, townhouse design, washer/dryer, etc.) to arrive at a base rent, these monthly rents can be displayed relative to their square footage, with a regression trend line then placed through the price/size points. Variations from the market norm (as depicted by the trend line) may be explained by location, curb appeal, management strength or weakness, specific unit location or views, or in some cases simply by mispricing.

Multifamily Housing: Colinas Gateway *(continued)*

To determine the base monthly rental rate each of the subject's floor plans should achieve, the analyst studies the position of floor plans offered by the competitors most like the subject in location, management, and general quality level. Perhaps this analysis translates to a premium to the market; perhaps, as in this case, to a discount.

For Colinas Gateway, the most relevant comparison is Concord, which also offers high-quality product but in a second-tier setting outside the primary clustering of competitors. Concord's rents, after major amenity adjustments, dipped 5 to 8 percent below the market norm for 1990s-generation product in the market area.

Table 3.1-8
Subject Unit Mix Based on Affordability

Floor Plan	A Percent Preferring Floor Plan[1]	Recommended Base Rent[2]	Rent Percentage of Income[3]	Minimum Income Required	B Percent Qualified for Preferred Floor Plan	A x B Affordability Index	Unit Mix Based on Affordability[4]
1BR-1B	13	$ 650	25	$ 31,200	100	12.9	13%
1BR-1B	20	690	24	34,500	100	19.9	21
1BR-1B	17	725	24	36,000	98	16.9	17
2BR-1B	14	810	25	38,900	100	14.0	14
2BR-2B	15	925	24	46,300	88	13.2	14
2BR-2B	17	1,045	23	54,500	94	15.9	16
3BR-2B	4	1,235	23	64,400	100	4.0	4
Total						96.8	100%

[1]Based on respondents who selected a preferred unit type.
[2]Base rents reflect the starting price for the most basic unit (i.e., one without custom features such as garages, views, fireplaces, or other features that may be available only in select apartments).
[3]Rent-to-income ratio for the least affluent households seeking each floor plan. The typical household will spend a lower share of income on rent.
[4]Affordability index reapportioned to equal 100 percent.
Source: M/PF Research, Inc.

Table 3.1-9
Recommended Unit Mix for Subject Community

	1BR-1B	1BR+den/2BR-1B	2BR-2B	3BR-2B
Presently Occupied, Target Market	41 %	15 %	41 %	3 %
Preferred, Target Market	45	20	30	7
Income Qualified for Preferred Floor Plan, Target Market	51	14	30	4
Under Construction	49	9	35	7
Recommended Mix	50 %	14 %	32 %	4 %

Source: M/PF Research, Inc.

Table 3.1-10
Unit Sizes: One-Bedroom/One-Bath Units

	Unit Size (Sq. Ft.)	Number Existing Units in Top Competitors	Current Occupancy (Percent)	Number Units in Future Competitors	Survey Preference
	<600	151	98.7	74	
	600–649	217	98.2	36	
Recommended	650–699	86	97.7	330	
Recommended	700–749	544	98.5	289	small = 13%
Recommended	750–799	469	99.1	98	mid-sized = 20%
	800–849	346	98.3	265	large = 13%
	850–899	296	96.6	91	
	900–949	22	95.5	82	
	950–999	26	100.0	0	
	1,000–1,049	35	97.1	0	

Source: M/PF Research, Inc.

Figure 3.1-5
Rents for One-Bedroom/One-Bath Units in the Market Area

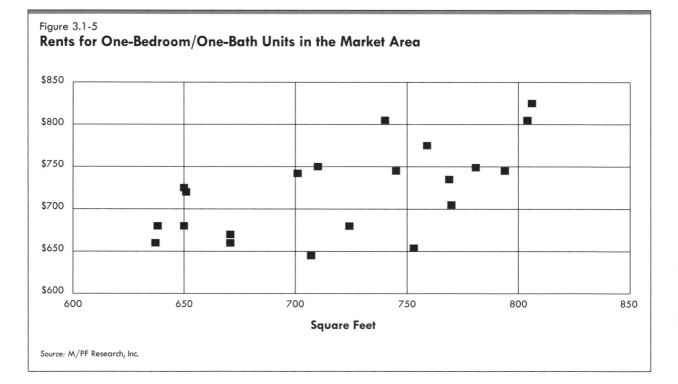

Source: M/PF Research, Inc.

Table 3.1-11
Recommended Apartment Product for Colinas Gateway

Floor Plan	Number of Units	Percent of Total	Unit Size (Sq. Ft.)	Base[1] Monthly Rent	Base Rent/ Sq. Ft.
1BR-1B	48	13	653	$ 650	$ 0.995
1BR-1B	74	20	718	690	0.961
1BR-1B	64	17	770	725	0.942
1BR-den	52	14	823	810	0.984
2BR-2B	56	15	1,052	925	0.879
2BR-2B	63	17	1,191	1,045	0.877
3BR-2B	15	4	1,302	1,235	0.949
Total/Average[2]	372	100%	887	$ 824	$ 0.929

[1]Base rents reflect the starting price for the most basic unit and include the following features as standard: Berber carpet, ceiling fan, ceramic tile entry, intrusion alarm, microwave oven, multiple phone lines, oval tub, track lighting, under-cabinet lighting.
[2]Averages are weighted by number of units.
Source: M/PF Research, Inc.

The range of rents seen at competitive projects in the one-bedroom segment is illustrated in Figure 3.1-5. The methodology described is used for each of the subject's floor plans to produce base rents at Colinas Gateway averaging 92.9 cents per square foot, or $824 per month, for units with a typical size of 887 square feet (Table 3.1-11).

Next, the value of amenities that survey results show as appropriate for some, but not all, units is added to the subject's rent potential. Also, the value of parking in a mix of private garages and carports is added. These extras boost Colinas Gateway's rent potential by 14.6 cents per square foot, yielding total achievable rents at an average of $1.075 per square foot, or $954 per unit per month.

Colinas Gateway is an example of applying the MPF method and using primary research to study the market potential of a proposed apartment project. The MPF technique works particularly well for determining market potential for multifamily residential development, especially in growing urban areas like Dallas. It might also be applicable to for-sale residential developments. By studying a market area's capture rate in relation to the metropolitan area, the analyst can gain an understanding of the competitiveness of the market area and at what rate it can continue to absorb new product.

For-Sale Subdivision Housing:
The McCall Tract (1997)

Adrienne Schmitz

The McCall parcel is a 22-acre site located in Fairfax County, Virginia, a suburban area about 20 miles outside of Washington, D.C. It is part of a 320-acre tract called McCall Farms, a property that has been developing for about six years. A total of 1,400 lots have been sold to individual builders, including 67 single-family lots, 745 townhouse lots, and 588 multifamily lots. As of 1997, 22 townhome lots and 500 multifamily lots remain undeveloped. No single-family lots remain in McCall Farms. All of the available lots are part of a flexible zoning designation, as is the subject property.

The immediate surrounding area experienced rapid development in the 1990s and is near buildout. It is a desirable location, but one where affordability drives the market. Young families form the largest proportion of new households, drawn by the reputation of the county school system, the convenience of commuting to nearby office parks, and major transportation routes into downtown Washington, D.C. They are also drawn by the relative affordability of the locale compared to most closer-in suburbs.

The specific site is well located within the market area. It is just off a major commuting route, but with enough of a buffer to shield the property from negative effects. The property is within walking distance of a new community shopping center and within a short drive to major shopping and other amenities, including a library, public golf course, and several parks. Aesthetically, the site is similar to others in the market area, with views of neighboring residential communities. There are no exceptional wooded areas or other unusually desirable views.

A homebuilder interested in purchasing the parcel wants to determine the optimal product type to meet current market conditions. The purpose of this study is to determine the most marketable residential product type and pricing structure for homes to be developed on the site.

Market Demand

First, the economics and demographics of the region are studied. It is important to understand the dynamics of the broad economy and whether it is in a growth cycle or trending downward. In this case, both the metropolitan area and the county are characterized by strong and moderately growing economies, a well-educated workforce, low unemployment, and high incomes. Further, the economic base is continuing to diversify, with increasing numbers of private sector high-tech jobs replacing federal government jobs.

In terms of analyzing demand for suburban residential development, the characteristics of the immediate market area are the more useful data. Typically, more than half of the purchasers in a new development come from a relatively small distance, often not more than a few miles. A market area's characteristics may reflect the region, or may be considerably different from the regional market, and therefore must be studied in depth. One way to identify the market area is by asking sales agents at competitive projects where their buyers are coming from. Many agents maintain detailed buyer profiles for their projects.

The number of buyers tracked might be relatively small. Unlike a large, master-planned community that can have hundreds, or even thousands, of sales per year, a builder's subdivision might sell 30 or 40 homes per year. This small sample size makes it difficult to apply the kinds of statistical methods that are valid for a larger sample. Instead of relying on sophisticated technique, the analyst must draw more from conversations with real estate professionals operating within the market area and from the analyst's experience in the market and in similar markets.

For the competitive projects surrounding the McCall site, about 60 percent of the buyers come from nearby communities, with most of the others relocating from out of state. Few buyers are drawn from other parts of the metropolitan area. It is therefore appropriate to use the county's demographic data supported with field survey data. (See Table 3.2-1.)

County population data indicate that growth in the immediate area was rapid between 1980 and 1990, with an average annual increase of 1,920 new households per year. Between 1990 and 1997, growth slowed to an average of 1,157 new households annually. Demographic projections indicate that over the next three years, growth in the market area will continue at approximately the same pace, with 1,133 new households per year in 2000. Of those, about 29 percent will be renter households, and the remaining 71 percent will be owner households. Thus,

Table 3.2-1
Demographic Summary of Market Area

Year	1980	1990	1997	2000
Population	70,800	125,200	148,100	154,000
Households	25,700	44,900	53,000	56,400
Household Size	2.75	2.79	2.79	2.73
Annual New Households		1,920	1,157	1,133
Percent Owners			71%	71%
Annual New Owner Households			822	804

the market for new for-sale housing is approximately 800 households per year.

The median household income in the market area is $68,000, which is somewhat less than the countywide median of $70,000. The largest income segment is the $50,000 to $74,999 range, accounting for one-third of the households. Table 3.2-2 shows the household income distribution.

Household income does not translate directly into housing affordability because many factors go into the equation besides income. Particularly when considering buyers who are moving from another owned home, who generally use equity from an existing home as a downpayment, affordability is difficult to determine on a market-area level. However, income does indicate an approximate portion of households that are in the general range of housing affordability.

Discussions with sales agents at currently selling new single-family projects in the market area suggest that the majority of single-family buyers fall into the $75,000 and over income bracket. From the income data in Table 3.2-2, it can be estimated that about 42 percent of the households are able to afford a new single-family home. With new households in the market area estimated at about 800 annually, about 335 of those households are able to purchase a new single-family home each year.

The average household size in the market area is 2.79 persons. This size is slightly larger than household size in the county as a whole and most likely indicates a higher proportion of family households. Conversations with local sales agents reveal that buyer profiles vary by the type of housing purchased, but buyers possess certain characteristics across the board. Most buyers are employed by the high-tech firms located in nearby office parks. The primary reason for purchasing a home in this market area is the convenience of the location. In all buyer groups, at least 60 percent are from the local market area.

Buyers of single-family homes in the market area naturally have higher-than-average incomes, ranging from $75,000 to more than $100,000. They are in their mid-30s to mid-40s, and most are families with one or two children. Townhome buyers include traditional families, blended families, divorced and single parents, retirees, and young couples. A wide range of ages and incomes is represented in this buyer segment. Condominium buyers fall into two disparate categories—young singles and couples buying first homes, and older move-down buyers. Families with children make up a very small part of this market. Incomes range upward of $35,000 and ages are

Table 3.2-2
Household Income Distribution

Income Range	Percent of Households
<$25,000	4.7
$25,000–49,999	19.9
$50,000–74,999	33.7
$75,000–99,999	18.7
$100,000 and over	23.1

split between those in their 20s and retirees, generally over 65.

Competitive Analysis

This section of the study examines projects currently being marketed that would compete with a project at the subject site. The purpose of analyzing existing projects is to gain an understanding of what sells best in this market area, in terms of both product characteristics and pricing.

Because the purpose of this particular study is to determine the best residential use for a property, all types of for-sale residential projects are included: single family, townhome, and condominium. Rental apartments are not included in the study because this type of development is not under consideration for the property. Also not included are custom home developments and most projects with fewer than 20 units because, with certain exceptions, these product types have minimal sales and do not affect the market significantly.

Numerous new projects are on the market in the surrounding neighborhoods. However, few lots remain in most of them, and little land remains available for devel-

opment of new subdivisions. Of the lots currently on the market, the vast majority are in townhome developments, where a total of nearly 800 lots remain.

From 1995 to 1997, sales have been variable throughout the metropolitan area, including this market area. Sales fluctuate dramatically from month to month and from one project to another. Overall, however, a well-conceived single-family project can expect sales of between 2.0 and 2.5 per month, and a townhome project can expect about 3.0 sales per month. Condominium projects are selling at an average of 4.5 per month.

Competitive Single-Family Projects

Single-family developments in the market area encompass a wide range of products and prices. (See Table 3.2-3.) Generally, projects in the McCall Farms market area attain prices that are lower than those to the south and east, and higher than those at the less-developed, farther out western edge of the county. No single-family projects are selling within McCall Farms. Average base prices (prices of homes without options or custom features) in single-family subdivisions in the market range from $225,000 for a basic, value-oriented home to $315,000 for an upscale home in a neighborhood backing onto parkland.

Table 3.2-3

Summary of Single-Family Projects

Project/Builder	Total Lots	Lots Remaining	1997 Sales/Mo.	Median Sq. Ft.	Median Base Price	Median $/ Sq. Ft.
Woodley/Williams	382	14	0.5	3,049	$315,000	$103
Monroe/Winchester	126	39	3.4	2,683	309,000	115
The Lakes/SMC	31	13	0.8	2,740	296,000	108
The Lakes/NVHomes	34	33	1.6	2,745	284,000	103
Holly Chase/Toll	106	76	4.0	2,588	284,000	110
Lakeview/Toll	88	1	2.5	2,617	278,000	106
The Lakes/Hovnanian	37	21	1.2	2,610	260,000	100
Century/Toll	102	32	2.2	2,500	257,000	103
Manors/U.S. Home	36	23	1.5	2,335	236,000	101
Sycamore/Centex	154	22	4.8	1,968	226,000	115
Autumn Glen/Richmond	124	18	3.1	2,378	225,000	95
Total / Average	**1,220**	**292**	**25.6 / 2.3**	**2,565**	**$270,000**	**$105**

Centex's Sycamore community leads in sales pace, with an average of 4.8 sales per month. The project is priced at the low end of the spectrum, and though floor plans are small for this market, with an average of only 1,968 square feet, they are open in feel and offer a good deal of style. The models at Sycamore are a new product line designed to capture a budget-oriented buyer. Prices average $226,000. Clearly, buyers are reacting favorably. The two other projects in this low price range, Manors and Autumn Glen, are not selling nearly as well, despite having better values on a per-square-foot basis. But homes at the Manors and Autumn Glen are lacking in style, and discriminating buyers reject the low-end look of these two projects in favor of Sycamore.

The second-best seller is Holly Chase, with an average of 4.0 sales per month. Priced toward the high end of the market at an average of $284,000, this project is by a builder with a reputation for good value. Sales are also strong at Monroe, where Winchester is building attractive, high-quality homes on one of the few wooded sites in the market area. Prices are the second highest in the market, averaging $309,000, but deemed worth it, as indicated by 3.4 sales per month. Buyers are often willing to pay a premium for wooded lots such as these.

These sales figures indicate that price is not the only determinant of marketing success. Buyers seek style, quality, and value when purchasing a home. In order to achieve success in a competitive market such as this one, a builder must assess the strengths of other builders in the market and develop a product line that meets buyer demands at competitive prices.

Currently, 11 single-family projects are actively being marketed that would be competitive with a new single-family product at McCall Farms. The active projects total 1,220 lots. Of these, 928 homes have been sold, leaving an inventory of only 292 lots on the market. At the current sales pace of 25.6 per month overall, that figure equates to an 11-month inventory of lots in existing subdivisions. An additional 203 lots are zoned for single-family development and will begin sales in 1998. Even with these additional zoned lots, about a 19-month supply of single-family lots remains in the market area. No land parcels await approval for single-family zoning.

Competitive Townhome Projects

McCall Farms and the surrounding developments are packed with townhome offerings. Six townhome projects are selling in McCall Farms, with another nine selling in other developments throughout the market area. These projects total 1,364 lots, of which 798 lots remain on the market. In McCall Farms, only 137 townhouse lots remain. (See Table 3.2-4.)

Average base prices in the market area range from $140,000 to $238,000. Within McCall Farms, prices cover a narrower range, from $152,000 to $189,000. The marketwide average price is $172,333, about $3,000 higher than average prices in McCall Farms.

With few exceptions, most builders are competing for the same buyers, with similar products and pricing. Townhouse units are typically three levels, 20 feet wide, with a one-car garage occupying most of the ground level. In this market area, townhomes are generally midlevel products with certain luxury features included. Features such as deluxe master baths, upgraded kitchens, molding packages, and upgraded carpeting tend to be the norm.

With 5.5 sales per month, Trafalgar's Carriage Hill is the market area's townhome sales leader. A highly desirable location coupled with a very well-designed product easily beats out the competition. The price, averaging $153,000, is misleading because most buyers are purchasing the optional three-level rear extension that adds $15,000 to $20,000 to the base price.

Other top sellers include Rockland, Rosewood, and Centex at McCall Farms, and Laing at Coppermill. Rockland's project just sold out. At $155,000, it offered one of the lower-priced products at McCall Farms.

Rosewood's newly opened project, on the other hand, appeals to the high-end buyer seeking a top-of-the-line townhome. With only 16 lots to develop and no direct competitors, what is likely to be a fairly narrow market should not hurt sales potential for Rosewood. Centex is positioned at the midrange of McCall Farms. Centex offers a good-sized unit with numerous customizing options. One such option is a very popular master-suite loft located above the second floor. The loft can be finished as either a study or a deluxe, oversized master bath. Unfortunately, new county building codes may preclude

Table 3.2-4
Summary of Townhome Projects

Project/Builder	Total Lots	Lots Remaining	1997 Sales/Mo.	Median Base Price	Median Sq. Ft.	Median $/Sq. Ft.
McCall Farms/Rosewood	16	14	5.0	$189,000	2,160	$88
McCall Farms/Engle	43	35	2.0	177,000	2,097	84
McCall Farms/Centex	85	10	5.0	175,000	1,899	92
McCall Farms/Equity	81	74	0.5	166,000	2,060	81
McCall Farms/Rockland	85	0	5.1	155,000	1,632	95
McCall Farms/Laing	116	4	4.8	152,000	1,557	98
Random Hills/Equity	44	35	2.3	238,000	2,395	99
Random Hills/Winchester	150	147	0.8	203,000	2,141	95
Fairway/Harmon	80	4	3.0	188,000	2,050	92
Ridgewood/Ryland	120	118	1.0	180,000	2,120	85
Penderbrook/Winchester	70	45	2.8	170,000	1,934	88
Coppermill/Laing	208	203	5.0	158,000	1,557	101
Carriage Hill/Trafalgar	96	42	5.5	153,000	1,272	120
Harmony/Pulte	116	57	4.0	141,000	1,560	90
Fairway/Richmond	54	10	0.5	140,000	1,632	86
Total/Average	**1,364**	**798**	**44.3 / 3.0**	**$172,333**	**1,871**	**$92**

further sales of lofts, and Centex has suspended the sale of lofts pending clarification of the new codes. Laing at Coppermill has nearly sold out. Laing, with an average base price at $158,000, offers one of the more attractive townhomes in its price range, easily outselling its lower-priced competitors.

At the current sales pace of 44.3 per month for the total market area, an 18-month inventory of townhome lots is now on the market. An additional 404 are zoned, and 668 lots are awaiting zoning approval. Most of these 1,072 new lots will enter the market over the next year or so, increasing the current inventory to well beyond what can be readily absorbed at the current sales pace. The oversupply of townhomes on the market likely will lead to slowed sales paces and discounted prices.

Competitive Condominium Projects

Only three condominium projects are selling in the market area. The Brighton is a garden-style, low-rise complex, and the Crescent is a secured, mid-rise elevator building with underground parking. Both offer luxury-style units of one- or two-bedrooms. The third condominium project is Fairmont, located to the south of McCall Farms. Fairmont is a garden-style development targeted to young, first-time buyers. (See Table 3.2-5.)

Average condominium prices range from $107,000 to $118,000, filling the niche below townhomes. On a price-per-square-foot basis, they vary widely. Elevator buildings are more expensive to build than walkups, and selling prices reflect the added cost. The average price per square foot at the Crescent is $142, compared with the Brighton at $118. The Fairmont, with average unit prices at $115,000, has a price per square foot of $101.

The three projects provide a good range of condo-minium products to appeal to the market split of buyers: young singles or couples just starting out and retirees downscaling to a lower-maintenance home. The Crescent, in particular, caters to the retiree market, with security, elevators, and underground parking. The Brighton and Fairmont both satisfy the young buyer seeking a more

Table 3.2-5
Summary of Condominium Projects

Project/Builder	Total Units	Units Remaining	1997 Sales/Mo.	Median Base Price	Median Sq. Ft.	Median $/Sq. Ft.
Brighton/Smith	184	107	3.5	$118,000	1,000	$118
Fairmont/FMD	108	89	3.8	115,000	1,140	101
Crescent/Smith	328	131	6.3	107,000	753	142
Total/Average	**620**	**327**	**13.6/4.5**	**$113,333**	**964**	**$118**

economical product. The Brighton's emphasis is on style, features, and recreational amenities, while the Fairmont maximizes space for the dollar.

The three projects total 620 units. Of these, 293 units have sold, leaving 327 units available for sale as of 1997. With a marketwide sales pace of 13.6 units per month, this number amounts to a two-year supply. Because the market area is largely a family-oriented locale, the market for condominiums is narrow, with the potential for successful absorption of not more than three competitors at any given time. Market conditions are not likely to change in the near term.

In addition to the units now on the market, an additional 328 units are zoned and 202 are awaiting zoning approval. All of these units could be developed as either rental apartments or condominiums. Conversations with the developers involved indicate that one of the zoned projects, with 200 units, is slated for development as a mid-priced, condominium-ownership, garden-style complex. The remaining 330 units in the pipeline will be developed as rental apartments. The current offerings, combined with zoned units that will be entering the market during 1998, will continue to saturate the market for some time, thus curtailing the viability of additional condominium products.

Table 3.2-6 summarizes existing, new, and planned housing units by type in the market area. Of existing homes, single-family dwellings comprise nearly 60 percent of the housing inventory in the market area. Townhomes account for 24 percent, and multifamily units are 18 percent

of the total. These ratios are fairly typical throughout the metropolitan area for outlying suburbs such as this one. However, those percentages shift dramatically in this market area for new units and undeveloped lots. Most notable is the increasing shortage of new single-family units being developed. Over the next few years, no new housing in the market area will be developed to satisfy demand from move-up buyers. At the same time, demand for move-up housing is likely to remain strong as the current batch of townhome dwellers mature, form families, and gain the income to support single-family homes.

Recommendations
The market for condominiums in this outlying suburb is very thin, and demand for the next three or four years will be accommodated by existing and planned projects. The townhome market is saturated and likely to remain so. Single-family development is declining significantly, while the market for such products is likely to remain strong. Thus, single-family homes are the obvious product to develop on this site. Because affordability is an important consideration, a zero-lot-line home or "patio home" would be an optimal product type for the site. No similar product is being developed or planned in the market area.

Product and Pricing
A patio home product would have the marketing advantage of a single-family home in appealing to family households. It would also have an affordability advantage

Table 3.2-6
Housing by Type in Market Area, 1997

	Single-Family	Townhouse	Multifamily	Total Units
Existing	31,400	13,000	9,750	54,150
Percent	58	24	18	100
Sold in 1997	307	532	163	1,002
Percent	31	53	16	100
On Market	292	798	327	1,417
Percent	21	56	23	100
Units Zoned	203	404	328	935
Percent	22	43	35	100
Pending Approval	0	668	202	870
Percent	0	77	23	100

because units could be priced lower than traditional single-family homes. Experience in nearby markets has shown that young families readily accept patio homes, generally preferring them over townhomes. A secondary market would be empty nesters, who find patio homes a good move-down product, because it offers the benefits of single-family living without the maintenance of a large yard.

Figure 3.2-1 plots average prices and square footage for all competitive single-family and townhome projects in the market area. A new patio home project should be positioned above most townhome projects but below most single-family comparables. An appropriate price range for the proposed development would be from about $200,000 to $240,000.

The lowest-priced model, in the $200,000 range, should offer about 1,800 square feet of living space for a per-square-foot value of $111. Because the product is more desirable than a townhome for this market, it is appropriate that the price per square foot is somewhat higher than similarly priced townhomes.

The project's higher-priced models must be competitive with single-family projects in the market area and must compensate for small lot sizes with more living space and/or features than comparably priced projects. A mid-priced model, in the $225,000 range, should include about 2,100 square feet of living area, for a per-square-

foot value of $107. This model will face little direct competition because the Sycamore and Autumn Glen subdivisions will be sold out before the subject project begins marketing, and Manors, a weak competitor, will have few homes left. However, those projects should be used as indicators of what buyers demand at this price point.

A third model, priced in the $240,000 range, should be targeted to the move-down market, helping to differentiate it from traditional single-family products and expanding the project's market appeal. This model should be designed with a first-floor master suite, ample storage space, and large rooms for entertaining. It should include at least 2,400 square feet of living space, for a per-square-foot value of $100.

In a relatively small project like this one, the key to developing the individual models is to span a wide enough market that the models do not compete with one another. At the same time, they should be within a narrow enough price range that a certain character and identity is maintained.

Projected Absorption

An estimated 335 households are projected to purchase new single-family homes in the market area each year, or 28 per month. If the project is well conceived and competitively priced to attract a range of household types and income levels, it should be able to capture a significant share of that market, especially because few other

Figure 3.2-1
Average Prices and Square Footage for Single-Family and Townhome Projects

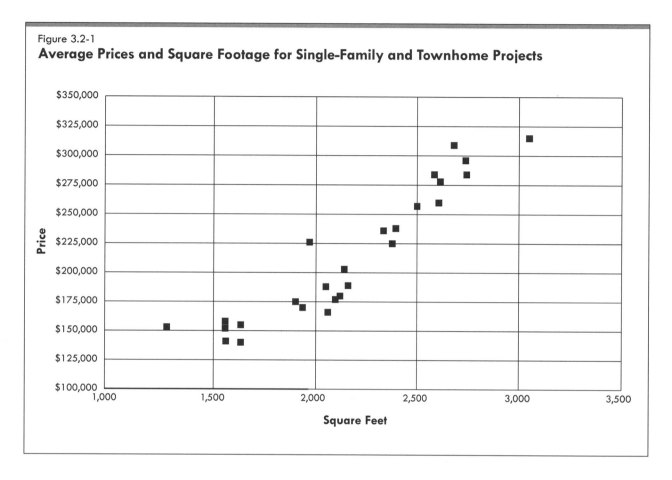

projects will be competing. If the subject project captures 10 percent to 15 percent of the market, it will achieve an average of three to four sales per month. This goal is not unrealistic, given that some of the better sellers today are achieving at least three sales per month while competing with a greater number of projects than the subject is likely to encounter.

Patio homes can be developed at a density of about six per acre, or a total of 132 units on the 22-acre subject site. With three sales per month, and a total of 132

units, the project will sell out in 44 months. If the project sells four units per month, it will sell out in 33 months.

This market study is just the first step in analyzing the potential for a new for-sale residential project. Additional research, including buyer surveys and/or focus groups, is required in order to fine-tune the product and pricing to suit the market during the time that the project is actually selling. As the project proceeds, additional market examination is conducted to reevaluate pricing and product design during the project's evolution.

A Master-Planned Community: Silver Knolls (1998)

John A. Walker

A market analysis for a large-scale, master-planned community or planned unit development (PUD) is typically more complicated than that for a single-product residential subdivision or commercial project, depending on the project's size and the mix of products proposed. Although some of the older PUDs around the country contained only a few product types (detached single-family homes, townhomes, and apartments or condominiums), today's projects sometimes include age-restricted sections, assisted living, and recreation-oriented residential units (golf course lots), as well as retail and office space.

In the case of the proposed Silver Knolls community in Orange County, New York, the developer prepared a plan to include market-rate, single-family detached units, townhouses, and condominiums, as well as an age-restricted section that contains several residential property types including an assisted living facility. In addition, the planned community will incorporate a retail center and an office park, both of which will function as integral parts of the overall development.

In performing the market analysis for Silver Knolls, the following issues are considered most critical in the evaluation process:

1. Because demand in Orange County alone will not be sufficient to develop the proposed project, what types of units and amenities will attract buyers looking in nearby Rockland County, New York, and Bergen County, New Jersey?
2. Because the commuting time from the site to Manhattan is less than one hour and fifteen minutes, how much demand can be expected to emanate from New York City versus northern New Jersey? Also, how does this commuting time affect the size of the market area?
3. How will potential homebuyers with young children perceive the difference in the quality of Orange County's school system compared to those of Rockland and Bergen counties? How might this perception influence the sales absorption and pricing of the units?
4. How will an age-restricted section function in this marketplace? How are other age-restricted projects

located a similar distance from New York City faring in the marketplace?
5. How much retail demand will be generated by the proposed residential development, and when should the developer attempt to bring it online in the project?
6. What effect will the proposed amenity package (including an 18-hole regulation golf course and a nine-hole executive course) have on the price and absorption of the proposed units?

All of these issues relate directly to the product mix, pricing and phasing of the project, and how it will function in the marketplace. These are the key questions to be answered by the market analysis.

Project Background

Silver Knolls is a distinctive community with an interesting history. Silver Knolls originally consisted of more than 17,000 acres of land in Orange County, New York, just north of the New Jersey border. The land has been the subject of intense interest from environmentalists and public officials because it is one of the largest undeveloped private land holdings in the New York/New Jersey CMSA.

The owner of the property, Silver Knolls Limited Liability Corporation (SKLLC), has developed small portions of the land over the past 30 years and had begun a comprehensive plan for development of its entire land holdings in the late 1980s. In 1996, SKLLC agreed to sell most of its landholding to several environmental organizations to be preserved for open space and watershed protection.

In an agreement with representatives of environmental groups and public officials, the owner retained control of approximately 2,220 acres of land contained in one large parcel of approximately 2,000 acres and a number of substantial out-parcels in areas where development has already occurred. Agreements with environmental groups and public officials limit development on the land that SKLLC retains to 3,000 residential dwelling units and 2.8 million square feet of commercial space, plus community and recreational amenities, including a golf course. The land retained by the owner already includes the following improvements: a ski slope, a conference center, the site of the New York Renaissance Festival, several residential communities, corporate offices, and two university research centers.

The Assignment

The owner of Silver Knolls retained a consultant to evaluate the market feasibility of developing a golf course and residential community on the 2,000-acre core property. In addition, the consultant was also asked to evaluate the market for the small commercial portion of the SKLLC holdings. The analysis covered the feasibility of a proposed 18-hole golf course, for-sale housing, housing for seniors, and commercial development that might be directly related to the development of residential units on the site. In order to evaluate the market feasibility of these components, the following steps were taken:

- Inspect the site and surrounding land area.
- Study regional and local economic and demographic trends and forecasts.
- Evaluate existing and proposed competitive golf courses, residential products, and commercial offerings in Orange, Rockland, and Bergen counties.
- Interview knowledgeable local and regional builders, lenders, Realtors, and economic development officials to help define supply and demand in the marketplace.
- Interview management, staff, and members of SKLLC's development team to obtain their vision and financial goals for the proposed development.

From an analysis of the information gathered, the following results were obtained:

- Definition of market areas for each product type, including the residential and age-restricted sections of the proposed community, the golf course, the retail space, and the commercial office space;
- Analysis of demographic-trend and household-movement information in order to measure the potential

demand for the residential, golf, retail, and office components of the community;
- Analysis of sales, absorption, pricing, and development data from similar residential communities, golf courses, retail centers, and office parks in the market areas in order to measure the potential competitive supply.

After completing a comprehensive review of the supply and demand information, the analysts were able to accomplish the following:

- Estimate the amount and type of development that could be absorbed at Silver Knolls based on analysis of supply and demand factors, and experience with similar large-scale development projects.
- Prepare specific recommendations regarding a development strategy for the property, the format for the proposed golf course, and the nature of residential and commercial development on the site.
- Make a formal determination of feasibility, and estimate the pricing and absorption pace for recommended product offerings.

Locational Issues

One of the most critical issues in assessing the potential for the Silver Knolls project is evaluating the project's location from several different perspectives. The focus of the locational analysis addresses five major issues: (1) commuting patterns, (2) quality of schools, (3) property taxes, (4) site characteristics, and (5) potential for special project amenities.

Commuting Patterns

The first locational issue involves analyzing commuting times to major employment centers in the region. Data from the 1990 census indicate that 32 percent of employed residents of Orange County commuted out of the county to work. Five percent of employed Orange County residents commuted to Manhattan, and 27 percent commuted to other suburban employment centers. Higher percentages of employees in neighboring Rockland County (44 percent) and Bergen County (40 percent) commuted outside their counties to work than those of Orange County. The largest single focus of commuting from Orange County is neighboring Rockland County, New York, followed by Bergen County, New Jersey; Manhattan in New York City; Dutchess County, New York; and Westchester County, New York.

Because the subject site is only 30 miles northwest of Manhattan and 15 to 20 miles north of employment concentrations in Bergen County, New Jersey, it is important to measure actual commuting times to those centers. Commuting times by automobile are less than one hour to employment centers in Rockland and Bergen counties, approximately one and one-half hours into Westchester County, and approximately one and one-half hours into New York City. Commuting by bus is faster than by car because of dedicated bus lanes in some areas. Bus lanes have cut commuting times from southern Orange County to Manhattan to less than 75 minutes. The bus commute is a major advantage for the proposed project because commuting times from many of the competitive communities in Middlesex and Monmouth counties in New Jersey are much longer, between 90 and 120 minutes.

Quality of Public Schools

The quality of schools serving any large residential community is a critical component in evaluating the potential for residential development. Although the seniors' and age-restricted sections of Silver Knolls are not likely to be affected by this issue, the nonrestricted units will be competing for buyers who regard school system boundaries as one of the major criteria in evaluating a home purchase.

The primary issue for the Silver Knolls property is the public's perception that Orange County schools are inferior to those in nearby Rockland County, New York, and Bergen County, New Jersey. During interviews, real estate professionals in New Jersey raised concerns about the quality of schools in Orange County compared to those in northern New Jersey. However, Scholastic Aptitude Test (SAT) scores in the Tuxedo and Monroe-Woodbury school districts (those serving the Silver Knolls site) were found to be comparable to those in most school districts in Rockland and Bergen counties, and average SAT scores for Orange County as a whole are actually above those for Rockland

and Bergen counties. Some districts in Bergen County, however, do have significantly better SAT scores than those found in the Tuxedo or Monroe-Woodbury districts.

The percentage of students going on to four-year colleges in the Tuxedo and Monroe-Woodbury districts is also below that of some neighboring districts. However, the Tuxedo and Monroe-Woodbury schools are on a par with those in Mahwah, New Jersey, where new-home development in Bergen County is concentrated, and with schools in Rockland County.

On the basis of this evaluation, the consultant concludes that school quality should not be a significant factor in deterring buyers from purchasing at Silver Knolls. Nevertheless, the perception of poor schools must be actively addressed in marketing materials and through cooperative efforts with the local school districts to ensure that these perceptions do not adversely affect sales.

Property Taxes

The property tax structure in New York and New Jersey is a complex overlay of school districts, towns, counties, villages, and various special districts for water, sewer, library, and so on. Property tax rates in Orange, Bergen, and Rockland counties were evaluated to identify differences that may influence homebuying decisions.

Of most interest is the difference in the property taxes between areas in northern Bergen County and Rockland County compared to Orange County. In the Mahwah area of Bergen County, the base property tax paid on a $250,000 home is $3,801. In Rockland County, taxes on a similar property range from $4,438 to $6,418. In Tuxedo, property taxes on the same $250,000 home would be $4,633 annually in the Tuxedo School District and $6,885 in the Monroe-Woodbury School District. Most homes in Silver Knolls would be located in the Monroe-Woodbury School District. In some areas, special district taxes such as fire, water, sewer, and police may also be charged; however, the overall tax differences between counties are not greatly affected.

The $3,084 per year difference in property taxes on a $250,000 home between Mahwah and Monroe-Woodbury school districts translates into $33,400 of home-purchasing power with an 8.5 percent fixed-rate mortgage. However, the average price for a 2,700-square-foot detached home in Bergen County is approximately $360,000, and the average price for a similar home in southern Orange County is about $300,000. Therefore, the difference in home prices between the two counties appears to more than make up for property tax differences between Mahwah and the Silver Knolls site.

Differences exist in income tax rates and allowable income tax deductions in New York compared to New Jersey. Real estate professionals active in both markets indicate that although New Jersey may have a lower income tax rate, deductions for home mortgage interest and property taxes in New York negate the difference for most homeowners.

Even though no significant differences appear to exist in the actual income or property taxes paid between prime Bergen County locations and the portion of Tuxedo where Silver Knolls is located, most Silver Knolls residents will pay property taxes at the high end of the range for the market area. The perception that New York income taxes are higher and that Silver Knolls residents will pay higher property taxes must be addressed through marketing materials that directly treat this issue. Taxes will also need to be considered when pricing homes at Silver Knolls.

Site Characteristics

The physical location of the Silver Knolls property—the Hudson Valley Highlands—provides a major competitive advantage over other communities in the market area. The property rises from cliffs overlooking the Hudson River toward the Catskill Mountains to the northwest. The area consists of tree-covered hills and valleys punctuated with mountain lakes and reservoirs. The character of the Silver Knolls site and the surrounding landscape is one of a mountain retreat rather than a typical suburb. This physical attribute will set the Silver Knolls community apart from many of its competitors.

Recreational Amenities

Recreational amenities are abundant in and around the Silver Knolls site. The proposed plan for Silver Knolls includes an 18-hole championship golf course, a nine-hole executive golf course, and community recreation centers with swimming pools, tennis courts, tot lots, and basketball courts. A number of lakes and reservoirs highlight the property, offering fishing and boating options, and a ski slope on the site provides winter recreation.

Economic and Demographic Issues

Because of the extended development and sales period required for a property as large as Silver Knolls, evaluating the long-term health of the economy of the region is of vital importance in the market analysis. Although short-term cycles may influence the year-to-year absorption projections for a community, the underlying stability of the economy is critical for the ultimate success of the project.

Employment Growth

After a period of decline in the early 1990s, employment in the New York/New Jersey CMSA has stabilized and is expected to continue to grow moderately over the next 20 years. Information from the U.S. Bureau of Labor Statistics indicates that modest job growth is underway in the New York/New Jersey CMSA, the market area, and in Orange County. Employment estimates for the market area and Orange County prepared for this study confirm that information. Estimates show job losses in the market area in 1990, 1991, and 1992, with employment increases thereafter. Orange County lost very few jobs in 1990 and more in 1991, but the county has seen solid job growth since then. These data indicate future employment growth in the market area in the range of 1 to 2 percent per year is likely. Although this level of job growth may seem unimpressive, when building on the large employment base in the market area, it represents growth in the range of 7,000 to 8,000 jobs per year. Forecasts call for total job growth in the New York/New Jersey CMSA in the range of 50,000 to 100,000 jobs per year, which will be concentrated largely in suburban employment centers.

Population and Household Growth

Population and household growth are expected to accelerate in Orange County as the area becomes more accessible to major employment centers. An estimated

4,900 to 9,100 additional households will be added to the county (23 percent of the market area) over the next five years, translating to annual household growth in the range of 980 to 1,820 households per year in Orange County. Allowing for a vacancy rate of 5 percent, this growth level will translate into 1,000 to 1,925 new housing units annually. Growth in the 2004–2006 period is forecast to continue at the same level.

Age and Income Characteristics

Age and income household characteristics indicate substantial demand for high-end, heavily amenitized communities as the baby boom generation reaches its peak income-earning years. Between 2002 and 2010, projections indicate a dramatic increase in the number of households aged 65 to 74, rising from 70,814 in 2002 to 85,765 by 2010. The next-largest increase is projected to occur in the aged 55 to 64 category, with nearly 6,800 additional households creating a rise from 85,999 in 2002 to 92,788 in 2010. In terms of income levels, the largest increases in the aged 55 to 64 group are expected in the $50,000 to $74,999 and the $75,000 to $99,999 categories.

Aging Markets

Although data on household growth characteristics indicate that the largest market at Silver Knolls is for households aged 55 and above, many of those households are simply aging in place and will not be entering the new-home market.

In order to estimate the characteristics of households likely to move in the market area, data from the U.S. Census Bureau's 1991 American Housing Survey for the New York Metropolitan Area have been analyzed. This survey provides information on the percentage of households, by age of householder, that moved in the previous year and the percentage that, over a four-year period, chose new owner-occupied or renter-occupied housing.

Data from the American Housing Survey indicate that young households move much more frequently than older households. For example, whereas more than a quarter of the households aged 25 to 34 move annually, only about 6 percent of the households aged 45 to 54 move annually.

The survey also reveals that a greater percentage of older households than younger ones select new housing until they reach age 65. For example, only 2.4 percent of movers aged 25 to 34 move to new housing, but 5.6 percent of movers aged 45 to 54 move to new housing. Finally, the survey suggests that the rate of homeownership among new-home buyers increases with age until age 65, when the rate begins to decline.

The consultant applied percentages from the American Housing Survey for the New York Metropolitan Area to the age distribution of households projected for the market area in 2001. This age distribution is used because it reflects the demographic characteristics of the market area at the time when Silver Knolls will begin actively marketing homes. The application of the American Housing Survey data produces a statistical estimate of the internally generated demand for new housing in the market area by age of householder. Local demand is converted into an estimate of total demand by assuming that households moving to new housing from outside the market area would have similar characteristics to those choosing new housing from within the market area. The age characteristics of new homebuyers for the market area are shown in Table 3.3-1.

When data on mover characteristics are considered, the demand for new homes in the Silver Knolls market area shifts to somewhat younger age groups. The largest single age group for prospective homebuyers is 35 to 44, with demand almost evenly distributed among the age groups from 25 to 64. In terms of demand for new rental units, demand is centered on the 25 to 34 and 35 to 44 age groups, with a significant portion of demand also coming from older renters aged 45 to 54. Comparatively little demand exists for new, owner-occupied or renter-occupied units from households aged 65 and over. However, those older households who are moving into retirement or assisted living communities are not typically identified in the housing survey. Therefore, they are typically underrepresented in the estimates, especially in areas that offer living choices for seniors from independent living units to assisted living and congregate care facilities.

The data presented in Table 3.3-1 show that the demand for homes in Orange County will be weighted

Table 3.3-1

Annual Demand Estimate for Silver Knolls Market Area

Age	Owner Demand			Renter Demand[1]		
	From Market Area	Total	Percent	From Market Area	Total	Percent
Under 25	0	0	0	162	280	16
25–34	321	555	23	253	434	24
35–44	389	673	27	257	443	25
45–54	315	544	22	197	338	19
55–64	328	566	23	37	64	4
65–74	28	49	2	27	45	3
75 & over	37	65	3	95	172	9
Total	**1,418**	**2,452**	**100%**	**1,028**	**1,776**	**100%**
	Estimated Annual Demand 2001 to 2006:	4,228				
	Estimated Owner Demand:	2,452				
	Estimated Renter Demand:	1,776				

[1]The demand for rental units in the market area is presented for informational purposes only since the proposed Silver Knolls contains no rental units.
Source: Legg Mason Real Estate Services, Inc.

in favor of owner-occupied housing and will be weighted toward buyers aged 35 to 44 and 45 to 64. Conclusions are based on the existing demographic makeup of the county and the trend over the past five years for more single-family housing to be permitted in Orange County than in the balance of the market area. Overall, the demographic and economic trends regarding the Silver Knolls project point to a strong market for the proposed residential, office, and retail components of the community.

Competitive Supply Issues

One of the main difficulties in analyzing the market for large-scale, master-planned communities is evaluating the existing and proposed competitive supply. Should the analysis include only other master-planned communities, or should it consider all of the surrounding projects?

In this analysis, residential competition is separated into several categories as follows:

- Projects within a 90-minute commute to Manhattan
  - Large-scale, master-planned communities
  - Golf course communities
  - Active-adult and senior-living communities
- Projects within Orange, Rockland, and Bergen counties
  - All residential projects with 50 or more units
- Projects within a 60-minute commute to other major metropolitan areas in the northeast
  - Selected active-adult golf course communities.

For the proposed golf course operation, the consultant analyzed surrounding golf courses and those tied to other large-scale, master-planned communities in the northeastern United States. On the basis of an overview of the site and surrounding market, the consultant determined that the competitive area for the commercial office space is Orange and Rockland counties in New York and Bergen County in New Jersey. The retail market area encompasses only the property and the communities within a five- to ten-mile radius.

With all of these categories to review, the consultant contacted major developers, local and state planning agencies, lending institutions, and builders' associations in order to identify the competitive residential communities, golf courses, office parks, and retail projects. After the list of projects was compiled, the following issues were researched:

- What are the most successful residential projects in terms of sales pace, and what locational and physical factors most directly affect sales?
- What residential product types are most appealing to move-up buyers, active retirees, and buyers at golf course communities?
- How are other golf courses operating in the marketplace (number of rounds, price per round), and how are they structured (daily fee, semi-private, or private)?
- What types of companies are relocating to Orange County, and what are their space needs?
- How much retail space exists in the surrounding market, and how much demand will be generated by Silver Knolls residents?

Residential Market Conclusions

A limited supply of new housing exists in the market area, particularly in Rockland and Bergen counties, which are mature and largely developed counties. No housing communities for active seniors exist in the market area. Development in Rockland County is concentrated in the north and west of the county and mostly consists of the large-lot communities that are favored by local zoning.

Sales paces are satisfactory despite relatively low-key marketing efforts. The market for new housing in Bergen County appears strong, and sales agents confirm that new homes are in great demand when they are available. The few large new-home developments being undertaken by major builders in Bergen County are selling very quickly, at a rate of eight to 12 units per month.

In Orange County, new home developments are somewhat more plentiful than in Rockland or Bergen counties. New projects are mostly small subdivisions by local builders without much sophistication in the way of design

or marketing. A significant difference exists between new homes in northern and southern Orange County. Homes in the north are typically smaller and lower priced, while homes being marketed in southern Orange County are larger, more expensive, and of better design. Marketing efforts are also more sophisticated in the south. However, some new-home developments in southern Orange County are still being undertaken in small subdivisions that cannot afford a significant marketing budget.

New homes in Orange County are being sold at about 75 percent to 80 percent of the cost per square foot of homes in Bergen County and are selling at a slower pace. They are priced comparably to mid-price offerings in Rockland County.

Although a number of new home projects are in the pipeline, the 6,500 units being processed for approval represent about two years of projected demand for new housing in the market area. In addition, the development approval process is difficult throughout the market area, and many of the projects seeking approval will never come to fruition because of this difficulty.

Forecasts show that annual household growth in Orange County will be in the 980 to 1,700 unit-per-year range, with demand for 1,000 to 1,700 new housing units annually. This demand represents between 23 and 50 percent of the household and housing unit growth in the market area, which was forecast at an average of 3,640 households and 3,847 housing units per year. The ability of Orange County to capture the higher level of growth is largely dependent on the ability of large development projects, such as Silver Knolls, to improve market perceptions of the county and to offer realistic housing alternatives in the southern portion of Orange County, which has the best access to employment centers located in the region.

Given the limited number of competitive new-home communities in the market area and the total lack of active-adult communities, the single-family products planned in Silver Knolls are estimated to capture 4 percent to 6 percent of the projected demand for new housing in the market area if they offer a high-quality product at appropriate prices. This level of activity would generate sales of 150 to 175 units annually, or a monthly communitywide sales pace of 12 units. This projection is realistic given that it is lower than what K. Hovnanian is currently achieving in Mahwah with only three product lines rather than the recommended nine product lines at Silver Knolls.

The projection of mover characteristics in the market area and the existing characteristics of households that have chosen to live in Orange County show that those choosing to live at Silver Knolls would likely be buyers rather than renters. Most will be at the older end of the age range of likely buyers (45 to 64), and most will be married couples with grown children.

A review of the effect of golf operations in master-planned communities shows that a golf course typically improves sales pace more than it increases home prices. Whereas homes on premium lots, with direct fairway or green frontage, command higher-than-normal prices (10 to 15 percent premiums), homes without golf course frontage command prices similar to those in comparable non-golf subdivisions. The difference is that golf course communities typically experience sales paces that are 15 to 20 percent higher than those of non-golf communities with similar housing products.

Residential Product Positioning

A product mix developed for Silver Knolls should focus on older couples seeking active-retirement detached homes. The golf course amenity should be used as an attraction for more affluent families and older buyers. Products should be positioned to maintain the current price differential between Orange and Bergen counties and to offer superior community amenities to spur sales pace.

Silver Knolls should open with modestly priced detached homes for active adults off the golf course and exclusive, high-end detached homes fronting the golf course in order to establish the community's image as an active retirement–oriented, detached-home community. After these initial product lines are established, the product lines should be broadened both upward and downward.

Table 3.3-2 presents the recommended product mix for Silver Knolls, which is organized in four distinct communities: (1) the community for active seniors, (2) the adult golf community, (3) the assisted living community, and (4) the family community. Each of these communities would be developed around a focal point and given a distinctive character through different housing products, amenities, signage, and landscaping elements. The active-adult community would be gated, with a full range of indoor and outdoor recreational facilities. It should be located near the village center to provide easy access to shopping and the potential for shared use of the major indoor recreation complex.

The recommended product mix for each neighborhood is described below. The projected sales pace for each product line is presented in Table 3.3-2.

Family-Oriented Community

GOLF COURSE LOTS
The golf course–related lots will be highly marketable and will likely sell at a rapid pace. It is recommended that the 120 single-family detached units (on 75-foot-wide lots) be priced in the $375,000 to $450,000 range for homes sized between 3,600 and 4,200 square feet. At this price level, units should sell at a pace of approximately 3.0 per month, selling out within four years.

The 14 two-acre lots on the golf course should be reserved for large custom homes priced in the $475,000 to $650,000 range. These homes should include 4,000 to 4,500 square feet of living space. They are projected to sell at a pace of 6.0 annually. At this rate, the 14 units will sell out within three years.

The 12 townhouse lots located on the golf course should also be reserved for a high-end product. These 30-foot wide units should be priced from $200,000 to $250,000 and should include 1,800 to 2,200 square feet of living space. The 12 luxury townhouse units should sell at a pace of one unit per month with a sell-out period of one year.

NON–GOLF COURSE LOTS
The family-oriented detached product (one-quarter- to one-third-acre lots with 75-foot widths), totaling 186 units, should be targeted to the move-up buyer. Recommended base prices for 3,200- to 3,900-square-foot homes range from $325,000 to $375,000. This range represents a

Table 3.3-2
Proposed Development Plan for Silver Knolls Community

Target Market	Housing Type	Total Units	Price Range	House Size Range (Sq. Ft.)	Price Per Sq. Ft.	Monthly Absorp-tion (Units)	Annual Absorp-tion (Units)	Build-out (Years)
Family-Oriented Community								
Golf Course Lots								
Single-Family Detached	75' lot width	120	$ 375,000 – $450,000	3,600 – 4,200	$104.17 – $107.14	3.0	36	4
Single-Family Detached	2 acre	14	475,000 – 650,000	4,000 – 4,500	118.75 – 144.44	0.5	6	3
Townhouse	30' width	12	200,000 – 250,000	1,800 – 2,200	111.11 – 113.64	1.0	12	1
Subtotal		146				4.5	54	
Non–Golf Course Lots								
Single-Family Detached	75' lot width	186	325,000 – 375,000	3,200 – 3,900	101.56 – 96.15	3.0	36	5
Total Non-Seniors' Units		**332**				7.5	90	
Seniors' Living Community								
Active Seniors								
Single-Family Detached	55' lot width	655	245,000 – 275,000	2,400 – 3,000	102.08 – 91.67	5.0	60	10
Single-Family Detached	65' lot width	117	275,000 – 300,000	2,700 – 3,300	101.85 – 90.91	2.5	30	4
Condominiums	Low to Mid-rise	240	140,000 – 170,000	750 – 1,200	186.67 – 141.67	10.0	120	2
Subtotal		1,012				17.5	210	
Assisted Living								
Multifamily	Low-rise	250	175,000 – 225,000	600 – 950	291.67 – 236.84	6.0	72	3.5
Cottages	5,000-sq.-ft. lots	53	200,000 – 250,000	900 – 1,100	222.22 – 227.27	5.0	60	2
Subtotal		303				11.0	132	
Total Seniors' Units		**1,315**				**28.5**	**342**	
Project Totals		**1,647**				**36.0**	**432**	

Source: Legg Mason Real Estate Services, Inc.

price per square foot of $102 for the smaller homes and $96 for the larger homes. These units are projected to sell at a rate of 3.0 units per month, selling out within 48 to 62 months.

Community for Active Seniors
The proposed age-restricted community will be well received in the marketplace, with demand for units emanating out of the market area as well as Manhattan and

central New Jersey. The property's setting and proposed amenity package will place it well above most other active-adult communities in the region. Also, its commuting times to employment centers in New York City and northern New Jersey are hard to match in this market.

The nine-hole golf course geared especially to seniors is strongly recommended to enhance the appeal of active-adult living at Silver Knolls. The championship 18-hole course proposed for Silver Knolls will be more difficult and more expensive than the active-adult crowd is used to. A moderately maintained nine-hole course for active-adult residents will be a positive selling point for the community and will help to differentiate it from other active-adult products.

AGE-RESTRICTED DETACHED LOTS

The bulk of the active seniors' section will include 655 homes on one-quarter- to one-third-acre lots with 55-foot widths. These homes should be priced from $245,000 to $275,000 for homes ranging in size from 2,400 to 3,000 square feet, for a price per square foot of $102 for the smaller homes and $91 for the larger homes. At these prices, units are projected to move at 5.0 per month, selling out within 120 months.

The section of 117 slightly larger single-family detached homes on 65-foot-wide lots could be marketed for prices ranging from $275,000 to $300,000, with a projected absorption pace of 2.5 per month and sell-out within 48 months.

AGE-RESTRICTED CONDOMINIUMS

A low- to mid-rise condominium section of approximately 240 units would be attractive to seniors looking for low-maintenance units in an active-adult community. Prices in comparable projects indicate that these units should be priced in the $140,000 to $170,000 range for units ranging from 750 to 1,200 square feet. These units will likely sell at a pace of approximately 10 units per month, with all 240 units selling within a 24-month time frame.

ASSISTED LIVING UNITS

The review of other assisted living projects in the market demonstrates that strong demand exists for the 303 proposed assisted living units in Silver Knolls (250 low-rise units and 53 cottages). The low-rise product should be developed in a garden-style configuration and priced in the $175,000 to $225,000 range. The absorption pattern at the nearby Fountainhead project suggests that these units should sell at a rate of 6.0 per month, with all 250 units sold within a 3.5-year period. The cottages would sell for $200,000 to $250,000 and would be absorbed within two years.

Commercial and Retail Absorption

Employment projections provided by the New York State Planning Office estimate that the Orange County office market will see an average absorption of approximately 500,000 square feet annually between 2000 and 2010. This level of absorption will require an equal amount of new construction because little space is available in the market today.

Because of its proximity to the active northern Bergen County commercial market and its convenient access to transportation, the Silver Knolls commercial property is in an excellent position to capture a significant portion of future demand. The demand will likely be dominated by companies seeking back-office operations and small professional companies searching for distinctive locations in order to attract a talented workforce. The uncongested, bucolic setting at Silver Knolls is likely to be very attractive to office users.

An office park with eight to ten small-scale, low-rise buildings, each with an average of 40,000 square feet of space, is recommended. The buildings would be developed over a ten-year period, translating to an average annual absorption of 44,000 square feet. The projected absorption pace would comprise 5 to 10 percent of the projected office/industrial absorption in the entire county between 2000 and 2010. The projected lease rates for this space are likely to be in the $22 to $27 per-square-foot range.

The retail component of Silver Knolls is planned to include less than 50,000 square feet of convenience retail space to serve the day-to-day needs of on-site residents. This amount is significantly below the retail space that ultimately will be supported by the Silver Knolls community at buildout. Comprising 1,647 households, residents of Silver Knolls will support the wide variety of retail space already in place in the area.

Assuming that the 1,647 households will have an average annual income of approximately $70,000 (in 1998 dollars), and that these households will spend approximately 40 percent of their incomes on retail goods and services, the residents of Silver Knolls will generate over $44 million in retail sales annually. With the projected sales performance rate of convenience retail space averaging approximately $250 per square foot, the planned 50,000 square feet of retail space will likely capture only $12.5 million of projected demand, leaving $31.5 million in annual retail sales to be spent at other retailers in the area surrounding Silver Knolls.

Conclusion

The market analysis described in this report demonstrates that the development of a high-end, 18-hole, daily-fee golf course and a residential community containing 1,647 units is feasible at Silver Knolls with the pricing and unit mix recommended. The first units should begin marketing in 2001. Silver Knolls can achieve a community sales pace of up to 210 active-seniors' units, 132 assisted living units, and 90 non-seniors' units per year if a diverse product line is offered. However, this pace will only be achieved at the peak of development when all phases of the community are active. The pace at startup and over the life of the project will depend on the number of product lines active at any given time.

Depending on the ultimate size, configuration, and development pace of the project, a development period of eight to ten years should be expected from the time sales begin until all homes are sold.

Projections related to Silver Knolls are based on the following conclusions regarding the critical issues identified in the first section of this study:

1. The physical attributes of the property and wide range of housing types will attract buyers from beyond Orange County.
2. The commuting time to Manhattan will allow the project to capture a significant portion (10 to 15 percent) of regional housing demand.
3. Although a perception exists that the schools serving the proposed project are of lower quality than those of surrounding areas, test scores refute the perception. However, this issue must be addressed in the marketing materials to eliminate any potential effect on price and absorption.
4. Because of a huge surge in households aged 45 to 64, the age-restricted market should grow rapidly over the near term.
5. Because the amount of residential development is limited, and a large amount of regional retail space exists nearby, only a neighborhood shopping center is likely to be supportable as part of the project.
6. Although premium golf course–frontage homes will command higher prices (10 to 15 percent higher than normal), the major impact of the golf course is likely to be increased sales.

Downtown Housing:
Old Town Square (1995)
Janet Smith-Heimer

The Old Town Square condominium project, located in downtown Oakland, California, illustrates market analysis techniques for pioneering projects. This project, the first market-rate housing to be developed in the commercial portion of downtown Oakland, had substantial city support and had been discussed by planners and developers for many years. However, because of the perceived risk of pioneering in a location suffering from the stigma of historic urban ills as well as a lack of demonstrable interest from buyers, the project concept had languished until the mid-1990s, when the city of Oakland issued a request for proposals and selected a developer (see *Urban Land* article on Old Town Square, 1997).[1]

Project Description
When the market study was commissioned as part of predevelopment in 1995, Old Town Square was proposed as a 400-unit, for-sale housing complex to be built in phases on a site encompassing three city blocks. Each block was planned to contain a mix of townhouses and stacked flats in a series of connected buildings organized around landscaped central plazas atop a podium parking garage. Old Town Square units were proposed to be offered through a lease/purchase program, whereby first-time buyers who lacked sufficient downpayments to enter the ownership market would rent their units for two years, allowing a portion of their rent to accumulate in an escrow account for downpayment purposes. The project was not designated for low-income families; rather, rents for the two-year rental period were to be set slightly above market rates, and standard market-rate underwriting criteria were to be used to qualify buyers of all income levels at the time of purchase.

Project Setting and Context
Several positive aspects of the site's location were expected to affect market demand. The site lies adjacent to a major employment center with upward of 60,000 daytime office workers and significant additional office development planned for the next several years. The site is within two blocks of a Bay Area Rapid Transit (BART) station, providing excellent commuter access to downtown San Francisco and the region. Within blocks of the project site, a growing array of urban amenities is available, including shopping, restaurants, an ice skating rink, and a large health club. Across the street from the first phase of Old Town Square, a mixed-use project with live/work units, specialty food and retail space, and a wholesale bakery had also been proposed (but is not yet under construction).

In addition, several blocks from the Old Town Square site, Oakland's Chinatown neighborhood offered a potential source of market demand. This neighborhood contains densely developed residential uses as well as a thriving ethnic retail area at the street level of almost every structure. However, many planners and developers believed that residents of Chinatown would not "cross Broadway," a major arterial, to settle in the area around Old Town Square.

Finally, the project site is located one block west of the Old Oakland office/retail district, a collection of beautifully renovated two-story historic Victorian structures. During the 1980s, the Old Oakland district had experienced moderately strong office absorption; however, the retail spaces absorbed very slowly. After the lender took control of the project, a new leasing strategy was employed that broadened the retail mix to include shops serving tourists and nearby Chinatown residents. This strategy succeeded in reducing vacancies, and Old Oakland is now attracting regional attention through its thriving weekly farmers market.

Purpose of the Market Study
The Old Town Square developers needed to address several key questions in order to proceed with the project and satisfy their lenders, including the following:

- What market segments should be targeted (e.g., first-time buyers, empty nesters, residents of Oakland, residents of San Francisco)?
- How deep is demand for market-rate ownership housing in downtown Oakland?
- Is there market interest in a lease/purchase financing arrangement?
- What amenities should be included in the project to maximize absorption?

To answer these questions, an in-depth market study moving beyond standard analysis of demographics, competitive supply, and demand factors was required. The analysis needed to specify unit attributes that would maximize marketability as well as clearly identify specific target market populations. These additional analytical goals were accomplished through a series of primary research efforts including two focus groups of different potential target markets and an extensive written survey of downtown Oakland office workers.

Traditional Market Study Components

The Old Town Square market analysis commenced with the traditional steps of demographic analysis, competitive supply analysis, and an estimate of overall housing demand in the targeted price range. These components demonstrated that the primary market area, defined as the city of Oakland, was characterized by a relatively stable population base with small household sizes, moderate to middle incomes, a high concentration of renter households, and moderate housing values and rents. Overall, the analysis indicated that the demographic characteristics of Oakland made it an excellent market for moderately priced, for-sale multifamily units such as those proposed by the subject project. A large number of renter households of moderate means were identified as a strong source of potential demand for the lease/purchase program being considered by Old Town Square developers. In particular, the study identified more than 8,000 middle-income renter households living in a nearby urban neighborhood known as Lake Merritt; these households were projected to provide an outstanding source of potential buyers.

With respect to competitive supply, Oakland had a very limited number of new condominiums available in the marketplace at that time. Only one new project, Parkwood Condominiums, was identified as potentially competitive. This project, which offered newly constructed, inexpensively priced units in a suburban setting, had been absorbing at a moderate pace. However, Parkwood's location was also its chief disadvantage. The apartment complex that previously existed at the same

site had burned down as a result of the devastating 1991 Oakland Hills fire. This history negatively affected the perception of many local residents regarding the site's future fire safety. One other planned project (which has since entered its marketing phase), the conversion of Park Bellvue Towers from luxury rental to condominium units, was identified as not competitive because of the project's high-rise design, location directly on Lake Merritt, and projected higher price range.

In-Depth Primary Research

During initial market analysis, two distinct target markets were identified: (1) urban dwellers, particularly renters living near downtown Oakland in the Lake Merritt neighborhood; and (2) downtown Oakland workers living elsewhere but seeking a residential location near their workplace. The latter group was considered to have strong potential interest in the Old Town Square project because market research of condominium buyers in other northern California downtowns indicated that these buyers made their location decision primarily to minimize their commute to their downtown job locations.[2]

Focus Groups with Urban Dwellers

To explore potential interest and perceptions of renters living near downtown Oakland, the focus group research method was selected. This approach allows the analyst to obtain an in-depth understanding of the location decision, interest in project amenities, opinions regarding a lease/purchase program, and related project design issues. A second focus group was conducted for urban renters residing in downtown San Francisco in order to explore their opinions regarding the downtown Oakland location.

METHODOLOGY

Focus group research is designed to elicit responses from participants that further illuminate consumer motivations and behavior. However, focus group research is qualitative, meaning that although it provides in-depth information about market preferences and opinions from carefully screened participants representing potential target markets, the technique is not statistically significant. The approach, based on well-established consumer market research, does not lead to a quantitative estimate of the size of the market, but rather helps to explain the purchase decision.

Recruitment for the focus groups was intentionally targeted to certain urban renter households earning at least enough income to qualify for Old Town Square units. Participants were also screened for age, gender, and familiarity with the for-sale marketplace.

Members of the Oakland focus group were recruited from the Lake Merritt neighborhood. Leaflets describing the purpose of the focus group and inviting participation were mailed to approximately 1,200 rental units selected from field research. Respondents telephoned the survey research firm and were screened through a series of questions that ensured all focus group members met a minimum income threshold, did not have a conflict of interest, and were balanced in terms of age and gender. Incentives to participate in the two-hour discussion included payment of $50 per participant and a dinner buffet.

The Oakland focus group was held during the evening of November 6, 1995, in a small conference room at the luxury Parc Oakland Hotel in downtown Oakland. All participants were renters, and all of them resided in the Lake Merritt neighborhood.

Members of the San Francisco focus group were recruited from large, middle-range and upper-end rental complexes located near the Financial District; these projects were targeted because of their proximity to the Bay Bridge/freeway connections to downtown Oakland. Approximately 1,000 invitations were mailed, and respondents were screened by a process similar to that used for the Oakland group. The San Francisco focus group was held during the evening of December 13, 1995, at the Park Hyatt in San Francisco's Financial District.

FINDINGS

The following summarizes the findings from the two focus groups:

Project Location

- Members of the Oakland focus group were very interested in the possibility of new ownership-housing

alternatives in downtown Oakland and responded positively to the proposed development site. Although participants were aware of security problems in downtown Oakland, concerns about safety were not a deterrent to seeking ownership housing in the area. The Oakland group placed a premium on cultural diversity and acceptance in the community. They were enthusiastic about cultivating an urban community at the Old Town Square site.

- In particular, the Oakland group cited factors such as the ability to "get by without a car," the proximity to BART and shopping, and the proximity to downtown Oakland jobs as positive factors influencing their interest in the Old Town Square site. Many of those same factors were already reasons for the participants' attraction to the Lake Merritt neighborhood where they lived at the time.

- The outlook of the San Francisco focus group contrasted sharply with that of the Oakland participants. San Francisco focus group members placed a heavy emphasis on security concerns and did not consider downtown Oakland an acceptable place to live. Although the San Francisco participants admitted to being unfamiliar with Oakland, they nevertheless conveyed a perception that crime and gang activity are commonplace, especially in the downtown area. None would consider living in Oakland unless their job were located there.

Design

- Proposed project design was discussed on a broad level in the Oakland focus group. Although the need for security was acknowledged, participants stated their wish for a project design that offered security while still being integrated into the urban fabric of the city. Group members also expressed a preference for low-rise, townhouse style units with abundant landscaping. "Good design," which participants defined as quality construction, workable floor plans, sound insulation, and architectural character, was considered critical to make the units "worth buying."

- Proposed project design was discussed In more specific detail with the San Francisco group. They preferred stacked flats rather than townhouses because of the security problems perceived with front doors at street level. Secured access to a lobby and other common areas was also preferred. Exterior halls were dismissed as "too much like a motel"; interior hallways were found to be the most secure alternative. Participants responded favorably to the addition of a loft-like bonus room in the two-bedroom floor plan and cited potential uses such as a home office, artist's studio, or guest bedroom. Podium parking was perceived as an appropriate design solution to allow adequate parking and to provide demarcation between the project and the street.

■ The San Francisco group also expected the project to provide ample amenities within the units, including microwave, air conditioning, dishwasher, fireplace, washer/dryer, pool, spa, workout room, and guest parking. This group also expected a grocery store, dry cleaner, café, and ATM to be located nearby.

Purchase Motivation

■ Oakland participants expressed a strong motivation to purchase a home, primarily because of a belief that their rent payments were equivalent to the cost of ownership. Other homeownership benefits cited included tax advantages and the security of having neighbors with a common, vested interest in the community. Barriers to purchase included the perceived lack of ownership units that are affordable, well located, and "good enough to buy" rather than rent. In addition, the group expressed uncertainty regarding downpayment requirements and felt skeptical toward lending institutions and their loan policies.

■ The purchase motivation was weak among San Francisco participants. Group members believed that they could rent a better unit than they could buy in San Francisco. Furthermore, participants cited examples of friends losing money on real estate transactions, as well as concerns about the nonliquidity of ownership.

Financing

■ Oakland participants were concerned about exclusionary lending practices, and they welcomed financing assistance. Although the Oakland group considered lease/option programs to be a legitimate financing tool, most did not understand the details of buyers' rights and responsibilities. The Oakland participants expressed anxiety about securing financing and reacted positively to the proposed lease/purchase program for Old Town Square.

■ Among San Francisco focus group members, the lease/purchase concept was perceived as an indication that the proposed project would be subsidized housing. The availability of such financing was not found to be a sufficient incentive to induce San Francisco participants to move to Oakland.

Marketing and Publicity

■ Because the San Francisco focus group members demonstrated little interest in housing located in Oakland, these comments reflect the views of participants in only the Oakland focus group. Although involvement from the city in announcing and promoting the project was considered positive, participants stated that caution should be exercised to ensure that the project would not be perceived as a public housing project. They suggested that the project be promoted as a complete, diverse, self-contained community that encompasses all four blocks, and not as simply one piece of a four-block plan. Respondents also mentioned a preference for "one-stop shopping" for financing with a lender who had established a relationship with the developer.

Conclusions

The Oakland focus group had an overall strongly favorable reaction to the proposed project, its preliminary design attributes, and the opportunity to purchase units through a lease/purchase program. At the end of the Oakland group meeting, several participants requested that they be notified when units were ready for sale. This positive reaction indicated that renter households in the Lake Merritt neighborhood were an excellent target for marketing the Old Town Square project.

The San Francisco group, however, did not represent a strong target market despite evidence that San Francisco renters had been attracted to other Oakland condominium projects. It was concluded that efforts to attract San Francisco dwellers across the bay to downtown Oakland would not be cost-effective, particularly for the first phase of the project.

Survey of Downtown Office Workers
For downtown Oakland workers, a written survey approach was used in order to obtain a broad sampling of this target market's opinions and interest in the proposed project.

METHODOLOGY
The survey methodology involved selecting employers for telephone contact, contacting the human resources or public affairs managers to request participation, delivering preprinted survey instrument forms to the contact person, requesting the contact person to distribute the forms personally to all employees at the organization, requesting the contact person to collect the forms by a specified date, and collecting the forms from the contact person for data entry. A mix of ten firms and government agencies was enlisted for participation, and 400 usable survey forms were returned.

Employers were selected for participation on a systematic basis. Specifically, the ten largest downtown employers were contacted for participation; two agreed to and did participate in the survey. In addition, a random sample of employers with ten to 250 employees and located within a five-block radius of the project was used, selected on the basis of data from Dun & Bradstreet. Approximately 20 employers were selected at random and contacted through this method, with eight agreeing to participate.

The survey instrument was prepared in draft form and pretested on three renter households. The instrument was designed to fit on both sides of one page of legal-size paper, so that the questions did not appear too lengthy and would be convenient to answer. The survey covered broad topics organized around previous purchase and housing location decisions, current interest and future plans to purchase housing, interest and opinions about the proposed project, desired project amenities, and basic demographic data for each respondent household.

Data were entered and tabulated using a simple database. Data were tabulated for three categories of respondents: all respondents, all respondents stating interest in the Old Town Square housing project, and a subset of interested respondents with qualifying household incomes exceeding $30,000 and current status as renters.

FINDINGS
The following summarizes the findings from the worker survey:

Profile of Survey Respondents
- A total of 400 usable surveys were returned. Of these, 206 respondents (52 percent of total) were willing to consider purchasing a unit at the subject project, including 180 with household incomes above $30,000. The subset of interested qualified renters totaled 64 respondents (16 percent of the total survey response).
- Of all interested respondents, 56 percent owned their housing unit. Most lived in single-family detached units and had two workers living in their household. Two-person households were the predominant household size, and the most frequently mentioned age of respondents was between 35 and 44.
- One of the most interesting aspects of the respondents' demographic profile was that 105 of the 206 interested households contained children, including 32 single-parent households and 73 couples with children. This finding was surprising because urban condominium projects typically do not attract significant numbers of families with children in other downtowns in northern California. The finding may be partially explained by the context of the survey's questions regarding interest in the Old Town Square project; these questions followed a series of queries on plans to move in the next five years. Some of these households with children may have been contemplating a move as children aged and left home, meaning that those households would become empty nesters seeking to minimize commute times or lower their housing costs.
- Household incomes for all interested respondents were concentrated in middle ranges, with 33 percent in the $30,000 to $50,000 household income range.

However, 75 out of the 206 interested respondents who reported their incomes earned $70,000 or more, including 28 households earning $100,000 or more.

■ Not surprisingly, among the interested qualified renter households, certain key demographic characteristics varied somewhat from all interested respondents. For example, the predominant interested qualified renter households contained only one worker, and the distribution of number of people in the household tended to be skewed more toward single-person households. Nevertheless, 24 out of the 64 interested, qualified renter households (36 percent) contained children, including 13 couples with children. The largest category, 37 out of the 64 respondents in the interested qualified renters group, reported incomes between $30,000 and $50,000, and 11 reported incomes of $70,000 or more.

Prior Homebuying Behavior

■ The survey instrument started off with a series of questions regarding past housing-selection behavior in order to test the importance of neighborhood factors as well as the effect of lack of a downpayment vis-à-vis the planned lease/purchase program for the Old Town Square project. Overall, 34 percent of all interested respondents and 59 percent of interested qualified renters had considered purchasing a unit in the previous five years, but had not followed through. Insufficient downpayment was the most frequently cited reason for not following through on the purchase effort; among interested qualified renters, insufficient downpayment represented 33 percent of the reasons cited. The next most frequently cited reason for all categories of respondents was that "units were too expensive." These two findings suggested clear market positioning for Old Town Square as an opportunity offering no downpayment and affordable prices.

■ Factors that affected the prior homebuyer cited by 90 percent or more of the respondents were neighborhood appearance and safety; unit price, size, and exterior appearance; and unit security features.

■ Walking to work was also an important factor, although cited less frequently than those shown above.

Future Relocation and Purchase Plans

■ Overall, 63 percent of all interested respondents said that they planned to move within the next five years, while 53 of the 64 interested qualified renters planned to move. Although most preferred a single-family home purchase, 35 percent of interested qualified renters planned to purchase a townhouse or condominium.

■ Both the "all interested" group and the "interested qualified renter" group most frequently stated a preference for a three-bedroom/two-bath unit. Among all interested respondents, the three-bedroom unit was preferred by 46 percent, while 39 percent of the interested qualified renters selected this unit type. For the interested qualified renters subset, some combination of a two-bedroom unit (with either one or two baths) proved to be the most popular (40 percent of respondents in this group preferred a two-bedroom unit).

Factors Affecting Interest in Old Town Square

■ One of the most appealing aspects of the Old Town Square project to downtown office workers was the ability to walk to work. The survey asked respondents a general question about the appeal of being able to walk to work, and 89 percent of interested respondents stated a positive reaction.

■ The availability of the lease/purchase program for Old Town Square was also clearly a major influence on interest in the project. When asked if the availability of such a program would make the respondent more likely to consider purchasing at Old Town Square, 76 percent of all interested respondents and an overwhelming 92 percent of interested qualified renters answered "yes." When considered along with the finding of insufficient downpayment as the most frequently cited reason for not buying a home during the past five years, this aspect of the proposed project appeared strongly favorable.

■ The survey also indicated that some potential buyers would not need or use the lease/purchase program because of their relatively high household incomes, previous equity from homeownership, and the number of potentially interested buyers who did not cite lack of downpayment as a constraint on past purchasing behavior.

Neighborhood Factors Affecting Opinions of Old Town Square

- Respondents were asked to rate a series of neighborhood factors that would affect their willingness to consider the Old Town Square project. Neighborhood appearance and neighborhood safety were mentioned as very or somewhat important by 90 percent of the respondents. Factors with less frequent mention (in the 60 percent to 90 percent range) included (in descending order of frequency) neighborhood amenities, distance to respondent's place of work, quality of schools, and distance to work of other household members.

Desired Project Amenities

- For all interested respondents, amenities mentioned by at least 90 percent of respondents as important were ample unit size and high-quality exterior appearance. Type and amount of parking were mentioned 88 percent of the time, followed by about 50 percent for fireplaces, then exercise room, on-site store, and on-site child care. A pool or spa amenity was mentioned by only about 35 percent of the respondents as an important feature of the project.

- On the basis of the frequency of various amenities mentioned, fireplaces were found to be an important amenity for some, but not all, interested buyers; therefore, fireplaces could be included in only the more expensive units as part of the price premium if fireplace construction costs become prohibitive.

- The exercise room was recommended for inclusion in the project because, although Old Town Square is located one block from a full-service health club, the presence of a small on-site exercise room was considered a good method of mitigating the perception of initial buyers that working out required a walk through an uncertain neighborhood after dark.

CONCLUSIONS

The downtown worker survey indicated that this market segment had strong interest in purchasing units at Old Town Square. The survey data suggested that buyer profiles would be a mix of single persons, couples, and households with children. Neighborhood appearance and safety were likely be the most difficult barriers perceived by these potential buyers. Unit amenities desired by many potential buyers included a bonus loft room, fireplaces, and an exercise room. On the basis of the survey, on-site child care, pool, and spa were not demanded enough to warrant their inclusion in the project.

Project Outcome

The market study recommended proceeding with the project and predicted strong market demand. Other recommendations included incorporating a bonus loft room into project design (which subsequently proved to be an important selling point) and weighting the unit mix toward two- and three-bedroom units, with as many townhouses as possible (subsequently, the three-bedroom townhouses were absorbed the most rapidly). Unit pricing and amenity recommendations were also made.

Old Town Square's first phase was then marketed very successfully, with more than 350 buyers making deposits for the 100 available units before construction. Almost one-third of the buyers did not use the lease/purchase program, but purchased their unit outright.

Notes

[1] Jane Bowar Zastrow, "Lease Purchase Programs for Affordable Housing," *Urban Land*, vol. 56, no. 9 (Sept. 1997): pp. 28–31, 89.

[2] Bay Area Economics (BAE) research summarized in *R Street Corridor Market Analysis* prepared by BAE for the Sacramento Housing and Redevelopment Agency in 1993, and *The San Jose Housing Initiative* prepared by BAE for the San Jose Planning Department in 1992.

R.R. Donnelley Building, Chicago, Illinois.

Chapter 4

Office and Industrial Development

Office and industrial development share certain similarities and, in fact, overlap in their definitions. Some of the flex and hybrid types of properties could be categorized as either office or industrial space, and potential users of these kinds of space would not necessarily limit their search by category. The methodology of market analysis for office and industrial space requires an understanding of the local business climate: Which industries are expanding and by how much? Which nodes or locations are desirable for particular industries and types of business activities? What are the specific space needs (amount, type, and price) of new and expanding businesses? Determining the requirements of industrial-space users is more complex than for office users. Whereas office space is a fairly simple function of amount of space per employee, industrial users are more varied in their activities and space needs, and the analysis requires a greater understanding of the target businesses.

Characteristics of Office Buildings

Office development runs the full gamut of building size, class, and location. About 20 percent of all employed Americans work in office buildings, mostly in service and information sectors.[1] Some office buildings are specifically targeted to distinct market niches: medical offices, banks, back-office functions (data processing, customer service, order taking, etc.). As for location, office buildings can be found in downtowns, suburban highway strips, office parks, and mixed-use developments. About 20 percent of all nongovernmental office buildings are owner occupied. The balance is owned by real estate services compa-

nies (institutions, insurance companies, REITs, partnerships, family businesses, and individuals) and leased to tenants.

Office space can be categorized according to several factors, including the following:

- Class;
- Location;
- Size and flexibility;
- Use and ownership;
- Features and amenities.

Class

Class is measured by evaluating a building's age, location, quality of finishes, building systems, amenities, lease rates, and tenant profile. Three classes of office space are usually defined. Class A, or investment grade, buildings are the most desirable; they feature high-grade finishes and amenities, which offer status to the businesses within. Class B and Class C buildings are often older properties that have not kept up with modern trends in design or features; however, older buildings can sometimes be renovated and repositioned as Class A properties. Most large, new buildings are Class A, but smaller, basic office structures with few amenities can be Class B from the outset. Definitions vary, but age, size, rent level, location, building materials, and amenities are all considerations.

Location

Downtown central business districts (CBDs) are usually prime locations that are characterized by high-density office buildings and high rents. Major service firms in fields such as law, accounting, and consulting as well as government tenants often prefer downtown locations. Located outside of the CBD, but still in the city, are often secondary office nodes that may center around hospitals, universities, or other business magnets. Suburban locations are more difficult to evaluate, and they appeal to a more diverse group of office users. Many of the mature suburban communities that ring large urban cores have their own concentrated "downtown" office cores that can even rival the CBD.

Size and Flexibility

In size, office buildings range from less than 10,000 square feet to more than 1 million square feet. The twin towers of New York's World Trade Center comprise 12 million square feet. Office buildings generally fall into three size categories: high-rise (16 stories or more), mid-rise (four to 15 stories), and low-rise (one to three stories). Floor plate size is important for tenants that need large contiguous blocks of space. Floor space flexibility is becoming increasingly important as more tenants opt for open floor layouts and more efficient use of space. Office floor plates generally range from 18,000 square feet to 30,000 square feet.

Use and Ownership

Buildings can be either single-tenant or multitenant structures. A single-tenant building may be owned by the tenant, in which case it is referred to as an owner/user building. A building constructed for a specific tenant is called "built-to-suit," while a building constructed for unknown tenants is a speculative or "spec" building.

Features and Amenities

One of the most important characteristics is the availability and cost of parking, or in urban cores, the proximity of mass transit. The importance of some of a building's features is defined by the target market. If the targeted tenants are high-tech firms, the electrical power and telecommunications infrastructure may be most important. If the target tenants are high-profile law firms, the architecture and quality of finishes in public areas may be the key factors. Some tenants may require on-site health clubs, restaurants, and retail outlets.

According to a survey of office tenants conducted by the Building Owners and Managers Association and ULI, rents and pass-through charges are the most important factor that tenants consider when signing or renewing leases. But the next most important factors were associated with the quality and productivity of the work environment: comfortable temperatures, indoor air quality, and acoustics and noise control. The next most important criteria relate to management responsiveness and maintenance. Today's tenants are less concerned with lavish lobbies and expensive exterior cladding.[2]

Characteristics of Industrial/Warehouse Buildings

The line between office and industrial space has blurred because so many businesses today require flexible space to accommodate a wider range of activities. Industrial development includes a continuum of real estate product types that range from research and development (R&D) space, which closely resembles office space, through unfinished warehouse space. Hybrid space mixes characteristics of office and industrial and does not fall neatly into one category of use. Most new industrial buildings are located in business parks, most of which are dominated by warehousing and distribution activities rather than production. Warehousing and distribution functions are characterized by relatively low ratios of employment to building square footage, an important factor to note when selecting market analysis methods.

Industrial space is classified in three broad categories: (1) manufacturing, (2) research and development, and (3) warehouse/distribution.[3] Most new factory buildings are designed and built to user specifications and are corporate owned. Laboratories, incubator space, and warehouse facilities may be single user or multitenant, speculative or built-to-suit. Although large retail store chains still tend to operate their own warehouses, multitenant bulk warehouses run by third-party logistics managers are increasingly common. Businesses that do not handle perishable items are moving to fewer but larger warehouse buildings.

Warehouse/distribution facilities are further distinguished by the percentage of space used for office functions (as opposed to package assembly, shipping, or storage). Small businesses often occupy flex space with a high degree of office finish (25 to 50 percent). Rents per square foot for high-finish industrial space are much higher than for bulk warehouses where less than 10 percent of the square footage is used for offices.

Because industrial space is low-rise and much of it is unfinished, warehouse buildings take less time to build than office structures do. As a result, smaller warehouse markets can quickly become imbalanced. Despite the relative ease of constructing bulk industrial space, the warehouse property market is less volatile than the office market. Rents and occupancy experience slow but steady increases during periods of economic expansion, and slight declines when recessions are underway.

Metropolitan areas often specialize in different types of industrial space. For example, San Jose, Boston, Austin, San Diego, Minneapolis, and northern New Jersey are well known as centers for high-tech research and laboratory space. Atlanta, Cincinnati, Columbus, Indianapolis, Kansas City, and Sacramento are warehousing meccas because of their location at the junction of two or more interstate highways. (See Case Study 4.3, Peachtree Industrial Park.) Port activity in Los Angeles, Oakland, Seattle, Miami, and Newark generates demand for warehouse space. Manufacturing space is concentrated in both large and small metropolitan areas in the Southeast and the Midwest.

Because of greater automation in warehousing activities, today's warehouse buildings are very different from those built in the past.

- Buildings with 100,000 square feet or more are common; a 300,000-square-foot warehouse is not unusual.
- "High cube" structures have ceilings at least 24 feet tall, with 32 feet desirable. Some facilities are as tall as 60 feet. High ceilings require more costly, sophisticated lighting systems.
- Technological capabilities are increasingly important; storage and distribution are now highly automated operations governed by the principles of just-in-time inventory control.
- Highly durable flat concrete floors are installed to accommodate taller stacking systems and heavier pallets.
- Warehouses have more truck docks, allowing simultaneous loading and unloading ("cross-docking"). At one time, the norm was one dock door per 10,000 square feet of warehouse space. New buildings now are providing one dock per 5,000 square feet.[4]
- Site plans provide for wider turning radii and longer parking bays to accommodate bigger trucks.
- Users may require both high docks and drive-in bays.

These new design standards suggest that much of the existing warehouse inventory is obsolete. The space

requirements previously listed, however, reflect the needs of large national and multinational firms. Local businesses, which often combine light assembly with distribution and storage functions in one facility, do not require (and do not want to pay for) state-of-the-art facilities. A flexible facility that can easily be expanded or reconfigured to accommodate tenant expansion will be preferable for both investors and users.

Manufacturing and laboratory space is usually designed to meet user specifications. The specialized nature of each facility poses problems when tenants move out or owners decide to shut down operations. Because of the high cost of retrofitting existing factory or high-tech buildings for new users, absorbing vacant manufacturing or R&D space takes longer than for warehouses.

Analyzing Office and Industrial Space Markets

Office and industrial developers and investors use market analysis to identify and evaluate opportunities for developing new projects, to attract investors and financing institutions, to reposition existing projects to attract different segments of the market, or to define a sales price for an existing property. To be most effective in planning a new development, the market analysis needs to be reexamined continually and updated throughout the planning and construction phases. Its performance projections—rent levels, timing of absorption, and occupancy—change as planning and design decisions are made, new information is gathered, and changes occur in the market, such as the possibility of a new competitor. A large tenant might move into the market. Its removal of a significant amount of space from the market would require upward adjustments in the market study's projected absorption, occupancy, and rent levels. Or a major tenant in the market might downsize or vacate. The addition of available space could necessitate downward adjustments in the rent, absorption, and occupancy projections.

From Macro to Micro Analysis

A commercial development often proceeds on the basis of a succession of analyses—from macroeconomic analysis (also called "market screening") to local market analysis to site analysis and project marketability analyses—serving to guide the developer in formulating and refining a development concept.

Many firms study office and industrial development, especially in the larger markets, and much information is available so that the analyst does not have to reinvent the wheel for every study.

Macroeconomic Analysis, or Market Screening

Market screening identifies potential development or investment opportunities by assessing the locational, economic, and market conditions of one or more large market areas. It generally focuses on broad elements such as the underlying economy of the market area and its prospects for growth, the growth potential of the office- or industrial space–using sectors of the economy, the availability and cost of labor, the development climate, and supply and demand factors in the regional office or industrial space market. What are the historical trends, by class and type of building, in net absorption, occupancy and vacancy rates, and rental rates? How much vacant space is currently on the market and how much space is planned or under construction? The following questions should be addressed:

- Who are the major employers in the submarket? Are they in industries that are expanding or contracting?
- What industries are expanding in the area?
- Are different types of tenants attracted to the smaller submarkets or office concentrations within the larger submarket?
- Is there interchangeability among submarkets and within submarkets?
- What types of tenants are attracted to the various areas and why? Is it back-office use, headquarters use, or small professional-tenant use?
- What size tenant is attracted to the various areas and why?
- What amenities are available to office buildings in the area? Are the amenities sufficient?
- What type of residential neighborhoods surround the area? Is executive housing nearby?
- Is the area able to draw support personnel from nearby areas? Is public transportation convenient to allow commuting by support personnel from other areas if not from nearby neighborhoods?

Figure 4-1

Year-End Office Vacancy Rates in United States

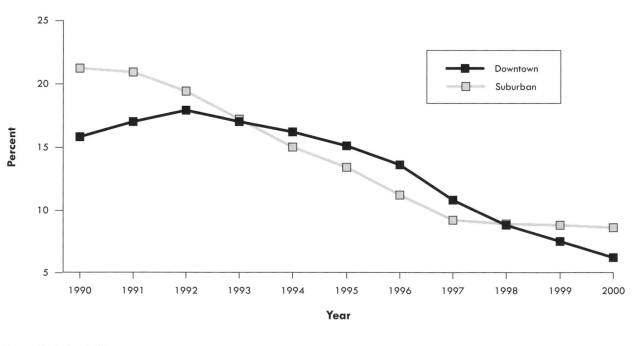

Source: CB Richard Ellis.

Local Analysis

Local analysis explores the dynamics of a single MSA. Typically, its purpose is to identify which submarkets, if any, indicate strong potential for new office or industrial space. It includes a description of the economic base of the metropolitan area, a review of development trends, and, usually, a detailed assessment of the strengths and weaknesses of submarkets—covering net absorption, occupancy, and rental rates by class of building, as well as demand by tenant size.

Within a metropolitan area, conditions can vary widely from one submarket to another. Analysts generally identify a submarket based on a major transportation node or a particular edge city or a district or neighborhood within a city. Industrial submarkets are often transportation based. For example, an airport might be the hub of an industrial submarket. Major highway corridors are often industrial submarkets as well.

Market Area Definition

In an area with an ample supply of comparables, the market area is defined first on the basis of location, then narrowed to include only the most competitive buildings within the previously defined market area. Sometimes it is necessary to broaden the market area by either location or product so that enough competitive product is delineated. The exact extent of the market area for any particular office or industrial project depends on many factors, such as the following:

- Location of competitive buildings;
- Street and road patterns in the area surrounding the building;
- Proximity to mass transit where applicable;
- Commute times from residential areas;
- Proximity to other facilities relevant to target businesses, such as universities or other institutions;
- Jurisdictional boundaries;
- For industrial property, proximity to airports and/or rail lines or interstate highways;
- Land use patterns;
- Physical barriers to access;
- Psychological or perceptual barriers to access, like unappealing or purportedly unsafe areas that must be traversed to get to the building.

The analyst must determine what factors to consider in defining the market area. For example, an office building located at a mass-transit station might be more competitive with buildings located at other stations than with nearby buildings that are beyond walking distance from the station. A definition of its market area would have to take that possibility into account. Urban and suburban locations tend to have quite dissimilar market areas. The market area for a downtown office building may encompass only a few blocks surrounding the building, whereas the market area for a suburban office project may encompass several suburban nodes, or edge cities, surrounding a central city.

Because shipping is usually a major function for industrial properties, industrial sites are more transportation driven than office sites. The market area for an industrial building might be the business parks surrounding an airport or an industrial strip along a rail yard. An R&D complex might depend on access to a university or other research center.

Identification of the market area for commercial real estate is less subjective than for residential or retail development. In many cases, generally accepted development corridors or nodes can be used as the market area for the study. These local submarkets are commonly used by brokerage companies and potential users, and data have already been organized by these submarkets.

Site Selection

Site selection is a crucial step in the development of an office or industrial project. The project's location directly affects the rent and occupancy levels it can achieve. Even office buildings located relatively near each other can experience significant location-based differences in rent and occupancy levels. A building within walking distance of a mass-transit station, for example, may be able to obtain substantially higher rents than buildings only two or three blocks away. Buildings with highway visibility can command higher rents than those without it. Land prices can reflect these large differences in the locational value of sites. Developers choosing sites based on price alone can find themselves unable to compete in the market, even at lower rents.

All of a site's qualities will affect the office building's potential for attracting tenants. Developers should compare the location, access, and physical attributes of alternative sites to identify potential opportunities and obstacles to development. This comparison should include a review of the rent and occupancy characteristics of the buildings located around each site. It should also note any differences in zoning or allowable development potential.

Office buildings should be located in areas with a sense of place. The synergy of a mixed-use environment—office uses alongside support uses such as restaurants, shopping areas, and club facilities—generates higher rents and better leasing. Infill or redevelopment sites in established office locations can offer the advantage of established amenities, available utilities and other infrastructure, and favorable zoning.

Suburban office buildings should be located close to freeways or roads that feed into the regional traffic system. Good access to adjacent roads is critical. Parcels located on prime highways may have great visibility, but they may not be accessible from those highways. Access for parcels located on major highways or frontage roads may be limited to side streets or even rear streets. The location, number, and arrangement of curb cuts into the parking lot can affect significantly the ease of access to a suburban office building.

Busy streets with high traffic counts may be popular with retail developers, but office developers may shy away from areas of heavy traffic. A site's topography plays an important role in project feasibility. For example, hilly sites may require extensive grading, which increases construction costs, but they may also provide excellent opportunities for tuck-under parking, which requires less excavation on a hilly site. In the case of business parks or industrial buildings, it is also important to look at the size, dimensions, and shape of a land parcel. Other factors include utilities, future expansion capability, and adjacent uses. Public approvals for office and industrial projects often hinge on traffic loading during peak hours.

Demand Analysis for Office Development

Good estimates of the total demand and demand for space with different characteristics are essential. Estimating future demand is an uncertain, often subjective, exercise and analysts should always keep in mind that short-term demand trends live up to their billing as short term. Developers with the ability to discern long-term trends are better able to put together developments that stand the test of time and retain their value.

Increases in demand come primarily from growth in office-using jobs. Unfortunately, employment data are not reported in most markets in a way that allows analysts to identify which or how many jobs are located in office environments, particularly at the submarket level. Nor are the data reported in a way that allows analysts to translate employment growth into a number of square feet of demand for office space. Still, analysts can glean important information from employment projections about the makeup and strength of the local

economic base, as well as a broad understanding of the market dynamics of office space demand.

Space per Employee

Market analysts often multiply the expected growth in office jobs by the estimated average square footage allocated per office employee to calculate the future demand for office space in the market area. The first step in this approach is to look at local employment patterns by industry or types of job. The U.S. Bureau of Labor Statistics (BLS) is a widely used source of data for this purpose. The BLS provides employment data for counties or metropolitan areas broken out by job categories based on standard industrial classification (SIC) codes.

All SIC-code job categories include some office-using jobs. Some, like finance, insurance, and real estate (FIRE) jobs, are strongly office based. But the BLS data do not distinguish between office jobs and nonoffice jobs. Some analysts use employment in one or two SIC codes, such as FIRE and business services, as a proxy for office employment. But this practice can produce widely inaccurate estimates of office demand. Analysts may do better by inferring from their own knowledge of the local economy the ratio of office to nonoffice jobs for each locally important job category. Analysts can gain an understanding of the makeup of a local economy by talking to major employers and other professionals who are knowledgeable about the local labor market.

Many state and local planning agencies estimate future employment levels. These estimates can be useful input in a demand analysis. The BLS data on employment growth by SIC codes do not include projections, but the U.S. Department of Commerce, through its Bureau of Economic Analysis (BEA), provides employment projections for metropolitan areas. The BEA forecasts form the basis of most state and local employment projections. A number of commercial forecasting firms offer employment projections as well. The appendix in this book lists some of these data providers.

After employment has been projected, the second step in the employment-forecast method of estimating the future demand for office space is to estimate the average amount of office space per employee. Analysts should be cautious and conservative in their assumptions in this regard. For many corporate office users, the amount of space allocated per employee is on a downward path. Many companies have cut back on space in order to reduce occupancy costs. An increasing number of companies are adopting open office space plans with fewer private offices. And technological innovations have eliminated the need for some office jobs altogether, although they have expanded the need for space for equipment in certain instances.

Virtual office arrangements are another factor decreasing the need for office space. Various arrangements allow workers to spend less time in the traditional office, such as telecommuting, hoteling (through which the worker reserves office space only for times needed), and working on the road or at customer sites without an office at all.[5] At one time, the average space allocation per employee was 250 square feet, which included a proportionate share of public space, corridors, and restrooms. That figure is no longer valid, and many buildings now average less than 200 square feet per employee. The amount of space varies significantly, however, by industry and location, and it is important to customize the figure to the specific market study.

For analysis of office space demand, the forecast of total regional demand is less important than the demand projected for the market area in which the project will compete. The analyst must clearly identify the relevant market area for a prospective project and construct as complete a picture as possible of employment trends, space requirements, and other demand factors for that market area.

The sources of demand for a proposed project generally can be segmented into two major categories: principal users and second-tier users. Principal users (a building's premium or marquee tenants) are generally large and growing firms. Potential premium

---

Table 4-1

Private Sector Employers with Significant Office Employment: 1987 U.S. Standard Industrial Classification System (SIC) and 1997 North American Industrial Classification System

1987 Standard Industrial Classifications		1997 North American Industrial Classifications	
Code	**Description**	**Code**	**Description**
47	Transportation services	51	Information (3)
48	Communications	52	Finance & Insurance
50	Wholesale Trade	531	Real Estate
60–65	Finance, Insurance & Real Estate	5324	Commercial/Industrial Equip. Rental & Leasing
73	Business Services (1)	54	Professional, Scientific & Technical Services (4)
781–782	Motion Picture Production & Distribution		exc. 5417 Scientific R & D Services
80	Health Services	55	Management of Companies & Enterprises
	exc. 805 Nursing Facilities & 806 Hospitals	561	Administrative & Support Services (5)
81	Legal Services	6114	Business Schools & Computer/Mgmt. Training
829	Schools & Educational Services n.e.c.	6116	Other Schools & Instruction
83	Social Services	6117	Educational Support Services
	exc. 835 Day Care & 836 Residential Care	621	Ambulatory Health Care Services (6)
86	Membership Organizations	6241	Individual & Family Services
87	Engineering & Management Services (2)	6243	Vocational Rehabilitation Services
		7113	Promoters of Entertainment Events
		7114	Agents/Managers for Artists
		813	Religious/Grantmaking/Professional Organizations

(1) Includes advertising, credit/collection, mailing, business equipment rental, personnel supply, computer & data processing, building services.

(2) Includes architectural, engineering, accounting, research, testing, management, & public relations.

(3) Includes publishing, motion picture & sound recording, broadcasting, telecommunications, information & data processing.

(4) Includes legal, accounting, payroll, architecture & engineering, design, computer, data processing, manangement consulting, personnel recruitment, marketing, environmental, advertising, public relations, marketing, photography, translators.

(5) Includes employment agencies, call centers, business service centers, credit/collection, travel agents, Investigators, security services, building services.

(6) Offices of physicians & other health care practitioners, outpatient facilities, diagnostic labs outside of hospitals & nursing facilities.

tenants may be essentially landlocked in their current locations, unable to expand into contiguous space because tenants that cannot be relocated occupy adjacent floors. If contiguous building floors are essential to their operations, moving becomes their only option. Developers must ascertain the presence of large, high growth firms in their market area, and their space needs. Other potential premium tenants may be firms preferring a particular location, such as law firms, which often are drawn to buildings with good courthouse access. Complementary users (a building's second-tier tenants) generally are smaller tenants, such as public relations companies, business consultants, and others that are drawn to a location near their major clients or one that provides access to potential clients.

Leasing Activity and Absorption

The analysis of net absorption trends in the market area can supplement and provide a cross-check for the broad-brush office-employment approach to calculating demand for office space. The absorption analysis should look at trends for different types of office space. Analysts must distinguish between net absorption and leasing activity. "Net absorption" is the change in occupied office space over a specified time period. "Leasing activity" is the amount of space that becomes leased or committed in a specified time period. Leasing activity does not account for space that has been vacated during the period, but net absorption does. A tenant moves out of 50,000 square feet of space in building X and moves into the same amount of space in nearby building Y: 50,000 square feet of space has been leased, but net absorption is zero.

Because both measures shed light on aspects of office space use, they are both relevant to the analysis. Most analysts argue that net absorption indicates the real strength or weakness of a market, whereas leasing activity indicates movement within a market area. By comparing trends in net absorption and leasing activity, analysts can reasonably describe the underlying strength and stability of an office market. For example, a market in which the rate of net absorption and the rate of leasing activity move in tandem over time is more stable than a market in which net absorption and leasing activity (or gross absorption) exhibit widely varying rates.

The market is said to be "churning" if it has a high rate of leasing activity and a low rate of net absorption. In a market characterized by churning, tenants are leaving space in one building and taking space in another, both within the market area. Although the market may seem to be growing, the amount of occu-

pied space increases little. Churning often occurs in overbuilt markets with falling rents. The availability of higher-quality space for lower rents, along with moving incentives offered by building owners, lures tenants away from their current locations.

Both office employment and net absorption are imperfect proxies for office space demand, and neither approach should be relied on alone in market analyses. When used together, however, the two approaches can provide a reasonable picture of trends in office space demand.

Straight-Line Projections

A straight-line projection of either office employment or net absorption is a notoriously unreliable method of estimating office demand. A straight-line projection uses recent trends as the basis for estimating future trends, and thus ignores the all-but-certain appearance of the next stage in the economic cycle. Nor can an analysis relying on recent historical trends take sufficient account of the predictable industrywide and local employment changes that are likely to occur for any number of reasons.

The straight-line projections of office space demand performed by developers and investment institutions in the 1980s contributed to the steep crash of commercial real estate in the early 1990s. Market studies should look beyond actual absorption and employment trends, and consider when national and local business cycles are likely to move into new phases and what effect that phasing will have on the demand for office space in the market area.

The demand analysis must go beyond general projections of future demand to identify and assess the sources of demand for the proposed office building. This analysis should include the identification of both potential tenants and market niches that need space—typical space and other requirements. This look at the demand picture entails the following steps:

- Interviews of brokers and other real estate professionals, business organization specialists, and major employers for their perceptions of the need for additional facilities in the market and the features that would be desirable in a new building;
- A determination of leasing trends in competitive properties—including vacancy rates, lease rates, and tenant types—to understand current demand;
- A determination of the services and amenities sought by potential tenants or potential types of tenants;
- An assessment of absorption trends to differentiate between new demand and mere churning.

Supply Analysis for Office Development

Measuring the competitive supply of office space is a less-subjective exercise than measuring demand. A supply analysis has essentially three components: existing space, likely future additions, and vacancy rates. Case study 4.1, an office building acquisition, illustrates the kinds of tables that need to be developed for office market studies.

The first step is to profile existing and proposed office space in the market area. The most basic feature of office space is its quality or class as measured by various characteristics including location, design, and amenities. Market studies should include an inventory of office space by class. It can be useful to categorize office space in the market by other property characteristics as well, such as size, style, location, lease rates and terms, ownership, tenancy (whether owner or renter occupied, whether in single-user or multiuser buildings), type and quality of building systems, and amenities included. A profile of buildings based on property characteristics not only delineates the competitive supply situation, but also provides important information about the local demand for office space and tenant preferences.

A field survey of competitive properties helps the analyst to verify published data and to gain personal insights. Building size, height, general quality, and tenant types are key factors to determine from the field survey. Some of the following building characteristics may be worth noting as well:

Exterior Building Characteristics

- How many floors: low rise (1–3 floors), mid rise (4–15 floors), or high rise (16+ floors)? High-rise buildings tend to be more prestigious and may offer exceptional views. Is the property midblock or on a corner? Corner properties are preferable to midblock properties that may lack good views and lose the benefits of their height.
- Is access to the building and parking easy or difficult? Do turn signals assist accessibility? Tenants obviously prefer that access be as easy and convenient as possible.
- Does the building have visibility from the street or highway?
- Are surrounding uses compatible? It is preferable to be located in an office core with buildings of similar uses.
- Does the building have curb appeal? Is the building well landscaped and well maintained? The initial impression of a building can affect tenant

leasing decisions; thus, it is important that the building have a timeless quality so it will be appealing to tenants over the long term.

- What type of parking exists: surface, attached garage, or subterranean? Is parking free or, if not, what is the monthly rate? Is the parking lot at capacity or can it hold additional cars? Are cars parked in tandem? Is executive parking or valet parking available? How far do employees or visitors have to walk in the open air or is parking attached? Covered or subterranean parking is preferable to surface parking, especially in cold or wet climates.
- What type of exterior does the building have? Polished granite, glass, concrete, brick? Does the exterior have a timeless quality? How will it look in ten years when the building is being sold? The appearance of the building should fit the rent level. In addition, it is important to invest in buildings that will remain able to attract tenants and that will achieve increasing rent levels over time.

Interior Public Space

- What is the number of elevators and elevator ratio (elevators per total square footage excluding the ground floor)? A preferred elevator ratio is one elevator per 30,000 to 40,000 square feet.
- What amenities does the building have? Some typical amenities are concierge service, a fitness center, a restaurant or deli, a conference room, dry cleaners, a card/sundry shop or other retail outlets, and banks. Smaller buildings do not have amenities in the building, but similar facilities should be located nearby. Ground-floor retail and specialty space in office buildings is often difficult to lease and should be minimized unless the market can support such amenities.
- Is the lobby a modern style or outdated? Has it been recently renovated? Is it well maintained? The image of the lobby must be appropriate for the type of tenants in the building. Today, many firms are sensitive to cost issues and therefore do not want to be in a building with an over-designed, expensive lobby.
- Are corridors modern looking? Are they wide or narrow? Spacious corridors are generally a minimum of six feet. How high are the ceilings? A preferred ceiling height is generally eight feet. Is tenant signage one consistent style?
- Are restrooms modern looking or outdated? Do they have stalls designed for the handicapped?
- Is the floor layout confusing or easy to navigate?

Tenants and Leasing

- What types of tenants occupy the building? The analyst can get a sense of the occupants by scanning the building directory. Are tenants concentrated in a particular industry? Government and medical tenants are generally a detriment to a Class A office building. Are the tenants prestigious or upstarts with tenuous credit? It is preferable to have at least 40 percent of the building secured by tenants with strong credit, but this rule of thumb does not hold true during economic downturns. Unless an investor is interested in single-tenant buildings secured by a strong credit, long-term lease, no one tenant should occupy more than 30 percent of the square footage of a building. This criterion protects an investor from a downsizing or a large move out that would severely undermine the cash flow and viability of the investment.
- Are leases staggered so that not all of the leases roll over at the same time?
- Who is the leasing agent for the building? Be sure to note the telephone number. In addition, when the analyst is driving the market and conducting a field survey, he or she should note any vacant parcels of land that could be developed for office use, any broker signs on vacant land, or any developer signs indicating a site for future development. After the analyst returns to the office, he or she should call the brokers listing vacant land to find out its selling price and what the zoning will allow or call the developer to find out what is under construction or planned.

Tenant interviews are useful if it is possible to perform them. Tenants can provide greater insight into the issues of the building and metropolitan area. The following is a list of sample questions to ask for office building tenants:

- Why did you choose to locate in the subject building?
- What other buildings did you consider?
- Has the building met your expectations?
- Do you have any problems with the building?
- Is building management responsive?
- Does your firm need to be in this submarket? Why? What other submarkets could you locate in?
- Are you planning to renew your lease in the building when it expires? Why or why not?

Following the field survey, the analyst calls the leasing brokers for the most competitive buildings to obtain the following information:

- Current asking rents, lease terms, and any concessions being offered (such as months of free rent or higher-than-standard tenant improvement allowances that might indicate soft markets); annual escalations based on CPI or another index, if included; history of vacancies, absorption, and base rent increases over the last few years. Rents are usually expressed in terms of annual rent per square foot.
- Pass-through charges that are billed directly to tenants based on the amount of space leased, such as utilities and property taxes. Some office buildings rent space on a triple net basis, with all expenses passed through directly to tenants. Others include certain utilities and taxes in the base rent, and charge tenants only for actual increases above and beyond the initial year of the lease.
- Floor/area ratio (building space to lot area). Suburban floor/area ratios are much lower than in central business districts, where higher densities are permitted. Single-story office structures in suburban business parks typically have floor/area ratios of less than 1.0. Mid-rise buildings could have ratios of 2.0 or more.
- Parking spaces per thousand square feet of office space. As recently as the 1980s, a parking ratio of four spaces per 1,000 square feet was considered typical, but today office tenants look for more parking spaces because more workers are packed into less space. Parking availability is more important in the suburbs than in downtowns where workers may use public transportation or park in commercial lots or garages.
- Capacity of heating, ventilation, and air conditioning systems has become a very important consideration.
- Telecommunications capabilities.
- Total building size, usable versus rentable space, size of a typical floor. Usable space may be limited by columns or mechanical systems that are part of the rentable space.

The previous checklist of building characteristics is more extensive than what the analyst will usually consider. This list, however, is useful for examining an existing property under consideration for purchase, sale, lease, or repositioning.

Sublet Space

Ascertaining the amount of space available for subleasing in a market area is an important element of the supply analysis. Such space is commonly referred to as "sublet" space. In the overbuilt markets of the early 1990s, it was common for tenants to vacate space before the end of the lease period in order to secure less expensive or more desirable space. In many cases, large amounts of sublet space should have indicated to analysts that markets were not as strong as overall leasing data indicated.

Sublet space, even if it remains vacant, is not technically vacant. It is under lease and the tenant is still paying rent. It is, nevertheless, empty space that is available to be leased. Tenants that vacate before the end of their lease term generally attempt to sublease the vacated space. Often, space available for sublease is offered at a discount and thus is less expensive than other vacant space. The availability of large blocks of sublet space can impinge significantly on the viability of existing and proposed office projects in the market area. It is important, therefore, to include an estimate of sublet space in the analysis of the competition that a prospective project will face.

Vacancies

Vacancy rate trends are another key item in the supply analysis. It is important to analyze movements in the market's overall vacancy as well as vacancy differentials within the overall market that indicate where and in what kinds of space vacancy rates are high or low, rising or falling. Are large blocks of space available for lease? Or is the supply of vacant space made up mostly of numerous, small chunks of space? How is vacant space distributed among classes of buildings? Are vacancies spread throughout the market area? Or are they concentrated in certain areas? The analyst should know whether space is leased and occupied or has a lease commitment. Often, a lender requires about 30 percent of a new office project (as much as 40 percent of an industrial project) to be preleased as a prerequisite for financing.

The analysis of vacancy trends also provides input for determining a potential project's "stabilized occupancy," which is the typical annual occupancy rate for the project after its startup period (and a key variable in assessing a project's feasibility). In the early and mid-1980s, office market analyses on proposed projects routinely projected stabilized occupancies ranging from 93 percent to 95 percent. As construction soared later in the decade and demand began to decline, however, the actual stabilized occupancies achieved by these new office buildings were well below their pro forma projections. Market studies for new developments today will have more conservative occupancy assumptions, even in markets where the overall vacancy rate is under 5 percent.

Demand Analysis for Industrial Space

Like office space demand, the demand for industrial space is often projected by estimating future employment in appropriate sectors. This method often works for projecting R&D demand, which is strongly tied to space needs per worker. But the link between employment and the demand for manufacturing and warehousing space is not clear. Such space is more closely associated with products than persons. A more appropriate method for forecasting such demand is based on projecting the gross metropolitan product (GMP). GMP is a measure of the output of a local economy, and much of this output is the goods produced and stored in industrial facilities. A proportional relationship is derived between the change in occupied industrial space and the change in GMP.

Others have used a model that studies the path of goods movement,[6] which is particularly suited to assessing demand for warehouse and distribution space. Demand for such space shows little correlation with employment trends but is influenced by the movement of goods from the place of production to the place of consumption. Measuring the growth of goods production in weight rather than dollar value provides a way to gauge the need for this kind of space. An accurate market analysis for industrial space requires a good understanding of the distribution process.

The growth of e-commerce is having an effect on warehousing and distribution needs. The demand for industrial space may actually increase, as fewer retail outlets distribute goods, but purchases are handled directly from distribution facilities. The design of new distribution facilities will have to take into account automated shipping and tracking functions and new methods of inventory control.[7]

Supply Analysis for Industrial Space

When the inventory for the supply analysis is compiled, properties should be categorized by type and configuration. Elements such as ceiling height, office buildout, column spacing, building depth, the number of docks and ground-level doors, and other functional components help to define the property's market. Site considerations, such as parking and the size of the truck apron, might also be important factors. Attention should be directed to those components that might give the property an advantage in the market. Air conditioning and oversized parking lots are examples of physical components that might garner a premium in market rents.

When an existing project is analyzed, a rent roll or, at minimum, a leasing summary should be reviewed. This procedure identifies tenants at the subject property and rental rates, lease terms, and other relevant factors. As with office space, most industrial property rents are quoted on an annual basis. A review of the subject property's physical characteristics reveals to the analyst how to analyze the competitive submarket. For example, should the analyst look at large, single-tenant warehouse properties with minimal office space, high ceilings, and lots of dock doors, or should the analyst look at multitenant warehouse facilities with oversized office buildout and ground-level doors? Only by understanding the subject property can the analyst answer such questions and properly analyze industrial space in the competitive submarket. Information on rents, tenants, and leases can help the analyst to position the property when current submarket conditions are studied later in the analysis. In the case of a project that is not yet built, the analyst's job, most likely, will be to recommend the characteristics that are most desirable for the market by examining comparable properties.

In addition to visiting the subject property, the purpose for touring the submarket is to examine competing industrial properties and to acquire a sense of the area's characteristics. Major points of access, transportation corridors, quality of industrial space in the area, general appearance, activity levels, and other spatial considerations should be reviewed during the site visit. It is also useful to schedule building tours with brokers and property managers active in the submarket. Such individuals are among the best sources for revealing the strengths and weaknesses of a submarket, as well as its subtleties.

Sources of Data

The U.S. Census Bureau's *County Business Patterns* includes economic data for counties, including the number of employees and business establishments by SIC code. These data can serve as a proxy for identifying the types and sizes of tenants in a county.

Most metropolitan areas have at least one real estate brokerage firm that maintains a database of office buildings or an office building guide. Some local governments or economic development authorities maintain such information. Obtaining such a list should be the first step in identifying competitive buildings. Usually, existing data are available on rents and occupancy on a building-by-building basis. Detailed data on construction activity, both underway and planned, may be available from a brokerage or

from one of the public agencies. Office inventories are usually compiled based on net rentable area; however, some landlords may quote lease rates based on gross or usable space.

For larger markets, national research firms (such as Torto Wheaton Research and National Real Estate Index) provide historic and current market data for submarkets and property class for a fee. These reports are usually updated at least twice annually. Analysts must supplement published information with field visits to competitive properties and interviews with leasing staff.

The inventory of competitive office supply must include planned projects that may come online and compete with the project under consideration. Such data are more difficult to obtain and are less reliable than are surveys of existing buildings. Some local economic development agencies and planning offices compile lists of proposed projects and track their progress through the approval and development pipeline. Officials in these agencies are likely to know about proposed projects and should be able to provide some details. Market analysts can confirm and expand on information from public agencies by questioning brokers and the executives of construction or development firms about building plans.

National and local commercial brokerages collect and publish data on the industrial market. Industrial data is, however, less comprehensive than office market inventories. Coverage can be inconsistent across metropolitan areas or among sources, or the analyst may need to pay a substantial fee to obtain the detail needed.

- CB Richard Ellis's *Industrial Vacancy Index of the U.S.* (published quarterly) covers only facilities with more than 100,000 square feet (although information on smaller buildings is often included in market reports prepared by its local affiliates).[8]
- Grubb & Ellis's coverage is defined locally; in some markets, buildings as small as 5,000 square feet are included, while in others the minimum size is 25,000 square feet. Although Grubb & Ellis's national industrial vacancy reports include multitenant, single-tenant, and owner-occupied space, other firms cover just investment properties.
- The National Real Estate Index's rent, price, and cap rate statistics are for Class A warehouse properties only.
- Torto Wheaton Research's *TWR Industrial Outlook* covers all three types of industrial properties, providing semiannual updates of rent, space availability, and construction activity both metrowide

and for subareas. It also includes two-year forecasts.

■ The Society of Industrial and Office Realtors publishes an annual overview of industrial property market conditions in both large and small metropolitan areas. This reference provides a breakdown of the percentage of industrial space that is manufacturing, warehouse, or high tech, with average rent information for each type. Recent absorption, operating expenses, and market trends are also highlighted.[9]

Office absorption is highly correlated with office employment. A subscription to Economy.com, WEFA, or McGraw Hill's DRI can provide historical and projected data on office employment by metropolitan area. However, if a subscription to one of the forecasting groups is too expensive, office employment can be approximated using the FIRE and 37.7 percent of Services categories from the BLS's *Employment and Earnings* publication. (See appendix for further information on data sources.)

Industrial brokers usually provide information on industrial availability, not vacancy. Because so much industrial space is corporate owned, vacant space is not always on the market. Available space is a better measure of full or partial buildings that could be acquired or leased. Manufacturing space tends to have the lowest availability among the three types of industrial buildings and shows little movement from year to year. In contrast, R&D space occupancy is the most volatile of industrial types.

Few market data sources provide industrial space information by subtypes. Most secondary market data are lumped into a single category labeled "industrial." Data portrayed in this fashion explain little about actual market trends and the performance of individual industrial property subtypes. Analyses based on such generalizations often result in flawed conclusions. Analysts often must make the best of imperfect data, but it is worth the time and trouble to identify a data source that characterizes the industrial market in the proper way.

The Integration of Demand and Supply Analyses

A comparison of the current rate of net absorption of office or industrial space with the existing (and planned) supply of space gives a fairly clear picture of the overall balance between demand and supply in the market. For example, if annual net absorption in the area has been averaging 50,000 square feet and 50,000 to 75,000 square feet of space is available, demand and supply are in balance. If, however, 100,000 square feet of space is available, the market has a two-year supply of office space; if the market contains 500,000 square feet of available space, it has a ten-year supply. This simple comparison of current demand and supply represents an expedient way of gauging the market's short-term supply/demand balance, but such a snapshot should never be relied on to predict future trends. To produce a study of real value, the market analyst must look for factors that could affect absorption of office or industrial space in the future and interpret current market conditions accordingly.

After the demand analysis has identified relevant industries in the market area and generated historical trend data for them, the market analyst must search out relevant clues by which he or she can extrapolate the future. Which local industries are poised to grow? To contract? What new office-using employers might locate in the area? Is the local government taking steps to attract certain types of industries? Are policy changes or program initiatives being considered at the federal or state level that will affect the growth of office employment or industrial-space users in the market area? Do tax or other cost differentials affect decisions in the market?

No easy and fast rules for understanding the market exist at this level. Analysts usually piece together the information they have obtained in interviews with local and regional government officials, civic leaders, employers, trade association representatives, and real estate professionals to arrive at their reasoned insights on the future of the area's commercial real estate market. In the end, a site-specific market analysis is only as good as its interpretation of the facts it so painstakingly gathers.

The main tasks in the integration of the demand and supply analyses are to determine how successfully the proposed project will compete in the market area and, specifically, to estimate what share of the competitive market it can be expected to capture. The marketability analysis and the market-share analysis are covered in the following sections.

Marketablity Analysis

Several of the preliminary steps involved in determining a proposed building's market competitiveness have been described earlier in this chapter. A market analysis is conducted to identify a site (or to assess the development potential of a specific site) and a target market. As part of the market study, the specific market area in which the project will compete for tenants should be defined precisely and a detailed inventory of the market area's existing and proposed buildings should be compiled. The inventory can be used to identify competitive projects.

Developers need to compare their prospective project with the buildings with which it will compete. The proposed building's advantages and disadvantages relative to the features offered by competitive buildings are evaluated in order to arrive at an achievable rent. The assessment of how the proposed building stacks up against the competition is really a matter of judgment by the development team, but the team's opinion should be based on the findings of the market analysis.

By looking at the competitive advantages and disadvantages of the proposed property, developers can arrive at an adjustment factor—negative or positive—that weighs the position of the proposed property relative to each competitive building. For each competitive building, the adjustment factor is applied to the rent charged in order to determine an indicated rent for the proposed project. The typical (or, in some cases, average) indicated rent of all of the competitive properties is then assumed to be the rent that the proposed project can expect to achieve, the rent that competitive analysis indicates is achievable. Case study 4.3 shows how marketability can be improved by repositioning an existing R&D facility.

Market Share and Absorption

The analysis usually includes an estimate of the proposed development's capture rate, or market share, so that absorption can be projected. It has already projected how much office or industrial space can be supported in the market area overall. Now the analyst must estimate the amount of the market that the prospective office project is likely to capture. Expressed as a percentage, this figure is estimated by comparing the subject project with competitive projects in terms of amount of space, location, price, amenities, special features, and strength of management. It is important to be realistic. A proxy for a building's fair-share capture rate is the share of competitive supply that it represents. This share-of-current-supply method is a good first cut at estimating a building's capture rate. A building may absorb more or less than its share depending on its competitiveness. Perhaps a location and amenities that make the building superior to the competition, or lower rents

that make it more competitive, will enable the proposed project to capture extra market share.

Another approach to fine-tuning the estimate of the capture rate for a proposed office project is to analyze how well the building meets the location, size, and other preferences of potential tenants. At this point, it is very important that target tenants and their space needs and preferences have been identified. If the project, as proposed, does not conform to the building characteristics sought by its target market, it should be redesigned to maximize its potential market share.

After a project's capture rate has been estimated, the analyst can calculate how long absorption will take. The basis for this estimate is demand projections and the lease-up experience of similar projects. Rental rates and terms should be estimated. The basis for these estimates is the rents achieved by the most comparable projects in the market area, adjusted for the proposed project's particular competitive position. Finally, stabilized occupancy, which is the typical annual occupancy rate for the project after its startup period, should be projected, based on local market conditions and the experience of similar buildings in the area. The analyst should clearly state whether absorption means leasing or occupancy pace. These various elements of the project—lease-up period, rental rates, and stabilized occupancy—together with operating expenses constitute the basic ingredients for the cash flow analysis that must be performed as part of the financial feasibility analysis.

Overview of Case Studies

Three case studies are included in this chapter. Case study 4.1 is an analysis of a Class A office building nearing completion in a desirable office corridor in suburban Chicago. The consultant has been hired by an investor who wants to purchase a building that will bring a stable cash flow over a ten- or 15-year period. The purpose of the market analysis is to familiarize the investor with the market and the subject property and to help determine if the subject suits the investor's needs.

Case study 4.2 analyzes a multitenant warehouse property in the Valwood submarket of Dallas. This case study uses the annual changes in GMP and population to model warehouse-space demand in the metro area, then applies a capture rate to the submarket. The case study also projects rent ranges for the submarket.

Case study 4.3 examines the Peachtree Industrial Park, a complex of four buildings in suburban Atlanta. The owner is selling the property and needs to determine a fair market value and identify how to reposition the property to improve its value and to better attract potential investors.

Notes

[1] Jo Allen Gause et al., *Office Development Handbook,* 2d ed. (Washington, D.C.: ULI–the Urban Land Institute, 1998).

[2] Building Owners and Managers Association (BOMA) International and ULI–the Urban Land Institute, *What Office Tenants Want: 1999 BOMA/ULI Office Tenant Survey Report* (Washington, D.C.: BOMA International and ULI–the Urban Land Institute, 1999).

[3] According to the Society of Industrial and Office Realtors (SIOR), roughly 59 percent of the nation's industrial inventory is warehouse space, 33 percent is manufacturing, and 8 percent is high tech. Torto Wheaton Research, which covers a smaller number of markets in greater detail, estimates that half of the nation's industrial space is warehousing, 32 percent is manufacturing, 8 percent is R&D, and the balance is specialized facilities.

[4] Marvin F. Christensen, Bill Wisener, and Darrel J. Campos, "Attributes of Tomorrow's Warehouse Structures," *Real Estate Review,* vol. 27, no. 3 (Fall 1997): pp. 51–57.

[5] Thomas Davenport and Keri Pearlson, "Two Cheers for the Virtual Office," *Sloan Management Review,* vol. 39, no. 4 (Summer 1998): p. 51.

[6] Glenn R. Mueller and Steven P. Laposa, "The Path of Goods Movement," *Real Estate Finance,* vol. 10, no. 2 (Summer 1994): pp. 42–50.

[7] John McMahan, "The Impact of E-Commerce on Real Estate," *Real Estate Issues,* vol. 24, no. 4 (Winter 1999): pp. 1–11.

[8] In the aggregate, the *Index* covers more than 5 billion square feet of industrial space. The largest market, Los Angeles, has 2,800 buildings, or nearly 5 percent of all the space in the United States in structures with at least 100,000 square feet.

[9] See Society of Industrial and Office Realtors and Landauer Associates, Inc., *Comparative Statistics of Industrial and Office Real Estate Markets,* published annually, Washington, D.C. Local brokers provide the information; more than 100 market areas are covered.

Office Building Purchase:
Suburban Chicago (1997)

Tsilah Burman

A real estate advisory firm has a client interested in acquiring Class A office buildings in major metropolitan areas. The client plans to hold the properties for the long term—ten to 15 years—and is seeking a relatively stable cash flow. The acquisition director has located a property that is for sale in suburban Chicago. The seven-story building, currently under construction, will contain approximately 270,000 square feet of leasable space. It is scheduled for completion in two months and is almost 100 percent leased on a long-term basis to several large tenants with strong credit. The building is the first phase of a multiphase, 42-acre office park. Construction of the 260,000-square-foot second building has begun, and design development for the third building is in progress. After completion, the office park is expected to include approximately 1.1 million square feet of Class A office space and potentially a hotel.

The market research director is asked to conduct a market study (1) to familiarize the client with the market, (2) to determine whether the property would be a good investment for the client, and (3) to determine whether any hidden risks have not been considered and underwritten.

As part of the data collection process, the research director makes a site visit to physically inspect the property and drives the submarket to assess the overall character of the area and to evaluate competitive properties. Additional data are obtained through conversations with owners, managers, leasing agents, and other real estate professionals familiar with the submarket. Published data sources are used for statistical information about the market.

The Chicago Economy

In analyzing demand, it is useful to begin on a macro, or city, level and move to a more micro, or submarket, level of analysis.

Chicago is the third-largest metropolitan area in the nation in terms of population, having reached 7.7 million in 1996. Although the rate of population growth in the future is projected to be less than the U.S. average, absolute growth will still be substantial (approximately 42,000 people per year or 212,000 over the next five years).

The Chicago economy is highly diversified and closely mirrors the U.S. economy. Greater Chicago's employment is expanding at an annual rate of 1.3 percent, trailing the national pace somewhat. Much of the reason for slower growth is that the labor market is constrained by a low unemployment rate of less than 5 percent. Leading the growth that is occurring are the service and construction sectors. The Chicago economy is expected to sustain its moderate expansion through the remainder of 1997. (See Table 4.1-1.)

It is important to look at absolute growth, not just the rate of growth. Although Chicago's employment growth

Table 4.1-1
Average Annual Growth in Chicago and the United States, 1992–2001

	1992–1996		1997–2001	
	Chicago	**U.S.**	**Chicago**	**U.S.**
Population Growth Rate	0.7%	1.0%	0.5%	0.9%
Employment Growth Rate	1.7%	2.0%	1.3%	1.6%
Absolute Employment Growth	80,300	2,725,000	52,300	1,775,000
Gross Metro Product	2.8%	2.7%	2.5%	2.8%

Source: CB Richard Ellis Investors.

rate is lower than the U.S. average, Chicago ranks second in the nation in absolute job growth, behind only Los Angeles. The region benefits from its position as the distribution, transportation, communication, and financial services center for the Midwest. It also benefits from having the second-largest concentration of Fortune 500 companies in the United States after New York. Commercial construction and capital investment have remained strong, but these sectors have softened from peak activity.

The outlook for the Chicago economy for the near term is not only buoyed by the enduring business cycle upturn, but also by the large number of new expansions and relocations in the metropolitan area. According to *Site Selection* magazine, Chicago led the nation in the number of new facilities during the past two years. In 1996 alone, the area attracted nearly 350 new facilities. Chicago's advantages include the following:

- One of the best transportation infrastructures in the nation;
- A central location in the United States; and
- Access to capital markets—Chicago is the financial center of the Midwest and ranked fifth in the United States in per capita commercial deposits.

Although Chicago is projected to grow more slowly than the nation in most categories, strong growth must be weighed against the potential for overbuilding. Many cities with strong growth profiles are also the cities where new construction has begun to occur in order to accommodate the growth. Many of these strong-growth cities are also more likely to experience overbuilding because of the greater availability of land.

Service Employment
The major drivers of growth in the Chicago economy have been its service industries as Chicago continues to diversify from its manufacturing roots into a service and distribution center for the Midwest. About three-quarters of employment growth over the past 12 months is attributed to growth in the service industries. Business services especially have been driving growth. This is primarily due to Chicago's concentration of headquarters operations, the

growth of the computer software industry, the concentration of financial services, and changes in the way businesses are being managed.

High-Tech Employment
Chicago has the third-largest concentration of high-tech employment after San Jose and Boston, and the outlook for Chicago's high-tech industries remains promising. Employment in high-tech industries has expanded by nearly 3 percent annually from 1991 to 1996. Chicago-based, large high-tech companies and startups are heavily concentrated in manufacturing of telecommunications equipment and software development, servicing the many major retailers and financial service firms headquartered in Chicago, as well as its large and increasingly technology-dependent traditional manufacturing industries. To Chicago's benefit, its high-tech industries have been much less tied to defense spending and, therefore, less vulnerable to cutbacks than those of some other regions.

Transportation
Integral to Chicago's status as a distribution and export center and a hub for passenger traffic is its transportation network. O'Hare Airport is the nation's busiest, handling 9 percent more passengers than the next-busiest airport, Atlanta's Hartsfield Airport. In addition, Chicago remains the nation's rail hub.

Summary of Metropolitan Area Economy
Over the long term, Chicago's growth potential will be constrained by the metropolitan area's high cost of doing business. Labor costs exceed the national average by 14 percent. Housing costs remain by far the highest in the Midwest, but are low relative to the major metropolitan areas in the Northeast and in California.

The key to Chicago's future lies in its transportation and distribution network, its strong export-oriented industries, as well as its status as the financial, commodity trading, and service center of the Midwest. The diversity of Chicago's economy and the growth of high-technology and communications industries are also important assets of the metropolitan area.

Overview of the East-West Corridor Office Market

The East-West Corridor office market encompasses approximately 12 miles stretching west of Chicago along the East-West Tollway from Oak Brook to Naperville. The market is the largest suburban office concentration in the metropolitan area, with more than 26 million square feet of space.

Large corporate tenants in the marketplace include some of the nation's largest businesses, such as the following:

- Amoco
- AT&T
- General Electric
- Kodak
- Lucent Technologies
- McDonald's
- Rockwell
- R.R. Donnelley
- Shell Oil
- Spiegel
- Swift
- Xerox

The East-West Corridor is home to 24 (9 percent of the metropolitan total) of the largest public companies in Chicago and 16 (6 percent of the metropolitan total) of Chicago's leading private firms. Many Fortune 500 companies have headquarters or satellite offices in the East-West Corridor market. In addition to the many corporate headquarters, the corridor includes nine college and university satellite or main campuses. Major research centers include Amoco's research facility, Argonne National Laboratory, and Fermi National Accelerator Laboratory. The corporate headquarters and national laboratories attract suppliers and subcontractors who want to be close to those facilities. In addition, such facilities have the potential to spawn new high-tech and other startup businesses.

Two major projects will also reinforce the corridor as a key business node:

1. Argonne National Laboratory was recently awarded $500 million of federal funds for a project involving its Advanced Photon Source facility. The lab was expected to hire approximately 5,000 people to staff the project.
2. McDonald's recently received approval for a 20-year expansion plan of its corporate headquarters

in Oak Brook. The state of Illinois is contributing $7.6 million for infrastructure improvements for the expansion. Nearby roads, intersections, and highway ramps will be improved near the headquarters. The expansion will add 7,000 jobs to Oak Brook.

Surrounding areas should benefit from the growth of subcontractors for the project at Argonne and suppliers to McDonald's.

Numerous factors add to the attractiveness of the East-West Corridor market as a business location. It has easy access to a diverse residential base, including very high end executive housing, as well as housing for middle-management and support personnel. Thus, office tenants locating in the market have a strong nearby labor base from which to draw. In addition, most of the market is located within DuPage County, an affluent county with good schools and infrastructure. DuPage County includes four regional malls, two of which are within the East-West Corridor office market's boundaries. Malls are desirable amenities for suburban office workers. Taxes are lower in DuPage than in adjacent Cook County, thus lowering occupancy costs for tenants.

Interchangeability exists within the East-West Corridor office market, but little exists with other suburban markets in the Chicago area. This market is truly the premier suburban market in the metropolitan area because of its size, the presence of many corporate headquarters, a diverse residential housing stock, easy accessibility from the tollways and other highways, and its depth of amenities.

The East-West Corridor office market has excellent accessibility to the entire metropolitan area from the East-West Tollway (I-88), the North-South Tollway (I-355), and the Tri-State Tollway (I-294). The advantages of being on the eastern end of the market, where the subject property is located, include being closer to downtown Chicago and O'Hare and Midway airports. Moreover, the eastern end of the market has more amenities, including full-service hotels, restaurants, a regional mall, and other retail facilities.

Within the East-West Corridor market area are several submarkets, including Oak Brook/Oak Brook Terrace, Downers Grove, Lisle, and Naperville. The Oak Brook area was built to be the residential and business home for major corporate users. The residential community has million-dollar homes with golf courses, polo fields, and Oak Brook Center, an upscale regional mall, as amenities. Smaller professional tenants, as well as a number of company headquarters, are located in Oak Brook and Oak Brook Terrace. As residential communities grew to the west and the Oak Brook office market tightened, the office market followed the residential growth west along the tollway with concentrations in Oak Brook Terrace, Lombard, Downers Grove, Lisle, and Naperville.

The Downers Grove submarket, in which the subject building is located, is closest to the Oak Brook/Oak Brook Terrace market, as well as the amenities of that area. Near the junction of I-88 and I-355, Downers Grove has easy access to both north/south and east/west highways. Further, the subject building is close to a four-way interchange on I-88, which allows tenants to travel both east and west, whereas many other buildings in the corridor are close to only a two-way interchange providing more difficult access to and from I-88. Being close to the center of the market, Downers Grove is sited advantageously to attract tenants from both the east and west ends of the corridor. The subject building can be directly accessed by 31st Street. This street is wide, containing four lanes in addition to turning lanes, and thus provides a back door to the Oak Brook core.

The eastern end of the office market tends to attract smaller tenants than the western part of the market. Whereas office tenants typically range from 3,000 to 7,000 square feet in Oak Brook, the typical size outside of Oak Brook is more than 7,000 square feet.

Because rents are higher in Oak Brook/Oak Brook Terrace than in the office concentrations farther east in Lisle and Naperville, less interchangeability tends to exist among these areas. However, because of its location in the middle of the corridor and close to many amenities, Downers Grove tends to have greater interchangeability with the other office concentrations. All these factors need to be considered when producing a market study.

Supply and Demand in the Submarket
The East-West Corridor office market contains more than 26 million square feet of space with a vacancy rate of 10.1 percent as of second quarter 1997. Class A buildings account for more than 23 percent of the market, or 6 million square feet. The vacancy rate for Class A buildings is 8.0 percent. Class A buildings have a vacancy rate of 8.0 percent in Oak Brook/Oak Brook Terrace, and 8.0 percent in Lombard, Downers Grove, Lisle, and Naperville. Currently, just under 4 million square feet of the Class A office space is in Oak Brook/Oak Brook Terrace; 2.2 million square feet is in Lombard, Downers Grove, Lisle, and Naperville. All the space under construction as of 1997 (850,000 square feet in four buildings) is in the western area of the East-West Corridor market. (See Table 4.1-2.)

Net absorption in recent years has been constrained by the lack of opportunities for large tenants to expand in the market because of the scarcity of large blocks of available space. As an indication of the pent-up demand, the subject building will be almost fully leased upon its completion. Moreover, the second building in the office park, which is not due to be completed until 1998, has already preleased 36,000 square feet. In addition, Hamilton Partners' 190,000-square-foot Arboretum Lakes building, which is also under construction and not due for completion until 1998, has 48,000 square feet of its space preleased. The strong preleasing points to a demand for large blocks of space in the market. Currently, 12 tenants in the East-West Corridor market are looking for office space of 50,000 square feet or more and 29 tenants are looking for space between 10,000 and 49,999 square feet.

Net absorption decreased from 1996 to 1997, primarily because R.R. Donnelley put the entire Corporetum Office Campus III building on the market for lease in anticipation of its move to the subject building. R.R. Donnelley will be increasing its square footage at the subject building by 15,953 square feet, another positive note.

The vacancy rate was increased slightly by the addition of Westbrook Corporate Center 4 in 1996. Raw space is still available in the building. Westbrook Corporate Center is on the far eastern end of the market in the Cook County portion. Taxes are higher at that building because it is in Cook County, but operating expenses are lower because of an innovative cooling system that makes ice at night.

Table 4.1-2

East-West Corridor Class A Office Market Building Characteristics (August 1997)

Building Name/ Address	Year Built	Floors	Square Feet	Vacancy (Sq. Ft.)	Vacancy Rate (Percent)	Asking Rent	Per Annum Escalations	Pkg. Ratio	Average Floor Size (Sq. Ft.)
Existing: Oak Brook/Oak Brook Terrace									
1 Westbrook Corp. Ctr. 22nd St. & Wolf	1985	10	221,456	8,848	4.0	$ 25.00 Net Electric	3%	3.8	22,100
2 Westbrook Corp. Ctr. 22nd St. & Wolf	1985	10	221,456	22,500	10.2	Negotiable	Negotiable	3.8	22,100
3 Westbrook Corp. Ctr. 22nd St. & Wolf	1989	10	216,096	21,600	10.0	Negotiable	Negotiable	4.1	21,600
4 Westbrook Corp. Ctr. 22nd St. & Wolf	1996	10	215,433	59,888	27.8	$ 25.00 Net Electric	3%	15.6	22,437
5 Westbrook Corp. Ctr. 22nd St. & Wolf	1990	10	216,096	0	0.0	N/A	N/A	4.1	21,600
Drake Oakbrook Plaza 2211 York Rd.	1981 1991R	5	126,000	0	0.0	N/A	N/A	3.5	25,000
Harger Woods Corp. Ctr. 701 Harger Rd.	1986	2	63,080	0	0.0	N/A	N/A	3.8	31,500
ATT Plaza 1111 W. 22nd St.	1984	8	225,316	18,042	8.0	$ 17.50 NNN	Negotiable	3.5	27,050
Commerce Plaza I 2001 Spring Rd.	1970 1986R	7	173,903	4,101	2.4	$18.00–20.00 NNN	3%	3.5	24,843
Oakbrook Terrace Tower 1 Tower Ln.	1987	31	633,946	80,000	12.6	$19.50–21.50 NNN	3%	3.2	22,436
The Crossings 1420–1520 Kensington Rd.	1985	3	294,593	20,734	7.0	$ 16.00 NNN	Negotiable	4.3	50,000
Oak Brook Regency Twr-E 1415 W. 22nd St.	1977 1993R	13	201,159	3,394	1.7	$ 22.50 Full Service	Negotiable	4.6	15,461
Oak Brook Regency Twr-W 1515 W. 22nd St.	1977 1993R	13	201,159	3,469	1.7	$ 19.50 NNN	3%	4.6	15,461
Mid America Plaza 1/2 Mid America Plz.	1985	10	407,190	50,953	12.5	$17.50–19.50 NNN	4%	3.3	26,000
One Park View Plaza 17-W110 22nd St.	1990	9	263,912	7,949	3.0	$ 19.00 NNN	Negotiable	3.4	29,323
One Lincoln Centre 18-W140 Butterfield Rd.	1986	17	294,972	15,587	5.3	$17.50–19.50 NNN	Negotiable	3.6	19,000
Subtotal/Average: Oak Brook/Oak Brook Terrace		**11**	**3,975,767**	**317,065**	**8.0**			**4.5**	**24,744**

(continued on following page)

However, the savings do not completely offset the higher taxes. The Westbrook Corporate Center campus is isolated, away from the office core and amenities of the Oak Brook market.

Rental Rates

Based on actual lease comparables for 1997 (see Table 4.1-3), rents for Class A office space in the East-West Corridor have ranged from $14.50 to $19.50 triple net

Table 4.1-2 *(continued)*

East-West Corridor Class A Office Market Building Characteristics (August 1997)

Building Name/ Address	Year Built	Floors	Square Feet	Vacancy (Sq. Ft.)	Vacancy Rate (Percent)	Asking Rent	Per Annum Escalations	Pkg. Ratio	Average Floor Size (Sq. Ft.)
Existing: Lombard/Downers Grove/Lisle/Naperville									
Unisys Center I 333 E. Butterfield Rd.	1984	9	189,930	3,760	2.0	$ 15.50 NNN	Negotiable	4.0	21,082
Unisys Center II 377 E. Butterfield Rd.	1986	9	184,420	28,618	15.5	$ 15.50 NNN	Negotiable	4.0	21,082
Esplanade at Locust Point 2001 Butterfield Rd.	1990	19	540,000	3,755	0.7	$ 20.50 NNN	3%	2.9	23,029
Corporetum Ofc. Campus III 750 Warrenville Rd.	1987	4	101,737	101,737	100.0	$ 16.50 NNN	3%	3.3	25,500
Two Arboretum Lakes 901 Warrenville Rd.	1986	6	145,600	1,639	1.1	Negotiable	Negotiable	7.6	25,433
Three Arboretum Lakes 801 Warrenville Rd.	1990	9	247,046	4,150	1.7	$ 21.50 Net Electric	Negotiable	3.0	27,444
Westwood of Lisle 2443 Warrenville Rd.	1991	6	148,063	9,763	6.6	$ 17.00 NNN	Negotiable	3.1	26,898
Central Park of Lisle 4225 Naperville Rd.	1990	6	292,500	11,941	4.1	$ 18.50 NNN	3%	3.8	50,000
Metrowest I 55 Shuman Bl.	1986	10	218,185	7,926	3.6	$ 17.50 NNN	3%	3.8	22,000
Park Lake Center 184 Shuman Bl.	1989	5	131,000	2,894	2.2	$ 16.00 NNN	3%	3.4	26,500
Subtotal/Average: Lombard/ Downers Grove/Lisle/Naperville		**8**	**2,198,481**	**176,183**	**8.0**			**3.9**	**26,897**
TOTAL/AVERAGE: EAST-WEST CORRIDOR			**6,174,248**	**493,248**	**8.0**				
Under Construction:									
Subject	Oct. 1997	7	259,116[1]	2,717	1.0	$ 17.00	2.5%	4.0	35,714
Subject Phase II	July 1998	8	252,499	222,499	88.1	$ 17.50 Net Electric	3%	4.0	35,714
Arboretum Lakes West 1011 Warrenville Rd.	Aug. 1998	7	190,300	142,300	74.8	$ 18.00 NNN	3%	N/A	27,200
Westwood of Lisle II 2441 Warrenville Rd.	Nov. 1997	6	148,423	148,423	100.0	$ 17.25 NNN	3%	N/A	24,777
Subtotal/Average Under Construction		**7**	**850,338**	**515,939**	**60.7**	**4.0**	**30,851**		
Other:[2]									
263 Shuman Bl.	1986	5	308,000	308,000	100.0	$ 16.00 NNN	35% CPI	3.3	61,000

N/A = Not Available
NNN = Triple Net
R = Renovation
[1]Office space only. Entire building NRA is over 333,000 sq. ft.
[2]Building off market due to bankruptcy will be coming back on the market but most likely with an anchor tenant.
Source: CB Richard Ellis Investors.

Table 4.1-3

Lease Comparables in the East-West Corridor Office Market

Building Name	Lease Date	Term in Yrs.	New/Renewal	Tenant Name	Sq. Ft.	Net Base Rent	Escalation	TI[1]
Two Arboretum Lakes	May 97	7	Renewal/Expan.	Caterpillar	10,502	$16.39	3%	$10
Westwood of Lisle	Apr. 97	3	Renewal	Richard Morton	8,150	15.50	$0.50	5
Oak Brook Regency Twr.	Apr. 97	5	New	Chase Manhattan Mort.	5,534	18.00	3%	17
One Lincoln Centre	Mar. 97	3	New	Interstate Real Estate	2,748	17.00	3%	As Is
Westbrook Corp. Center	Mar. 97	5	N/A	Nike	21,000	17.95	2%	30
Arboretum West	Feb. 97	10	New	Mercedes Benz	48,000	15.50	2.5%	25
Mid America Plaza	Jan. 97	5	N/A	Network General	16,000	18.00	3%	10
The Crossings	Jan. 97	5.4	Renewal	Allstate Insurance Co.	13,162	15.75	2%	17
Park Lake Center	Jan. 97	4.5	New	Exec. Mktg. Services	1,581	19.50	3%	12
Lincoln Centre	1st Qtr. 97	3	N/A	MONY	2,500	17.00	3%	N/A
Arboretum	1st Qtr. 97	5	N/A	Bristol Myers	6,500	17.75	3%	N/A
Central Park of Lisle	1st Qtr. 97	5	N/A	E&J Gallo Winery	7,900	17.75	3%	N/A
Mid America Plaza	1st Qtr. 97	5	N/A	CareAmerica	4,000	16.00	3%	N/A
Unisys Center	1st Qtr. 97	5	N/A	PCN Mortgage	60,000	14.50	3%	N/A
Total/Average		**5.1**			**207,577**	**$16.90**	**3%**	**$16**

[1]Tenant improvements.
N/A = Not available.
Source: CB Richard Ellis Investors.

per square foot on an annual basis. Rents have increased more than 60 percent from their low of $9.75 for Class A space in 1991 to a weighted average of $16.90. Much of the range in rents is accounted for by the size of the lease—the larger the lease, the lower the rent. Rents quoted for space in Class A buildings typically range from $17.50 to $20.00 per square foot. The majority of tenants have rent escalations of 3 percent annually in their leases. Rental rates are projected to show strong increases above inflation over the next couple of years. Future growth of rents will, however, be dependent on how much new construction actually comes on line.

Significant potential for speculative development exists in the East-West Corridor. Because of this fact, it is conservatively estimated that rents in the market area will fall below inflation in the fourth and fifth lease years because of overbuilding. It is, however, possible that lender discipline and preleasing requirements may act to keep construction under what is conservatively projected. In a market with potential new supply and rising vacancy rates, the key is to provide long-term protection of the income stream. The long-term leases of the majority of tenants in the subject building provide rent insulation, thus complying with the consultant's strategy for investing in such a market.

Potential Supply of Office Space

In addition to evaluating current competitors, it is important to compile as much data as possible concerning projects coming on line in the market area. The following four buildings are under construction in the market area:

Project	Square Feet
1. The subject building	259,113
2. Phase II in the subject building's office park	252,499
3. Arboretum Lakes West	190,300
4. Westwood of Lisle II	148,423

Compared to the other buildings under construction, the subject building and Phase II are the farthest east, are closer to more amenities, have greater access to I-88 with a four-way interchange, and are able to draw from both the east and west ends of the market. In addition, the subject building and the Phase II building are a notch above the others in quality.

The potential supply of office space in the East-West Corridor is primarily located within master-planned office parks, including the following:

- The subject office park;
- The Esplanade (Hamilton Partners);
- Lincoln Centre (Lincoln Property Co.);
- Corporate Lakes (Quadrangle);
- Arboretum (Hamilton Partners);
- Corridors (Alter Group);
- Central Park of Lisle (Duke REIT); and
- Cantera (LaSalle/Amoco).

No shortage of developable office sites exists in the market area. Demand seems to be keeping pace with the supply being brought to market. Announcements of new construction will need to be monitored on a regular basis to assess current and future supply and demand conditions.

Building Characteristics

The subject building is a seven-story office building under construction in Downers Grove. The height of the building is appropriate for the market, where most newer buildings contain from six to ten floors. The building has a floor plate of 35,714 square feet, larger than that of most of the competitive projects, which typically have floor plates ranging from 22,000 to 27,000 square feet. The larger floor plate is more attractive to larger tenants, which the subject building was able to draw. Central Park of Lisle, which has a floor plate of 50,000 square feet, has also leased well. The subject building was designed with standard bay depths on the length of the building to allow easy divisibility for smaller tenants when the building is re-leased.

The new buildings in the marketplace in the 1990s are functional and have appealing treatments, but they eschew the glitz and emphasis on high-end finish of buildings from the 1980s. In this market, amenities within the building are required. All of the better buildings have a deli or convenience store, a fitness facility, and a conference room. With these amenities, the subject building is competitive.

Because of the extreme climate of the Chicago area, covered parking is a major attraction for any building. The subject building has a parking ratio of 4.2 spaces per 1,000 square feet of leasable space, a higher ratio than much of its competition. Most of the parking is covered and located in an adjacent structure. There is covered access to the building only from the executive parking level. The parking structure is expandable; one additional deck can be added if future need arises.

Sale Transactions

Building sale prices have been increasing in the East-West Corridor market. The average sale price in 1995–1996 was $146 per square foot. The average sale price in 1997 had increased to $172 per square foot, an increase of nearly 15 percent from 1995–1996. The current average cap rate on sales is 9.6 percent. (See Table 4.1-4.)

The majority of buildings sold from 1995 to 1997 were purchased by REITs. Sale prices have reached the level of replacement cost, thus spurring new construction.

Office Market Conclusion

The subject building is a well-located, attractive, and competitive office project. The building addresses the key concerns of tenants in the market, which are amenities within the building, covered parking, and accessibility.

Table 4.1-4

Office Building Sale Comparables in the East-West Corridor

Building Name/ Location	Sale Date	Square Feet	Sale Price	Price Per Sq. Ft.	Cap Rate (Percent)	Buyer
Central Park of Lisle (ofc spc only)	May 97	292,500	$61,550,000	$210.43	10.00	Duke Realty Trust
Corporetum Office Park	May 97	323,728	50,500,000	156.00	9.00	Prentiss REIT
Regency Towers	May 97	402,318	58,250,000	144.79	8.88	Archon
Westbrook Corp. Ctr.	May 97	1,090,537	182,100,000	166.98	9.75	Beacon REIT
Oakbrook Terrace Tower	Apr. 97	633,946	127,300,000	200.81	10.60	Zell/Merrill
300 Park Place	Apr. 97	152,500	28,900,000	189.51	9.25	TMW
Crossings at Oak Brook	Feb. 97	294,593	40,000,000	135.78	9.84	CarrAmerica REIT
Subtotal 1997		**3,190,122**	**$548,600,000**	**$171.97**	**9.62%**	
Unisys Center	Dec. 96	374,350	51,000,000	136.24	9.50	CarrAmerica REIT
Lincoln Center	Nov. 96	294,972	51,000,000	172.90	9.25	Cornerstone REIT
AT&T Building	Aug. 96	225,316	35,000,000	155.34	9.67	Beacon REIT
Westwood of Lisle	Mar. 96	148,063	19,400,000	131.03	9.17	MetLife
Park Lake Center	July 95	131,000	15,250,000	116.41	12.15	LaSalle Advisors
Subtotal 1996/1995		**1,173,701**	**$171,650,000**	**$146.25**	**9.95%**	

Source: CB Richard Ellis Investors.

The East-West Corridor is the prime suburban office market in the Chicago area because of its

- Excellent transportation network through I-88, I-355, and I-294;
- Accessibility to a diverse range of housing (for executive, middle-management, and support personnel);
- Depth of hotel, retail, and restaurant amenities; and
- Many corporate headquarters, which are well-established and wedded to their location in the marketplace.

In the subject scenario, new construction has begun in the market, thus the submarket can be assumed to be well into a recovery period and entering the construction phase of the cycle. A risk to the investment is the availability of land for future office development and the potential risk of overbuilding. The client, however, is reasonably protected from this risk because the building has been preleased at market rents on a long-term basis to strong credit tenants. The client's objective of a steady cash flow is thus reasonably ensured. In addition, although supply is projected to be plentiful, demand is also projected to be strong, keeping vacancy in check.

The office market has performed well and should continue to do so in the future, but it will need to be monitored on a regular basis with respect to the rate at which new construction is added to the market.

Warehouse Property:
Valwood (1998)

Marvin F. Christensen

The subject property is a 140,000-square-foot, multi-tenant warehouse property in Dallas, Texas. Built in 1994, the property has 24-foot ceiling clear heights, an office buildout of 10 to 15 percent on average, and offers one dock door for every 10,000 square feet of space. Truck courts measure 120 feet. (A truck court is the area from the edge of a loading dock to the edge of the truck maneuvering area.) The building can be subdivided into units as small as 20,000 square feet, or it can function as a single-tenant facility. As of 1997, the facility is 100 percent occupied by three tenants, two 35,000-square-foot users and one 75,000-square-foot user. Both of the small users are in the first year of a five-year lease. The large user's lease expires at the end of 1998. Annual rents for the 35,000-square-foot spaces are $3.35 per square foot, triple net, with a 5 percent escalation at midterm. Rent for the 75,000-square-foot space is $3.25 per square foot, triple net. There is no rent escalation.

Because the proposed investment is a multitenant warehouse building, the consultant acquired industrial inventory data from a secondary source that segments the market by warehouse and flex properties as well as across 17 industrial submarkets. The subject property is located in the Valwood submarket. A tour of the submarket shows Valwood to be one of the primary locations for industrial space in the Dallas metropolitan area. The submarket's centralized location and its ready access to Dallas/Fort Worth Airport provide a competitive advantage over most other industrial areas. Early discussions with industrial brokers active in the submarket indicate that larger, single-tenant users are moving to new locations on the suburban fringe.

Analyzing Existing Market Conditions

The purpose of analyzing existing conditions is to establish a baseline for market projections. A good starting point is to review the industrial market data obtained from secondary sources. Inventory levels, absorption and construction trends, and vacancy rates are the main factors that should be reviewed at the metropolitan and submarket levels. Additional quarterly data can be obtained on gross leasing activity for recent periods. Published bro-

kerage reports and other sources of market information should be reviewed to supplement the historical review of the market.

How much inventory exists in the industrial market? How much inventory exists in the submarket? Who are the tenants? How much space has been absorbed annually over the submarket's history? How much space has been developed? Is the submarket's vacancy rate increasing or decreasing? Answers to these and other questions will allow the analyst to formulate an impression of where the submarket is in its property cycle.

Secondary Sources of Data

One secondary source of information that can be helpful is lease comparables. Lease comparables or "comps" are lists of lease transactions for a specific area or property type that are usually obtained from brokers. Comps should be used with caution. They are often outdated or weighted in favor of a set of transactions to the exclusion of others in the market. Comp data may not fully reveal the lease terms or the dates leases begin and end. Comp lists with such limitations should be avoided.

Real estate professionals are turning increasingly to the Internet to obtain secondary market data and information. Working through the growing volume of material available on the Internet takes patience, but some sites are worth the effort. See the appendix for a list of public and private data sources that are useful.

Various real estate periodicals—*Commercial Property News; Plants, Sites & Parks; Office Buildings*—are good sources for becoming familiar with national and regional market events, including market outlooks, investment trends, and property sales and major lease transactions. A worthwhile source for targeting searches to individual markets is www.amcity.com, which links users to various city business journals.

Talking with Brokers

Information on the submarket's tenant base, effective rents, and lease terms is best obtained by collecting primary data from a telephone survey of industrial brokers. Collecting primary data is often an overlooked step in market analysis. Clearly, secondary data have a distinct advantage in that they are relatively inexpensive and easy to obtain. But their weakness is that they may not be timely or accurate. This is problematic for market analysis, where an accurate read of current market conditions is critical to making plausible forecasts.

The survey of industrial brokers is intended to provide the analyst with a timely assessment of the submarket beyond that obtained through the review of secondary data. Acquiring firsthand information helps the analyst to understand more fully the current state of the industrial submarket.

Industrial brokers active in leasing space in the submarket are the main respondents for the survey. Other potential interviewees include property managers, appraisers, and developers.

When interviews are conducted with brokers, it is especially important to acquire data on effective rents as opposed to asking or contract rents. Asking rents are those rents a landlord advertises and would like to obtain; contract rents are those rents recorded on the lease; and effective rents are contract rents less any rent concession in the market. Effective and contract rents tend to be the same when market conditions are healthy, but effective rents may be considerably lower than contract rents in a weak market.

It is important to have brokers specify the type of lease on which rents are based. In a net lease, the tenant pays the rent as well as all of the expenses for the operation of the building—typically taxes, insurance, and maintenance. With a gross lease, the tenant pays the rent while the landlord pays all or part of the operating expenses. Industrial properties may be rented as "industrial gross," where the tenant pays the rent and a portion of common area maintenance expenses.

Interviewing brokers is a time-consuming and labor-intensive undertaking, but it is an excellent way to formulate an up-to-date picture of the health of an industrial submarket. Some respondents will be helpful; others will not. Sufficient time should be devoted to this valuable process.

Analysts should keep in mind that brokers may be prone to overstating the positives and understating the negatives. Brokers are in the business of leasing and selling real estate. Putting a positive spin on market and submarket conditions aids them in reaching those ends. Analysts must remember that interviewing industrial brokers will be of value only if the interviewer gains a complete picture of submarket conditions.

In the subject case study, the analyst was able to form an impression of how the Valwood submarket has evolved in recent years from the market history obtained from a secondary data source (see Table 4.2-1). The historical sketch indicates that Dallas and the Valwood submarket recovered from a period of high vacancies in the early 1990s. Vacancy rates remained comparatively low—in the 6 to 7 percent range, although some upward movement in vacancy is obvious in Valwood.

A characterization of submarket rents and lease terms was obtained through a survey of brokers and a review of leasing comparables (see Table 4.2-2). Because the subject property can accommodate various tenant sizes, warehouse rents in three size categories were surveyed. Discussions with brokers also permitted a breakdown of industrial tenants in Valwood by industry group to be made (see Figure 4.2-1).

A review of existing market conditions indicates that Dallas and the Valwood submarket are in a growth phase of their market cycle. Market conditions are typified by low vacancy rates and increasing warehouse space inventory through new development. Leasing trends, however, show that warehouse spaces in excess of 75,000 square feet are leasing more slowly than smaller spaces. Larger distribution firms are moving to submarkets outside of Valwood, leaving its larger spaces vacant. Meanwhile, users of less than 50,000 square feet continue to locate to Valwood because of its functional space and centralized location.

Rents are at attractive levels and unencumbered by concessions or high tenant improvement allowances. Annual rents for spaces of 100,000 square feet or more range from $3.00 to $3.25 per square foot, net. Annual rents for spaces of 40,000 square feet or less range as high as $4.25 per square foot, net (see Table 4.2-2). Rent escalations for longer-term lease transactions (five years or more) offer further evidence of a healthy market environment. The analyst concludes that the subject property

Table 4.2-1
Space Inventory for Dallas and Valwood

Type	Valwood		Dallas	
	Sq. Ft.[1]	% Vacant	Sq. Ft.[1]	% Vacant
Flex	9.1	5.6	37,464	9.0
Warehouse	42.6	7.6	202,185	7.2
All	51.7	7.1	239,650	7.5

Year	Sq. Ft.[1]	% Vacant	Sq. Ft.[1]	% Vacant
1989	39.6	12.1	NA	NA
1990	39.3	10.0	192,391	13.0
1991	39.5	11.0	192,952	12.0
1992	39.3	9.4	192,648	11.0
1993	39.5	6.0	192,949	10.0
1994	39.8	4.5	192,180	8.0
1995	41.1	5.0	192,548	7.0
1996	41.6	7.6	202,186	7.2
1997	44.3	6.8	213,248	6.4

NA = Not available.
[1]Square feet in millions.
Sources: M/PF Research and RREEF Research.

Table 4.2-2
Warehouse Rents and Lease Terms for Valwood[1]

	Multitenant	Multitenant	Single Tenant
	Less than 20,000 Sq. Ft.	20,000–40,000 Sq. Ft.	100,000 Sq. Ft. or More
Annual Rents	$3.50–$4.25/Sq. Ft. (NNN)	$3.25–$3.50/Sq. Ft. (NNN)	$3.00–$3.25/Sq. Ft. (NNN)
Term	3–5 Years	3–5 Years	5–10 Years
Escalations		Flat for 3–5 Years; Midterm Increase for Longer Terms	
Free Rent		1–2 Months/Lease Term	
Tenant Improvements		$0.50–$1.00/Sq. Ft. Overall $2.00–$3.00/Sq. Ft. Office	
Expenses		$0.85–$1.05/Sq. Ft.	

[1]Rents and terms for new warehouse properties with minimum 24-foot clear heights and office buildout of 10% to 15%; under 10% for single tenant.
NNN = Net of taxes, insurance, and utilities.
Source: RREEF Research.

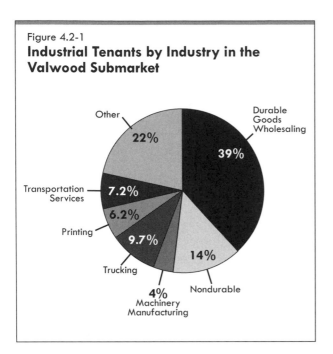

Figure 4.2-1
Industrial Tenants by Industry in the Valwood Submarket

- Durable Goods Wholesaling 39%
- Nondurable 14%
- Machinery Manufacturing 4%
- Trucking 9.7%
- Printing 6.2%
- Transportation Services 7.2%
- Other 22%

is typical of the submarket, both in terms of its spatial/functional characteristics and its lease terms.

Analyzing Industrial Space Demand

Changing patterns in an area's economic and demographic makeup generate corresponding shifts in the need for industrial space. The objective of the demand side analysis is to translate projected economic and demographic trends into projected levels of annual net absorption in the metropolitan market and in the submarket.

Analysts often employ some form of econometric model to project absorption. Econometric models can be powerful analytical tools, but they do have limitations. To develop a properly specified econometric model, sufficient time-series data must exist. Without adequate data, the problems of misspecification and omitted variables can reduce the value of econometric forecasting. Also, it is difficult to forecast with econometric models because the relationship between variables can change because of factors not fully captured by the model.

In practice, demand models for industrial space often emulate office demand models, where a change in metropolitan office employment is the prime determinant of office net absorption. Unfortunately, the connection between industrial employment and industrial space demand is not as clear cut. Employee and space-use relationships among the different industrial subtypes vary greatly, making space-per-worker applications problematic. Even within individual industrial subtypes, the relationship between the number of employees and space use can be decidedly different. Equally important, the prime determinant of space demand in industrial analysis, especially for a warehouse property, is inventory flow, not jobs.[1] Unfortunately for the industrial market analyst, no data sources provide inventory data at the metropolitan or local levels.

As a result, analysts conducting industrial warehouse analyses should review other measures of metropolitan growth, such as Gross Metropolitan Product (GMP) or changes in total population or households. GMP, because it measures the output of a local economy, is arguably the best proxy for warehouse space absorption. Warehouse/distribution properties store much of this output either during product manufacturing or during shipment to consumers.

The Metropolitan Absorption Calculation

Calculating net absorption at the metropolitan level consists of multiplying the annual percent change in GMP and the annual percent change in metropolitan area population (or households) by the appropriate space demand parameter. In its simplest form, a proportionality relationship is derived between the change in occupied stock (net absorption) and percent changes in GMP and in population. The resulting demand parameters indicate that for every 1 percent increase in GMP, a corresponding percentage increase will occur in occupied industrial space. The same holds true for the population measure.

Submarket Capture Rate

After space demand is calculated for a metropolitan area, a final step is to estimate what share of metropolitan absorption will be captured by the submarket. Often, analysts simply calculate a submarket capture rate by using a fair-share approach. A fair-share capture rate is simply the proportion of metropolitan space inventory located in a submarket. For example, if a submarket holds 9 percent of a metropolitan area's industrial space inventory, then its capture rate is 9 percent.

Other methods of determining submarket absorption are largely subjective and are accomplished by examining the historical share of submarket net absorption in relation to metropolitan area net absorption over time. Observing the submarket's share of annual absorption should provide the analyst with an idea of how well the area stacks up against other submarkets. It is likely that the amount of industrial space absorption captured by a single submarket will vary from year to year. The analyst must be careful not to exaggerate absorption levels during strong markets or to underestimate absorption during market slowdowns. Understanding where the broad metropolitan market and the submarket are in their respective property cycles can help the analyst determine the best capture rate for each year of the forecast period.

Sources of Data

Economic and demographic data at the metropolitan-area level are readily obtainable from several national data sources, including Regional Financial Associates; DRI-McGraw Hill; Woods and Poole, Inc.; and other private forecasting firms. Each of these firms offers a broad range of data depicting historical and future growth trends on a year-by-year basis.

Regional and local public planning or economic development departments may also be good sources for economic and demographic data. Most often, public sources formulate projections for jobs, population, households, and other variables at five-year intervals, but some of the larger jurisdictions produce annual forecasts. One advantage of these sources over private data providers is that the data are usually free.

Absorption in Valwood

In studying the Valwood property, the analyst based projections for warehouse space absorption in the Dallas metropolitan area on changes in GMP and population. He also looked at total employment growth as an indicator of demand-side activity in the market. The data, obtained from a national forecasting and economic consulting firm, indicate that growth in Dallas will slow in 1998 and 1999 before expanding more rapidly over the longer term.

The projections for GMP and population were then used in modeling metropolitan-area warehouse space absorption in Dallas. The model indicates that for every 1 percent increase in GMP, occupied space will increase by 0.26 percent. A 1 percent increase in population results in a 0.24 percent increase in occupied space. Metropolitan net absorption should average approximately 6.1 million square feet annually through 2007.

Submarket absorption was calculated for each year of the forecast period by applying a capture rate to metropolitan-area absorption. Valwood captured from 15 to 20 percent of metropolitan absorption between 1989 and 1997. Submarket absorption during this period was buoyed by Valwood's strategic location adjacent to the Dallas/Fort Worth Airport, its central location in the metropolitan area, and a substantial increase in warehouse construction since 1993.

Valwood's locational advantages are expected to remain in place over the long term. The submarket will continue to witness further warehouse construction, although building volumes are expected to be more modest in the near term because of increasing vacancy rates. These factors, along with the general desirability of Valwood as a distribution location for small tenants, suggest a capture rate of between 10 and 15 percent in the near term, and between 15 and 20 percent long term. Net absorption in Valwood should equal between 9 million and 10 million square feet over the next ten years.

Analyzing Supply

Analyzing the future supply of industrial space in a submarket centers on three tasks. The first is to identify properties that are currently being built. The easiest way to accomplish this is to drive around the competing submarket and record the number of projects under construction and their site locations. Follow-up calls to sponsoring developers should then be made to obtain information on project sizes, expected completion dates, costs, and rents. The broker and developer surveys discussed earlier are another way to obtain this information. If time allows, industrial building permit data should be studied at the local planning or building departments.

Next, proposed industrial development projects must be researched. Many proposed projects that have not broken ground have received development approvals from the local municipality. These "entitled projects" can be identified through a review of local planning and building department records. Other proposed or announced projects that have not yet received development approval can be identified through discussions with local brokers or developers. Local business newspapers can be a good source for identifying industrial development project announcements. Clearly, an analyst who is thoroughly familiar with a market area is at an advantage in the data collection process because he or she can compile a database of both existing and pipeline projects, then update it for new market studies, rather than having to begin anew.

Projecting changes in industrial space supply in a submarket through the first two to three years of the forecast period is a time-consuming but straightforward exercise. The need for entitlements offers some advance notice of projects and suggests future levels of building. Analysts who follow through on the various leads the entitlement process provides should be confident in the reasonableness of their shorter-term supply-side projections.

Projecting changes in the supply of industrial space beyond two or three years becomes more uncertain. Aside from using an econometric model to project submarket construction, the analyst can take a more practical approach involving an assessment of factors that influence development. These factors include land availability, cost of building, and public policy considerations.

The analyst must answer the following questions: How much land is available for industrial space development? How many years before the available land supply is exhausted? How much rent is required to support the development of an industrial building? Are current market rents supportive of new construction? Does existing public policy—development plans, zoning—preclude or limit industrial development in the submarket? How much time does it take to gain the necessary entitlements for an industrial project?

Answers to these questions will not reveal how much space will be built in the latter years of a forecast period. They will, however, provide the analyst with a framework for making a long-term projection of industrial space supply.

Warehouse space construction in Dallas is occurring in a number of submarkets, including Valwood. Six projects totaling approximately 1.5 million square feet are anticipated to be completed in 1998, three of them early in the year (see Table 4.2-3). Another 2 million to 3 million square feet is expected to enter the market during the 1999–2001 period.

Market conditions, including land availability, development costs, and public policy, are highly supportive of warehouse construction. In particular, market rents of $3.50 net per year are high enough to support the development of larger and, to a lesser extent, medium-sized warehouse properties. As a result, the analyst projects warehouse construction levels to remain high through the forecast period.

The Outlook

A final step in the analysis is to present an outlook for the submarket along with a projection for rents. In deriving a submarket rent projection, the analyst must identify both the direction and magnitude of rent change during each year of the forecast period.

To accomplish this rent projection, annual volumes of industrial space absorption and annual volumes of space construction are compared and measured by projected vacancy rates. Vacancy rates provide a general assessment of the future health of the submarket and an indication of whether or not rents will change. A useful convention for industrial analyses is to assume that a submarket with a vacancy rate of between 6 and 8 percent is a submarket in equilibrium. A market in equilibrium is often a market that will witness upward movement in rents.

Table 4.2-3
Warehouse Construction Pipeline in the Valwood Submarket

Building Name	Size (Sq. Ft.)	Developer	Completion
Completed Early 1998			
2515 Tarpley Road	36,000	Group R.E.	Mar. 1998
1808 Monetary Lane	67,200	Industrial Prop.	Mar. 1998
Valwest Parkway	75,000	Valwest	Mar. 1998
	178,200		
Under Construction			
Frankford Trade Center #6	709,920	Argent/Meridian	Jul. 1998
Luna Distribution Center III	260,000	Lucy Billingsley	Aug. 1998
Luna Distribution Center IV	260,000	Lucy Billingsley	Aug. 1998
	1,229,920		
Planned			
Frankford Trade Center 1–14	2,433,774	Argent/Meridian	
Luna Distribution Center II	250,000	Lucy Billingsley	
	2,683,774		

Source: RREEF Research.

A review of historical rent changes can be helpful in trying to sort out a credible rent projection. Looking at past increases or decreases in submarket rents relative to demand and supply may give some impression of how rents move in a particular submarket.

The extent to which rates can increase is also tied to the difference between market rents and "economic" rents. Economic rents are the rent levels needed to support new construction for competitive space. A submarket is more apt to see stronger rent increases when market rents are well below economic rents. Typically this situation exists in the recovery stage of the market cycle, when vacancy rates are falling and the gap between market and economic rents is wide, which allows for significant rent spikes.

Projecting rents is a complicated task. Rent changes are influenced not only by market fundamentals related to demand and supply,[2] but also by market perceptions. A well-formulated market analysis will have assessed and measured the market fundamentals that influence rent. Conversely, market perceptions are not readily measured and, therefore, less easily addressed by market analysis, even though they may influence changes in rent as much as a change in market vacancy.

Given the complexities associated with projecting rents, care must be taken not simply to crank through a model and derive a point forecast of future rents. Point forecasts convey the impression of a high degree of accuracy that is not attainable in market analysis. More credible forecasts are those structured as a range, offering a best and worst projection for any one year.

Projections for warehouse space net absorption and supply in Valwood (noted as completions in Figure 4.2-2) show an upward trend in submarket vacancy through 2001. The supply-side analysis shows that warehouse construction in Valwood will outpace absorption, even though the Dallas economy continues to expand at a healthy rate. The imbalance in supply should correct itself by 2002 as development activity eases and absorption remains positive. Nonetheless, the threat of continued additions to supply in Dallas and Valwood is a long-term concern.

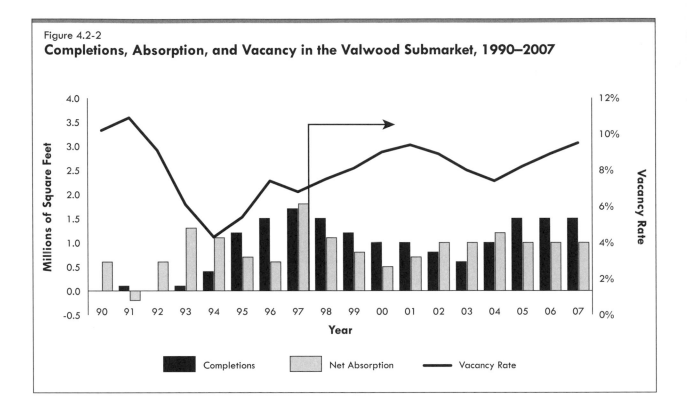

Figure 4.2-2
Completions, Absorption, and Vacancy in the Valwood Submarket, 1990–2007

In light of these trends, submarket rents in Valwood will experience only modest growth (see Table 4.2-4). In fact, larger properties of 100,000 square feet or more are not anticipated to realize any increase in rents because much of the submarket's increase in supply is occurring in this property segment. Anecdotal evidence from discussions with local brokers suggests that as much as 80 to 90 percent of Valwood's warehouse vacancy is in larger buildings.

The near-term prognosis for warehouse space in the 25,000- to 40,000-square-foot category is more positive. A lack of supply in this property segment should allow modest rent increases of up to 4 percent. Space of this size is well suited to Valwood's expanding tenant base of small and medium-sized users.

Spaces of 25,000 square feet and less should enjoy the strongest rent gains. A minimal amount of inventory in Valwood caters to users in this segment of the market. Cost constraints on building, along with steady demand, should allow rents to move up in each year through 2003.

The rent projections for Valwood can reasonably be applied to the subject property, given its similarity to other competitive warehouse facilities in the submarket. The subject property's smaller 35,000-square-foot spaces appear to have good prospects for garnering future rent increases, while the 75,000-square-foot space has less upside. As indicated in the market analysis, large users are leaving Valwood, pushing up the vacancy rates among large spaces. It will be difficult to re-lease the entire space if the existing user leaves, or to raise rents if the existing lease is renewed. Reconfiguring the 75,000-square-foot space to accommodate smaller tenants may make the most sense long term, especially if the large user leaves.

Table 4.2-4
Projected Change in Warehouse Rents[1] in the Valwood Submarket

	100,000 Sq. Ft. and More		Multitenant 25,000–40,000 Sq. Ft.		Multitenant 25,000 Sq. Ft. and Less	
	Rent Range	% Change	Rent Range	% Change	Rent Range	% Change
Current	$3.00–$3.25		$3.25–$3.50		$3.50–$4.25	
2Q 1999	3.00–3.25	0–0	3.25–3.50	0–0	3.65–4.40	3–5
2Q 2000	3.05–3.30	0–2	3.30–3.55	0–2	3.80–4.60	3–5
2Q 2001	3.15–3.40	2–4	3.45–3.70	3–5	3.90–4.75	2–4
2Q 2002	3.30–3.55	3–5	3.60–3.85	3–5	4.00–4.90	2–4
2Q 2003	3.45–3.70	3–5	3.75–4.00	3–5	4.10–5.05	2–4
2003–2007:	Changes in rent will depend on future levels of construction and absorption.					

[1]Rents are calculated using the midpoint of the forecast range.
Source: RREEF Research.

Concluding Note

Industrial market analysis offers a framework for projecting the health of industrial markets over time as measured by conditions of demand, supply, and rents. The analytical process balances quantitative techniques and qualitative approaches, market knowledge and experience with judgment and intuition. No one can analyze an industrial market or submarket and expect to foretell its conditions with complete certainty. Future conditions are always a step ahead of current facts. Nonetheless, the combined approach of market analysis—the blending of art and science—can offer meaningful insights about future submarket conditions and the prospects for investing successfully in industrial real estate.

Notes

[1]Glenn R. Mueller and Steven Laposa, "The Path of Goods Movement," *Real Estate Finance,* vol. 11 (Nov. 2, 1994): pp. 42–50.

[2]Richard J. Buttimer, Jr., et al., "Industrial Warehouse Rent Determinants in the Dallas/Fort Worth Area," *Journal of Real Estate Research,* vol. 13 (Nov. 1, 1977): pp. 47–55.

Flex/R&D Property:
Peachtree Industrial Park (1998)

Steve Laposa

Flex/R&D refers to the group of commercial property types that include showrooms, business service buildings, research and development buildings, or flexible space that can be used for a range of industrial to office activities. Generally flex/R&D properties are less than three stories with a minimum of 25 percent, but less than 75 percent, office space.

Several market research issues are particularly relevant for flex/R&D investments. Successful research, or attention to these issues, can help identify market risks and opportunities, and thus the pricing and valuation of a flex/R&D property. These issues are

- Location risk. What demographic and spatial linkages exist in a submarket area for flex/R&D properties? For example, white-collar and high-tech employment, universities, concentration of small firms, or enterprise zones can be important generators for flex/R&D development.

- Real estate risk. How does the composition of flex/R&D properties for a submarket, as a percentage of total industrial space, compare to the market? For example, if in a given market flex/R&D properties are 5 percent of the total industrial stock, and 10 percent of the total industrial stock for a submarket, what does that imply? For some flex/R&D tenants, substitution of one- or two-story Class B and C office space may also meet their needs. Therefore, a researcher may need to analyze more than just competitive flex/R&D properties.

Property Description

The owner of Peachtree Industrial Park is selling the property. The following market analysis is being prepared to help the owner develop appropriate pricing assumptions.

The subject property consists of four flex/R&D buildings located in Peachtree Industrial Park, about five miles east of I-285 and one mile north of I-85 in a northern suburb of Atlanta. The industrial park contains a total of 16 industrial and flex/R&D properties. The park is nicely landscaped and provides good road access and parking. Each building has two dock-high doors and two drive-in doors

for trucks at the back of the building. The average parking ratio is 2.9 spaces per 1,000 square feet of building area. This ratio has worked out well except for Group 10 Communications, a tenant in Building 104, which is a phone center that requires a parking ratio of at least 4.5 spaces per 1,000 square feet of building. The subject buildings are well maintained, with 70 percent of the roof square footage less than four years old. The buildings are 88 percent leased; one 45,000-square-foot space is available in Building 103. Table 4.3-1 summarizes the major characteristics and tenants of the subject properties.

Demand Analysis
Atlanta Metropolitan Area Economy

The Atlanta metropolitan area enjoys one of the top-performing economies in the United States. (See Table 4.3-2.) Well-developed distribution networks, a large concentration of headquarters operations, and inexpensive housing compared to other major metro areas place it at an advantage. However, Atlanta is beginning to face stiff competition from other lower-cost southern metro areas.

In 1998, Atlanta's job growth is up from a year ago in every industry. With the exception of manufacturing jobs, which increased by 0.9 percent in the past year, job growth in all sectors has increased by at least 2 percent. Services showed the greatest growth with an impressive 5.5 percent increase. According to a recent survey, companies are more likely to expand or relocate to Atlanta than they were four years ago. The share of surveyed executives who preferred Atlanta to ten other major metro areas nearly doubled, from 16 percent to 31 percent. Atlanta's top competitors are Chicago and Dallas.

Transportation employment has increased by more than 40 percent during the current economic expansion (1991 to 1998), a pace that is nearly twice the national average. Ongoing expansions of cargo facilities at Atlanta's Hartsfield International Airport will enable further growth, especially because more international carriers are starting cargo service through Hartsfield. According to airport estimates, cargo volume is projected to triple by 2015. By 1999, Norfolk Southern Railroad is expected to relocate

Table 4.3-1
Subject Buildings in Peachtree Industrial Park

Property	Year Built	Clear Height	Building Size (Sq. Ft.)	Tenant	Tenant Sq. Ft.	% Office Buildout	Lease Expiration	Effective Gross Rent
Building 101	1980	16 ft.	100,000	Apex Healthcare	12,000	90	9/00	$ 9.75
				Quick Delivery Co.	30,000	12	8/02	6.25
				Wake Up Bakery	18,000	10	6/99	6.50
				Uniform Supply	12,000	30	2/07	8.00
				Atlanta Printing Co.	28,000	20	10/02	6.50
Building 102	1986	15 ft.	90,000	A1 Pool Supply	30,000	20	6/00	7.00
				Fancy Business Interiors	60,000	30	5/04	8.00
Building 103	1985	15 ft.	120,000	Computer Repair, Inc.	35,000	45	3/99	8.00
				Sonoma Credit Services	40,000	80	7/08	10.50
				Vacant	45,000	0		
Building 104	1986	16 ft.	80,000	Group 10 Communications	40,000	85	6/02	8.50
				Energy Electrical	20,000	50	5/03	7.25
				American Office Supply	20,000	35	4/01	7.50
Portfolio Total/Average[1]			**390,000**			**88%**		**$ 7.90**

[1]Weighted average.
Source: PricewaterhouseCoopers.

Table 4.3-2
Economic and Demographic Trends

	Atlanta	U.S. Average	Rank among Largest 100 Cities in U.S.
Forecast Absolute Employment Growth (1998–2003)	182,500	—	4
Forecast Annual Employment Growth (1998–2003)	2.3%	1.3%	11
Forecast Annual Population Growth (1998–2003)	2.2%	0.9%	4
Percentage Change in GMP or GDP (1998–2003)	3.4%	2.4%	10
Unemployment (12/98)	3.2%	4.5%	20
Economic Diversity	High	1.0	2
Cost of Doing Business	0.96	1.0	48
1998 Total Employment	1,955,200		
1998 Population	3,639,700		
GMP = Atlanta's Gross Metro Product; GDP = U.S. Gross Domestic Product			

Source: PricewaterhouseCoopers.

650 office jobs from Philadelphia to Atlanta following its purchase of Conrail. The company also plans to build a $97 million intermodal facility in Atlanta by 2000.

Population growth has been greatest in the suburban fringes of the metro area, with negative growth occurring in most of the inner areas surrounded by I-285. Exceptions are Buckhead and the northern quadrant of the city, and a small, slow-growing area to the east of the downtown.

Office employment growth is strongest in the northern submarkets, where growth from 1993 to 1998 has averaged 5.9 percent annually, compared to 3.2 percent for the metro area. Flex/R&D employment growth has been more concentrated in the Northcentral and Northeast submarkets, which each gained at least 2,200 new flex employees. This increase equates to 4.5 percent annual growth and compares to 2.2 percent for the metro area.

Overall, Atlanta's economic strengths include a diverse economy, above-average per capita income, strong in-migration and population growth trends, and affordable housing. On the downside, the metropolitan area is facing increasing competition and is outgrowing its infrastructure.

Northeast Submarket Economic Drivers
The Northeast submarket provides easy access to I-85, which is a major distribution route, and to a fast-grow-ing and affluent population base located on the north side of Atlanta. Retail and distribution companies are prominent in the submarket (see Figure 4.3-1). Although some of these companies occupy office space for their headquarters and operations services, many use flex/R&D space. More than 54 percent of the sub-market's employees work in office properties—a typical ratio for Atlanta. Back-office jobs that typically require low-cost office space account for more than half of the office market. The submarket also has an above-average concentration of flex/R&D jobs; about 9 percent of the employment base is in this sector. (See Figure 4.3-2.)

The Northeast submarket is home to a variety of companies, most of which employ fewer than a thousand people. The largest employers in the submarket are the Gwinnett Hospital (1,300 employees) and Boeing (1,200 employees). Neither employer holds a dominant position in the submarket.

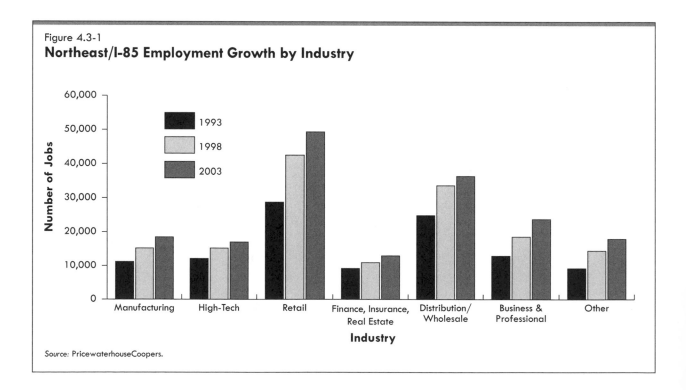

Figure 4.3-1
Northeast/I-85 Employment Growth by Industry

Source: PricewaterhouseCoopers.

Flex/R&D Property: Peachtree Industrial Park *(continued)*

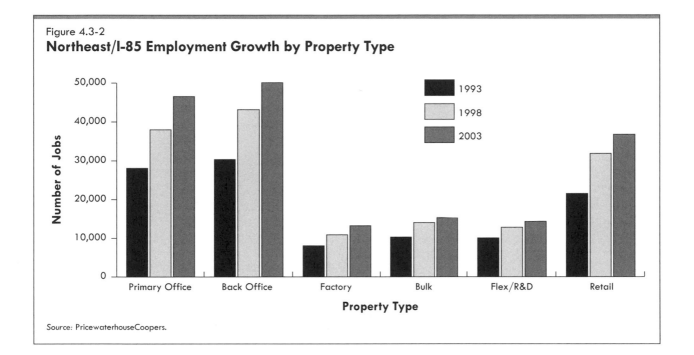

Figure 4.3-2

Northeast/I-85 Employment Growth by Property Type

Source: PricewaterhouseCoopers.

Economic Forecast

The consensus of both local and national economists is that the Atlanta economy will continue to be a top performer in the United States for several years. However, a number of factors are expected to cause the economy to slow from an average annual growth rate of 5.9 percent during the late 1990s to 3.4 percent during the next five years. (U.S. economic growth is expected to slow to 2.4 percent annually from 2.9 percent annually during the same time period.) During the 1990s, the Atlanta economy has generally outpaced the U.S. economy, but it followed the same patterns of acceleration and deceleration in growth over time.

U.S. economic growth has already begun to slow and is expected to continue slowing for a number of reasons. First, corporations have already used profit-boosting resources such as lower interest rates, outsourcing, revising benefit plans, and merging with other companies. Second, with unemployment rates at historically low levels, wages have begun to rise, contributing to lower growth in

corporate profits. Furthermore, the world economy is experiencing a significant slowdown and uncertainty in the capital markets. Manufacturers are already showing signs of weakness as the number of new and unfilled orders is not increasing and payrolls are declining. Export growth has nearly stopped because of the collapsing Asian economy and soaring U.S. dollar. High-tech producers have been especially hard hit.

The diversity of Atlanta's economy will help it weather some of the expected U.S. economic slowing. Less than 5 percent of the local economy is dependent on exports, compared to 8.5 percent for the United States. Additionally, only 1 percent of the Atlanta economy is linked to Asian exports, compared to a U.S. average of 2.3 percent. With unemployment at only 3.2 percent, the market is dependent on in-migration from other areas to sustain growth. Although net migration has slowed slightly since the early 1990s, the metropolitan area has generally been able to attract at least 60,000 residents each year, for an annual total population growth rate of about 2.7

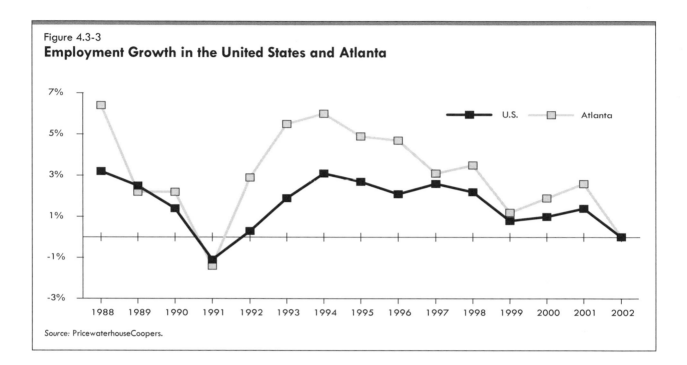

Figure 4.3-3
Employment Growth in the United States and Atlanta

Source: PricewaterhouseCoopers.

percent. Total employment growth is expected to slow from 4.8 percent during the past five years to 2.3 percent during the next five years compared to a U.S. average slowing from 2.5 percent to 1.3 percent during the same time period. (See Figure 4.3-3.)

In the Northeast submarket, retail jobs will continue to grow with the proposed addition of a new 1.1 million-square-foot shopping mall. The market's access to I-85, which is a primary national distribution route for cargo, will also continue to attract distributors and wholesalers. Additionally, the area's access to high-income households, a growing population base, retail amenities, and a concentration of technology companies will contribute to demand for office and flex/R&D space.

Market Area Analysis
The Atlanta Industrial and Flex/R&D Markets

Atlanta contains more than 325 million square feet of industrial space, making it the eighth-largest industrial market in the United States. Warehouse properties, which total more than 270 million square feet in Atlanta, are the largest component of the industrial market. Flex/R&D properties equal 32 million square feet, or 10 percent of total stock. National and regional distributors are attracted to the metropolitan area's central location in the southeastern United States, its prime access to rail, a major international airport, and I-85 and I-75, which are major distribution routes for cargo. In addition, the large and fast-growing population base and a highly educated workforce attract local service companies and high-tech operators, many of whom need flex space.

Atlanta's Northeast submarket, which includes 92.3 million square feet of industrial space, or 28 percent of the market inventory, is by far the largest and most active in the region. The submarket is followed in size by the Fulton industrial submarket, which is located west of the city and is the older industrial area. That submarket contains 61 million square feet of industrial space. The third major submarket is the Airport or South submarket, which contains 53 million square feet of industrial product.

Flex/R&D properties are highly concentrated in the Northeast and Northwest submarkets, which account for 61 percent of the metropolitan area's 32 million-square-foot flex market. Flex/R&D properties account for 12 percent of total industrial stock in the Northeast submarket. Gross asking rents in the Northeast market average $8.25 per square foot, followed by the Northwest at $7.94 per square foot. For the metropolitan area, gross asking rents average $7.45 per square foot.

In contrast to markets such as San Jose, California, which are highly dependent on high-tech users, the Atlanta flex/R&D market is more oriented to small service companies, telecommunication companies, and local distributors. The average size of flex/R&D tenants in the market and submarket is 15,000 square feet.

Flex/R&D Market Trends in the Atlanta Metropolitan Area

Since 1980, net absorption of flex/R&D space has been greater than 400,000 square feet annually. Vacancy rates peaked at 13.6 percent in 1991 after construction exceeded demand for seven years. Since 1991, absorption has averaged more than 750,000 square feet per year. Although the Olympics generated some demand in 1995–1996, absorption trends remained strong in 1997, with 952,000 square feet of flex/R&D space absorbed (see Table 4.3-3).

During 1998, 925,000 square feet of new product was delivered, including nearly 580,000 square feet of speculative space. As of year-end 1998, approximately 55 percent of the new space was leased, and an additional 650,000 square feet had broken ground. Net absorption slowed slightly as the national and local economies began to slow. Absorption activity this year has been concentrated in Atlanta's Northeast and Northwest submarkets, which accounted for more than 68 percent of total flex/R&D absorption. The Northeast alone accounted for 48 percent of market absorption.

Flex/R&D Trends in the Northeast Submarket

The Northeast submarket includes 92 million square feet of industrial space, made up of 80 million square feet of warehouse space and 11 million square feet of flex/R&D. Approximately 59 percent of the space is leased, and the

---

Table 4.3-3
Atlanta Flex/R&D Market

	Inventory (1,000 Sq. Ft.)	Construction (1,000 Sq. Ft.)	Net Absorption (1,000 Sq. Ft.)	Vacancy (%)	Gross Rents (per Sq. Ft.)
1993	28,739	54	704	13.1	$6.10
1994	28,871	132	719	11.0	6.40
1995	29,376	505	878	9.5	6.90
1996	30,404	1,028	858	9.8	7.00
1997	31,418	1,014	952	9.7	7.30
1998	32,343	925	816	9.7	7.45
1999	33,083	740	330	10.7	7.52
2000	33,503	420	565	10.2	7.64
2001	34,183	680	596	10.2	7.68
2002	34,703	520	565	9.9	7.80
2003	35,123	420	678	9.1	8.20

Source: PricewaterhouseCoopers.

remainder is owner occupied. Attesting to the national distribution routes of many of the tenants in this market, nearly 57 percent of the warehouse space is large bulk distribution with minimum clear ceiling heights of 24 feet and sizes in excess of 250,000 square feet. (See Table 4.3-4.)

The Northeast submarket has accounted for 44 percent of the metropolitan area's flex/R&D absorption and has been the site of 47 percent of new construction from 1993 to 1998. Of the new leases signed in the past year, 60 percent of the tenants came from within the Northeast submarket, 10 percent came from office buildings, 15 percent came from the Northwest submarket, and the remaining 15 percent were from other submarkets or locations outside of Atlanta.

The Northeast submarket is showing some signs of oversupply, but construction is slowing. As of year-end 1998, 470,000 square feet of space was delivered in the Northeast submarket. The average size of the buildings being delivered is 93,275 square feet. Of this new space, 38.5 percent is vacant. Nearly 50 percent of the first-generation space (space that has not been leased before) took more than nine months to lease. However, very few

projects are in the pipeline. Proposed projects include the recently announced 60,000-square-foot project to be built by Industrial Development Trust in their Peach Road office park, about five miles from the subject property. The Smith Company has announced two 100,000-square-foot projects in the Tech Industrial Park, which is located ten miles farther east on I-85. None of the above projects has broken ground, although one of the Smith Company projects has gone out to bid.

Vacancy rates in 1998 are 11.8 percent, up from 11.6 percent a year earlier. Current gross asking rates for flex/R&D properties in the submarket average $6.50 per square foot for warehouse space, and $11.50 for office space, for an average blended rate of $8.25. Operating expenses in both the market and submarket average $3.15 per square foot. No unusual concessions such as free rent are being offered.

The Atlanta Class B/C Office Market

Because several of the tenants in the subject property use a high percentage of office space, some Class B/C office properties, particularly single-story office

---

Table 4.3-4
Northeast Flex/R&D Submarket

	Inventory (1,000 Sq. Ft.)	Construction (1,000 Sq. Ft.)	Net Absorption (1,000 Sq. Ft.)	Vacancy (%)	Gross Rents (per Sq. Ft.)
1993	9,383	0	262	15.8	$6.90
1994	9,411	28	401	11.8	7.00
1995	9,667	256	593	8.0	7.70
1996	10,171	504	36	12.2	7.80
1997	10,614	443	453	11.6	8.10
1998	11,084	470	393	11.8	8.25
1999	11,437	353	159	13.1	8.25
2000	11,636	199	272	12.3	8.37
2001	11,969	333	287	12.3	8.42
2002	12,219	250	272	11.9	8.50
2003	12,422	203	326	10.7	8.71

Source: PricewaterhouseCoopers.

buildings, could compete with the subject property. Atlanta contains more than 97 million square feet of office space, making it the ninth-largest office market in the United States. More than 12 million square feet of new completions has been added to the market since 1996, causing vacancy rates to increase from a low of 5.4 percent in 1997 to 7.1 percent by year-end 1998. The majority of the new construction has occurred in the northern submarkets, particularly North Fulton, where vacancy rates jumped to more than 21 percent in 1997.

Class B/C office properties comprise 46 percent of the office market. The Northlake (just south of the Northeast submarket) and Northwest submarkets are the largest, comprising 41 percent of the Class B/C market. The Northeast submarket, which includes 4.5 million square feet of Class B/C office space, or 10 percent of the market, is the fourth largest of the nine office submarkets in the metropolitan area. Class B/C office vacancy rates range from 5.4 percent in Northlake to 34 percent downtown.

With the exception of North Fulton, where vacancy rates exceed 17 percent, the vacancy rate for Class B/C office space in all of the northern submarkets is less than 12 percent. Gross asking rents for Class B/C office space are by far the highest in the small Buckhead submarket, with 1.8 million square feet of Class B/C office space averaging $18.79 per square foot. This submarket is followed by North Fulton at $16.38 per square foot and Northwest at $15.45 per square foot. The Northeast submarket generates Class B/C office space gross asking rents of $15.15 per square foot, which are below the metro area average of $16.07. It is likely that the tenants in the Northeast submarket are more cost-conscious than those in the Buckhead submarket, where tenants tend to be financial companies and other image-conscious firms. Operating expenses for Class B/C office properties average $6.25 per square foot.

Class B/C Office Space Trends in the Metropolitan Area

In the metro area, Class B/C office space net absorption has been positive, and generally close to or greater than one million square feet annually since 1980. One exception was 1996, at which time several Olympics-related tenants vacated space after the Olympics. Although absorption has been positive, vacancy rates reached a peak of 17.4 percent in 1993 because of excess construction. (See Table 4.3-5.)

During 1998, 1.7 million square feet of new speculative product was delivered, half of which was located in the North Fulton submarket. This submarket also accounted for half of the metro area's Class B/C office space absorption. The construction pipeline is slowing in response to significantly higher vacancy rates in some areas. As of year-end 1998, only 540,000 square feet of new Class B/C office space has broken ground in metro Atlanta.

Class B/C Office Space Trends in the Northeast Submarket

The Northeast submarket includes 7.0 million square feet of office space, 4.5 million square feet of which is Class B/C. The submarket has accounted for 18 percent of the metro area's Class B/C office space absorption and has been the site of 28 percent of new construction from 1993 to 1998. (See Table 4.3-6.)

The Northeast submarket is showing some signs of oversupply, and construction is slowing in response. As of year-end 1998, 476,000 square feet of space was delivered in the Northeast submarket. Of this new space, 22 percent is vacant. Nearly 60 percent of the first-generation space took more than nine months to lease. The average size of the buildings being delivered is 122,000 square feet. No unusual concessions are being reported.

Very few projects are in the development pipeline. One new project is being developed by Northcentral Insurance Company, which has started a 240,000-square-foot building. Completion is expected by October 1999. As of fall 1998, the building was fully leased.

Recent Flex/R&D Sales

At least 15 flex/R&D buildings were sold in the past two years. Projects that have sold in the Northeast submarket are listed in Table 4.3-7. As the market recovered in the early 1990s, the number of sales increased steadily from almost none during 1990 to 1992. Cap rates for well-positioned projects dropped from 10.5 percent in 1994 to between 9 percent and 9.5 percent currently. Uncertainty

Table 4.3-5
Metropolitan Atlanta Market Class B/C Office Space

	Inventory (1,000 Sq. Ft.)	Construction (1,000 Sq. Ft.)	Net Absorption (1,000 Sq. Ft.)	Vacancy (%)	Gross Rents (per Sq. Ft.)
1993	41,297	10	1,840	17.4	$14.83
1994	41,331	34	903	15.3	15.01
1995	41,647	316	1,572	12.2	15.36
1996	42,265	618	657	11.9	15.39
1997	43,555	1,290	1,067	12.0	15.59
1998	45,255	1,700	1,550	11.9	16.07
1999	45,995	740	626	12.0	16.17
2000	46,415	420	1,073	10.5	16.28
2001	47,095	680	1,133	9.3	16.38
2002	48,445	1,350	1,073	9.7	16.49
2003	49,845	1,400	1,288	9.6	17.02

Source: PricewaterhouseCoopers.

Table 4.3-6
Northeast Submarket Class B/C Office Space

	Inventory (1,000 Sq. Ft.)	Construction (1,000 Sq. Ft.)	Net Absorption (1,000 Sq. Ft.)	Vacancy (%)	Gross Rents (per Sq. Ft.)
1993	3,407	0	189	10.2	$13.02
1994	3,407	0	21	9.6	13.45
1995	3,457	50	195	5.3	13.85
1996	3,577	120	70	6.5	14.99
1997	4,063	486	397	7.9	15.09
1998	4,539	476	282	11.3	15.15
1999	4,779	240	114	13.4	15.24
2000	4,829	50	195	10.3	15.34
2001	5,019	190	206	9.6	15.43
2002	5,019	0	195	5.7	15.53
2003	5,019	0	234	1.0	16.02

Source: PricewaterhouseCoopers.

Table 4.3-7
Recent Flex/R&D Sales in Northeast Submarket

Building	Year Built	Total Net Rentable Area	% Office	Vacancy (%)	No. Bldgs.	Avg. Bldg. Size	Location	Sale Price per Sq. Ft.	Sale Date
Techwood Industrial Technology Drive	1987	270,000	23	12.5	3	90,000	Good	$54	6/98
Glesser Park 670–682 Downers Drive	1984–1985	250,000	45	9.0	4	62,500	Fair	61	2/98
Lakewood Park 21-56 E. Lake Ave.	1994–1996	340,000	60	2.0	6	56,667	Excellent	71	10/98
McKinley Place 340 McKinley Drive	1985	220,000	25	11.0	2	110,000	Good	48	12/97
Norwood Industrial 210 Katy Road	1979–1984	750,000	30	17.0	8	93,750	Fair	38	9/97
Total/Average		**366,000**	**37%**	**11.7%**		**82,583**		**$54**	

Source: PricewaterhouseCoopers.

in the capital markets caused by the slowing economy and volatile international markets caused several deals to fall through in late 1998. Although interest rates dropped by the end of 1998, cap rates did not follow because lenders became more conservative and investors started requiring higher risk premiums.

In the Northeast submarket, land suitable for flex/R&D is priced near $2.50 per land square foot with a 40 percent building coverage-to-land ratio ($6.25 per building square foot). Depending on the quality of the building and the percentage of office buildout, construction costs for the basic shell building, including hard and soft costs but excluding tenant improvements and leasing costs, are estimated at $49 per square foot on average.

Northeast Submarket Flex/R&D Forecast
The Northeast corridor is expected to experience continued strong demand. Although the market is starting to show some signs of excess supply—such as slowing in leasing and increasing vacancy rates—new construction has already begun to slow as well, which should help rebalance the market. However, absorption is also expected to slow somewhat because of the weaker economy. Local brokers report that one weak link is the Route 316 corridor, located ten miles east of the subject property, where absorption of newly developed space has been slow and leasing concessions have reportedly reentered the market.

Because rents are already high enough to justify new construction and because construction is expected to continue at a pace that will keep both flex/R&D and Class B/C office space vacancy rates generally above 10 percent, market rents are expected to remain flat, or at a maximum, near the rate of inflation, which is forecast at about 2.5 percent through 2003. In addition, effective rents for the office portion of flex buildings are near the rate for low-end Class B/C office buildings, offering little advantage for flex/R&D over competitive office properties.

Competitiveness Analysis and Marketability
The subject properties, Buildings 101 to 104, are of similar quality, age, and size to most competitors. Gross asking

rents at the competitive properties are all within a fairly narrow range, from a low of $7.65 per square foot at the 20-year-old Bucher Building, to a high of $8.42 per square foot at Three Memorial Center. Three Memorial Center receives the highest rents in this survey because it is the newest building and offers a prime location. Vacancy rates in the competitive buildings vary from a low of 7 percent in Three Memorial Center to 16 percent in the Bucher Building, where a small tenant just vacated space to move to a larger facility in the Northeast submarket. Tech Park generally has higher vacancy rates and lower rents than Peachtree Industrial Park because it is located about ten miles east of I-285, which is farther from the population base and amenities such as shopping and restaurants. Rents for the subject property are slightly below average, but with improved leasing and management, it is possible that these rents could be increased. (See Table 4.3-8.)

Strategy for Positioning Peachtree Industrial Park

A small parcel of land is available close to Building 104. The leasing manager has discussed the parking problem with Group 10 Communications, and the company might be willing to assist in defraying the costs of paving part of the site to provide extra parking. Further negotiations will be necessary.

The current leasing staff has done a good job in staggering the leases so that the lease expirations are fairly spread out (see Table 4.3-9). Only 25 percent of the space will roll in the next two years, and at least one of those spaces is currently rented at below-market rates. If the market continues to improve, even slightly, it may be possible to bring this tenant up to current market levels at renewal, or to lease the space to new tenants willing to pay market rates.

Given that the average tenant size in this market is only 15,000 square feet, the 45,000-square-foot space avail-

Table 4.3-8
Competitive Projects

Building	Year Built	Total Net Rentable Area	% Office	Vacancy (%)	No. Bldgs.	Avg. Bldg. Size	Location	Parking Ratio	Avg. Asking Rent
Peachtree Industrial Park Buildings 101–104	1980–1986	390,000	43	12.0	4	97,500	Good	3.1	$7.90
Peachtree Industrial Park Buildings 112–114	1988–1989	310,000	56	8.0	3	103,333	Good	2.9	8.20
Tech Park 820 Guildner Drive	1983	375,622	34	14.0	5	75,124	Fair	2.5	7.80
Three Memorial Center 840 Guilder Drive	1994	280,000	45	7.0	3	93,333	Excellent	3.5	8.42
Memorial City Place 21 Katy Road	1983	150,418	53	11.0	2	75,209	Good	2.7	8.10
Bucher Building 55 Katy Road	1978	36,000	61	16.0	1	36,000	Fair	3.2	7.65
Total/Average Competitive		**1,542,040**	**49%**	**10.8%**		**80,083**		**3.0**	**$8.01**

Source: PricewaterhouseCoopers.

Table 4.3-9

Peachtree Industrial Buildings 101–104 Lease Rollover

Year	Square Footage Rolling (x 1,000)	Percentage of Total Space
1999	53,000	14
2000	42,000	11
2001	20,000	5
2002	98,000	25
2003	20,000	5
2004	60,000	15
2007	12,000	3
2008	40,000	10
Occupied Space	345,000	88
Total Space	**390,000**	**100**

Source: PricewaterhouseCoopers.

able in Building 103 could be subdivided to make it more attractive for leasing. Building 103 is 150 feet deep by 800 feet long. The rectangular shape of the building makes it fairly easy to subdivide. Two of the dock doors are within the 45,000-square-foot vacant space. If the space is divided into more than two spaces, the extra costs of installing another dock door in the back of the building may need to be considered, depending on the tenants' needs.

In conclusion, the buildings are of quality construction in a well-located and well-positioned business park. The biggest risk facing the property is the amount of new construction coming online. Because the construction pipeline is slowing, the volume of new product should slow in the next year, but such new product will be met by less demand as the economy slows down. Effective net rents in the submarket are not expected to decline, but, with continued competition from new product, should grow at rates at or below the rate of inflation. If the subject property is successfully repositioned as described above, rents at the property could grow at a slightly faster rate.

Fashion Valley Center, San Diego, California.

Chapter 5

Retail Development

The retail market analyst must understand the real estate as well as the retailing business and its customers. Retail real estate includes both shopping centers and freestanding stores. The ULI definition of a shopping center is "a group of commercial establishments planned, developed, owned, and managed as a unit."[1] Store space, whether in malls, strip centers, or on Main Street, is most commonly tabulated as gross leasable area (GLA)—the total floor area that a tenant occupies exclusively, including any space used for storage or offices.[2]

The U.S. Census Bureau and the International Council of Shopping Centers (ICSC) classify stores in two main groups: GAFO and convenience. GAFO is an acronym for stores selling general merchandise (discount and conventional department stores), apparel and accessories (including shoes), furniture and home furnishings (including electronics), and "other" (specialty shops selling books, toys, luggage, jewelry, or sporting goods). Convenience stores include supermarkets and other food stores (such as bakeries or butcher shops) and drugstores. Home improvement, hardware, and building supply stores are often classified with convenience stores.

Although much of America's store space is now found in shopping centers, freestanding retailing (in individual buildings or street-front business districts) provides additional competition. Well-capitalized retail chains are often able to build their own stores—and attract customers—without being in a shopping center. Although they can benefit from being close to other shopping attractions, freestanding stores usually enjoy lower rents. Freestanding retailers do not have to pay for common area maintenance, mall

marketing, and management. Also, some chains want exclusive control over store siting, design, and parking, which is not always possible in a multitenant shopping center. Traditional neighborhood business districts, sometimes called "town centers" are enjoying a revival. Compact, pedestrian-oriented environments attract both local residents and visitors, especially in upscale neighborhoods.

Available data on retail space and sales trends focus on large malls, but it is important to remember that more than 70 percent of shopping center space is found in centers with less than 400,000 square feet such as small convenience centers, as well as neighborhood and community strips. (See Figure 5-1.) In 1999, only 730 centers had more than 800,000 square feet and only 14 new centers of this size opened around the country in 1999. Many reasons exist for the relatively small number of big malls.

- They require many years of advance planning, including a lengthy (and often acrimonious) public approval process.
- They are more difficult to finance than smaller centers.
- They are rarely finished within two years of ground breaking. General economic conditions, as well as the financial stability of key tenants, can change dramatically during that time frame.
- Most markets are already served by regional malls and cannot support additional major malls.

On the other hand, small centers are comparatively easy to plan, finance, and build. More often than not, market analysts are asked to evaluate proposed new neighborhood and community centers or to determine whether expansion or renovation, or both, of an existing center makes sense in light of the market's demographics and competition.

Types of Shopping Centers

ULI and the ICSC describe seven key types of shopping centers. Each consists of "anchor tenants" (bigger stores that draw shoppers) and "in-line" or "mall shop" space (small tenants, usually a mix of national, regional, and local stores and service businesses).

1. *Neighborhood centers* sell convenience goods (food, drugs, cards, and sundries) and provide personal services (dry cleaning, hair and nail care, travel agent, and video rental) that meet the day-to-day living needs of the immediate area. Takeout food and small sit-down restaurants are also common in neighborhood centers. They tend to be smaller than 100,000 square feet in size, but can range from 30,000 to 150,000 square feet. Usually anchored by a supermarket, larger neighborhood centers serve a two- to three-mile radius and need ten to 15 acres of land, including parking.

2. *Community centers* also provide for daily necessities, but add more apparel and specialty store space. Key tenants are usually a supermarket and a discount department store. Home improvement stores, hardware, lawn and garden, gift items, banks, and larger eating establishments are also featured in community centers. A typical community center is 150,000 square feet, but may range in size from 100,000 to more than 300,000 square feet and occupy 30 or more acres. Trade areas range from three to six miles.

3. *Power centers,* developed in large numbers between the mid-1980s and late 1990s, are also known as super-community centers. They range in size from 250,000 to more than 1 million square feet, and offer at least three "big-box" or "category-killer" stores, each having at least 25,000 square feet of space. Such stores offer in-depth merchandise selection at attractive prices. Less than 20 percent of power center space consists of small stores; some have no in-line space at all. These open-air centers prefer locations near large malls and draw shoppers from a radius of five miles or more.

4. *Regional centers* focus on general merchandise, apparel, furniture, and home furnishings. They are usually enclosed, with two or three department stores. They may have movie theaters, a food court, and restaurants. Typical size is 400,000 to 800,000 square feet. Regional centers draw 80 percent of their sales from within ten miles.

5. *Super-regional malls* have at least 800,000 square feet of GLA, three or more department stores, and a range of entertainment offerings. A typical size is 1 million square feet, but the largest malls are closer to 2 million square feet. Each department store has at least 100,000 square feet of space. Many super regionals need more than 100 acres of

Figure 5-1

Number of Shopping Centers by Size, 1993 and 1999

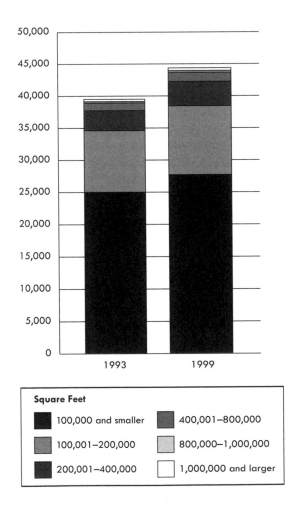

Square Feet

- 100,000 and smaller
- 100,001–200,000
- 200,001–400,000
- 400,001–800,000
- 800,000–1,000,000
- 1,000,000 and larger

Source: National Research Bureau Shopping Center Database and Statistical Model.

land. In densely populated areas, their trade areas can be as small as five miles, but in typical suburban locations, they draw from ten miles or more.

6. *Outlet centers* are collections of discount stores directly operated by manufacturers. They sell out-of-season items and production overruns. Many outlet centers also include discount stores or close-out operators. Most are single story, open-air strips, but some use renovated older buildings. They are usually less than 400,000 square feet with no traditional anchor tenants.

Originally, factory outlets were limited to tourist destinations and highway locations far from regional malls. (Full-line department stores did not want vendors to sell directly to their customers at lower prices, and vendors were willing to comply.) Outlet stores are now locating at the fringe of large metropolitan areas. Some apparel manufacturers now produce goods especially for their outlet stores.

7. *Value-oriented hybrid malls* combining large discount and off-price anchors with smaller factory outlet stores and themed entertainment are a special case. The largest such center, Sawgrass Mills in suburban Fort Lauderdale, Florida, opened in 1990 and now contains more than 2 million square feet of space. Since 1990, however, the trend has been away from such large centers, and newer ones are closer to the 1 million-square-foot range. A good value-oriented hybrid mall can draw shoppers from as far away as 60 miles, but its primary trade area is typically within a half-hour's drive.

Store Mix in Shopping Centers

In a regional or super-regional mall, the full-line department stores are referred to as the anchors. Anchors might also be entertainment centers or large specialty stores. Most regional or super-regional malls have three or more anchor tenants. The anchor chains often design and build their own buildings, executing a ground lease with the mall owner. Some anchor stores own their land and a portion of the parking lot. The arrangements could be different for each anchor in a given center. (Over time, the percentage of department stores that own their buildings has increased.) As a result, it is important to understand whether sales statistics include the department stores. Some mall managers report sales for an entire center. Others report sales only for space owned by the mall, covering only in-line or mall shops.

A combination of operating economics and shifting consumer preferences dictates a shopping center's desired tenant mix. In newer super-regional malls, anchor tenants account for 50 to 70 percent of total GLA. Although mall shops pay higher rents per square foot than anchor tenants do, leasing agents find it increasingly difficult to find successful credit tenants for smaller store spaces. And as independent department store chains continue to be acquired by the largest operators (notably Federated, May Company, and Dillard's), older regional malls may find themselves with empty anchor space. Today, it is not at all unusual to find discount department stores or big-box category killers taking over vacant anchor space in enclosed malls.

ICSC statistics indicate that family apparel stores (such as Old Navy and the Gap), family shoe stores, and furniture and home furnishings stores (such as Crate and Barrel and Pottery Barn) are occupying an increasing share of mall shop space. At the same time, the proportion of space devoted to women's ready-to-wear and men's and boys' shops is declining. Among non-GAFO tenant types, entertainment—in the form of theme restaurants and ever larger multiscreen movie theaters—has become more important, whereas drugstores are moving out of regional malls. (In fact, the pharmacy chains' newest prototypes are freestanding buildings located on strip-center outlots where they may feature drive-up prescription windows that cater to time-pressed customers.)

Retail Market Analysis

With the emergence of new types of shopping centers and retail tenants, the market study is not as simple as it once was. What was once primarily a quantitative study of retail space needs has now become heavily qualitative, relying on the kinds of survey techniques described in chapter 2. In all situations, however, the developer must be sure the market can absorb the increase in retail space that is being proposed. Success may require providing a new shopping center type, a more up-to-date merchandising mix, a more current design concept, or stronger tenants.

Measuring a project's market potential is the first exploratory step in determining the feasibility of a shopping center. The developer's first aim is to match the location, size, and composition of the center to the needs of the trade area. To do so, the developer usually tries to obtain an accurate economic analysis of the trade area, based on a market survey, from which he or she can derive a tentative plan for a shopping center.

A shopping center cannot generate new business or create new buying power; it can only (1) attract customers from existing businesses within or beyond the trade area that are not meeting market expectations because they are obsolete or poor quality; (2) fulfill a demand that has not been met within the market area; or (3) capture the increase in purchasing power that results from population, household, employment, or income growth. New retail space can cause a redistribution of business outlets and consumer patronage, but it cannot create new consumers. A new center can, however, alter consumers' shopping habits. Each new center must be justified by gauging the purchasing power available to it in light of the nature of its competitors.

The following key elements are typically part of a comprehensive market study for a shopping center. The extent to which all of these elements are examined depends on the resources available, the complexity of the proposed center, and the level of sophistication desired. Although household expenditure data and sales figures for competitors should form the core of the analysis, those statistics are the most difficult to obtain, and the analyst will need to rely on a combination of available data and estimates based on experience.

Demand analysis includes the following elements:

- An economic base analysis for the metropolitan area showing general characteristics of the market, including overall economic trends, employment trends, projections of economic activity, and growth patterns;
- Delineations for primary, secondary, and peripheral trade areas and accessibility patterns;
- Population, household, and employment growth trends and projections for each trade area, as well as household characteristics such as household type (families, singles, etc.), lifestyle data, and ages, including trends and projections;
- Income characteristics for each trade area, including household, family, and per capita totals, and disposable income trends, purchasing power, and future projections (today, three year, and five year);
- Demographic data for any sources of patronage other than the resident population in the trade areas: tourists, workers, and convention and business travelers;
- Expenditure patterns and trends by type of goods and services in the trade areas.

Supply analysis includes the following elements:

- Location, characteristics, and sales figures of competitive retail centers, by type of center, in the trade areas;
- Retail space availability, absorption, and sales trends by retail categories in the trade areas;
- Characteristics and status of proposed and planned retail developments in the trade areas, as well as availability of other vacant, zoned sites that could likely become competitive retail development;
- Estimated market share (capture rate) and sales per square foot, and recommended characteristics, anchors, and sizing of the center or centers, depending on the scenarios being considered.

In addition, a retail analyst may investigate other indicators of future market-area growth potential, such as land availability and costs for housing, sales tax revenue growth, and bond programs for road and utility infrastructure.

Defining the trade area for retail development is based on road and transit access (or sometimes pedestrian access) and is limited by distance, travel time, and the location of similar competitors. A demographic study of the supporting population's income and composition will decide the type of retail outlets in demand in the trade area. The demographics and other characteristics of the trade area's population will strongly influence the tenant composition. Income levels play a major role in shoppers' choices. Do major segments of the population consist of families or singles, blue-collar or professional workers, college-educated young people, aging baby boomers, or retirees? Do households own their homes or rent? Accurately analyzing population traits and any changes in the composition of the population is of paramount importance in evaluating the feasibility of any retail location. The number, composition, density, growth rate, income, expenditures, buying habits, and lifestyles of the population can be translated into market potential. Much of this information can be extracted from census data (including metropolitan area supplements), sales tax reports, consumer expenditure data compiled by the Bureau of Labor Statistics, statistics gathered by the jurisdiction's planning and economic development offices, and—usually the easiest and most cost-effective—market area data purchased from vendors like Claritas or CACI. Much must be interpolated and evaluated, however, and many assumptions must be made.

The Importance of Key Tenants

Seasoned developers know the trade area characteristics that suit the type of center they want to build. But until developers know what key tenants are obtainable, they can only surmise the type or size of center that may be feasible. For example, if the top-volume supermarket chain operating in the area is not represented in the vicinity of the proposed center, and that chain is interested in striking a deal with the developer, then a certain pattern of success can be projected with some confidence. In contrast, if the major volume-producing chains have already established stores in the vicinity, leaving only poorer producers available for the proposed site, the size of the center, its success, and other factors will be evaluated differently. Only someone well versed in leasing will be able to resolve the selection of key tenants. For a regional shopping center proposal, the strength of the key tenants interested in the site selected determines the size, character, and success of the center and even the price that can be paid for the land.

In retail development, the anchor tenants are essentially the customers; they are comparable to the homebuyers in a residential development. Just as the residential analyst identifies segments of potential homebuyers, it is often up to the retail market analyst to identify potential retail tenants. What anchor tenants are not already represented in the market area? Which ones are looking to expand in the area? Which ones would be appropriate for the proposed center and suitable for the target market? The experienced retail analyst is familiar with the expansion plans of national and regional chains and understands what they look for in trade area demographics, which other tenants they like to be near, and what space requirements they have. Several trade publications provide useful information. For example, each listing in the *Directory of Leading Chain Stores* gives the number of new outlets planned for the year, the standard store size, types of locations preferred, and estimated sales figures.

A developer must be equipped with hard data to interest prospective tenants, to identify the site, to sketch the proposed plan, to satisfy the community, to obtain zoning approval, and to secure financing. The end result is matching the location, size, and composition of the center to the demands of the trade area. However, the market study is analogous to the chicken and egg conundrum. A potential key tenant will not be interested in a center until a market analysis has been completed, but a thorough analysis cannot be made until the kind of key tenant that the trade area will attract is known. As a consequence, two types of analyses must occur simultaneously: one is to interest potential key tenants in anchoring a prospective center; the second is to determine the number and types of customers who may be brought to the center. The customer draw influences the volume of business that can be expected by other major and supplementary tenants.

Obtaining commitments from major tenants is fundamental to determining project type and size, estimating project costs, and framing leasing arrangements with other tenants. Such commitments are key to the economic feasibility of a project. Without key tenants, no shopping center—neither a small neighborhood center nor a regional center—can materialize. Although specialty centers often do not have traditional anchor tenants, tenanting is still crucial because a cluster or group of tenants probably will function as the anchor tenant.

Citrus Park Town Center in Tampa, Florida, includes 1.1 million square feet.

Pursuing and choosing appropriate anchor tenants requires a clear understanding not only of the type of store that will benefit the center but also of locations that such tenants seek and will accept. A good location for one type of retailer may not be a good location for another. For example, a power center located on a commercial strip is appropriate for a destination-type tenant such as a home improvement warehouse. A specialty department store, in contrast, needs to be in a regional center, surrounded by other specialty stores. Each center's ambience, character, and level of finish is also quite different. Upscale retailers want to be located in a well-lit, attractive mall of high-quality design and finishes. Home improvement stores are more concerned with ease of entrance, egress, loading, and overall vehicle access and convenience. Perhaps most important, the location and type of center will have a strong impact on a retailer's drawing power, sales, and rent structure. Anchor tenants have a very clear understanding of the types of locations and shopping center concepts that will meet their requirements, and a well-conceived market study makes these distinctions and requirements clear.

When a retailer considers a new market, reevaluates existing stores, or analyzes new or existing markets, two questions arise: How many stores of this genre can the market support? What is the minimum number of stores needed to gain a foothold in the market? Often, the first retailer in a market will capture enough of the market potential to thwart additional competition until sufficient growth allows a second store, either the first retailer's or a competitor's. Additionally, many major retailers are public companies, which find that embarking on an aggressive expansion program is the only way to maintain the corporate objectives of continued expansion and earnings growth. Last, a retailer's distribution center may be underused or an investment in some new technology may require spreading the cost to all the existing stores in the chain; the more stores, the lower the cost per store, even though some stores may be marginal performers.

Big-box tenants, which provide the anchors in power centers and community centers, are a special case. Their corporate goal is to drive out competition altogether—hence the name "category killer." It is not uncommon for these stores to be built in such profusion that they saturate a market and eliminate the competition, which leaves large vacancies in the least-competitive centers. Having won the competition, the winning big-box chain may then close some of its own stores that had been built solely to establish market dominance. As a result, when developing a power center, choosing the strongest anchors as tenants is particularly important. (See ULI's *Developing Power Centers* for a detailed description of tenants in power centers.)[3]

Trade Areas and Market Segments

The character of a prospective trade area and the nature of the competition within it will shape the character of a shopping center, including its type, quality, and tone. The trade area traditionally is the geographic area that provides the vast majority of the steady customers necessary to support a shopping center. The delineation of trade areas is more complex than in the past because of the variety and volume of shopping centers already present in most markets. It is further complicated by the existence of multiple consumer markets that are attracted to a center by their affinity for the type of goods sold and the environment in which they are sold, rather than because the center is located within a prescribed distance of their home or workplace. Trade area boundaries are determined by a variety of factors, including shopping center type, accessibility, physical barriers, location of competing facilities, and driving time and distance limitations. Defining a trade area is never as simple as drawing concentric circles around a potential site although potential retailers often want to know the statistics in terms of "rings" to screen potential locations.

Because new shopping centers do not create buying power, they must attract existing customers from their trade areas and capture a portion of new buying power as those areas grow. Hence, the extent of the area from which a new center can be expected to draw most of its customers, whether they are residents, workers, tourists, or business travelers, must first be established. Within a shopping center's trade area, customers closest to the site patronize the center most frequently, with customer influence diminishing gradually as the distance increases. Trade areas are usually divided into two or three categories or zones of influence. The following general guidelines should be modified depending on the type of center and other factors:

- The primary trade area is the geographical area from which the center will derive its largest share of repeat sales. This area typically extends to 1.5 miles for a neighborhood center, three to five miles for a community center, and eight to 12 miles for a regional mall. Driving time within the primary trade area ranges correspondingly from five minutes to 30 minutes, and 70 to 80 percent of the center's regular customers are drawn from this area. In denser areas like older suburbs or urban areas, the distances can shrink by as much as 50 percent. Some newer specialty centers, such as entertainment centers and off-price megamalls, have much larger trade areas and may draw from an entire metropolitan area. Some outlet malls actually derive the majority of their patronage from tourists passing through or from day-trippers.
- The secondary trade area generates from 15 to 20 percent of the total sales of the average shopping center. The extent of the secondary trade area is heavily influenced by the existence of similar centers nearby and, as a result, the extent of secondary trade areas varies widely depending on center type and size, as well as on the competition. For the largest centers, the secondary trade area

may extend three to seven miles beyond the primary trade area.

- The tertiary or fringe trade area forms the broadest area from which customers may be drawn. A small but sometimes significant share of a center's customers may be drawn from tourists and other travelers who do not live in the market at all. This is particularly true for large specialty centers, downtown centers, factory outlet centers, and entertainment centers. Although customers in the tertiary trade area must travel greater distances, they may be attracted to a center because it is more accessible or it provides special merchandise, greater parking, more stores, better value, or higher-quality goods or it has a more attractive ambience than closer centers. For the largest centers, driving time from the tertiary market area to the site can be an hour or more, extending 15 miles beyond the primary trade area in major metropolitan markets. In smaller markets, or rural areas, it may extend as far as 50 miles or more.

Geographic distance and travel time must be differentiated. The competitive relationships among retail areas largely control the movement of shoppers in an urban area, and this situation can vary widely. Distance alone is therefore not a reliable criterion for establishing the extent of a trade area. In addition, a shopping center's trade area may extend farther in one direction than in another. Natural barriers, such as lakes, rivers, hills, parks, and other open space or undevelopable land, as well as constructed barriers or psychological barriers such as railroads, freeways, and large institutional uses, can act as boundaries to the trade area.

The size of a trade area also depends on a site's accessibility from streets, highways, and transit stops, where relevant. Travel times should be set by actual trial runs over key access routes, with the runs made during peak and off-peak times and under weather conditions typical of the area. Driving times, traffic lights, roadside hazards, and barriers are all factors in measuring accessibility. Any proposed changes in existing routes must also be considered.

If a factory outlet or off-price megamall is being considered, the market analyst generally should survey a larger trade area than if a traditional center of the same size were being considered. Similarly, if a downtown entertainment center is proposed, the market analysis should reflect the fact that the center will draw from far beyond the primary trade area. An entertainment center will draw heavily from metropolitan area residents, downtown workers, business travelers, and tourists. Further, the market analysis for such a center should also take into account the drawing power of other downtown anchors and attractions, such as museums, sports facilities, and historic sites; the overall character of the downtown environment (in terms of appearance and safety); and how well the proposed center meshes with this environment, because all these factors can directly affect the center's potential to succeed or fail. The tradeoff is that a large trade area usually means smaller capture rates.

Using geographic information system (GIS) imagery and readily available software programs, a map of the trade area can be plotted easily on the basis of geographic coordinates. Such a map puts into perspective the current and proposed access routes, the population density of developed areas, any commercial locations and competitive facilities, and the topography and land use features. The availability of GIS technology allows an analyst to easily test different scenarios, trade area sizes and configurations, and assumptions to determine the optimum type and size of shopping center to be developed. Many major retailers have been using GIS as a tool for site-selection strategies. GIS enables retailers to examine sites objectively and quickly. Variables that can be weighed include census and traffic counts, household income, and competitors' locations.

Purchasing Power

The income level within the trade area is critical to the success of a proposed center in terms of total dollars available but, more importantly, in relation to disposable income by retail categories. Disposable income estimates for households in the trade area can be derived by applying a factor of consumer expenditures to household income figures, or estimates can be purchased from one of the private data providers. The percentage of income spent on retail purchases varies by income, as does that share of income that is disposable. The Bureau of Labor Statistics indicates how much households (BLS uses the term "consumer units") spend by income group for each major category of goods and services: food, food services, general merchandise, clothing and accessories, shoes, home furnishings, home appliances, building materials, hobbies, gifts, jewelry, liquor, drugs, automotive parts and accessories, and a range of personal services. Potential consumer expenditures in each of these categories can be estimated from the per household purchasing power available in the trade area.

The key factor for determining demand for retail is the total number of people multiplied by the average per capita expenditure within each retail category, which yields the total sales potential of an area. A comparison of the total potential retail sales and the total actual sales in existing retail areas shows whether excess purchasing power is available that either is not being spent or is being spent in surrounding trade areas. Purchasing power that leaves the local market area is often called "leakage." In either case, such a situation clearly indicates unmet potential for new retail development. Even without excess potential, there may still be an opportunity for new retail activity if some of the existing retail stock is not meeting the demands of the market. Given the rapidly changing demands of consumers, and the large stock of older retail space in many regions, obsolete space is increasingly common. Estimating the amount of uncaptured trade potential, the expenditure potential that can be drawn from obsolete space to the proposed center, and the variation in expenditure patterns by different income groups will help to determine the size, type, and development concept of the proposed center.

In growing trade areas, its not uncommon for centers to be built that exceed the size needed to meet current demand. Such centers depend on the continued growth of population and purchasing power for success. In such cases, the area's future purchasing power must be carefully estimated and factored into the area's total available purchasing power. The full sales potential of centers that rely heavily on future trade area growth may not be reached for a decade as the market matures around them. Thus, the market study must take into account the center's anticipated underperformance in the early years to reap the benefits when the center and its market reach maturity. Developers of new communities in isolated fringe areas may have to construct some convenience retail facilities before the size of the market fully justifies them in order to be able to market the community. Potential homebuyers need to see that basic goods and services are available before deciding to move into a new community.

The risk increases if a center is located too far on the leading edge of growth or is too aggressive in its projections of purchasing power. National economic trends and cycles can slow or stop growth for years, rendering carefully made projections inaccurate. Given the increasingly competitive nature of the shopping center industry, entry into the market more often requires riskier and earlier decisions, and developers must secure a site that will benefit from future trade area growth and beat the competition to the market.

Inner-City Communities

Many developers and retailers perceive that doing business in inner-city neighborhoods is risky and unprofitable. Yet, the untapped market potential of these communities is vast. Lower incomes are offset by high population densities, yielding greater aggregate buying power in a concentrated area than in most suburban neighborhoods. Further, studies suggest that retail spending rates are proportionally higher for inner-city residents than for suburbanites. And because few competitors exist, capture rates are likely to be considerably higher for retailers that do enter inner-city markets. The traditional ways of collecting and measuring retail market data tend to underestimate the potential of these communities for several reasons.

■ Most data are based on the U.S. Census and Consumer Expenditure Survey data. These sources tend to undercount low-income households and their spending power. For example, such statistics do not include the unreported income (for babysitting, home repairs, and other informal business activity) that makes up a large portion of household revenues.

■ Because retailing is so minimal in inner-city neighborhoods, little data is available on sales. Also, the lack of existing retail options leads to considerable purchasing power leaking into wealthier areas with better retail facilities. Statistics do not accurately measure this phenomenon.

■ Purchasing patterns differ among the various ethnic communities. These specialized niche markets are just beginning to be studied, understood, and targeted by retailers.

In 1998, a national study of inner-city shoppers found that inner-city shoppers actually spend more on certain goods than their suburban counterparts.[4] Many companies that have developed outlets in inner-city locations have found success. For example, McDonald's estimates that their volume in inner-city Los Angeles exceeds their national average by over 25 percent.[5] One key to success is to understand the market niche and its buying patterns. A representative of Home Depot, which has opened stores in inner-city Chicago, New York, Los Angeles, and Denver sums it up: "We don't sell riding lawn mowers at inner-city locations."

Forecasting Sales

A new shopping center will not attract all the business in its trade area (primary, secondary, and peripheral), but it will draw on three sources: patrons from existing stores in its trade area; customers seeking goods and services currently not offered in the trade area; and, in the future, new residents, workers, tourists, and business travelers. The portion of spendable income that is unsatisfied by what is currently offered reveals the extent of potential sales that are leaking to other communities.

The increasing complexity of shopping centers combined with a multiplicity of overlapping trade areas requires that the analyst use multiple methods to estimate potential sales. Thus, the analyst can project the range of anticipated sales at the proposed center, and the developer can plan for different scenarios using expected, lower-than-expected, and higher-than-expected sales. Several ways of estimating sales are presented in the following paragraphs.

A number of computer programs exist that can help forecast sales volume for individual retail stores. In some cases, they rely on an analog model in which market share for a new addition is compared with existing stores having roughly similar site and trade area characteristics. Using a regression model to project new-store sales, existing-store sales can be adjusted by factors expected to influence sales at a specific new location. Other, simpler methods bracketing estimated potential sales volume can also be used. First, a retailer may compare sales per square foot of other stores in its chain and assume a similar productivity per square foot for a new store, adjusted for variations in trade area characteristics. Second, a retailer may estimate the volume achieved by its competitors in the trade area and then redistribute those sales based on its entry into the market. Third, a retailer may estimate market share on the basis of market shares achieved in other comparable locations.

Several methodologies historically have been used to determine the viability of retail facilities. The choice of which model to apply rests partly in the underlying motivation of the potential consumer. If the trip purpose will be shopping—that is, to acquire needed goods and services—some variation of a gravity model may be useful. If the purpose is recreational shopping combined with entertainment activities—for example, to see a movie, to enjoy lunch or dinner out, or generally to be entertained—a comparable project/per capita analysis is more appropriate.

The Gravity Model

The gravity model combines store sizes and geographic-distance relationships. Reilly's Law of Retail Gravitation, formulated in 1929 by William J. Reilly at the University of Texas, states generally that

when two cities (or retail centers) compete for retail trade, the breaking point for the attraction of such trade will be more or less in direct proportion to the population of the two cities and in inverse proportion to the square of the distance from the immediate area of each city. In effect, this law states that people will travel to the largest shopping center most easily reached, assuming the centers offer the same types of goods and services, except in the case of neighborhood centers, where customers are most interested in convenience, not size.

Experience-Based Models

The gravity model has major weaknesses, because where people shop is determined by far more complex factors than the location and size of a center. Store quality, image, ambience, prices, and customer service are some of the many factors that draw customers independent of size and distance. Increasingly, the synergistic effects of the center's multiple stores, services, and entertainment attractions are what draw shoppers, because most people do not make a separate trip for each need. This phenomenon is the "bundling effect," and the gravity model does not lend itself very well to analyzing that effect. Estimating the bundling effect is very difficult, except through past experience with similar retailing concepts. For such analysis, one must rely on a sophisticated understanding of how consumers behave, how strongly various types of anchors attract customers, and which mix of retailing concepts and specific tenants have the strongest and most long-lived appeal. A better methodology is one that bases projections on experience at comparable retail centers.

The projection of potential sales volume at a new shopping center presupposes a clear understanding of other shopping centers against which it will compete—both existing and planned. They include suburban shopping centers within and beyond the trade area, retail facilities in the central business district(s), and street-front retailers throughout the trade area, the last of which might exercise a strong though varying influence on shoppers throughout a metropolitan area.

In the past, clear tenant distinctions existed among shopping center types, but since the 1980s shopping center types have become less distinct from one another and tenants that used to be found only in regional malls are increasingly found in other types of centers and vice versa. For example, urban street retail is thriving again in some locales and drawing major chain retailers that once considered only regional mall locations. In addition, new types of hybrid shopping centers and others filling newly identified niches are emerging—even in markets that by traditional measures are saturated with retail space. Older centers are being repositioned as home-furnishing centers with tenants that feature furniture, linens, shades and blinds, lighting, and so on. Sales at these centers will depend on some existing centers' inability to meet the changing demands of today's consumers or retailers, with the result that some of their business will be cannibalized by emerging centers. Case study 5.3 is an example of experience-based modeling used to determine the potential of a new entertainment retail center.

Location Decisions

Location is of paramount importance in the success of all shopping center types. The site must qualify by virtue of its trade area characteristics, the income level of the households in the area, competition, highway access, and visual exposure. Location and access are interrelated but separate aspects. The site must be easy to reach and its roads must have the extra capacity to avoid congestion during periods of high traffic volumes. The site must be easy to enter and safe to leave for customers and employees, or it must be able to be modified to make it so. Ideally, the site also should represent an impregnable economic position. Its superior access, greater convenience, better merchant array, and improved services should make it impractical for another similar project to be developed nearby.

Recommended distances between shopping centers cannot be precisely established either for centers of the same type or for centers of different types. After all, it is not mere distance between centers, but population density, customer convenience, accessibility, and diversity of merchandise that count. For example, multiple convenience and neighborhood centers can operate successfully within the trade area of a regional center or even be located next to or across the road from it. Likewise, power centers and other types of community centers often are developed across from or next to regional centers to tap the already established shopping patterns of the regional center's customers. Such coexistence is possible because the two types of centers offer distinct ranges of merchandise. Shoppers at a neighborhood center want convenience in buying everyday goods and services, whereas customers of the regional center are primarily comparative shoppers who are looking for and comparing general merchandise in terms of price, quality, size, color, and style.

Sources of Data

The trade area's population and projected growth are key determinants of a proposed shopping center's viability. Secondarily, the composition of the population according to age, income levels, and family and household sizes is helpful in refining the center's characteristics. The U.S. Census of Population and Housing (taken each decade) and the Census of Retail Trade (conducted every five years as part of the economic censuses) offer basic statistics. (See appendix for specific reference works and sources.) Projections for the trade area's population are often based on estimates for metropolitan area zones made by various planning agencies. It is important to understand the underlying assumptions in the population projections because they often vary depending on source and methodology. The market analyst can use them to create an independent assessment of the market's growth potential.

Because the retail development industry has become much more complex and retail centers are being targeted to increasingly specific market segments and niches, the need for timely, accurate, and sophisticated demographic data has increased significantly, and firms specializing in demographics and psychographics have become an important source of data. Many of those firms offer sophisticated analyses, including the use of a statistical technique known as "cluster analysis." These demographic groups are based on lifestyle and psychographic information (as well as basic age, sex, and income data) in recognition of the fact that people with different lifestyles shop differently.

Statistics on the physical characteristics and market performance of shopping centers are more widely available than for freestanding space or street-front retailing.

- Every two years, ULI's *Dollars & Cents of Shopping Centers*® provides information on sales performance by size and type of center (and for individual store types), based on surveys of more than 1,000 U.S. shopping centers. From time to time, ULI also prepares reports on specialty centers such as high-end fashion malls or downtown retailing in mixed-used projects.
- The ICSC reports monthly mall shop sales for regional and super-regional centers. It also publishes annual summaries and special reports on sales trends, tenant mix, and other aspects of regional mall operations.
- Shopping center directories (national and regional) are published by Chicago-based National Research

Bureau (NRB) and are available on CD-ROM and in paper copy. Centers are listed by state, metropolitan area/county, and municipality in alphabetical order. Descriptive information includes center size and type; anchors and smaller tenants; year built/renovated/expanded; and contact names for owners, managers, and leasing agents.

- NRB also publishes national and regional statistics on the number of shopping centers, average size, and sales per square foot in six size categories. It also reports the number of new-center openings each year.
- Commercial brokers, local chambers of commerce, newspapers, and business journals often prepare lists of the larger shopping centers.
- Retail tenant directories provide information on retail tenants and their needs.
- The summer issue of *Stores* magazine shows sales figures for all major chain retailers.

Although the NRB's shopping center directory is updated every year, tenant mix changes frequently and new competition is always being added. Any shopping center lists or directories should always be checked in the field. Follow-up telephone contacts with center managers or leasing agents will be necessary to learn about future expansion or renovation plans and anticipated changes in tenancy, as well as rent levels and common area maintenance charges.

In addition to those private sector sources, the U.S. Census Bureau publishes monthly and annual statistics on retail sales nationally and for a selected number of large metropolitan areas on a yearly basis. These estimates are based on store sampling and do not distinguish between freestanding stores and mall tenants. Sales are tabulated by SIC (Standard Industrial Classification) code.[6] Additional retail sales and establishment information can be found in publications from the Census of Retail Trade, conducted every five years. State information on sales-tax receipts for municipalities is often used as a proxy for retail sales and can be compared on an annual basis.

Shaping the Character of the Center

After the trade area has been drawn and the potential retail sales have been projected, the character of the proposed center begins to take shape. Developers typically specialize in certain center types, and the most successful of them develop long-term relationships with favored anchors and other key tenants. The advantages for developers are that they understand how these tenants do business, what kind of deals they are looking for, what their location and business requirements are, and under what circumstances they will perform well. These tenants are somewhat predictable partners, and their presence lessens the risks of development. Developers are also able to leverage key tenants' demand for the best locations in the center with locations that are not as good, making it easier to fill secondary space. Retailers also benefit from long-term relationships with shopping center developers. Their investors demand expansion and sales growth, and long-term relationships with key developers create a continuous source of new locations, as well as the opportunity to strike more favorable deals on rents and other charges.

The shaping of a shopping center's character usually begins with a determination of the key anchor tenants. Table 5-1 lists typical anchors by type of center. Retail analysts prepare lists of probable tenants, including anchors and key tenants, while the market analysis is being conducted. Increasingly, developers strive for a mix of local and national tenants. National tenants, also called "credit tenants," provide the strong credit ratings needed to finance a shopping center, while local tenants provide the offerings that give the center its special character. In most areas, some local merchants are stronger than others, and the local standing of a merchant should be taken into consideration. For example, a majority of customers might prefer one supermarket chain over another. Popular, established merchants are likely to draw more patrons to a new center, thereby strengthening its appeal.

Identified market segments in a trade area, combined with national shopping center trends, often suggest a special character for the proposed center that would allow it to depart from the traditional neighborhood, community, or regional center tenant mix and to include special tenant categories that could be supported because of the presence, or absence, of such segments in the market. For example, in a market with a large number of young single professionals demand for food-service tenants will likely be greater, because busy adults without children tend to eat out more often. Additional market analysis could quantify those potentials.

In any market study, assumptions should be conservatively made, clearly understood, and based on realizable goals. They are critical to the validity of the study because the primary purpose of a market survey is not to convince prospective tenants that the trade area needs and can support a proposed center, but to find out whether the area can support a new shopping center of the type being considered. Key

Table 5-1

Typical Shopping Center Anchors by Type of Center

Convenience	Neighborhood	Community	Regional/Super Regional
Minimart	Supermarket	Junior department store	Full-line department store
Restaurant	Drugstore	Discount department store	Fashion department store
Beauty parlor	Discount department store	Supermarket	Megaplex cinema
Dry cleaners	Restaurant	Off-price superstore	Entertainment center
Fast-food outlet	Furniture store	Variety store	Food court
Medical/dental office	Hardware store	Family apparel store	Large-format specialty store
	Automotive store	Furniture store	Large-format off-price store
	Liquor/wine store	Sporting goods store	
	Video rental outlet	Drugstore	
	Bank	Office supply store	
		Cinema	

Source: Dollars & Cents of Shopping Centers®: 2000 (Washington, D.C.: ULI–the Urban Land Institute).

tenants will conduct their own market studies because their criteria and assumptions will likely be different from the developer's in some respects.

Overview of Case Studies

This chapter features four case studies, each illustrating a different type of retailing and different methods of analysis. La Cantera, case study 5.1, is a value retail center to be built by a major national retail developer in suburban San Antonio. The concept capitalizes on a unique tenant mix and its location within a larger entertainment complex to draw customers from a very wide trade area.

Case study 5.2, the Granby Street District in downtown Norfolk, Virginia, is an urban redevelopment project that is part of the revitalization of what was once a thriving downtown. Similar to downtowns throughout the country, Norfolk's retail core declined during the 1960s and the 1970s as suburban shopping centers seized much of its customer base. Beginning in the 1980s, revitalizations like Granby Street's captured the imagination of local governments and developers throughout the nation, and the trend continues today. The market analyst faces difficulties identifying and quantifying market potential for these pioneering projects because of untested markets and a lack of comparables.

The Lake at Riverdale, case study 5.3, is a retail/entertainment complex that features a cinema as an anchor. The market analysis uses a combination of several methodologies, including psychographic analysis and focus groups to fine-tune the concept. For comparables, the analyst found it necessary to go

well beyond the boundaries of the market area and to draw from a national list of successful projects.

Case study 5.4, Wilanow Town Center, in Warsaw, Poland, depicts an emerging retail market that is replacing the old state-owned shopping facilities. In researching markets outside the United States, analysts often face a lack of data and must rely more heavily on interviews and other primary research for documentation. Projects in emerging locations, such as inner-city neighborhoods, often present similar situations and the analyst must invent creative approaches to the market analysis.

Notes

[1] ULI–the Urban Land Institute, *The Dollars & Cents of Shopping Centers®: 2000* (Washington, D.C.: ULI–the Urban Land Institute, 2000), p. 3.

[2] GLA is measured from the centerline of joint partitions and outside wall faces.

[3] W. Paul O'Mara, et al., *Developing Power Centers* (Washington, D.C.: ULI–the Urban Land Institute, 1996).

[4] PricewaterhouseCoopers LLP and the Initiative for a Competitive Inner City, *The Inner-City Shopper: A Strategic Perspective*, 1998.

[5] "Retail Rebounds in Inner-City L.A.," *Chain Store Age*, vol. 76, no. 9, p. 196.

[6] See U.S. Bureau of the Census, Current Business Reports, in *Annual Benchmark Report for Retail Trade*. The old SIC system will soon be replaced by the NAICS (North American Industry Classification System). Shifting classifications will complicate comparability with earlier years' sales statistics. Although most retailers will still be classified in Sectors 44 and 45 (Retail Trade), restaurants (formerly Eating and Drinking Places) will now be grouped in Sector 72 (Accommodations and Food Services).

A Value-Retailing Center:
La Cantera (1992)

Mark E. Kissel

In the highly competitive environment of retailing, retailers and developers alike struggle with the inherent conflict between following the path of proven success or blazing a new direction that may deliver big returns. In shopping center development, the right location and the right demographics may not guarantee a successful project. Developers must be cognizant of how their project will compare to competitive projects—directly or indirectly. Project layout, architecture, an unusual combination of tenants, and complementary uses, particularly entertainment, are all elements of a project's design that can be used to differentiate a center from competitive centers.

The proposed project, La Cantera, was designed to be a unique destination differentiated from competitive shopping centers by its value-oriented tenant base coupled with one-of-a-kind tenants and a location adjacent to a major theme park–entertainment complex. Thus, the development strategy was, to some degree, to draw shopper sales from other San Antonio centers, to attract the San Antonio tourist, and to generate "cross-shopping" business with the adjacent entertainment complex.

Location and Site

The La Cantera site is located at the intersection of Loop 1604 and I-10, at the far northwest corner of San Antonio's city limits, 15 miles northwest of the central business district (CBD). The shopping center site is one component of a larger entertainment complex. The recently developed theme park—Fiesta Texas, which features amusement rides, musical entertainment, and various food services—is adjacent to the La Cantera site. In addition to the existing theme park, several other large-scale projects are proposed as follows:

- Between one and three Branson, Missouri–style, celebrity theaters;
- A multiplex theater with eight to 12 screens, plus the possible inclusion of a specialized film format;
- Several hotels to serve different market segments, including a 500-room hotel/conference center adjacent to an 18-hole golf course, a 350-room hotel to serve Fiesta Texas, and a 150-room budget hotel;

- A variety of dining experiences, including themed dinner theaters, specialty restaurants, a fine-dining format, entertainment clubs, and a microbrewery;
- A cable television and radio network that would air musical events at Fiesta Texas, offering increased exposure and revenue through broadcasting rights.

Market Area

San Antonio ranked 30th among the 281 metropolitan areas in the 1990 census, with a population of 1.3 million. Most noteworthy are its population growth rate, exceeding that of the state of Texas (1.99 percent versus 1.79 percent), and its large Hispanic population. San Antonio is home to about 684,000 Hispanic residents, making it one of the largest Hispanic markets in the United States, both in actual and relative (53 percent) terms.

San Antonio's economy experienced a boom-to-bust cycle during the 1980s. The low of the cycle hit bottom in 1988, and the economy has since rebounded. San Antonio's unemployment rate has declined because several high-technology firms and back-office operations of national corporations have entered the job market. Unemployment rates have declined from the 7.0 to 7.9 percent range that prevailed during 1986 to 1989 to the 6.0 to 6.9 percent range that has existed since 1990. Employment in the early 1990s in San Antonio is dominated by the service, government, retail, and finance, insurance, and real estate (FIRE) sectors.

The area within a ten-mile radius of the site demonstrates the quality of growth in the northwest quadrant of San Antonio. The 1992 population of 415,200 has grown at the rate of 3 percent per year with a median household income of $34,000. In contrast, at a distance of 20 miles or more from the site, the demographics tend to reflect the metropolitan area at large, with a population growth rate of approximately 1.7 percent and a median household income of $29,000. The household income within a ten-mile radius—reflecting the income characteristics of the northwest quadrant—is 21 percent higher than the household income for the overall market. These income demographics enhance the marketability of the La Cantera site. Furthermore, the northwest quadrant of the San Antonio market is home to three important employment generators: South Texas Medical Center, a health care and education center with 17,900 employees; USAA, a worldwide insurance and financial services corporation with 9,600 employees; and the University of Texas at San Antonio, with an enrollment of 16,800 students and 1,200 full-time employees and 2,300 part-time employees.

For most shopping centers, the consideration of radius-based geography above a 20-mile radius is not relevant to the dynamics of a typical regional mall trade area. Most traditional regional shopping centers capture a large proportion of their patrons from within a 20-mile radius. A shopping center with a distinctive tenant base and physical design, however, functions differently from a traditional regional mall because such a center attracts a large proportion of its patrons from within a 40-mile radius. Because the proposed center at La Cantera could potentially attract patrons from an area broader than the three-county area of the (MSA), this analysis used a six-county region, consisting of 1.35 million people. (See Table 5.1-1.)

Tourism is a key economic activity in San Antonio and would add to the customer base of the proposed shopping center. At present, San Antonio accommodates approximately 5.3 million overnight visitors annually. The continued success of the tourism industry depends on extending the stay of overnight visitors and converting day-trip visitors into overnight visitors. The second critical element of success is complementarity. As long as the entertainment venues complement each other's activities, a tourist conceivably can plan to visit every venue. If the complementarity of the venues turns into direct competition, each of the competing attractions will suffer. Carefully nurturing the existing attractions by continual facility renewal, and understanding the long-term synergy of all the venues, creates the successful entertainment mix.

The level of tourism activity and the mix of the entertainment venues factor into what is termed the "inflow" part of the trade area and sales analysis. In essence, inflow customers reside outside of the trade area, and for a variety of reasons—from attending a convention to taking leisure tours of historical sights—pass through the trade area and, thus, have a higher than usual probability of shopping at the proposed retail center.

Retail Market History

The suburbanization of San Antonio produced long-lasting effects in the retail community. The department store business consolidated from three local stores to two out-of-town stores, Dillard's and Foley's. Mall activity in the 1980s included expansions by North Star and Ingram Park, and the development of Rolling Oaks. North Star ultimately became the region's premier mall as well as the largest shopping center, at 1.2 million square feet. Central Park, North Star's neighbor and at one time near equal, was never able to keep pace with North Star's expansion and, hence, quickly became an outdated and underperforming shopping center.

Other retail development in the 1980s consisted of value centers, power centers, outlet centers, and urban centers. Discount and value stores paved the way for the development of value and power centers. What launched value retailing into a position challenging the department store business was not the national chains, but two local retailers, 50-OFF and Solo Serve. Although both stores relied on an off-price merchandising strategy, they served different customers. 50-OFF targeted low- to moderate-income customers, while Solo Serve catered to moderate-income customers with more of a fashion orientation. The two chains complemented each other's business and greatly expanded their store bases during the 1980s, capturing a surprising share of retail expenditures. In fact, entry into the San Antonio market by national off-price stores has been somewhat limited because of these two chains.

With respect to value-oriented retail development, Walzem Plaza represents one of the best examples of a 1980s value center. This center opened in 1981 and today incorporates a mix of national and local value tenants, including Service Merchandise, Solo Serve, Office Depot, and Weiner's. Westlakes Mercado, due west of the San Antonio CBD, opened in 1983 with Montgomery Ward and Target as anchor stores plus a number of off-price and value-oriented small tenants.

Exchange Place, near Ingram Park, evolved into a power center with value and category-dominant tenants such as Circuit City, Ross Dress for Less, and Pier 1 Imports. Adjacent to North Star, The Pavilions at North Star opened

Table 5.1-1

Radius Demographics, La Cantera Site: Loop 1604 and I-10

Demographic Attributes	5-Mile Radius	10-Mile Radius	20-Mile Radius	30-Mile Radius	40-Mile Radius
Population					
1990	72,454	388,421	1,168,916	1,272,829	1,373,935
1992	80,152	415,224	1,208,450	1,318,301	1,424,347
1997	99,415	482,245	1,308,432	1,433,097	1,551,471
Annual Growth (%)					
1990–1992	5.18	3.39	1.68	1.77	1.82
1992–1997	4.40	3.04	1.60	1.68	1.72
Households					
1990	29,339	151,329	405,057	441,119	475,849
1992	32,656	162,882	422,836	461,213	497,831
1997	40,950	191,766	467,283	511,449	552,785
Annual Growth (%)					
1990–1992	5.50	3.75	2.17	2.25	2.28
1992–1997	4.63	3.32	2.02	2.09	2.12
Average Household Size					
1980	2.45	2.54	2.81	2.82	2.82
1990	2.44	2.52	2.79	2.79	2.80
1992	2.41	2.49	2.74	2.74	2.75
Annual Growth (%)					
1990–1992	(0.20)	(0.39)	(0.36)	(0.53)	(0.36)
1992–1997	(0.25)	(0.24)	(0.36)	(0.36)	(0.36)
Median Household Income					
1990 ($)	$35,753	$30,885	$26,149	$26,150	$25,967
1992 ($)	38,554	33,554	28,848	28,826	28,632
1997 ($)	44,108	38,872	34,255	34,221	34,030
Annual Growth (%)					
1990–1992	3.84	4.23	5.03	4.99	5.01
1992–1997	2.73	2.99	3.50	3.49	3.51
Households with Income >$35,000					
1990: # of Households	14,899	66,067	144,626	157,116	167,889
% of Households	50.78	43.66	35.71	35.62	35.28
1992: # of Households	17,824	77,768	168,693	183,635	196,484
% of Households	54.58	47.74	39.90	39.82	39.47
1997: # of Households	25,272	107,242	227,484	248,646	266,815
% of Households	61.71	55.92	48.68	48.62	48.27
Annual Growth (%)					
1990–1992	9.38	8.49	8.00	8.11	8.18
1992–1997	7.23	6.64	6.16	6.25	6.31

Sources: Urban Decision Systems; Kissel Consulting.

in 1990 with a similar roster of tenants. In the northwestern suburbs, Trammell Crow developed Bandera Festival, a 188,000-square-foot value/convenience center anchored by Kmart and Solo Serve.

One of the more interesting developments was completed by locally based H.E. Butt, the dominant grocery chain in San Antonio. Within a half mile of Exchange Place, H.E. Butt developed a power center, called the Market Place, featuring an expanded format of its own grocery store, H.E.B., Office Depot, and value retailers such as Clothestime. Like the Pavilions and Bandera Festival before it, the design of the Market Place was a cut above the typical San Antonio open-air center. H.E. Butt designed the building to resemble an ore mine by using a corrugated metal facade. Although the design may be somewhat provocative, H.E. Butt created a fresh new look for an open-air shopping center that represented a distinctive departure from the usual, mediocre design of many San Antonio community shopping centers.

Outlet retailing came to the San Antonio area with the construction of the Mill Store Plaza in New Braunfels, Texas, in 1986. Anchored by Westpoint Pepperell, this 245,000-square-foot manufacturers' outlet mall captured tourist and intercity traffic traveling between San Antonio and Austin. With a distance of only 22 miles separating Mill Store Plaza from the junction of Loop 410 and I-35, San Antonio shoppers found Mill Store Plaza's location convenient, particularly for big-expenditure shopping trips.

With so much attention on suburban development between 1960 and 1980, the San Antonio CBD was largely a forgotten place until the early 1980s, when the DeBartolo Corporation embarked on a highly creative downtown project. The result, Rivercenter, connected an existing Dillard's department store, the Alamo, and the River Walk—the developed riverfront of the San Antonio River—with a three-level retail complex of boutiques, restaurants, and tourist attractions, plus a Lord & Taylor department store (which Foley's later assumed) and a Marriott hotel. By successfully linking the established urban amenities through a fun and upbeat retail environment, Rivercenter became a major attraction for tourists and residents alike. This development activity is summarized in Table 5.1-2.

By the end of the 1980s, the retail market had experienced significant growth, more than 3.1 million new square feet of major retail development. The decade did not pass, however, without several major changes in the market. As value retailing grew, conventional retailing contracted, primarily caused by the expense of corporate mergers and a long-term shift by consumers to stores offering value. By the close of the 1980s, retailing names such as Joske's, Frost Brothers, Wolfe & Marx, Rhodes, and Liberty House had all disappeared from the San Antonio retail landscape.

The largest retail development of the 1990s occurred not in San Antonio proper, but in San Marcos, Texas, approximately 18 miles northeast of the Mill Store Plaza in New Braunfels. Adjacent to I-35, the Prime Group built 310,000 square feet of outlet space in two phases. The tenant mix at this project, San Marcos Factory Shops, is an impressive collection of upscale manufacturers' outlet stores, such as Donna Karan, Mondi, First Choice, and Coach, and mid-scale tenants such as VF Outlet, Corning/Revere, Bass, and Springmaid/Wamsutta.

Most recently, a prominent manufacturers' outlet developer, Tanger Factory Outlet Centers of Greensboro, North Carolina, received approvals to construct approximately 100,000 square feet of outlet space adjacent to San Marcos Factory Shops.

Current Retail Assessment

The value-retailing trend continues unabated in San Antonio, while department stores search for new merchandising strategies. Table 5.1-3 summarizes the impressive growth of value retailing in San Antonio to date and reinforces two prevailing themes of San Antonio value retailing.

■ A compact growth period. The only value stores in operation before 1980 were Kmart and Solo Serve. Most important, their rapid growth demonstrated unabashed customer acceptance.

■ A reputable representation of local retailers. Because of their larger store size, national retailers control about 80 percent of the value-retailing space in San

A Value-Retailing Center: La Cantera *(continued)*

Table 5.1-2

Growth in Major Shopping Center Space, San Antonio, TX, Market, 1960–1992[1]

Period	Major Shopping Centers[2]	Square Feet	Square Feet for Period	% of Market
1960–1969	North Star	670,000		
	Northwest	270,000		
	Crossroads	732,000		
	McCreless	468,000		
	Central Park	672,000	2,812,000	31.6
1970–1979	South Park	620,000		
	Windsor Park	1,061,000		
	Ingram Park	978,000	2,659,000	29.9
1980–1989	North Star Expansion	597,000		
	Ingram Park Expansion	148,000		
	Walzem Plaza	246,000		
	Westlakes Mercado	440,000		
	New Braunfels	245,000		
	Rivercenter	779,000		
	Rolling Oaks	650,000	3,105,000	34.9
1990–1992	San Marcos	310,000	310,000	3.5
Total		**8,886,000**		**100.0**

[1]Definition expanded to include shopping centers in New Braunfels and San Marcos, TX.
[2]"Major" refers to malls with approximately 250,000 square feet or more.
Sources: National Research Bureau; San Antonio Express-News; Kissel Consulting.

Antonio. The store size of a typical Kmart, Target, or Wal-Mart averages 85,000 to 95,000 square feet. On a store-unit basis, however, local retailers operate about 45 percent of the locations. Even though local retailers clearly trail behind the national retailers in sales (by virtue of the amount of selling space), their market presence is highly unusual in comparison to other major metropolitan markets.

One of the objectives of a retail analysis is to identify retail or shopper demand. Demand can be demonstrated directly by showing that it indeed exceeds retail supply. In other words, the dollar or expenditure value of the retail goods and services that the trade-area population can potentially purchase is greater than the dollar or expenditure value of retail sales that occur within the trade area. This is the fundamental relationship of retail demand and supply within a store or shopping center trade area. Retail demand can also be demonstrated indirectly by showing that demand from *outside of the trade area*—in the form of sales from other stores or shopping centers (that is, the "transfer" effect)—or from *outside the market* (for example, tourist dollars) will augment trade-area demand and, thus, support the proposed shopping center.

Table 5.1-3

San Antonio Value Retailers

Type of Value Retailer/ Market Niche	Market Store	Estimated Total Scope	Units	Square Feet
Off Price				
Middle to Upper	Stein Mart	Regional	2	60,000
	Solo Serve	Regional	11	253,000
	Tuesday Morning	National	3	30,000
Middle	Marshalls	National	3	75,000
	Ross Dress for Less	National	3	75,000
	Burlington Coat	National	1	65,000
Lower to Middle	50-OFF	Regional	9	180,000
	MacFrugal[1]	National	4	60,000
Discount				
Middle	Weiner's	Regional	12	180,000
	Target	National	6	570,000
Broad	Kmart	National	11	990,000
	Wal-Mart	National	5	500,000
Wholesale Membership				
Broad	SAM's Club	National	3	360,000
Total			**73**	**3,398,000**

[1]Pic N Save changed the name of its four San Antonio units to MacFrugal in fall 1992.
Sources: Solo Serve; 50-OFF; Kissel Consulting.

In the case of San Antonio, the developer had correctly identified a market niche for the kind of shopping center that was proposed. From a retail analysis perspective, the niche was predicated on an indirect demonstration of demand. In short, the project concept of combining a distinctive collection of tenants—value-oriented and "one-of-kind" stores—with proximity to a major entertainment complex creates a retail destination that arguably would attract residents of the metropolitan market, tourists, and visitors to the entertainment complex. Hence, the retail demand demonstrated by the trade area would be supplemented by the retail demand of tourists and theme-park patrons.

The proposed shopping center synthesizes several evolving trends in San Antonio shopping center development with national development trends that have yet to arrive in San Antonio. The fusion of those trends creates a

shopping center development product termed the "unique destination center." This term defines the shopping center product envisioned by the developer. The unique destination center includes the following elements:

- Merchandising clarity. The shopping center consists of retailers that present a powerful selection of merchandise and/or merchandise at exceptional value. These two attributes, selection and value, draw shoppers to a destination almost regardless of distance. An integral part of selection and value is brand names. In other words, a store sells a stunning selection of brands within a particular product category and/or desirable brands are offered at unbelievably low prices. The only shopping centers in the greater San Antonio area to offer this kind of clarity are the outlet centers. Within San Antonio, only individual stores offer clear selection (like Circuit City) and/or value (like Solo Serve).

- **Identity.** Merchandising clarity certainly helps to establish identity. However, if merchandising clarity is duplicated, a shopping center's sense of identity or distinction diminishes. Both uniqueness and merchandising clarity define a shopping center's identity. Within San Antonio, only the outlet centers and Rivercenter come close to a truly unique identity. Nonetheless, two outlet centers with a handful of merchants duplicated in both centers now exist. The opening of the San Marcos center did split the outlet market: New Braunfels now tends to target lower- to middle-income shoppers while San Marcos tends to target middle- to upper-income shoppers. Neither of these centers, though, presents one-of-a-kind or retail outlet tenants.

- **Architectural appeal.** Shopping centers are places; they represent points or areas of commerce. When a place has aesthetic appeal, it generates enthusiasm for visitation. Regardless of whether a place is a restored colonial village or a contemporary shopping center, the design of the place stimulates interest from the market. In the case of the unique destination center, the design does not take precedence over the quality of the retail experience but rather enhances the experience by providing an attractive environment for the shopper.

- **Location.** When a center is unique, can there be a right location within an entire metropolitan area? The right location is one where several major interstate highways intersect or where a popular and well-known destination is adjacent to an interstate. In either case, a location close to the metropolitan area is preferable because it keeps driving to a minimum for the largest number of consumers.

A unique destination center—that is, a shopping center with merchandising clarity, identity, aesthetic appeal, and a good location—does not exist today in San Antonio. The opportunity for such a center exists at the La Cantera complex. With value retailing now established and maturing in San Antonio, a unique destination center would synthe-

size the existing value-retailing and development trends with new retail formats not presently in the market, at a celebrated location.

The advantages of the La Cantera site are twofold. The first advantage relates to the adjacent theme park. The proposed location is well recognized throughout the market because of the Fiesta Texas theme park. The second advantage is that the site is at the edge of the metropolitan area. This location turns out to be an advantage, given the desirability of leasing to outlet tenants. Manufacturers' outlets are one tenant constituency of the unique destination center that actually prefers locations at the periphery of a metropolitan area as opposed to suburban or urban sites.

The La Cantera location has one disadvantage. With respect to the entire San Antonio market, a location at Loop 1604 can be perceived as inconvenient from the perspective of the northeast, southeast, and southwest quadrants of the market. To counter such a perception, La Cantera must be positioned from the outset as convenient to I-10. In addition, La Cantera must be known as San Antonio's value center, unlike New Braunfels and San Marcos, which require a much farther drive.

Powerful selection and value can overcome any locational disadvantages. For La Cantera to succeed, it needs an innovative and distinctive mix of retailers in a fun environment. These qualities are key to a unique destination center that will firmly position La Cantera as San Antonio's distinctive shopping venue.

Sales Potential

A sales forecast for the La Cantera site is based on the following assumptions:

- First and foremost, leasing will focus on merchandising La Cantera with tenants that offer all of the qualities of a unique destination center. Value and selection are clear. Merchants are distinctive and readily identifiable. The notion of clarity of offerings and uniqueness of value is critical to draw patrons from beyond the local area and to establish loyalty among the local patrons.

■ La Cantera will lure five to seven high-profile tenants from San Marcos Factory Shops. Not only must La Cantera cannibalize San Marcos Factory Shops' tenant base, but also it must create ambivalence among available tenants about where to locate their store. In other words, the possibility of a third choice (in terms of location) vis-à-vis San Marcos Factory Shops and Tanger's recently announced project creates a better opportunity for La Cantera now. If the leasing of La Cantera begins *after* San Marcos and Tanger have split the available tenants, then La Cantera will lose a significant strategic edge. Hence, the leasing of La Cantera must begin posthaste.

■ Leasing will achieve an occupancy rate of at least 80 percent for opening in fall 1994.

■ Access to I-10, the primary traffic carrier, and Loop 1604 will be smooth and easy to understand.

■ A major *bilingual* marketing campaign of print (including major newspapers in San Antonio and Austin), broadcast, and outdoor advertising will create region-wide awareness.

■ No new competing centers, traditional or outlet, will open in Bexar County during the sales projection year of 1994–1995.

■ The national and local economies will maintain their present level of growth or will improve.

■ Fiesta Texas will steadily increase its attendance levels; Sea World will reverse its downward trend and experience a modest rise in attendance.

Sales for La Cantera are estimated for the 1994–1995 period by analyzing the market's expenditures. Rather than undertake a detailed sales and trade area analysis, the client requested a more generalized method. An expenditure analysis meets the stated objective. The analysis follows a five-step process:

1. Accept a radius definition as an adequate representation of the trade area. The client did not want drive times used to define the trade area.

2. Estimate total expenditures for the trade area. From the expenditure estimate, derive retail expenditures for department store–type merchandise (DSTM) alter-

natively referred to as general merchandise, apparel, furniture, and other merchandise (also known as GAFO). Table 5.1-4 summarizes steps 1 and 2.

3. Apply three different scenarios—low, medium, and high—of estimated market shares against the retail expenditures. Also apply three different scenarios —low, medium, and high—of the ratio of market sales to inflow trade.

4. Calculate the "equilibrium level" of square footage for each of the three sales scenarios. The equilibrium level is based on a sales productivity benchmark for a regional shopping center as published in the Urban Land Institute's *Dollars & Cents of Shopping Centers*®.

5. Enter the square footage of the proposed project and account for the space allocated for food service (which is not considered a DSTM expenditure). The last row produces three different estimates of sales productivity based on the project's size, food sales, ratio of inflow to market sales, and market penetration. Table 5.1-5 summarizes steps 3, 4, and 5.

In the case of La Cantera, inflow business is projected to provide 15 percent of the center's sales, which reflects the "mid" sales scenario. Given La Cantera's access to I-10 and Loop 1604, the center will successfully attract patrons from beyond a 40-mile radius. The percentage of sales from the primary trade area, a 20-mile radius, is similar to a Mills-brand shopping center (a shopping center whose tenant base is a hybrid of different kinds of value retailers) and is thus quite different from traditional regional shopping centers.

Table 5.1-5 illustrates the supply/demand analysis process. For opening year 1994–1995, the forecasted sales productivity of $269 per square foot, +10 percent/–15 percent, yields total sales of $107.6 million. The disproportionate range, +10 percent versus –15 percent, indicates the possible effect of Tanger's project on La Cantera. Ultimately, the tenants, not the mall itself, provide customers with the benefits of shopping. Because tenants play the key role in the success of a shopping center, if La Cantera cannot secure quality tenants because of prior commitments to San Marcos' Phase III or Tanger, then La

Table 5.1-4

Expenditure Overview, La Cantera Site

Expenditure Components	5-Mile Radius	10-Mile Radius	20-Mile Radius	30-Mile Radius	40-Mile Radius
Average Household Income					
1990	$48,220	$40,184	$33,997	$33,811	$33,487
1992	$52,599	$43,613	$37,098	$36,871	$36,509
1997	$63,259	$52,133	$44,660	$44,371	$43,922
Estimated 1995 Income	$58,758	$48,542	$41,466	$41,203	$40,791
Annual Growth (%)					
1990–1992	4.44	4.18	4.46	4.43	4.41
1992–1997	3.76	3.63	3.78	3.77	3.77
Households					
1990	29,339	151,329	405,057	441,119	475,849
1992	32,656	162,882	422,836	461,213	497,831
1997	40,950	191,766	467,283	511,449	552,785
Estimated 1995	37,406	179,644	448,969	490,729	530,111
Annual Growth (%)					
1990–1992	5.50	3.75	2.17	2.25	2.28
1992–1997	4.63	3.32	2.02	2.09	2.12
TOTAL 1995 Income Potential ($x000)	$2,197,870	$8,720,195	$18,616,936	$20,219,737	$21,623,987
1995 Expenditure Potential ($x000), by Radius	$373,638	$1,482,433	$3,164,879	$3,437,355	$3,676,078

By Geographic Band	5-Mile Radius	5–10 Mile Band	10–20 Mile Band	20–30 Mile Band	30–40 Mile Band
1995 Expenditure Potential ($x000), by Area	$373,638	$1,108,795	$1,682,446	$272,476	$238,722

Sources: Urban Decision Systems; U.S. Bureau of Labor Statistics Consumer Expenditure Survey; Kissel Consulting.

Cantera will have difficulty positioning itself as the destination of value and selection.

The sales forecast of $269 per square foot demonstrates bona fide market potential for a unique destination center in San Antonio.

Recommendations

The prospects for retail success at the La Cantera site look very positive. The five following factors support this conclusion:

- In terms of demographics, the northwest corridor demonstrates strong population growth and relatively high household incomes.
- Since the 1988 economic low, the economy turned upward as evidenced by a stabilization in retail occupancy rates and the ability of the market to attract new businesses from outside the market area.
- Between 1980 and 1990, the San Antonio MSA's employment base increased by 28 percent, an addition of 146,000 jobs, easily outpacing the nation's growth rate of 22 percent.

Table 5.1-5

Sales Analysis Overview, La Cantera Site

Market Area	Retail Sales Potential (000)	Capture Rates (%)			Project Sales Range (000)			Sales Distribution (%)		
		Low	Mid	High	Low	Mid	High	Low	Mid	High
Primary Trade Area[1]	$3,164,879	1.85	2.50	3.15	$58,550	$79,122	$99,694	80.00	72.50	65.00
Extended Trade Area[2]	511,199	1.00	1.75	2.25	5,112	8,946	11,502	10.00	12.50	15.00
Total Trade Area	3,676,078	1.73	2.40	3.02	63,662	88,068	111,196	90.00	85.00	80.00
Inflow Trade					12,186	24,487	39,301	10.00	15.00	20.00
Total GAFO Sales ($000)					70,736	103,609	138,995			
Benchmark Productivity (from ULI)[3]					$207	$207	$207			
Supportable GLA (sq. ft.)					341,719	500,528	671,471			
Proposed GLA (sq. ft.) for GAFO Goods					396,000	396,000	396,000			
Proposed sq. ft. vs. Supportable sq. ft.[4]					1.16	0.79	0.59			
Sales per sq. ft.					$179	$262	$351			
Food GLA (sq. ft.)					4,000	4,000	4,000			
Food & Service Sales ($000)					$1,400	$1,560	$1,700			
Total Mall GLA (sq. ft.)					400,000	400,000	400,000			
Total Mall Sales ($000)					$74,736	$107,609	$142,995			
Total Project Sales per sq. ft.					$187	$269	$357			

GLA = gross leasable area; GAFO = general merchandise, apparel, furniture, and other merchandise
[1] Based on a 20-mile radius.
[2] Based on a 20- to 40-mile band.
[3] ULI 1990 median productivity for a regional shopping center (average size of 518,000 sq. ft.) adjusted to 1995.
[4] A value greater than 1.00 indicates excess space; a value less than 1.00 indicates a shortage of space.
Sources: Urban Decision Systems; U.S. Bureau of Labor Statistics Consumer Expenditure Survey; Kissel Consulting.

- The strength of biomedical, high-technology, tourism, and financial services industries offsets, if not exceeds, the weakness in manufacturing in the local economy.
- Together with the economic upturn, increased work in the biomedical and high-tech community, prudent management of tourism venues, and continued disposition of Resolution Trust Corporation–controlled real estate will further enhance growth.

Given the favorable demographic and economic conditions for retail development in the northwest corridor, this analysis projects strong potential for a unique destination center at the La Cantera site. Assuming the development of 400,000 square feet of retail space (of which 396,000 square feet is for department store–type merchandise and 4,000 square feet for food establishments) and an opening year (1994–1995) sales productivity of $269 per square foot, total annual mall sales should yield $107.6 million.

Considering the market, economic, access, and competitive issues relating to the La Cantera site, this analysis concludes that the client should proceed with the development of a unique destination center at the subject site, based on three compelling factors:

1. The site's proximity to Fiesta Texas ideally positions La Cantera adjacent to a proven traffic generator at a location well known throughout the metropolitan area.

2. The northwest quadrant represents the best mix of demographic quality and economic development within the San Antonio market.

3. Well-merchandised and well-packaged value retailing simply does not exist in San Antonio. Within the market, Solo Serve stands alone as the only formidable off-price competitor. The stores of a unique destination center can answer Solo Serve's challenge through more sophisticated merchandising and a better selection of branded merchandise. San Marcos Factory Shops has established a successful, well-packaged retail complex more than 45 miles outside of San Antonio. A unique destination center at La Cantera, however, can accomplish the same success at a closer-in location with a more diverse tenant base. As noted previously, La Cantera's leasing program must begin immediately to avoid the prospect of narrowing tenant availability caused by Tanger's project approval and San Marcos' planned expansion.

In summary, the San Antonio market presents an attractive opportunity for developing a value-oriented shopping center. A shopping center project based solely on the proposition of offering a roster of off-price tenants, however, is not the optimal market strategy. This type of product already exists in San Antonio. A tenant base that combines different kinds of value tenants including one-of-a-kind stores at a distinctive location creates the product differentiation that can distinguish La Cantera from competing shopping centers. Thus, the product strategy that best establishes a clear identity for La Cantera is to create a unique destination center, a shopping venue characterized by personality, entertaining fun, and great value that draws customers from within and outside the market area.

Street Retail:
Granby Street District, Downtown Norfolk (1998)
H. Blount Hunter

The Granby Street district of downtown Norfolk, Virginia, is a main-street retail zone that is being rejuvenated within the city's central business district (CBD). Granby Street was once Norfolk's primary retail corridor, with several department stores and numerous specialty shops. As occurred in many cities throughout the country, suburban development during the 1960s and 1970s drained Granby Street of its retail vitality.

During the 1980s and into the 1990s, Norfolk's downtown waterfront was restored to prominence as a site for entertainment and dining with the development of the Waterside Festival Marketplace and adjacent Town Point Park. The office core grew and prospered, and city planners wisely added several regional-scale cultural and recreational venues to enhance the mixed-use appeal of downtown. New hotels and a conference center were developed along with other tourist attractions and facilities.

In March 1999, MacArthur Center, a 1 million-square-foot enclosed shopping center anchored by Nordstrom and Dillard's department stores is scheduled to open adjacent to the Granby Street district. This upscale specialty center will draw millions of shoppers to the general vicinity of the Granby Street district for specialty apparel and other comparison goods not readily available in traditional malls in the suburbs.

In preparation for the opening of MacArthur Center, Norfolk's Department of Development commissioned a comprehensive retail and restaurant market assessment for the Granby Street district. Their goals were the following:

1. Quantify the special retail and restaurant sales potential associated with current patrons of downtown Norfolk.
2. Develop a merchandising strategy for the Granby Street district that is compatible with the adjacent regional center and the existing waterfront festival marketplace.
3. Provide usable, fact-based leasing data for the public and private sector.

Fundamental Considerations

Whether located in a CBD or another type of urban setting, street retailing offers a significant growth opportunity for local and national retailers, restaurateurs, and service providers. Across the nation, merchants are capitalizing on the extraordinary level of activity occurring in and around vibrant and revitalizing urban areas.

Initiating street retail activity often requires greater effort than is necessary for traditional suburban retail centers for the following reasons:

- Retail thrives in high-traffic areas. Street retailing functions best in areas that are crossroads locations for a broad mix of destination uses by a wide variety of consumer segments. Only limited retail development can be expected in single-purpose downtown areas inhabited solely by daytime employees. In such instances, street retailing will be confined to restaurants and to convenience-oriented shops and services with minor representation of comparison goods.
- Even in busy urban areas, retailers are often unable to perceive the full extent of consumer potential represented by all users of a downtown area. Although the daytime workforce is readily visible, other downtown patrons go unnoticed. It is ironic that the daytime workforce is often the only customer segment that is considered by prospective merchants, yet this segment typically generates less than 25 percent of sales in robust urban retail areas.
- Street retail areas suffer from the lack of a strategic merchandising plan with centralized execution. Unlike suburban retail centers, which are controlled by single developers, street retail areas are usually held by multiple property owners, which results in fragmented merchandising and leasing efforts.
- Unlike retail development of suburban greenfields, real estate in urban areas must often undergo remedial environmental action in order to compensate for private sector neglect of buildings and municipal neglect of infrastructure and streetscape. Retail activity will be slow to occur in the absence of environmental enhancement, which may be perceived as highly speculative by both public officials and private investors.

Developing an appropriate knowledge base for stimulating street retailing requires a systematic approach that includes the following steps:

- Quantify current users and create profiles of trip motivations, demographic characteristics, and economic effects using primary and secondary consumer research.
- Quantify aggregate retail and restaurant expenditure potential associated with the current level of use through primary and secondary research as well as experience from other, similar cases.
- Translate aggregate expenditure potential into an estimate of supportable square footage, assuming a range of sales productivities that allows for economically viable retail and restaurant operations.
- Compare the estimate of supportable square footage to existing total space inventory and prevailing level of vacancy.
- Generate a merchandising plan based on user profiles and the existing retailers and restaurants. Identify high-impact leasing opportunities, that is, those with the potential to significantly redefine the image and usage patterns of the district.

Establishing a Trade Area and User Profile

The most fundamental question posed by prospective tenants of any retail site is, "What is the trade area for this shopping center?" Suburban shopping center developers have become adept at defining residential trade areas based on sales generated by individual zip codes in areas contiguous to the shopping center. However, promoters of street retail areas and downtown districts often fail to answer this question adequately.

Without an accurate trade area definition, many prospective tenants of street retail erroneously assume that the trade area of an urban retail district consists primarily of its daytime-worker population supplemented only by the residents within a narrow radius of one to three miles. This assumption significantly underassesses the drawing power of a downtown area and can result in an unrealistically low measure of the economic vitality and the level of consumer expenditure potential available to merchants in an urban environment.

Trade areas are not necessarily defined in geographic terms. A trade area can be defined geographically, using

zip codes or counties, if telephone research was designed and conducted with an accurate representation of the distribution of local population by zip code or county within the MSA.

A more accurate means of addressing the level of consumer expenditure potential that is available to an urban retail district is to establish an annual estimate of visits, or "person trips," that flow into the downtown area by tracking its actual users and then generating economic and demographic profiles of those users. Total estimated person trips into the study area is an effective means of portraying the drawing power of a downtown. These data can be used to generate a geographic trade area for downtown retail as well as to create the following user profiles:

- Net reach, or percentage of a cohort that travels to the subject area, and frequency of use among key demographic groups;
- Share of annual usage related to nonwork versus work trip motivations;
- Comparative profiles of frequent users versus infrequent users.

Downtown users tend to fall into three relatively mutually exclusive market segments. These segments form the basis for estimating the annual number of person trips as well as expenditure potential as follows:

1. Residents of the entire MSA who visit downtown for discretionary purposes (i.e., nonwork trips);
2. Office workers and other employees who come downtown for work purposes;
3. Visitors from outside the MSA, including tourists, business travelers, convention delegates, and day visitors, who visit for a variety of reasons.

Collectively, these three market segments form the universe of potential customers for street retail. The size of each market segment is easily discernible using statistics available from local government agencies in most communities. Each segment's level of interaction with downtown can be quantified using a combination of primary and secondary data sources.

1. The population of adult residents of the overall MSA is available as updated census data from most local planning agencies. The analyst should make certain that the geographic basis used to represent the local resident market area is consistent throughout the analysis.

2. A count of office workers and other employees is generally available through the municipal economic development agency, state employment commission, or local chamber of commerce. Periodic employment counts are available from the U.S. Census Bureau.

3. The annual count of overnight visitors can be gleaned from statistics compiled by metropolitan convention and visitors' bureaus or state tourism agencies. Another estimate of visitor count can be constructed using hotel room counts combined with occupancy data. The day-trip component of total annual visitation is elusive and is typically estimated by applying a multiplier to the hotel-based visitor count.

The annual average frequency of downtown visits by members of each market segment must be measured in order to construct a comprehensive estimate of annual downtown usage. "Reach" and "frequency" of use by local residents from the MSA can be determined by proprietary consumer research. "Reach" represents the share of each customer segment that has visited downtown Norfolk at least once for nonwork purposes in the past six months. "Frequency" equals the average number of nonwork downtown trips by members of each segment. Frequency includes nonusers and users. Aggregate estimates of person trips generated by daytime employees and visitors are generated by standard usage estimates.

1. Random telephone interviewing within the MSA is used to measure the reach and frequency of downtown visits by local adults. Alternative sources of usage information are Scarborough- or Belden-type media/shopper studies or community-based omnibus polls, which are generally available through newspapers in larger communities. The results of the consumer research conducted among residents of the communities in the Norfolk MSA are shown in Table 5.2-1.

2. Office workers and other employees are assumed to make approximately 200 trips annually into a downtown area when vacations, holidays, and sick leave are factored out. Generating the economic impact and demographic profiles of this market segment requires sampling by means of primary consumer research.

Table 5.2-1

Downtown Norfolk's Penetration of Key Customer Segments and Average Annual Frequency of Nonwork Visits

	Reach or Penetration (%)	Average Frequency (Visits)
Age Group		
18 to 24	38	7.4
25 to 29	35	11.8
30 to 39	43	11.2
40 to 49	37	10.8
50 to 59	41	12.2
60 to 69	25	3.4
70 and up	23	5.6
Household Income		
Under $25,000	21	5.6
$25,000 to $34,999	29	6.6
$35,000 to $49,999	36	8.6
$50,000 to $74,999	42	8.4
$75,000 to $99,999	49	13.4
$100,000 and up	75	30.2
City of Residence		
Norfolk	50	24
Portsmouth	34	8.4
Virginia Beach	40	8.2
Chesapeake	47	10.6
Suffolk	18	12.4
Southside Average	41	12.4
Newport News	23	4.2
Hampton/Poquoson	32	4.2
Williamsburg/James City Co.	14	2.2
York County/Yorktown	35	9.2
Peninsula Average	27	4.6
MSA Average	35	9.2

Source: H. Blount Hunter Retail & Real Estate Research Co.

3. Downtown visitation by out-of-town visitors is best measured by convention and visitors' bureaus or state tourism agencies by means of exit-intercept research at hotels, airports, and follow-up research. It is reasonable to equate downtown visitation with usage rate for the most-visited attraction or venue located within the downtown area. Most tourist studies incorporate spending assessments and demographic profiles of out-of-town visitors.

For Norfolk's Granby Street district, the size of each market segment is presented in Table 5.2-2. The adult population of the Norfolk MSA is 1.2 million persons. Random telephone interviews within the MSA, with calls allocated in proportion to the population of each munici-

pality, indicate the average frequency of nonwork visits to the downtown is 9.2 trips per year, equating to 11.04 million person trips. In addition, the tourism sector contributes 2.86 million person trips per year based on visitor research conducted by regional and state tourist development authorities. Downtown workers, who number about 36,000, account for 7.2 million trips annually, assuming an average of 200 work days per year.

An interim result of the analysis is a fact-based estimate of actual usage, stated as person trips, of the downtown area over the course of a year. The analyst estimates that downtown Norfolk draws 21.1 million person trips annually from a combined market of local residents, tourists, and downtown workers and students. A full two-thirds of these trips are not work related.

Table 5.2-2
Estimated Annual Person Trips to Downtown Norfolk

	Segment Size	Current Annual Usage Frequency	Projected Annual Person Trips
Nonwork Trips			
Local Residents (adults 18+)	1,200,000	9.2	11,040,000
Tourists/Day-Trip Visitors/ Business Travelers/ Meeting & Convention Delegates	11,000,000	0.26	2,860,000
Work Trips			
White-Collar Workers/Students/ Other Employees within 1 Mile	36,000	200	7,200,000
Total Trips			**21,100,000**
Nonwork Trips	13,900,000	66%	
Work Trips	7,200,000	34%	
Total Trips	21,100,000	100%	

Source: H. Blount Retail & Real Estate Research Co.

Assessing Retail and Restaurant Demand

Assessing retail and restaurant demand requires objective expenditure data and subjective evaluations of the probable capture rate, or share of expenditures, that can be expected by retailers and restaurateurs in the study area. The basis for objective evaluation is existing behavior patterns and industry benchmark data, and the analyst's experience from similar retail districts provides the basis for subjective judgments.

At this stage of analysis, two questions are critical:

1. What share of all downtown person trips is the subject street retail district likely to capture?
2. What will be the average expenditure of each patron, once drawn to the street retail district?

Dual assessments of retail and restaurant demand are typically prepared. The first reflects potential and probable sales, assuming capture of current downtown users. This analysis is followed by future potential and probable sales goals, assuming a projected increase in downtown users. This case study focuses exclusively on the initial assessment of demand based on current downtown users (i.e., existing annual person trips).

Analogous experience provides a starting point for projecting the share of downtown person trips by each market segment that can be captured by the street retail district. Influencing factors include the following:

- The overall size of the downtown area and the magnitude, or critical mass, of the subject street retail district;
- The connectivity of the street retail district with key activity generators within the downtown area, such as employment centers;
- The predominant time of usage of downtown facilities compared to retail and restaurant hours of operation;
- The proximity of the street retail district to key visitor attractions and facilities such as hotels and convention centers;
- The existing or planned anchors within the street retail district.

The expertise of the analyst is critical in applying analogous experience to this stage of assessment. Any inclination toward unrealistic capture rates will yield an overly optimistic assessment of market demand. Expressions of aggressive capture may have a place, however, in the supplemental calculation of future potential.

Average expenditure (per capita spending) is also subject to analogous experience. The content of the retail mix determines the amount of expenditure assumed in the assessment of sales potential. Average expenditure per capita should be stipulated for each market segment.

Most rejuvenating street retail districts face modest initial average expenditures by customers because comparison-shopping goods will be minimally represented In favor of impulse-oriented specialty items. As the merchandise content of a street retail district evolves, projections of potential sales can reflect increasing average expenditures.

Table 5.2-3 represents the conversion of estimated downtown trips into expenditures. For the Granby Street district, the analyst determined that consumer expenditure assumptions should reflect a mix of casual restaurants and specialty shops to supplement other comparison-goods merchandise available elsewhere in the downtown area. From the calculations previously described, the analyst

---

Table 5.2-3

Annual Retail/Food Expenditure Potential Analysis by Market Segment

	Market Segment Count	Person Trip Count	Annual Utilization Rate	Per Visit Per Capita Spending Factor	Total Sales Potential
Residents					
Norfolk MSA Residents over Age 18	1,200,000	1,680,000	1.40	$30	$32,400,000
Tourists/Convention Delegates					
Overnight Hotel Guests (net persons)	6,400,000	640,000	0.10	20	12,800,000
Overnight Non-Hotel Guests (net persons)	2,600,000	260,000	0.10	20	5,200,000
Day-Trip Tourists	2,000,000	100,000	0.05	20	2,000,000
Subtotal	11,000,000	1,000,000			$20,000,000
Office Workers/Daytime Employees					
White-Collar Workers in Downtown Norfolk	25,000	6,500,000	26.00	25	16,250,000
Other Employees within 1 Mile of Downtown	11,000	110,000	10.00	25	2,750,000
Subtotal	36,000	6,610,000			$19,000,000
Total Annual Sales Potential					**$71,400,000**

Source: H. Blount Hunter Retail & Real Estate Research Co.

determined that Norfolk MSA residents account for 1.68 million annual person trips to the Granby Street district. At a per capita spending factor of $30 per trip, this market segment will account for $32.4 million in annual sales.

The 11 million visitors displayed in Table 5.2-2 are broken down into three sectors in Table 5.2-3. Overnight hotel guests comprise 640,000 person trips, with a per-visit spending factor of $20, equating to annual sales potential of $12.8 million. Non-hotel guests and day-trip tourists comprise the remaining potential from tourists, for a total annual sales potential from the tourism market segment of $20 million.

Office workers and other daytime employees are the smallest sector, and despite accounting for the greatest number of person trips, still generate the smallest share of sales potential, estimated at $19 million. The total annual sales potential for downtown Norfolk is thus estimated at $71.4 million.

In Table 5.2-3, Annual Utilization Rate refers to the estimated average number of person trips generated, by market segment. It is derived by dividing the person-trip count by market-segment population count and reflects the analyst's experience in evaluating the performance of strong urban areas of varying sizes across the country. Similarly, the Per Visit Per Capita Spending Factor reflects the analyst's experience with main-street retail districts, as well as retail/restaurant developments within numerous downtown settings. These spending factors vary according to the specific circumstances of the study area and are influenced by factors such as the presence of department stores and the extent to which the study area is expected to become a destination for comparison-goods shopping (apparel and other mall-type goods).

Determining Supportable Square Footage

From the calculations shown in Table 5.2-3, aggregate annual sales potential for the Granby Street retail district is determined to be $71,400,000. Sales potential must be translated into supportable square footage of retail space. This extrapolation can be accomplished by creating a matrix that incorporates the aggregate sales potential and a range of sales productivities (sales per square foot) rang-ing from $150 to $300, the range of productivity that is generally considered both acceptable and realistic.

The range of sales productivities used in the matrix must reflect the retail dynamics of the local market. If a base of retailing exists in the study area, the analyst should use current productivity as a guideline when establishing a productivity target for new businesses. Because the Granby Street district is essentially void of contemporary specialty retailing, the analyst did not have a preestablished sales productivity base to use as the basis for new tenants. Instead, he relied on reasonable productivity within the Norfolk MSA as the basis for setting a goal of $250 per square foot for future sales productivity. This assumption affects the projected amount of supportable square footage, as well as rent economics. The temptation to increase the projected amount of supportable square footage by selecting a low level of productivity conflicts with rent economics if assumed sales productivity translates into unrealistic rent-to-sales ratios.

In some circumstances, the existing volume of retail and restaurant sales in the study area may be learned through tax records or from the business improvement district (BID) or management organization. When existing sales are known, the amount of supportable square footage can be based on net incremental sales (the difference between projected sales and current sales). The resulting amount of net supportable square footage can be compared to the existing vacancies to determine how much of the current supply of retail space can be filled, and whether a demand for new construction is indicated.

In the Granby Street district, projected demand will support 285,600 square feet of retail space at $250 per square foot sales productivity. In Table 5.2-4, a range of sales volumes, representing a conservative level of 15 percent below projected sales and an aggressive level of 15 percent above projected sales, have been cross-indexed against a range of sales productivities to determine supportable square footages. The range of sales productivities corresponds to reasonable sales levels for retail and restaurant investment in a variety of retail settings, as well as the range of sales productivities currently generated by retail centers and districts within the Norfolk MSA.

Table 5.2-4

Supply and Demand Analysis Sales Productivity Matrix (Supportable Square Footage Assuming Three Sales Volumes and Five Levels of Sales Productivity)

Sales Volume	$150 per Sq. Ft.	$200 per Sq. Ft.	$250 per Sq. Ft.	$300 per Sq. Ft.	$350 per Sq. Ft.
$60,000,000	400,000	300,000	240,000	200,000	171,429
$71,400,000	476,000	357,000	285,600	238,000	204,000
$82,000,000	546,667	410,000	328,000	273,333	234,286

Source: H. Blount Hunter Retail & Real Estate Research Co.

Creating a Merchandising Strategy

A comprehensive merchandising strategy precedes the leasing effort. Promulgation of a broad merchandising strategy is an important element of creating a strategic vision and plan for a street retail district. Consensus must be reached among key stakeholders, including property owners, the directors of the BID or management organization (if present), and the host municipality.

Optimally, the merchandising plan for a street retail district will respond to the retail and restaurant interests of current and potential users of the downtown area in a way that simultaneously contributes to the district's extended drawing power and enjoys maximum insulation from competition from other retail and restaurant clusters. A "void analysis," which is often recommended by retail analysts for determining underserved retail merchandise categories, is arguably applicable because its greatest usefulness applies to assessing demand for comparison goods with predictable annual household spending based on data from the U.S. Census Bureau's Consumer Expenditure Survey. However, this analytical process is only appropriate for suburban retail development or for an urban study area that has overwhelming majority support from a nearby residential market. For most urban street retail districts, comparison-goods retailing will be secondary to specialty retailing where consumer spending is not well documented by any published government data.

The foundations for a merchandise strategy are drawn from

1. Prevailing themes in the larger downtown environment such as local history, maritime heritage, significant architecture, content of visitor attraction and cultural venues, and programmatic elements of marketing and/or special event organizations within the downtown area;
2. Demographic and psychographic characteristics of current and potential users;
3. Existing strong signature businesses in or near the street retail district;
4. Untapped niches in the competitive retail and restaurant landscape of the metropolitan area.

For the Granby Street district, key merchandising themes that emerged included history, maritime heritage, performing and visual arts and culture, entertainment, and casual and fine dining.

The Next Steps

Armed with a fact-based set of user profiles, realistic sales projections, and a comprehensive merchandising strategy that illustrates key themes, private sector and municipal stakeholders can proceed with leasing and development actions, as well as marketing and promotional activities.

1. High-impact leasing and development opportunities should be identified for priority effort. These opportunities should have the potential to contribute to major image transformations for the street retail district. These kinds of tenants may be considered as being comparable to the anchors of a regional shopping center in terms of their potential for positioning the district and generating destination traffic.

2. Marketing and promotional activities can be organized in support of generating targeted traffic concentrated specifically within the street retail district. Strategies and tactics may be designed around the dual goals of increasing spending by current users and generating new person trips by nonusers. For example, a BID could undertake activities such as concerts or "Taste of the Town" dining promotions as a means of bringing people into the heart of the study area.

3. Periodic reevaluations of market conditions should be undertaken to measure progress and to refine future goals.

Results

After completing the market analysis, promoters of the street retail district—like their suburban retail center counterparts—are able to answer the following ten questions most critical to retailers, restaurateurs, and site selectors:

1. Who are the customers?
2. How many customers are there over the course of a year?
3. Where do they come from?
4. What motivates them to come to this area?
5. How often do they come to this area?
6. Who are the best customers?
7. What do they do when they are here?
8. How much do they actually spend?
9. How much are they capable of spending?
10. How large a critical mass of retail and restaurant space can be supported given current levels of usage?

The Granby Street market study provides significant leasing data for the Downtown Norfolk Council, the retail development staff of Norfolk's Department of Development, real estate brokers, and property owners. The study identifies the penetration and frequency of use by age group, by income level, and by residency. It estimates the market share from residents, tourists, and downtown workers, and provides an estimate of supportable square footage and expected sales per square foot. All of these statistics paint a positive outlook for development of street retail in the Granby Street district.

Reinvestment by key property owners has occurred as building owners have recognized the need for basic property improvements as a prerequisite for generating tenant interest. Investment by new property owners has occurred as aggressive landowners have acquired the holdings of passive or absentee property owners. New business openings are perhaps the most exciting results of newly generated interest in the Granby Street district. As expected, restaurants are leading the return to the district; specialty retailers are following.

Within six months of the release of the study, there has been significant local and national tenant interest in the area. The following results have been realized:

- A major property owner began renovation of a 22,000-square-foot building for a national chain tenant.
- Four vacant buildings underwent facade upgrades as the first step toward making them more attractive to potential tenants.
- A florist relocated from the suburbs.
- Two upscale bistros have opened and a 50,000-square-foot dining/entertainment center is underway.
- A minimum of three national restaurant chains expressed interest in locating in the district.
- The Downtown Norfolk Council (a voluntary member organization) initiated efforts to convert to a BID to maximize property-owner interests in the Granby Street district.

Retail Entertainment Center:
The Lake at Riverdale

Jill Bensley

Four years ago, Bill Johnson's dream was to create a place where people in Riverdale, an upscale suburban community, could come with their families to meet friends, stroll, relax and unwind, shop, eat, and play. His firm's previous retail projects had succeeded in the town: an 80,000-square-foot center with a big-box bookstore, several fast-food restaurants, a home store, and several service shops; and a 50,000-square-foot center just up the road, with a six-screen cinema, the best local restaurant, and several convenience shops. But this project would be far bigger, and far more elaborate.

Today, going over the second-year sales volumes, Johnson was struck with the extraordinary figures. Sales were so impressive that he suspected a miscalculation: $500 per square foot for the retail; $550 for the restaurants; $125 for the cinema and $175 for the game center. Overall sales averaged just under $460 per square foot, well above the productivity of typical retail centers.

He checked the projections in the feasibility study; sales were significantly higher than predicted. The feasibility consultant had explained to him that this project could not be viewed as a conventional shopping center. The methodology, she said, is totally different. It involves data collection, analysis and projections of many diverse market segments, projection of discretionary spending for recreation and entertainment, and surveys of many types of restaurants, game centers, cinema, and retail venues in the market.

Riverdale, A Town on the Edge

The town of Riverdale is located in the shadow of a major metropolitan area; it is an edge town. Residents can drive 40 minutes and sample the finest restaurants, stores, cinemas, performing and visual arts, and nightclubs in the United States. But Riverdale residents had left the busy urban sprawl to settle here and create the type of life they had earned. They built a glamorous performing arts center so residents would not have to go downtown. They created the best school system in the state. And they enjoyed one of the highest income and quality-of-life regions in the state.

About one mile away, a 1.5 million-square-foot regional mall with five anchor department stores is achieving sales

of $380 per square foot. How could potential demand be measured for Johnson's dream center, The Lake at Riverdale? The following pages summarize the process used to conduct the market feasibility analysis.

Project Description
The plan for the new center included a program of 270,000 square feet of gross leasable area with the following uses:

Type of Use	Square Feet
15-screen cinema	75,000 (5,000 seats)
Retail	100,000
Food and beverage	60,000
Nightclub	10,000
Family and children's attraction	25,000
Total	270,000 square feet

Going into the project, two anchor tenants had been secured. The upscale grocer had been looking for a location in the area, as had the cinema.

New Methodology
As entertainment-themed projects began to evolve, it became obvious that the commonly used gravity model (see page 147) would not apply. The first studies conducted for a specialty retail center attempted to measure performance of other entertainment-anchored centers with retail components in like areas of the country. It was extremely difficult to construct a model based on limited data. As more centers were developed, performance indicators were established measuring attendance, per capita expenditure at the center, trip purpose (i.e., dining, strolling, visiting, shopping, etc.), percentage of attendance from residents versus overnight visitors, and market penetration rate of visitors.

In the early 1980s, Disney Development Company proposed a whole new concept in urban entertainment. It conducted market research and feasibility testing on a new "urban entertainment center" planned to include a major regional shopping center, an indoor theme park, cinemas, nightclubs, and food and beverage venues. The project underwent extensive feasibility testing, including a complete gravity model for the retail component, a modified theme park study for the ride component, and separate analyses for the restaurants and nightclub components. After these studies were complete, a massive amount of consumer research (telephone surveys and focus groups) was conducted to test the new products. In the end, the project was abandoned because of several factors, including difficulties with the site, the demographics of the close-in population, and the construction cost of building the attraction.

It is from this exercise, however, that a new methodology for testing retail entertainment center feasibility emerged. The methodology combines a detailed comparable project analysis, market and site analysis, and consumer research to develop probable levels of attendance and expenditure. This model has been successfully employed to test the feasibility of several new projects in the marketplace, including The Lake at Riverdale.

Demand Analysis—What's Missing in Riverdale?

The methodology derived to predict market feasibility of retail entertainment centers is based on the following three key assumptions:

1. The product is not a retail center.
2. Consumers are extremely discriminating in their choice of entertainment and leisure experiences.
3. People are missing a collective human bonding experience in their lives.

The first is easy to understand. The second and third are much more subtle. According to focus groups and opinion polls, today's consumer sees goods as interchangeable. Thus, in order to get a consumer to shop at a location, it is necessary to differentiate the product and presentation from those of competitors. Shopping today is not about goods and services; it is about experiences. Further, consumers—especially female consumers, who comprise approximately 75 percent of primary purchasers at shopping centers—are afraid to shop at night for safety reasons. The female consumer is sick of waiting in lines, and she is busy and harried in her dual-earner household. She needs shopping and recreation provided in a convenient, high-quality, entertaining package.

Modern consumers view shopping in two ways, the "have to" shopping and the "want to" shopping. A retail entertainment developer's job is to make the "have to" shopping into the "want to" shopping. The developer must provide a safe, fun, emotionally bonding experience, within an entertaining, changing themed environment.

When viewed with these factors as background, it is easy to conclude that a huge void exists in Riverdale for this product.

The Many Markets

Demographic analyses for a retail entertainment center must consider the overall population and identify the appropriate submarkets. For example, the extended market area in this case is the market-containment area of those living within 25 miles of the site. From that distance, an estimated 80 percent of total sales will be generated, based on comparable market analyses. A closer market-containment area is also important, that is, the 10-mile radius. According to studies of centers with retail and entertainment elements in suburban locations, this market can comprise from 60 to 75 percent of the sales at the center. If this were an urban downtown, the market area would be extended considerably. Further, overnight visitation could be a major market segment. However, in this suburban location, no tourism exists and the closest visitor area is more than 20 miles to the west.

Demographic factors to consider include the size of these two market-area populations, the number of households, the average household size, and their income characteristics, levels of educational attainment, and employment characteristics including occupations.

Within these market segments, various submarkets must be quantified and qualified. For example, a game center will attract young males; thus one must know the number of males aged 12 to 24 within the market areas. Nightclubs need a market area with large numbers of people aged 18 to 35. Fast-food retailers need to know the size and characteristics of the nearby office population. And all retailers must know all they can about their female consumers.

The Submarkets

THE FEMALE CONSUMER

Because women purchase between 70 and 85 percent of all goods sold at a shopping center (according to a 1996 survey by the Mass Retail Association), they are a formidable segment for retail entertainment products. Characteristics such as the number of working women, family structure, and presence of children under 17, must be quantified.

In this case, the population is family dominated; 67 percent of households include children. Bucking national trends, only 45 percent of the women in this market work. These factors must be kept in mind when programming the center.

OFFICE WORKERS

This market segment, estimated at 50,000 workers within three miles, provides demand for food service at lunch and some convenience retail; they are also prospective consumers for the cinema, if the workers live nearby. In this case, most workers live within ten miles of their worksite. This lucrative market segment, if large enough, can generate demand for a fast-food food court, which, if executed well, can also serve busy mothers with children in the after-school shopping hours.

UNIVERSITY STUDENTS

The state university located five miles north of the site boasts an enrollment of 20,000. This market segment has a large appetite for nightclubs, movies, low-rent bars, and beer halls, and will occasionally browse in a bookstore. The analyst must remember, however, that the university bookstore provides students with most of their retail academic needs.

PASSING MOTORISTS

The site is located at an off-ramp of the freeway. Average daily traffic is approximately 80,000 vehicles. Although these motorists will probably not create a large share of business for restaurants, movies, or retail, the center will be a constant billboard for these passing motorists, who will return to the center as a destination at another time.

Psychographics

Because a retail entertainment center sells lifestyle and experience, not goods and services, it is important to know just who customers are, what they like to buy, where they vacation, and other characteristics. Psychographic analysis is an inexpensive way to identify and target like groups.

A sample psychographic analysis is provided in Table 5.3-1. The summary section at the top of Table 5.3-1 highlights the largest psychographic groups in the Riverdale market and will be used to test the proposed plan and to target tenants. Each category has a detailed explanation associated with it. For example, the Upward Bound category is defined as upper middle-income, family-oriented, college-educated non-Hispanic white households, aged 25 to 54, living in single-family homes. Second City Elite are affluent, college-educated, white-collar executive, mostly non-Hispanic white couples, aged 35 to 64. Table 5.3-1 shows all of the high-income clusters in the market area. It is notable that Riverdale is a very high-income market area, with 93.6 percent of its households falling within the higher-income segments.

Focus Groups

Many retail entertainment projects will offer products new to the market. Modeling projected attendance, per capita expenditure, and affordable rents can be problematic with no market comparables available. In the case of The Lake at Riverdale, the developer is considering a family entertainment center sponsored by a large national company. Collectively, the owner and developer will conduct a series of five focus groups to determine response to the concept, pricing, hours, food and beverage choices, and other important factors. Carrying the research this far may appear unnecessary, but because initial investment in tenant improvements will be so significant, testing the concept as thoroughly as possible is important to ensure that the investment is worth the risk.

Supply Analysis

Surveying and quantifying comparable projects for a retail entertainment center is more art than science. Because the project includes many categories of shopping

Table 5.3-1

Higher Income/Expenditure Potential Lifestyle Clusters in the Riverdale Market Areas, 0–10-Mile Band

Cluster	Population Distribution (%) 0–10-Mile Band
Total Population	100.0
SUMMARY OF FOUR LARGEST CLUSTERS	
Upward Bound (C1)	52.0
Second City Elite (C1)	23.4
Winner's Circle (S1)	5.6
Blue Blood Estates (S1)	5.1
Subtotal	**86.1**
SUMMARY OF HIGH-INCOME CLUSTERS	
Educated Affluent in Suburbs (S1)	
Blue Blood Estates	5.1
Winner's Circle	5.6
Executive Suites	2.2
Pools and Patios	0.0
Kids and Culs-de-sac	0.0
Subtotal	**12.9**
Couples/Singles in Upscale White-Collar Suburbs (S2)	
Young Influentials	0.0
New Empty Nests	1.0
Boomers and Babies	0.0
Suburban Sprawl	0.0
Blue-Chip Blues	0.0
Subtotal	**1.0**
Middle-Income, Child & Post-Child Families in the Inner Suburbs (S3)	
Upstarts and Seniors	0.0
New Beginnings	0.0
Mobility Blues	0.1
Gray Collars	0.0
Subtotal	**0.1**

Cluster	Population Distribution (%) 0–10-Mile Band
Educated, White-Collar Singles & Ethnic Families in Upscale Urban Areas (U1)	
Urban Gold Coast	0.0
Money and Brains	0.0
Young Literati	0.0
American Dreams	0.0
Bohemian Mix	0.0
Subtotal	**0.0**
Educated, Young, Mobile Families in Exurban Satellites & Boom Towns (T1)	
Country Squires	0.4
God's Country	3.6
Big Fish Small Pond	0.0
Greenbelt Families	0.2
Subtotal	**4.2**
Educated, Affluent Families & Retirees in "Second Cities"/ "Edge Cities" (C1)	
Second City Elite	23.4
Upward Bound	52.0
Gray Power	0.0
Subtotal	**75.4**
Total Higher-Income Population	**93.6**

Sources: NDS/UDS Data Services and JB Research Company.

and entertainment, it is important to assess the competition in each category. This research means collecting sensitive sales information from local cinemas, restaurants, specialty retailers, game centers, nightclubs, and other categories of potential tenants.

Projects to survey include all entertainment-oriented districts and centers in the local area. Retail experience at regional malls is not relevant; however, cinema and restaurant sales at the regional mall are. More to the point, any shopping district, such as a downtown offering restaurants, bars, nightclubs, and retail, represents competition. And any recently developed retail entertainment centers are also considered competitive. Factors to research include square footage of each center, year opened, tenant list, estimated sales per square foot, rents, overages, terms, and future plans.

Estimated annual attendance at each of the projects surveyed is a key factor to research. In many cases, this figure is not known, even by the owner or operator. Estimates and sometimes educated guesses are the best one can do under these circumstances. However, the number is critical to the analysis, because it will be used to determine an array of market penetration rates upon which to base attendance at the proposed project.

A comparable project survey is given in Table 5.3-2. With the data provided in this table, per capita expenditure can be calculated, and market share for each center can also be determined. Market share analysis can be derived using demographic ring analysis, which must be ordered from a data service. (See appendix for list of sources.) These factors will be used to project attendance and per capita expenditure for The Lake at Riverdale.

For this exercise, the analyst used the *Zagat* restaurant guide, which surveys every major U.S. metropolitan area annually. Although the subject location is in the suburbs, the guide was helpful in pointing out the most popular spots. Local guides can also be purchased to identify top nightclubs, nightspots, and bars in the region.

Obtaining sales volumes at individual restaurants and retail stores is difficult, sometimes impossible. Brokers, other analysts, and knowledgeable sources can assist in identifying sales achieved in the best nightclubs and restaurants. For cinemas, movie grosses for individual locations can be purchased from Entertainment Data, Inc., Los Angeles.

Table 5.3-2
Retail Entertainment Center Experience

Center	Gross Leasable Area (Sq. Ft.)	Sales ($000)	Attendance (000,000)	Sales per Sq. Ft. ($)	Sales per Capita ($)
A	240,000	$312,000	17.0	$1,300	$18.35
B	136,100	51,000	16.1	375	3.19
C	219,000	98,600	13.0	450	7.58
D	248,000	108,800	10.0	439	10.88
E	231,200	55,700	10.3	241	5.41
F	200,000	85,500	10.5	428	8.14
G	173,400	55,000	3.8	317	14.47
H	89,000	35,500	4.8	399	7.40
I	150,000	100,000	6.0	667	16.67
J	164,000	30,000	4.0	183	7.50
K	138,000	60,000	3.0	435	20.00
L	144,000	60,300	4.0	419	15.08
M	255,000	58,000	4.0	227	14.50

Source: JB Research Company.

National and Regional Comparable Projects

For this exercise, the analyst chose four national models that have been operating for several years in the marketplace and ordered demographics of ten-mile markets for each. The results presented in Table 5.3-3 give a good background on the size and character of the primary markets of these successful centers. The smallest market surveyed includes a population of approximately 300,000. The subject market, with 450,000, is on the low side, but still within range of the comparables.

The table also provides telling data regarding income and occupational characteristics. For the most part, all of these centers have high median household incomes, high home ownership, and are extremely white collar. Comparing the subject market with the others shows that it is close to the profile of an area that can support a retail entertainment project.

Projected Attendance and Per Capita Revenue

Projected attendance at the proposed project can be derived from the data collected and analysis conducted in the supply and demand analysis. The comparables indicate penetration rates ranging from a low of 10 percent in a large urban market to a high of 400 percent in a small suburban market. The Lake is most similar to the suburban project.

The 200 to 400 percent penetration of the 25-mile radius market exhibited by the suburban projects is a function of multiple monthly visits by locals. Also responsible for this high penetration are weekly lunchtime visits from nearby office workers. Interviews of visitors at one national comparable project indicate that 25 percent of patrons returned to the project at least weekly (52 visits annually), while many only visited once or twice a year. At The Lake, cinema, retail, specialty, nightclub, restau-

Table 5.3-3

Demographic Characteristics of Retail Entertainment Center Markets

	Reston Town Center, Reston	Mizner Park, Boca Raton	Country Club Plaza, Kansas City	The Spectrum, Irvine	Main Street, Miami Lakes	The Promenade, Westlake
10-Mile Market Area						
Population (000)	482	529	786	848	1,111	295
Households (000)	175	248	333	300	384	100
Families (000)	125	150	200	585	272	76
Per Capita Income ($)	32,862	26,730	17,708	26,349	13,014	31,024
Median Household Income ($)	71,622	38,534	33,076	56,115	32,203	65,224
Average Household Income ($)	90,269	56,830	41,542	74,022	37,521	90,916
Home Ownership (percent)	72.7	73.8	59.6	61.6	58.0	76.7
Occupation, White-Collar (percent)	80.7	66.0	64.6	70.0	53.8	72.8
Median Age (years)	34.4	45.7	35.3	31.8	35.3	34.6
Racial Characteristics (percent)						
Non-Hispanic White	83.6	86.1	74.8	81.0	65.3	86.0
African-American	5.5	11.5	21.1	2.0	28.7	1.9
Asian	0.2	1.3	0.5	10.5	1.6	6.7
Hispanic Origin	6.0	6.5	5.0	26.2	46.2	13.2

Source: JB Research Company.

rants, and children's attractions will draw customers back several times each month.

Several ways exist to apply this methodology to derive a penetration rate for The Lake. First, the most comparable projects must be identified in terms of market size, character, and retail program. An average can be calculated, or data from the two most likely candidates can be averaged. This methodology generates a reasonable market penetration on which to base projections. These mathematical manipulations yield a 175 percent penetration of the 2.0 million 25-mile market, or projected annual attendance of 3.5 million.

Projected Per Capita Expenditure

Per capita expenditure is the mathematical average of the total number of visitors divided by gross revenue at comparable centers. In the demand analysis, this number was derived on the basis of estimates of attendance and gross sales. The exercise provides a range of per capita expenditures.

To choose the appropriate per capita for The Lake, it is necessary to analyze the projects with similar programs and to apply information about industry average pro-ductivity for the various tenants. An additional exercise is provided in Table 5.3-4, which applies expected sales productivities by tenant. In fact, the analysis indicates that projects with cinemas produce the highest per capitas, theoretically because they generate more activities (e.g., dinner and a movie, movie and a drink, movie and browsing at retail shops, etc.).

With the projected annual visits as high as 3.5 million and per capita expenditure at an estimated $26 annually, gross sales are projected at nearly $91 million in a stabilized year. Sales per square foot on this basis are approximately $336 including the cinema. Sales net of the cinema, which has a much lower yield than the retail and restaurant, are at $417 per square foot.

Financial Analysis—Projected Rents, EBDITA, and Return on Investment

The financial analysis at this point provides a rough estimate of the return on investment. In this case, the firm expects a 12 to 15 percent cash-on-cash return, excluding land and financing. The developer estimates hard and soft costs to be approximately $210 per square foot. Total project cost on this basis is $56.7 million.

Table 5.3-4
Estimated Gross Annual Sales, Retail Entertainment Center

Program	Sq. Ft.	Estimated Productivity	Annual Gross Revenue
Cinema	75,000	$125	$ 9,375,000
Restaurants	60,000	400	24,000,000
Retail	100,000	513	51,250,000
Nightclub	10,000	225	2,250,000
Children's Attraction	25,000	150	3,750,000
Subtotal/Average	**270,000**	**$336**	**$90,625,000**
Sales Per Square Foot, Overall			$336
Sales Per Square Foot, Net of Cinema			$417
Estimated Annual Attendance			2.5 million to 3.5 million
Estimated Per Capita Expenditure			$25.89–$36.25

Source: JB Research Company.

Retail Entertainment Center: The Lake at Riverdale *(continued)*

An estimated rent roll is given in Table 5.3-5 and assumes rents based on local, regional, and national comparables. Those rents are cross-checked with expected sales to determine affordability by the tenant. Gross rent is approximately $7.6 million, net of $6.1 million EBDITA (earnings before depreciation, interest, taxes, and amortization). Under these assumptions, return on investment is 12 percent, a moderate, but acceptable, rate of return.

The first analysis to determine return suggests that the project should continue. The relatively low return is expected to be bolstered by percentage rent collections, which will be considerable, parking subsidies from the city of Riverdale, and favorable financing.

Summary

The following assumptions and conclusions are key to understanding the market for entertainment retail:

- An identified need must exist in the marketplace for a people-gathering locale, a place to see and be seen.
- Trip motivation is recreation and entertainment, not shopping.
- The commodity sold is an experience, not a good.
- Project cost will always be higher than conventional retail.
- Sales volumes must be similar to or greater than those for a regional shopping center because of high development costs.
- Average per capita expenditure on an entertainment trip is less than half the average per capita expenditure on a shopping trip. Therefore, the center must create repeated experiences for local patrons.
- Several market segments must be identified, quantified, and qualified.
- Psychographic analysis is a requirement of the market study.
- Focus groups are necessary to test new development types.

- The supply analysis must include profiles of successful bars, restaurants, cinemas, game centers, and specialty retail locales in the market.
- Because competitive projects may not answer questions regarding performance, key competitive data may have to be interpolated or estimated.
- If entertainment retail is successful, sales will surpass a comparable model.
- Consumer safety and perception of safety are a key component of success. Convenience is also crucial.
- Return on investment may not tabulate well at first. The project often needs municipal subsidy and stores contributing overage rents to earn a healthy return.

Table 5.3-5

Stabilized Year Operating Pro Forma Retail Entertainment Center

Program	Sq. Ft.	Base Rent per Sq. Ft.	Annual Rent
Cinema	75,000	$24	$1,800,000
Restaurants	60,000	36	2,160,000
Retail	100,000	29.50	2,950,000
Nightclub	10,000	24	240,000
Children's Attraction	25,000	18	450,000
Subtotal	**270,000**		**$7,600,000**
At weighted average 8.0 vacancy non-cinema space			($464,000)
Expense: Management Fee, G & A, Other @ 7%			($532,000)
Net Operating Income			**$6,604,000**

Source: JB Research Company.

Town Center:
Wilanow, Warsaw, Poland (2000)

Anne B. Frej

Conducting market research in countries outside the United States can be tricky, especially if public sources of information are unreliable or if they provide less detail than is required to draw conclusions. In countries with newly emerging economies such as those of central Europe, historical data are also lacking because commercial real estate markets have been in existence only since the early 1990s. This case study of the Wilanow Town Center in Warsaw, Poland, illustrates the methodology used for retail research when data availability is an issue.

Project Description

The Wilanow Town Center project is planned as the heart of a new community to be developed at the southern edge of Warsaw. This large new community of 420 acres will be developed by several different companies and is anticipated to include a mix of uses including low-density residential neighborhoods, shopping facilities, offices, and public facilities. The master plan places a major focus on leisure activities with plans for a skating rink, water features, and open space areas. At buildout, the community is expected to house a population of 10,000 to 15,000 residents. The retail and entertainment components are estimated to attract 8 million to 12 million off-site visitors per year.

The Wilanow Town Center to be developed by IDM encompasses about 27.1 acres and is planned to include a variety of complementary uses. The shopping center component of the project will include a hypermarket, a two-level shopping gallery, a multiplex cinema, and a food court, with a total area of around 914,962 square feet. Completion is expected by December 2003. Given the wide variety, high quality, and large size of its retail and entertainment offerings, the development is planned to serve local residents as well as the wider market of the surrounding areas.

The developer, IDM, is headquartered in Warsaw, Poland. IDM invests in, develops, leases, and manages urban retail centers and larger retail mall projects throughout central Europe. The principals of IDM have worked in the region since 1989 on a variety of real estate projects supported by European institutional investors.

In May 2000, the Real Estate Consulting Services Group of Arthur Andersen in Warsaw completed a market feasibility analysis for the proposed shopping center for the Wilanow Town Center. The purpose of the study was to provide an objective assessment of the project for IDM's internal decision-making team. Data on the estimated market area's spending power and resulting figures for supportable floor space were used by the company as a guide in determining the optimum project size and mix of uses.

Site Assessment

The site is located in the Wilanow area, a prestigious and wealthier-than-average residential district characterized by high-end single-family homes, parks, and historical monuments, including the Wilanow Royal Palace. This baroque palace and park, originally established in the 17th century and rebuilt after World War II, is located only a few blocks from the proposed development site and plays an important role in all planning and design decisions for the project.

The main advantages of the shopping center site include the positive image of the surrounding neighborhood and excellent access to the center of Warsaw, several miles to the north. Many shoppers in Warsaw, as in other cities of central Europe, tend to use public transit in the form of buses and trams because car ownership is still relatively low. Therefore, an assessment of public transportation service and frequencies is an important component to a shopping center market analysis.

Analysis indicates that site disadvantages include the low-density character of the surrounding area, the lack of existing infrastructure, and possible constraints to future development because of the presence of protected areas such as parks and forests in the immediate area. These disadvantages were examined in depth to determine how they would affect project feasibility.

Existing master plans and zoning regulations are purposely quite general in Warsaw. Therefore, interviews with local authorities are often the best way to obtain up-to-date information on planning regulations and infrastructure improvements affecting a project. Interviews with local officials and planning staff, as well as staff of various transportation-related authorities, reveal important information about the future development opportunities in the surrounding area. The schedule for a proposed sewage treatment plant was one of the most important questions to be answered because it significantly affects the growth potential of the entire area. The schedule for construction of a major bridge over the Vistula River was also crucial to ascertain because it could greatly facilitate access for households living in areas to the east.

Defining the Market Area

Market areas were defined for the proposed shopping center on the basis of drive times to the site, population concentrations, physical features, competing retail schemes, and local shopping patterns. The primary market area surrounding the site was estimated to encompass populations within a 12- to 15-minute drive of the site. The secondary market area was defined as populations within a 15- to 20-minute driving radius of the site. Because of strong competition from two existing shopping centers, the subject's west and southwest borders were not expected to extend significantly beyond the primary market area.

Base data on market-area populations were obtained from 1999 government statistics for the subareas of Warsaw known as *gminas*. *Gmina* data provide the smallest population breakdowns possible, but unless their boundaries coincide with market area's boundaries, which is unlikely, subarea populations must be estimated by other means. At the simplest level, such methods can include visual surveys to estimate the percentage of the population of the area that is included within the market-area boundaries. No age breakdown or income data are available for subareas; they must be extrapolated from citywide data.

Population projections for city subareas may also be unavailable or unreliable in countries outside the United States or western Europe. In the case of the proposed shopping center at the Wilanow Town Center, this information was considered crucial to a realistic determination of the future feasibility of the project. The surrounding market area of the project is still relatively unpopulated but could

grow dramatically in the future. To estimate population growth up to 2003, when the shopping center is planned to enter the market, the consultants projected growth trends on the basis of land availability, residential densities allowable under current zoning, and proposed infrastructure plans. They conducted interviews with planning authorities of the relevant subareas, as well as with residential developers active in the area.

As a result, the consultants determined that the primary market area would grow to approximately 270,000 people in 2002, whereas the secondary market area would grow to 416,000 people by that year. For the longer-term period 2003 to 2007, the primary market area was estimated to grow by some 50,000 people. This figure was recognized as highly speculative and dependent upon public and private investment in infrastructure, but it was considered a useful estimate for general planning purposes. For example, in Wilanow, the population is expected to grow significantly after the local sewage system is upgraded and important arterial streets are improved, but the exact timing for those improvements is uncertain. In other parts of the market area, growth potential will be limited by decreasing availability of land and local plans that restrict the density of new residential developments.

Spending Potential

On the basis of government statistics for the city of Warsaw, the average annual per capita expenditure for residents of the primary and secondary market areas was estimated at $3,300 in the year 2002. Of this total sum, the expenditures on shopping center–type goods were estimated at $2,046. These citywide figures were recognized as potentially conservative for the residents of the more affluent Wilanow area; however, no indicators were available from which to make a more reliable determination of income within the market areas.

Breakdowns of expenditures by category (such as food, fashion, and entertainment) were based on official statistics for Warsaw and Poland as a whole. The data were collected by household surveys dating from 1997;

therefore, adjustments were necessary to take into account recent changes in shopping patterns. It was recognized that since 1997 Poland has moved closer to the norms in other European countries because of growth in the proportion of expenditures on clothing, household goods, and leisure activities relative to spending on food.

The total market-area expenditure on shopping center–type goods (the amount of expenditures available to retailers in the area) was calculated by multiplying the number of residents by expenditures per capita within the primary and secondary market areas. This figure is estimated at $555,591,300 for the primary market area and $851,197,380 for the secondary market area.

To estimate the share of expenditures that could be captured by the proposed shopping center, the consultant analyzed a number of factors, including the size and character of the proposed center, existing and proposed competition, access to the site, and European industry norms. The estimates for market share for the primary market area ranged from 10 percent for restaurants and 15 percent for food to 40 percent for clothing and footwear. As is typical in any region, capture rates for the secondary market area were much lower because of retail competition and greater distance to the site for shoppers within that area. The capture rates used in this analysis are relatively high compared to those used in similar analyses in the United States because they take into consideration the lack of competition and lower opportunities for growth that cause Poland's relatively low ratio of modern shopping space per capita. As a result of these calculations, the total captured market expenditure expected for the center from both the primary and secondary market areas was determined to be $226,800,668.

Estimating Supportable Floor Space

To determine the amount of floor space that could be supported at the new shopping center, Arthur Andersen divided the figure for captured market expenditure by estimates of turnover (sales per square meter) for categories such as food or clothing. These figures are crucial to a realistic analysis but are extremely difficult

to quantify in an immature market. In Poland, no published sources exist, and retailers, both local and international, are very reluctant to reveal sales data. In the United States, in contrast, these data are readily available (ULI's *Dollars & Cents of Shopping Centers*® is one example). To estimate turnover, the analysts interviewed a variety of retailers active in the Warsaw market and compared these data to norms in the United States, Great Britain, and Germany to come up with estimates for Poland. On the basis of these assumptions, they further estimated that the total potential supportable gross leasable floor space for the proposed Wilanow Town Center Shopping Center was 895,000 square feet.

The breakdown by category is shown graphically in Figure 5.4-1.

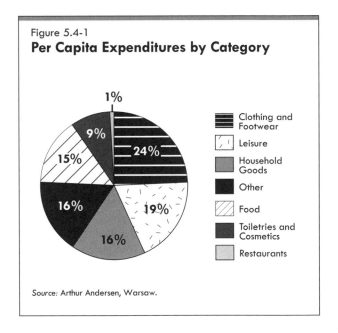

Figure 5.4-1
Per Capita Expenditures by Category

Source: Arthur Andersen, Warsaw.

Supply Analysis

An analysis of Poland's retail market provided useful background information and a basis for projecting future trends. Poland's retail market has undergone substantial changes in recent years, particularly in the larger urban areas. From just a small number of state-owned and small

Wilanow Town Center, Warsaw, Poland.

private enterprises at the beginning of the 1990s, the country's retail inventory has grown to encompass a rapidly increasing number of domestic and international retailers.

Poland's first phase of retail development in the early 1990s focused on supermarkets. This trend continues today because Polish consumers still spend a high percentage of their overall expenditures on food (33%). Most of the recently constructed shopping centers throughout the country feature a supermarket or hypermarket as the anchor store. The next generation of retail developments, including the proposed Wilanow Town Center, will feature a smaller proportion of food offerings and more choices for comparison shopping and entertainment.

Warsaw's total retail inventory stands at about 3.7 million square feet, but less than 20 percent of this can be considered modern shopping center space suitable for international retailers. About the same amount is made up of hypermarkets, which focus on food items in addition to a range of consumer durables and clothing.

An undersupply of good-quality retail space has meant that vacancy rates at shopping centers have remained at less than 5 percent in recent years. But starting in 2000, the amount of new space entering the market began to show a large increase.

Competitive Analysis

On the basis of an analysis of existing and proposed shopping centers in Warsaw, the most direct competition to the proposed Wilanow Town Center was projected to come from Galeria Mokotow, a 516,684-square-foot shopping center scheduled to open in 2000. As illustrated in Figure 5.4-2, other potential retail centers are not competitive because they are smaller scale, farther than ten or 15 minutes drive from the site, or unlikely to proceed in the near term.

Because of its potential competitiveness to Wilanow Town Center, Galeria Mokotow was analyzed in greater detail than other existing and proposed retail facilities

identified in Warsaw. This center is located approximately 12 minutes drive from the project site, so the primary market areas for the two overlap slightly.

Galeria Mokotow entered the market in late 2000. As the first example of the second generation of shopping centers in Warsaw, it features a supermarket and various fashion and home anchor tenants rather than the earlier format of one major hypermarket and a limited range of smaller shops. The project leased quickly in the months before its completion, and it achieved higher-than-expected rents.

Although Galeria Mokotow had the advantage of entering the market several years before Wilanow Town Center, it was not expected to have a significant effect on the proposed project. Wilanow Town Center is planned as a major regional shopping center that will be able to take advantage of its location in a larger new community with on-site residents, daytime office workers, and leisure uses that will be able to attract shoppers from a wide area.

Conclusions

Market-area analysis indicates that more than sufficient spending power exists in the primary and secondary market areas to support a major retail center of approximately 861,000 square feet at the Wilanow Town Center. In its early years of operation, it will be important for the center to capture expenditures from the densely populated neighborhoods to the west and north of the site.

After 2005 to 2007, the population of the primary market area is likely to grow significantly because of the expected completion of infrastructure improvements that will encourage new residential development. In addition, the completion of a new bridge across the Vistula River and improvement of new roads serving the Wilanow area will facilitate access to the site from locations to the east and could increase the size of the secondary market area. The acquisition of additional land should be considered for expansion of the retail and leisure uses at the center several years after it opens.

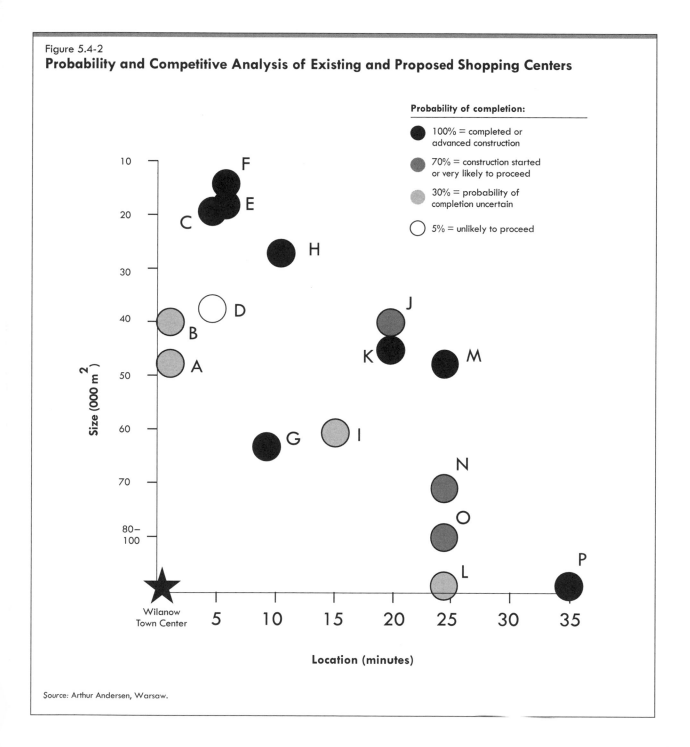

Figure 5.4-2
Probability and Competitive Analysis of Existing and Proposed Shopping Centers

Probability of completion:

● 100% = completed or advanced construction

● 70% = construction started or very likely to proceed

● 30% = probability of completion uncertain

○ 5% = unlikely to proceed

Size (000 m²)

Location (minutes)

Wilanow Town Center

Source: Arthur Andersen, Warsaw.

Marriott Wardman Park Hotel, Washington, D.C.

Chapter 6
Hotels and Resorts

The success of a hotel depends on the developer's and the operator's understanding of the dynamics of each segment of market demand. Equally important is an understanding of consumer trends such as the demographics and values that influence demand within each market segment. An accurate hotel market analysis calls for a close look at (1) the location of the subject site with regard to market demand generators such as tourist attractions, (2) the growth of business demand within the market area, (3) the sources and strengths of transient travel, (4) the location of competitive properties and their physical and operational characteristics, (5) current and future travel patterns, and (6) special local conditions and trends.

Increasingly, hotel demand is dependent on convention and meeting business, plus tourists' ability to easily obtain information and reservations. Affinity clubs, like Hilton Honors and Starwood Preferred Guest, are very important in building brand loyalty.

Product Types

Hotel development has followed paths taken by other types of commercial real estate in the United States. In the first half of the 20th century, most hotel development occurred in downtown areas where most office and retail development was also taking place. Then, highways began to change development patterns and demand for hotel rooms accompanied the outward movement of offices, stores, and residences. Today the trend is reversing somewhat, with downtowns being reinvigorated and again attracting new

commercial, institutional, and residential development, thus renewing demand for downtown hotels.

Beginning in the 1970s, hotel product became more segmented and specialized as developers and operators attempted to define more narrowly their potential markets and to develop facilities targeted specifically at those markets. The two principal methods of classifying hotels are by location (downtown, airport, resort) and by the market niches they serve. Hotels are probably more accurately described on the basis of markets served than by locations, which have blurred somewhat because of urban sprawl and evolving land use patterns.

Locationally, the primary distinction is downtown hotel versus suburban hotel. Other frequently used categories include airport hotels (those located on airport grounds or near airports) and highway hotels (those located outside city or suburban nodes along travel routes). Classifiers sometimes include resort as a locational category, but the term "resort" more accurately refers to the facility's amenities than to its location. Resort hotels can be located almost anywhere, but the vast majority are found in either waterfront or mountain locations.

Some major niche hotel categories are described in the following sections. It is important for market analysts to understand that most hotels appeal to overlapping market segments and to delineate each of those segments when assessing a property's market potential.

Convention Hotels

Probably the best-known type, the downtown convention hotel generally contains 400 to 500 rooms and considerable banquet and meeting space. In many cases, convention hotels are physically connected with or adjacent to large convention centers. They usually include several eating establishments of varying styles and price ranges. Many also include substantial amounts of retail space.

Convention hotels generally feature large lobbies to handle the check-in and checkout functions that occur in a concentrated period at the beginning and end of every convention. It is common for up to 10 percent of the guest rooms to be suites. Guests can use the living rooms of the suites as hospitality rooms, or the hotel can furnish them as meeting spaces for small groups. Many convention hotels have set aside concierge floors for valued patrons or for those paying higher rates. With controlled access, concierge floors offer separate check-in areas, lounges, extra in-room amenities, and complimentary snacks, beverages, and services.

Luxury Hotels

Luxury hotels tend to be located in large metropolitan areas, places frequented by visitors willing to pay a premium price for accommodations. Most have fewer than 300 rooms, and the few larger luxury hotels tend to cater more to corporate travelers and overseas visitors. Such hotels are distinguished by high-quality furnishings, amenities, and services. Many, but not all, house fine restaurants. Their high ratio of employees to guest rooms affects the economics of operations. Although luxury hotels may accommodate some meeting and banquet business, they do not target large groups.

Commercial Hotels

Commercial hotels are generally smaller than convention hotels, offering between 100 and 500 guest rooms. Although meetings may represent an important part of their business, the groups that are served generally are smaller than those using convention hotels. Compared with convention hotels, most commercial hotels provide less public space and a less-extensive array of food and beverage outlets.

Budget/Economy Facilities

At the opposite end of the spectrum are the economy hotels, which go by many names, including budget, hard budget, limited service, and economy. Hotels at this level are a response to the emergence of more value-conscious travelers in the late 1970s and 1980s,

when many businesses began to control travel expenditures more carefully. At the same time, tourist travel expanded rapidly, but much of the growth came from a price-sensitive portion of the market.

The first economy hotels were built along highways outside metropolitan areas, on inexpensive land. They have since moved into suburban areas, airports, and even some downtowns. The original economy properties were one- and two-story structures with exterior corridors. Generally, they contained 50 to 150 rooms.

The economy hotel offers limited services, and average room rates are typically 20 to 50 percent below the rates of full-service facilities in the same area. Economy hotels usually do not have restaurants or banquet space, recreational facilities, or many other amenities found in more traditional hotels. The economy segment of hotel chains has expanded greatly since 1970. That year, only half a dozen chains operated fewer than 200 budget hotels. By 2000, more than 40 chains operated more than 9,200 budget properties. The segment has diversified as well, and it now offers at least three separate tiers of product:

- Upper Tier. Hotels at the high end of the budget segment offer more upscale furnishings and decor, and generally charge rates closer to market-area averages. These hotels are generally larger—usually more than 100 rooms. Though the guest rooms are small, the level of quality is often close to that of commercial hotels.
- Middle Tier. Mid-economy hotels generally have 60 to 125 guest rooms and charge rates that are usually 25 to 40 percent below the rates of full-service hotels. Their corridors can be either external or internal.
- Lower Tier. Economy hotels at the lower end have room rates that are about 50 percent below market. They generally have 50 to 125 modestly furnished rooms and exterior corridors.

Economy properties tend to operate at higher occupancy levels than do full-service hotels, and they achieve income-to-expense ratios that are significantly higher as a consequence of lower staffing requirements and the lack of food and beverage facilities, the latter of which generally operate at fairly low profit margins.

All-Suite or Residence Hotels

All-suite hotels came into existence as a separate category in the 1970s. Their guest spaces are larger than normal (usually containing more than 500 square feet) and have a living area separate from the bedroom. Some all-suite facilities offer a compact, or even full-scale, kitchen.

The all-suite hotel was developed to meet the needs of business travelers who spend a lot of time on the road and long-stay guests like corporate personnel who are relocating or consultants who are on a project that will last some time. Many leisure travelers, especially families, also find these facilities desirable. This product category varies widely from property to property. Still, all-suite hotels generally take one of three basic forms:

1. Urban. Urban all-suite hotels are usually mid- to high-rise structures containing 200 to 300 suites, a size generally considered small enough to retain a residential atmosphere and large enough to provide the desired level of service.
2. Suburban. Usually found in areas containing a concentration of office buildings, such as edge cities or built-up highway corridors, suburban all-suite hotels generally have four to eight stories.
3. Residential. In contrast, residential all-suite hotels usually occupy two-story structures and resemble apartment complexes more closely than hotels. Guest spaces are large, with separate living and sleeping areas, full kitchens, exterior entrances, and a variety of amenities and services. As long-stay hotels strive to become more homelike, the line between hotels and apartment properties has blurred. Residential all-suite facilities usually attract guests who stay longer and, because of the higher occupancies and smaller staffing needs attributable to low guest turnover, they are often more profitable than regular hotels.

Executive Conference Centers

Although many hotels market themselves as conference centers, truly dedicated conference centers are designed to provide a setting free of distractions for executive and professional meetings. Usually located in rural areas or in suburban office communities near major metropolitan areas, they combine meeting and conference facilities with lodging in a way that can accommodate groups in a self-contained learning environment.

Conference centers usually contain 200 to 400 guest rooms and a large number of dedicated conference and meeting rooms. They provide a carefully designed and more or less isolated learning environment, with comfortable seating, suitable lighting, audiovisual equipment, conference support services,

and living and recreational facilities to occupy the hours when conferences are not in session. The food offered is typically of a sufficient quality and variety to make leaving the facility unnecessary. Conference centers offer more extensive recreational facilities than those in traditional hotels. In most cases, occupancy by transient guests is a relatively small part of the operations.

Resort Hotels

Resort hotels cater to both vacation travelers and meetings or conferences. The emphasis is on recreational amenities both on site and off. A resort hotel might feature golf, water sports, skiing, or health spa facilities. Resort hotels have been built in conjunction with theme parks, casinos, and other attractions.

Resort hotels usually include a range of restaurants and meeting and banquet space. Depending on the climate of the resort area, lodging demand may be prone to seasonality, with distinct peak and off-peak periods. Peak periods generally yield maximum published room rates and high occupancy levels. In contrast, off-peak periods are characterized by lower published room rates and reduced occupancy levels. In certain market areas, intermediate periods marked by moderate demand are referred to as "shoulder seasons."

Other Hotel Products

The catalog of hotel products contains some other noteworthy entries. Mom-and-pop hotels usually are fairly small, older motels often located along older highways. B&Bs (bed-and-breakfasts) are usually small inns (fewer than 20 rooms) that are heavy on charm and provide breakfast as part of the room price. Boutique hotels are small, mostly urban hotels (usually fewer than 125 rooms) that cater to upscale clientele desiring a high degree of luxury and personalized service. Condominium hotels offer hotel services and amenities within a condominium ownership structure, usually a timeshare.

A hotel might serve more than one market segment, increasing its potential and making the project less susceptible to market downturns. However, broadening the target market might cause an increase in competition from other hotels. It might also weaken the product's appeal to those originally targeted. Some examples of crossover niches include amusement park hotels, such as those at Disney World, combining family entertainment with conference business, or Las Vegas casino hotels, combining adult-style entertainment with family-oriented activities. In many cases, convention business overlaps with other market segments.

Hotel Market Analysis

Hotel market analysis is similar to that for other product types in terms of the basic methodology. However, some important differences exist. Hotel demand is not generated by the hotel itself, in most cases, but by local businesses, convention facilities, tourist attractions, and other draws that bring travelers to a location. These demand generators must be understood to properly analyze the hotel market. Unlike other kinds of real estate, which respond to relatively local demand, hotels cater to patrons from outside the local area.

Determining the Market Area

For most types of real estate development, the market areas for supply and demand are either identical or overlapping. For hotel development, however, the two market areas are distinctly different, sometimes varying greatly in location and size. For example, the competitive supply for a convention hotel is the inventory of hotels with a similar price range and location in relation to the local convention center. The market area might encompass a ten-minute walking distance from the subject site. But the demand for lodging might come from a national or even an international base of convention travelers. A beach resort hotel with a regional draw would compete with similarly priced and amenitized hotels along the same strip of beachfront. Patrons might be drawn from a nearby metropolitan area or from several surrounding states.

To determine the boundaries of the market area, the analyst needs to identify (1) the location of competitive hotels, (2) the segmentation and origination of the facilities' major sources of business, (3) the trends in travel patterns for vacation, commercial, and convention visitors to the proposed site, (4) the proximity and scope of major demand generators, (5) the expenditure patterns of area visitors, and (6) existing socioeconomic boundaries. For a business hotel, a generator would be business and commercial centers, whereas for a resort hotel, the generators would be nearby theme parks, ski slopes, beaches or lakes, golf courses, sports facilities, and the like. The sources of demand for a resort lodging facility may be segmented into three major categories, which, in descending order of importance, include vacation or pleasure travelers, convention travelers, and commercial travelers. The following methodology is useful in identifying and assessing the sources of lodging demand:

- Interview representatives from the local tourist and convention bureaus and chambers of commerce to identify the number, length of stay, expenditure patterns, typical group size, lodging demand, and seasonality of tourists and convention delegates. (Note that these agencies sometimes overstate tourist statistics. In addition, they frequently do not maintain a research program that adequately quantifies travel patterns.)

- Interview corporate travel officers, meeting planners, association executives, wholesale tour operators, travel agents, brokers specializing in group or corporate travel, incentive-travel organizers, and spokespersons for travel clubs in feeder cities. Determine their clients' lodging needs, perception of the area, frequency of visits to the area, primary reasons for visiting, typical group size, and seasonality of travel plans. Find out their clients' views of the competitive strengths and weaknesses of existing properties in the subject area and other market areas, the services and amenities they seek, the magnitude of their typical lodging budgets, their future travel plans, and their perceptions of the need for additional local lodging facilities.

- Conduct an occupancy and room rate survey, or purchase data from a hotel association or consultants such as PKF. Examine trends over the last three to five years.

- Identify and speak with officials of comparable hotels to determine their properties' number of guest rooms, average annual occupancy, average annual room rate, market mix of guests, and type and class of facilities. If no comparable properties exist in the market area, locate similar facilities in nearby market areas and then adjust the associated data for the subject location.

- Assess existing capacity and arrival and departure patterns at the major airport within the market area and then determine the mix, seasonality, and growth rate in the number of airport passengers. Data on airline arrivals must be adjusted to reflect stopovers at hub airports.

- List the major tourist attractions, community special events, regional and state fairs or expositions, athletic events, and the like, and determine their typical needs for lodging facilities. Interview attraction or event organizers, hotel operators, tourist bureaus, and others.

The market analyses for roadside motels are approached differently. Such properties, typically located at highway interchanges, serve as a convenience for travelers making an overnight stop on their way elsewhere. For that product type, analysis based on traffic counts usually suffices. Major motel chains typically devise rules of thumb for estimating the minimum number of vehicles required for a new hotel outlet. They also tabulate the inventory of surrounding uses that are desirable amenities for the proposed motel.

Demand Segments

In general, market segments are defined in terms of purpose of trip, seasonality, length of stay, price sensitivity, the nature of the facilities and amenities required, and the number of rooms required. In measuring demand, analysts used to consider that people traveled for only two purposes: business or pleasure. But today, marketers identify more specific purposes for travel. Is the business traveler on his or her own or attending a conference? Is the conference a training meeting or an executive retreat? Is the business traveler attending a trade show or convention? Is the pleasure traveler part of a tour group or traveling independently? Is the visitor from the United States or abroad? Is this stop the final destination or part of an extended trip? The responses to such questions help define the distinct demand segments available to a hotel. Some of the major demand segments are described as follows:

■ Commercial Market. The commercial market segment, made up of individuals and groups of both domestic and international business travelers, typically represents a major source of demand for downtown and suburban hotels and a minor source for resorts. Business travelers include managers at all levels, sales representatives, official trainees, and recruits. A crucial criterion in the selection of lodging facilities is location. Primary locational considerations include proximity to centers of business activity and ease of access to and from airports. The typical length of stay is approximately one to two days with demand typically concentrated on Monday through Thursday nights. In some markets, particularly resort areas, however, some commercial visitors extend their stay through the weekend to enjoy the resort and its amenities. Seasonality and price sensitivity are limited concerns. Within the commercial travel sector, further delineations can be made.

♦ Corporate/Commercial Individuals. This demand segment consists of individuals whose purpose is related solely or predominantly to their jobs or businesses.

♦ Corporate Groups. This segment is distinguished from the corporate individual segment by virtue of its booking rooms on a block basis. The specific purpose of travel is likely to be a company-sponsored meeting or training session in the hotel or at a nearby location. Because of the nature of the clientele and the source of business, room rates for this segment are negotiated and specify the number of rooms booked and the time of year that the rooms are available.

♦ Convention and Association Groups. Conventions and association meetings can have thousands of attendees, many of whom travel as corporate groups or book rooms on a block basis through the sponsoring organization. A major trend in the operation of resort hotels has been the marked shift to conference business as one of the principal contributors, if not the principal contributor, to resort occupancy. Although a limited number of resort hotels rely almost entirely on occupancy by independent travelers, most have mounted major efforts to attract conferences and business meetings as an economic necessity. For most large resort hotels, between 45 and 70 percent of occupancy now takes the form of group business.[1]

■ Tourists and Leisure Travelers. This demand segment encompasses most pleasure travelers and includes many family groups. Double or higher occupancy of rooms is common. Travel tends to occur at peak periods of demand. Lengths of stay vary widely from single-night stopovers a day's drive from home to vacations lasting a week or longer at a resort thousands of miles from home. Market segments include the free independent traveler (FIT) market, the group market, and the wholesale market.

♦ FIT Market. The FIT market segment consists of destination tourists and other transient travelers. Destination tourists represent visitors who have selected a vacation destination and arranged for their accommodations either directly with the hotel or through a travel agent. Because individuals book their own accommodations, little or no discounting is available beyond that offered to affinity club members.

A range of sight-seeing opportunities and on-premises recreational amenities and facilities, such as beach frontage, casino gaming, swimming pools, tennis courts, and golf courses, attracts the FIT segment. In addition, a strategic location near recreational and entertainment centers, such as theme parks, world-class golf courses, snow-skiing areas, watersports venues, shopping opportunities, cultural activities, or spectator sports facilities, can be important in effectively marketing to the FIT segment. Peak seasons and weekends account for significant FIT demand. The FIT market encompasses many demographic subsegments, including singles, couples, and families—all in a variety of price ranges.

◆ Wholesale Market. The wholesale market segment extends to tourists who purchase discount packages that include any combination of hotel, airfare, food and beverage, automobile rental, tours, and discounts at retail outlets. Travel agents and tour operators, the primary vendors of discount packages, typically negotiate room rates with a range of properties on an annual basis. The negotiations specify the number of rooms booked and the time of year that the rooms are available. Accordingly, room rates are generally much lower relative to other demand segments.

Discount packages are popular, particularly among European tourists, because of the assurance that travelers' full range of needs will be addressed without unexpected expenses. Some consumers purchase discount packages based on the price/value relationship while others like the convenience of making a single purchase for all their vacation needs. Wholesale travelers are generally extremely price sensitive and therefore tend to travel during off-peak seasons. As with the FIT market segment, the wholesale market segment looks for the availability of a range of on-premises recreational amenities and facilities coupled with a strategic location near recreational and entertainment centers.

■ Other Kinds of Stays. In addition to the major demand segments, the following niches can be identified:

◆ Long-Term Guests. Hotels can serve as temporary residences for executives, corporate employees, or others who have relocated to an area and need lodging until they can make permanent living arrangements. They can house consultants, auditors, or other workers assigned to projects lasting several weeks or months. Families often accompany relocating employees. Increasingly, lodging facilities that specialize in longer stays, such as Residence Inn and Extended Stay America, are filling this need.

◆ Contract Demand. Airlines contract with hotels for crew lodging and emergency housing for stranded travelers. They typically reserve a block of rooms for this purpose and negotiate a very low rate. Businesses with employees who travel to perform low-budget jobs also frequently negotiate contract rates with hotels, which usually are heavily discounted. Construction crews, disaster relief workers, and truck drivers are typical kinds of contract guests.

◆ Government and Military Personnel. Government workers and members of the military travel with generally modest per diems and thus tend to strongly prefer low-rate rooms. They gravitate to establishments that offer special discounts to government and military personnel.

◆ Getaway Guests. Downtown and suburban hotels catering to weekday corporate guests pioneered the getaway concept to bolster sagging weekend occupancies. The practice has been adopted by virtually all nonresort hotels. Typically, guests are offered a package plan that includes the room, some meals, entertainment of some sort, and other perks. Rates often are discounted substantially.

Fluctuations in Demand

Nationally, annual room occupancy averages in the 65 percent range,[2] but varies considerably by region, season, and product type. Of all demand characteristics, fluctuation in demand is the one most frequently overlooked. In a sense, the guest rooms and space that a hotel offers are perishable commodities. One day's nonsales cannot be made up at a later date. A careful analysis of demand trends for each segment of the market for a specific project permits a realistic projection of annual occupancy. Commercial travel remains relatively constant throughout the year, whereas the volume of pleasure travel changes with the seasons, peaking in the summer quarter when many families take vacations.

In the United States overall, August is the month of peak hotel demand. June is usually second, followed by October, a popular month for meetings and conventions. The demand for hotel rooms reaches its lowest point in December, when business travel declines because of the holiday season.

Seasonal profiles for particular geographic areas tend to be weather related. The seasonal fluctuations

Table 6-1

Top Hotel Market Performers: 2000

Highest Occupancy Rate (Percent)		Highest Average Room Rate	
San Francisco	88.3	New York	$180
Seattle	87.6	San Francisco	150
Boston	86.8	Boston	146
New York	86.5	Chicago	118
San Diego	85.7	San Diego	116
Minneapolis/St. Paul	82.3	Oahu	115
Anaheim-Santa Ana	81.5	New Orleans	109
Denver	80.7	Philadelphia	107
Chicago	78.8	Washington	107
Los Angeles/Long Beach	78.6	Seattle	105
Oahu	78.2	Los Angeles/Long Beach	104
Norfolk/Virginia Beach	77.3	Miami	102
Orlando	74.7	New Orleans	89
Washington	74.7	Norfolk/Virginia Beach	89
Miami	70.3	Anaheim/Santa Ana	88

Source: Smith Travel Research, *Lodging Outlook,* October 2000.

in demand in some resort destinations are so extreme that some hotels stay open for only part of the year. Rocky Mountain ski lodges and New England shore resorts are highly seasonal, for example. But the purely seasonal resort has become a rarity today. Some resorts have successfully made the transition from seasonal to year-round operations by identifying market segments that could be attracted in their off-seasons. For example, ski resorts have added recreational amenities to attract summer tourists. Others have pursued group meetings business for the non-ski season.

Measuring Demand

Knowing the demand segmentation and seasonal patterns for the demand in a given market is the beginning. But the analyst must evaluate the potential for a new hotel's projected demand based on population growth, new commercial or industrial development, new tourist attractions or recreational development, changes in transportation networks, and new competitive—or synergistic—lodging facilities.

Demand is affected by many factors. Growth or decline in the supply of competitive hotel rooms, shifts in market segmentation, and renovation or repositioning of competitive hotels all affect demand. Analysis must include historical market performance

as well as solid forecasts of the supply of competitive hotel rooms and the demand for rooms by market segment. Research should include an analysis of whether the target market is able and willing to pay the room rates projected and an analysis of what target hotel guests want in terms of facilities, design, amenities, and services.

In assessing the market for an existing hotel, two key measurements are its penetration and yield. A hotel's "penetration" is its share of demand (occupied rooms) in relation to its share of supply (available rooms). Table 6-2 provides an example of the penetration and yield analysis for an existing 300-room hotel being considered for purchase. It presents a picture of the historical and projected performance of the competitive market for the subject hotel and its performance within the market. In 1998, for example, the subject hotel's share of demand was 17.46 percent (165 ÷ 945), and its share of supply was 20.0 percent (300 ÷ 1,500). Thus, its penetration was 87.3 percent (17.46 ÷ 20.0). Comparing the property's occupancy rates with the overall market rates is another method for calculating penetration (55 ÷ 63 = 87.3 percent). Penetration rates are useful for determining whether a hotel is performing up to its potential, and whether its performance has improved or slipped in relation to the overall market.

A hotel's "yield" in this analysis is its revenue per available room (revPAR) divided by the market's revPAR. It reflects the property's relative position in terms of occupancy and room rate. RevPAR is derived by multiplying the average daily room rate[3] by the occupancy percentage. In 1998, the yield for the subject property was 70.6 percent ($53.35 ÷ $75.60) based on its $53.35 revPAR ($97 × .55) and the market's $75.60 revPAR ($120 × .63).

The table shows strong growth in demand over the past several years in this market area. Demand is projected to grow at more modest levels over the next several years, with the exception of 2002 when a new hotel will be added to the market. New hotels in strong markets often create demand (supply-induced demand) or accommodate previously unsatisfied demand. The average room rate has grown modestly, a trend that is projected to continue except while new supply is being absorbed.

Demand may shift because of developments in transportation, technology, or environment. A thriving motel corridor might decline when a new highway replaces an existing one. Hotels adjacent to a convention center might become locationally less desirable when a new convention center is built, even if the new center is only a few blocks away. New tech-

Table 6-2

Penetration and Yield for a 300-Room Hotel

| Year | Average Daily Rooms | | | | Occupancy Rate (%) | | Average Daily Room Rate | | Performance of Subject | |
| | Available | | Occupied | | | | | | | |
	Market	Subject	Market	Subject	Market	Subject	Market	Subject	Penetration[1]	Yield[2]
1998	1,500	300	945	165	63	55	$120	$97	87.3%	70.6%
1999	1,500	300	1,005	168	67	56	123	97	83.6%	65.6%
2000	1,500	300	1,065	174	71	58	125	97	81.7%	63.4%
projected										
2001	1,500	300	1,097	—	73	—	128	—	—	—
2002	1,650	300	1,163	—	71	—	128	—	—	—
2003	1,700	300	1,186	—	70	—	130	—	—	—
2004	1,700	300	1,210	—	71	—	136	—	—	—

[1]The hotel's share of demand (occupied rooms) divided by its share of supply (available rooms).
[2]The hotel's revPAR (revenue per available room) divided by the market's revPAR.

nologies may eventually make business travel obsolete, although such predictions have yet to materialize. Miami Beach is an example of a thriving tourist destination that went through a long decline and then rebounded when the historic architecture of South Beach became a new draw for tourism. Today, old hotels are being restored, new ones are being built, and room rates and occupancy rates are soaring.

Demand Generators

The link between new commercial, industrial, recreational, or transportation development and increased hotel demand is fairly direct and easy to quantify. More difficult to project is supply-induced demand, which is the new room demand that can emerge simply because a new lodging facility opens that meets some previously untapped market. Room demand is affected not only by local, regional, and sometimes national economic trends, but also by hotel marketing strategies and changes in the competitive supply of hotel rooms.

Business and leisure travel are both tied closely to the health of the economy. When analysts project lodging demand potential, they must analyze the market's economic and demographic trends. A review of various economic and demographic data can provide evidence on whether the economy of a specific market area will grow, stabilize, or decline. The analyst should focus on the most relevant economic data to the subject property. Not all trends need to be examined for every market study. The following economic indicators might be considered as part of the hotel market analysis.

- Employment. The characteristics of an area's workforce and employment data by establishment provide an indication of the performance of the local economy and of the type and amount of room demand it may generate.
- Office and industrial space. Data on the amount, vacancy rates, and rental rates of a market's office and industrial space are useful measures of its potential.
- Income. A market's income levels are a good indicator of its demand potential. The amount of disposable income available determines how much spending can be devoted to leisure travel.
- Retail sales. Analysts use retail sales data to gauge the purchasing power of both visitors and residents.
- Attendance at major attractions. Historic and projected attendance figures by local or out-of-town origin of the visitors for demand generators such as theme parks, convention centers, and other attractions are valuable for determining potential demand for lodging.
- Airport activity. Reflecting both local business activity and the overall economic health of a market, airport passenger volumes and other data on airport activity can be good indicators of current and potential lodging demand.

- Hotel operating trends. Trends and projections of hotel operating statistics are clearly an important market indicator.
- Travel spending. Expenditures for travel are another good indicator of current and potential room demand. However, local data are not usually available.

Competitive Supply

An analysis of the inventory of the existing and proposed competitive lodging supply in the market area helps predict the likely success of a new lodging facility. For each existing and proposed facility that, because of its location, size, and room rate, will compete with the subject hotel, the analyst should quantify the number of rooms, location, affiliation (chain or independent), orientation (convention delegates, business travelers, vacationers, etc.), amenities, average annual room rate, average annual occupancy, and competitive strengths and weaknesses.

Proposed hotels should be scrutinized to determine what innovations they are bringing to the market that may change the standards for the entire market. In Las Vegas, for example, several major new theme resort hotels built in the early 1990s were larger and more upscale than any hotels previously built in the city. They raised the bar on luxury amenities and created new competitive standards for hotels. To remain competitive, any proposed hotel in Las Vegas must respect these innovations and anticipate those of tomorrow.

The ultimate result of the market analysis process is the identification of an opportunity, that is, currently underserved market demand. A new or expanding airport generates new opportunities for hotels. Sometimes hotel owners and operators already in the market can easily identify the underserved market. For example, at the Pebble Beach Resort in Monterey, California, the resort's owners became acutely aware that they could not adequately serve the expanding conference business with one small hotel in a high-demand golf resort setting. To tap this demand, they developed the Spanish Bay Resort on an adjacent site; the resort's original hotel was positioned as a group meeting hotel while the Pebble Beach Lodge was positioned as a hotel for the free independent traveler, although both properties can be used jointly for larger meetings. In this case, the market analysis process was simplified by the fact that supply was severely restricted in an environmentally sensitive, world-class resort location.

Demographics and Psychographics

Targeted marketing will be the watchword for the coming decades. Particularly when assessing a resort or luxury hotel's leisure-market potential, the analyst needs to approach demand in terms of the demand for the enjoyment of a particular amenity or lifestyle that is to be offered and marketed to the visitor. The analyst must determine what recreational and leisure pursuits interest specific market segments as defined by geographic area, income level, and psychographics. For these reasons demand analysis for leisure-travel markets must go beyond the quantitative methods of demographic and economic analysis and inevitably must involve some original research and surveys. Specifically, the analysis must determine what combination of leisure pursuits, settings, and accommodations are underrepresented in the market.

From a broad perspective, it is critical to gather and evaluate data on recreation and sports participation rates to understand what the potential market prefers in leisure activities and whether the market encompasses underserved segments. The National Sporting Goods Association conducts an annual national survey to determine the recreation and sports participation rates for 54 separate recreation or sports activities. The data can be used to identify emerging trends in recreational patterns.

Most activities in the survey can be accommodated both within and outside a resort; however, resorts can offer especially attractive environments for many of the activities. Swimming, the second-ranking activity, is a perfect example of a recreational activity that can be more attractively offered in a resort than in most urban areas. Many activities are poorly suited to urban areas but lend themselves well to a recreational or resort setting. These include fishing, camping, hiking, hunting, mountain biking, backpacking, Alpine skiing, canoeing, snorkeling, climbing, kayaking or rafting, and scuba diving. Other activities such as bicycle riding, boating, golf, and tennis can be accommodated attractively in both urban and resort environments.

A resort must carefully assess how it can differentiate its recreational offerings to attract a market with access to the same offerings in an urban setting. Usually, the setting itself is the primary means of differentiation, but other design and programming features should be considered when assessing market potential.

Surprisingly, resorts often fail to accommodate some of the simplest activities in an appealing fashion.

For example, exercise walking—the top-ranking activity in the survey—merely requires an aesthetically pleasing pathway or trail. Yet, it is striking how many resorts do not provide attractive walking facilities.

Synthesis of Demand and Supply

After the competitive projects have been analyzed, the performance of the subject property should be projected. The most commonly used method is fair-share analysis, in which a percentage of market capture is estimated for the subject based on the number of rooms in the subject divided by the total number of rooms in the market. Projected market share must be tempered by qualitative factors, such as location, quality, and reputation. Case study 6.1 illustrates fair-share analysis.

Sources of Data

Federal, state, and local government agencies are the primary source for most of the economic and demographic data used by hotel market analysts. Numerous private data sources provide data on competitive projects and hotel markets. PKF's annual *Trends in the Hotel Industry* which covers hotel statistics for major U.S. cities. Travel statistics, including spending data, are available from the U.S. Travel Data Center, local chambers of commerce, the U.S. Department of Commerce, and various trade associations. Smith Travel Research publishes *Lodging Outlook*, a monthly mar-

ket summary. These and other sources are described in greater detail in the appendix.

Overview of Case Study

This chapter includes a case study for a 250-room full-service hotel to be built in downtown Austin by a large national hotel chain. The case study shows how published data sources are combined with field survey data to provide the necessary information for the analysis. One of the factors explored is seasonality of demand. In this case, demand is partly derived from state government, which meets only in odd-numbered years, creating an unusual kind of seasonality for this hotel market. The study illustrates how important it is to understand the nuances of the market before drawing conclusions.

Notes

[1] J. Richard McElyea and Gregory L. Cory, *Resort Investment and Development: An Overview of an Evolving Market* (San Francisco: Economics Research Associates, 1998).

[2] Smith Travel Research, *Lodging Outlook*.

[3] Average daily room rate is the total room revenue for a given period, divided by the number of occupied rooms during the same period. It reflects discounts and other rate reductions. Rack rates, or published rates, are the highest rates charged for the room and are the rates listed in hotel directories.

A New Hotel:
Downtown Austin (1997)
John M. Keeling

The Project

A major hotel chain proposes to build a new 250-room full-service hotel in downtown Austin, Texas. The hotel will have about 10,000 square feet of meeting space, including a 6,000-square-foot ballroom. It will offer a resort-style pool with a view of Town Lake. The hotel will provide services and amenities typical of a four-star property.

The Austin economy is quite strong. In addition to being the state capital and a university town, Austin has experienced rapid growth in technology-related industries. The area's computer industry has reached a critical mass where existing companies attract both suppliers and industrial consumers to the area. Approximately 200 high-technology semiconductor companies are located in the area, providing 22,000 jobs. In addition, more than 160 computer and electronics companies and 600 software firms employ more than 20,000 and 17,000 workers, respectively. Austin has become Texas's "Silicon Gulch," offering clean industry and using a highly educated workforce as well as research facilities of the University of Texas. The university's campus is located downtown, as is Austin's convention center, and the state capitol. With its scenic hills, limestone rock formations, and numerous waterways, Austin is known for its high quality of life and as a nonresort tourist destination.

Methods

The following steps are followed when conducting market research for a hotel project:

- Define the product to be evaluated.
- Identify the properties to be included in the competitive analysis and evaluate their strengths and weaknesses relative to the proposed facility.
- Collect information on the competitive properties through interviews with property managers and/or owners and by accessing available databases.
- Evaluate the strengths and weaknesses of the proposed site.
- Assess the strength of the area economy and the likelihood of change in hotel demand from historic patterns.

- Estimate future hotel market performance.
- Based on the subject's strengths and weaknesses relative to its competitors, estimate its ability to penetrate the various market segments and the resulting occupancies and average room rates.

Competitive Supply

More than 160 hotels exist in the Austin metropolitan area offering more than 18,500 guest rooms. The proposed development is a 250-room, full-service, chain-affiliated hotel to be located in downtown Austin. Hotel properties have been identified that are likely to compete with the subject because they share similar characteristics of location, size, and quality. A great deal of information on hotel properties can be collected from readily available publications. Among the more useful publications are

- Directories of the various hotel chains;
- *Mobil Travel Guide;*
- *American Automobile Association Tour Book;*
- *Hotel & Travel Index;*
- *OAG Business Travel Planner;*
- *Official Meeting Facilities Guide;*
- Publications by local chambers of commerce, hotel associations, or convention and visitors bureaus;
- Internet Web sites for the various chains or individual properties.

In this case, the competitive properties are described in Table 6.1-1.

Fortunately for those conducting hotel market research, an excellent national database provides accurate and timely data on most markets in the United States. For a reasonable fee, Smith Travel Research (STR) "Standard Historical Trend" reports provide a six-year history of aggregate occupancies and average room rates by month, as well as year-to-date information for a designated market area. Of course, not every property in every market is tracked by STR. Professionally managed and chain-affiliated hotels tend to be included whereas smaller, owner-operated hotels and motels tend not to participate. For this case study, every hotel in the competitive set is a participant. Typically, one or more of the properties needed for information will not be participants. In certain markets, such as South Beach in Miami Beach, Florida, where most of the competitive properties are small and entrepreneurially managed, not enough STR participants exist to generate a report. A summary of data from an STR report for the competitive set follows in Table 6.1-2.

A number of facts are immediately apparent from these numbers. First, supply has been static. No new rooms have been added to the market that would compete directly with a new project. Room rates have demonstrated very strong growth, two to three times the rate of inflation, while increases in demand have remained low. If one were to conclude that demand is not increasing very fast, however, it would likely be an incorrect conclusion. Rather, it appears that the market has reached capacity and additional demand cannot be accommodated within the competitive set and must seek room accommodations outside of the set.

Table 6.1-1
Competitive Hotel Properties

Property	No. Rooms	Year Open	Total Seats		Square Footage		Mtg. Sq. Ft. per Guest Room
			Restrnt	Lounge	Ballroom	Total Mtg.	
DoubleTree Guest Suites	189	1987	120	30	2,166	4,942	26
Driskill Hotel	177	1886	110	60	2,535	18,000	100
Embassy Suites	262	1985	80	—	1,026	2,380	9
Four Seasons	292	1987	90	60	7,029	18,021	62
Holiday Inn Town Lake	320	1967					
Hyatt Regency	446	1982	60/170	70	10,290	25,000	56
Marriott at the Capitol	365	1986	155	45/80	9,600	14,750	40
Omni Austin Center	304	1986	162/68	45/50	3,500	22,000	72
Radisson Town Lake	280	1965	300	20	6,080	9,600	34
Sheraton Waller Creek	254	1985	105	65	4,224	11,370	45
Total	**2,889**						

Source: PKF Consulting.

Table 6.1-2
Summary of Standard Historical Trends in Downtown Austin Market Area

	1992	1993	1994	1995	1996	1997	Annual % Change
Occupancy	71.2%	74.0%	75.3%	76.3%	72.6%	75.5%	
Room Rate	$74.41	$80.15	$86.13	$96.23	$103.20	$110.79	8.3
Supply	1,054,485	1,054,485	1,054,485	1,054,485	1,054,485	1,054,485	0.0
Demand	751,067	780,096	794,119	804,671	765,793	795,808	1.2

Source: Smith Travel Research.

This unaccommodated demand is called "turn-away demand" and is important because the addition of new hotel rooms in the market will have the opportunity to recapture this lost demand.

Although the STR reports are excellent for providing both a good statistical overview and a historical context, they are insufficient for gaining useful insights into the dynamics of the market. For this information, on-the-ground fieldwork is required. It is important to conduct interviews with hotel managers and marketing directors in order to get a qualitative as well as a quantitative sense of the market. From these interviews, the researcher should learn what the makeup of the competitors' business is; what percentage of business comes from individual business travelers (IBT), leisure travelers, conventions, in-house groups (groups that use the meeting facilities of the hotel and do not require a convention center), and any special sources of demand such as airlines, medical facilities, contracts, and government. Table 6.1-3 provides a breakdown of 1997 market segmentation for the competitive set.

Of particular importance in property interviews is gaining an appreciation of how each hotel competes. Interviews with property managers should include questions regarding the strengths and weaknesses of their hotels. Managers are also a good source for understanding the strengths and weaknesses of their competitors. Although property managers may be less than candid when discussing their own weaknesses, they have no reticence in discussing those of their competitors. Other important data to gather include information about the last renovation and any planned changes to the property that might alter its future competitive position. Each property representative should be asked which hotels they consider to be competitors. The competitive set initially selected by the researcher should hold up after discussions with the property representatives. A researcher may discover that a property thought to be competitive is not considered to be so by the other hotel managers. Or one may discover a hotel that at first did not appear to compete with the project, but based on interviews, does on some level.

The researcher should ask for operating information about each property, including occupancy and average room rate information for at least the past few years and up to five years if possible. It is also useful to ascertain the property's anticipated performance for the current year. The degree of candidness obtained will vary from property to property. In general, the more professional the management, the more comfortable it is with sharing information.

Combining the market segmentation information accumulated during interviews with the statistics from STR results in the analysis described in Table 6.1-4. This analysis reveals some additional information. It appears that all of the growth in the market has occurred in the group segment. The IBT segment is stagnant, while the leisure segment has declined. This analysis confirms earlier observations that the market is at capacity. Returning to the STR data, the seasonality of the market can be determined. (See Table 6.1-5.)

Very little seasonality occurs in this market, which is typical for a largely commercial area like downtown Austin. Also typical in a commercial market, December and January are soft months. Although many commercial markets see

---

Table 6.1-3
Competitive Hotel Market Segmentation

	Individual Business Travel (%)	Group/ Convention (%)	Leisure/ Tourist (%)
DoubleTree Guest Suites	47	34	19
Driskill Hotel	40	39	21
Embassy Suites	60	13	27
Four Seasons	33	34	33
Holiday Inn Town Lake	60	15	25
Hyatt Regency	23	59	18
Marriott at the Capitol	40	30	30
Omni Austin Center	40	50	10
Radisson Town Lake	40	30	20
Sheraton Waller Creek	48	42	10
Market Average[1]	**41.6%**	**35.5%**	**21.4%**

[1]Weighted averages.
Source: PKF Consulting.

Table 6.1-4
Summary of Estimated Competitive Market Conditions

	1993	1994	1995	1996	1997	Annual % Change
Rooms Available	1,054,485	1,054,485	1,054,485	1,054,485	1,054,485	0.0
Room Nights of Demand						
IBT	335,000	345,900	349,600	318,100	331,000	(0.3)
Group	265,900	267,800	270,000	272,900	282,200	1.5
Leisure	179,000	180,700	184,900	163,000	170,000	(1.3)
Total Demand	779,900	794,400	804,500	754,000	783,200	0.1
Market Occupancy	74.0%	75.3%	76.3%	72.6%	75.5%	
Average Daily Rate	$80.15	$86.13	$96.23	$103.20	$110.79	8.4

Source: PFK Consulting.

some seasonality in the summer months, Austin's summer occupancies are buoyed by strong summer leisure visitation. When the same analysis is performed in a tourism-driven market like Scottsdale, Arizona, or Aspen, Colorado, it reveals dramatic differences in occupancies between in-season and out-of-season periods.

A type of seasonality that is particular to Austin is its even-year, odd-year seasonality. According to the Texas constitution, the state legislature may meet only in odd-numbered years, except when a special session is called by the governor. The data display this seasonality, but because the market operates at near capacity, the seasonality is not pronounced. (See Table 6.1-6.)

After the existing lodging market is clearly understood, it is time to look to the future. Are any changes occurring in the market that would either benefit or harm the prospects of the project? Competitive interviews may have revealed information about planned or rumored developments. A search should be conducted with the local government to see if building permits are on file for new properties. The researcher should try to determine the likelihood of any rumored development actually being built because not all planned developments will actually be constructed. Full-service and center-city properties in particular are much more difficult to bring to fruition than suburban limited-service properties. An important factor in assessing this probability is the sponsor of the project. If it is an experienced hotel developer with a proven track record, the project's completion is more likely than if the sponsor is an individual with no development experience. The researcher needs to understand how far the project is in the development process. Most property sponsors claim their project is imminent when it is far from certain. Do they

Table 6.1-5
Seasonality Analysis

	Occupancy Range 1992–1997 (%)	Seasonal Index
January	61.0 – 67.2	85
February	73.7 – 82.8	107
March	76.3 – 88.6	111
April	76.4 – 84.2	109
May	78.1 – 84.9	110
June	74.1 – 79.6	102
July	73.4 – 83.0	104
August	69.5 – 75.5	98
September	68.2 – 78.0	100
October	75.4 – 86.8	108
November	68.4 – 75.6	99
December	48.1 – 52.5	69
Annual	**71.2% – 76.3%**	**100**

Source: Smith Travel Research.

Table 6.1-6
Odd-Year, Even-Year Seasonality

	Year	Occupancy	Year	Occupancy	Year	Occupancy	Average
Even Years	1992	71.2%	1994	75.3%	1996	72.6%	73.0%
Odd Years	1993	74.0%	1995	76.3%	1997	75.5%	75.3%

Source: Smith Travel Research.

own the site or just have an option? Have they had a market study prepared? How far along are they in the design process? Do they have a financing commitment? From whom? Both permanent and construction financing? Is their equity in place? Often, sponsors claim that a project is financed and ready to go; they "just" need to line up their investors. Many projects fail at this stage.

If it is determined that a project is likely to be built within a period that will affect the proposed project, the researcher must evaluate the project's competitiveness with the proposed subject. Will it be similar in concept, facilities, and location? To the degree that it varies from the subject, its competitiveness may be significantly diminished. If the proposed hotel is to be a full-service four-star hotel, a limited-service hotel may not be at all competitive, even if it is only a block away.

During interviews, it was discovered that the Radisson Town Lake is adding 135 two-room suites, a conference center, an expanded health facility, and a business center with completion anticipated in July 1998. Also, the former Stephen F. Austin Hotel, which has been closed for some time, is being renovated and will reopen with 188 rooms in October 1998. The reopened hotel will include 5,000 square feet of meeting space, a full-service restaurant, and a cigar bar. It will operate as an independent hotel. The impact of both of these properties must be considered in the analysis. A new Adam's Mark hotel has been rumored for several years, but according to the corporate office, although the firm would like to be in Austin, it has no site or current plans. A Ritz-Carlton hotel has also been rumored, but the firm is currently focused on developments in New Orleans, Dallas, and Houston. Proposed 100-room expan-

sions at the Four Seasons and the Marriott are reportedly on hold. Although the Marriott has land available, an expansion would require a variance from the city.

The researcher must estimate whether the demand for lodging is growing or decreasing, and by how much. To do this, one could examine past market trends, particularly over the past few years. This review is useful in markets where new development can occur with few constraints. In the case of downtown Austin, significant barriers to new development exist, and no competitive hotel has been added to the market since 1992. With the market effectively operating at capacity, historical growth rates will understate future growth of demand.

Demand Analysis

At this point, only the competition, or "supply," has been examined in this evaluation of the hotel market. It is also necessary to study the users of hotel rooms, or "demand." Interviews with corporate meeting planners, association executives, and other users of local hotels are necessary to broaden the understanding of the market. From these interviews, the researcher will get a consumer's-eye view of how the existing properties serve the market. The researcher should learn where employees, customers, and suppliers stay; why they choose one hotel over another; how often they require meeting facilities, and the size and nature of their meetings. If possible, the researcher should discuss the proposed hotel to size up the likelihood of the interviewee using the facility. During interviews it may be discovered that an important demand generator always uses full-service hotels or never uses full-service hotels. In one market, for example, it was determined that a major demand generator only stayed at hotels that used a soft drink manufactured by a related company.

Other indicators of growth should be determined, such as airport activity, job formation, convention attendance, and population growth. Data are generally available from chambers of commerce, economic development agencies, and area improvement districts. Also, published economic and demographic information are available from Sales and Marketing Management's annual "Survey of Buying Power" published each August for the previous year. The firm of Woods & Poole, Inc., is also an excellent source of economic and demographic information. Large real estate brokerage firms often track office, retail, and industrial space absorption for cities and suburbs.

Employment growth, office and industrial space absorption, new business formations and relocations, airport activity, population growth, and commercial building permits are all factors to be considered in looking at growth of IBT demand. To estimate growth in group demand, convention attendance, airport emplanements, tourist visitation, visitor counts at attractions, and population growth should be studied. Leisure growth should consider tourist visitation, visitor counts at attractions, and population growth.

According to Austin hotel managers, 1995 was a banner year when everything came together (legislative year, state basketball tournaments, the South by Southwest Music Festival, and a record number of convention bookings). Most of those interviewed anticipated the drop in occupied rooms in 1996 as well as the significant increase in average room rates. Capacity constraints are evident from Tuesday through Thursday from mid-January to mid-May and during football weekends and special events.

With occupancies as strong as they have been in recent years, hotel managers are reluctant to commit discounted, group rooms for future bookings at the convention center. This policy has been especially hard for the center, which has lost a significant amount of business because of a lack of commitments for nearby rooms.

Future growth in room demand will be influenced by several factors. Notwithstanding the fact that 1998, 2000, and 2002 will be on the even-year down cycles reflecting nonlegislative years, capacity constraints during peak periods will affect overall maximum occupancies. In 1999, 2001, and 2003, commercial demand should displace group demand at many hotels during those legislative years. The years 1998 and 2001 will receive boosts with the introduction of the additional rooms at the Radisson and Stephen F. Austin hotels, as well as the subject 250-room property. The addition of rooms to the downtown Austin market will enable previously unaccommodated demand that overflowed to other areas to return to the Austin market area.

Demand for hotel rooms in a given market can be categorized in one of three ways:

1. Demonstrated Demand—demand that can be quantified as existing occupancy levels at competitive hotels;
2. Unaccommodated Demand—demand that desires accommodations in the competitive market but is turned away because of capacity constraints;
3. Created Demand—demand that does not presently seek accommodations in the competitive market, but could be persuaded to do so through marketing efforts, room rates, location, available facilities, services, and amenities.

An evaluation of economic indicators in the Austin market indicates that the growth in each market segment will occur as shown in Table 6.1-7.

Table 6.1-7
Demand Growth

Year	Individual Business Travelers	Group/ Convention	Leisure/ Tourist
1998	2.0%	0.0%	0.0%
1999	2.0%	1.0%	0.0%
2000	2.0%	2.0%	1.0%
2001–2005	2.0%	1.0%	1.0%

Source: PKF Consulting.

Table 6.1-8
Market Supply and Demand

Market Segment	1997 Demand	1998 % Change	1998 Demand	1999 % Change	1999 Demand	2000 % Change	2000 Demand	2001 % Change	2001 Demand
Individual Business Travel									
Demonstrated	331,024	2.0	337,600	2.0	344,400	2.0	351,300	2.0	358,300
Created			5,900		13,600		18,900		24,300
Group/Convention									
Demonstrated	282,200	0	282,200	1.0	285,000	2.0	290,700	1.0	293,600
Created			5,000		11,500		23,000	1.0	23,300
Leisure/Tourist									
Demonstrated	170,000	0	170,000	0	170,000	1.0	171,700	1.0	173,400
Created			3,000		6,900		10,200	1.0	10,300
Total	**783,224**	**2.6**	**803,700**	**3.4**	**831,400**	**4.2**	**865,800**	**2.0**	**883,200**
Rooms Available	1,054,485	4.9	1,106,311	6.0	1,172,380	7.8	1,263,630	0.0	1,263,630
Market Occupancy	74.3%		72.6%		70.9%		68.5%		69.9%

Source: PKF Consulting.

The new rooms being added to the market at the Radisson, the Stephen F. Austin, and the subject 250-room property will accommodate individual business traveler and leisure demand that was turned away during peak periods. Additionally, the Stephen F. Austin and the subject property will have marketing staffs to sell group business that might otherwise have been accommodated outside Austin. A capture rate of two fill nights per week, 50 weeks per year, for the new rooms can be assumed. The rooms were distributed to the demand base at their respective percentage segmentation. (See Table 6.1-8.)

Estimating Performance for the Subject

After the likely performance of the competitive projects is established, the next step is to estimate the performance of the subject hotel. This projection is usually accomplished through a fair-share analysis. "Fair market share" is the percentage of demand allocated to a given property based on the ratio of its available guest rooms to the total number of rooms in the competitive market. In this case,

the fair market share of the subject property is calculated as follows:

Size of subject property	250 rooms
Number of rooms in competitive set	3,462 rooms
Fair market share	250 ÷ 3,462 = 7.2%

Market penetration is based on the attributes of a hotel relative to the competitive market. Historic penetrations of properties in the competitive set are considered, as well as any potential changes caused by changing property attributes or marketing strategies. A penetration rate of 100 percent or greater indicates that a property is capturing more than its fair market share, while a penetration rate of less than 100 percent indicates that the property is losing fair share to its competition. Properties with large amounts of meeting space tend to penetrate the group segment at higher levels than properties with less space. In general, a property's attractiveness to the various market segments will determine how it will penetrate each segment. The primary competitive supply has penetrated its fair share of room demand at the rates shown in Table 6.1-9.

The subject hotel is anticipated to be similar in quality to the Marriott at the Capitol. The hotel will have the equivalent of 40 square feet of meeting space per guest room. It is anticipated that it will achieve its fair share of demand from the IBT segment. Although it will be attractive to small groups, the hotel is seen primarily as a facility that will cater to individual business travelers. Accordingly, it is estimated that the subject will penetrate the group segment at less than its fair share or 90 percent. With its resort-style pool, the subject should be quite attractive to the leisure segment. It is expected that the property will penetrate this segment at 130 percent of its fair share. The resulting property occupancies are calculated in Table 6.1-10.

After a likely occupancy for the subject property has been arrived at, the next step is to apply the achievable room rates that were obtained from the market research to the various market segments to estimate annual room revenue. Taking the stabilized year, 2003, the calculation would be as shown in Table 6.1-11.

This method of determining a hotel's anticipated performance is the most widely used; however, it does not apply in all circumstances. It works well when the subject property will compete against a number of other properties. In such cases, the relationships between the properties can be discerned and the appropriate penetration rates applied. However, this method fails in circumstances when few or no competitive properties exist, as is often the case with resort destinations, executive conference centers, and large convention hotels. In Phoenix and Scottsdale, Arizona, where there are a large number of existing resorts, this penetration model would be useful. It would not work, however, in markets where there are few or no existing comparable and competitive properties. The methodology for evaluating such projects is beyond the scope of this case study.

Table 6.1-9
Penetration Rates of Competitive Supply

Property	Individual Business Traveler (%)	Group/Convention (%)	Leisure/Tourist (%)	Overall (%)
DoubleTree Guest Suites	115–120	85–90	70–75	105–110
Driskill Hotel	70–75	80–85	70–75	90–95
Embassy Suites	140–145	35–40	125–130	95–100
Four Seasons	80–85	100–105	165–170	100–105
Holiday Inn Town Lake	135–140	35–40	110–115	85–90
Hyatt Regency	55–60	165–170	85–90	100–105
Marriott at the Capitol	95–100	85–90	145–150	105–110
Omni Austin Center	95–100	140–145	45–50	100–105
Radisson Town Lake	100–105	90–95	100–105	95–100
Sheraton Waller Creek	105–110	110–115	40–45	95–100

Source: PKF Consulting.

A New Hotel: Downtown Austin *(continued)*

Table 6.1-10

Estimated Property Performance

Year	Market Segment	Market Demand	Fair Market Share Percent	Fair Market Share Demand	Market Penetration Percent	Market Penetration Demand	Occupancy (%)
2001	IBT	372,400	7.2	26,800	100	26,800	
	Group	305,500	7.2	22,000	90	19,800	
	Leisure	180,500	7.2	13,000	130	16,900	
	Total	**858,400**	**7.2**	**61,800**	**103**	**63,500**	**70**
2002	IBT	379,900	7.2	27,400	100	27,400	
	Group	311,600	7.2	22,400	90	20,200	
	Leisure	182,200	7.2	13,100	130	17,000	
	Total	**873,700**	**7.2**	**62,900**	**103**	**64,600**	**71**
2003	IBT	387,500	7.2	27,900	100	27,900	
	Group	314,700	7.2	22,700	90	20,400	
	Leisure	184,100	7.2	13,300	130	17,300	
	Total	**886,300**	**7.2**	**63,900**	**103**	**65,600**	**72**

Source: PKF Consulting.

Table 6.1-11

Estimated Rooms Revenue by Market Segment

Market Segment	Occupancy	Occupied Rooms	Room Rate	Rooms Revenue
IBT		27,900	$120	$3,348,000
Group		20,400	100	2,040,000
Leisure		17,300	135	2,335,500
Total/Average	**72%**	**65,600**	**118**	**7,723,500**

Source: PKF Consulting.

Centro Vasco da Gama, Lisbon, Portugal.

Chapter 7

Mixed-Use Developments

Mixed-use development is complex for both the developer and the market analyst. It involves more than the sum of the parts. The developer must strategize the proper placement and timing of components. The market analyst must evaluate each use individually and understand the synergies created—both positive and negative.

Mixed-use was a common development pattern throughout history until after World War II, when suburbanization and separate-use zoning became the norm. By the 1970s, mixed land uses were again becoming an important development form, and today mixed-use developments are often the preferred form for both developers and local governments. The smart-growth and new urbanism movements encourage mixed-use development because it enhances opportunities for improved pedestrian accessibility through increased density and mixing of activities, both of which shorten the distances between destinations.

Since the 1976 publication of ULI's first book on mixed use—*Mixed-Use Developments: New Ways of Land Use*—both the concept of mixed-use development and the actual product have grown and evolved tremendously. However, the original definition developed in 1976 still holds today. Mixed-use developments are characterized by

- Three or more significant revenue-producing uses (such as retail, office, residential, hotel, and entertainment/cultural/recreation), which in well-planned projects are mutually supporting;
- Significant physical and functional integration of project components (and thus a relatively close-knit and intensive use of land), including uninterrupted pedestrian connections;

- Development in conformance with a coherent plan (which frequently stipulates the type and scale of uses, permitted densities, and related items).

Three or More Significant Revenue-Producing Uses

Although many real estate projects have more than one use, mixed-use developments as defined and discussed in this chapter include at least three major revenue-producing uses. The three or more uses should be significant (for example, retail space should offer more than site-serving convenience facilities) and should produce revenue (for example, to amortize costs over time and to provide a reasonable return). In most mixed-use projects, the primary revenue-producing uses are usually a combination of retail, office, and residential or hotel facilities. Other revenue-producing uses are also possible in a mixed-use project, including wholesale trade marts, arenas, convention centers, performing arts facilities, and museums. In the case of the last, revenue may need to be derived in part from philanthropic sources for the project to be viable. The important factor is that they be significant uses that draw their own users to the project.

Three or more significant uses together in one development usually implies a project of considerable scale and impact. Although smaller-scale projects have been developed, the typical sizes of the components of a mixed-use project usually exceed 100,000 square feet; thus, total project square footage usually exceeds 300,000 square feet, sometimes running as high as several million square feet.

Developers often seek a minimum critical mass for mixed-use developments to create the requisite public image and market penetration. The size and diversity of uses in these projects, if effectively programmed and designed, can result in a project that becomes a significant new place on the urban landscape. Thus, many mixed-use developments are much more than simply developments; they are exercises in place making. A good mixed-use development can turn a lesser location into a prime one.

Sometimes, mixed use can make possible a socially desirable, but economically risky, use because the more profitable uses can carry the less profitable ones. For example, a performing arts center becomes feasible when paired with an office complex. A mixed-use project is sometimes favored by a locality and has improved chances of getting zoning approval. This favorability is not always the case, however, since some localities are still tied to old notions of separate-use zoning.

Physical and Functional Integration

The second descriptive characteristic of mixed-use developments is a significant physical and functional integration of the project's components and, thus, an intensive use of land. All components should be interconnected by pedestrian links, although this integration can take many physical forms, as follow:

- A vertical mixing of project components into a single megastructure, often occupying only one city block;
- Careful positioning of key project components around central public spaces (for example, a street, park, plaza, atrium, galleria, or shopping center);
- Interconnection of project components through pedestrian-friendly connections (such as sidewalks along streets, interior walkways, enclosed corridors, underground concourses, retail plazas and mall areas, escalators, and even aerial bridges between buildings).

Integrated, shared parking is a key component, improving land-use efficiencies and reducing costs. Pedestrian circulation and orientation are critical elements in the planning process, because without them, the project will not work as a whole and will not achieve the desired synergies and sense of place that are the hallmarks of mixed-use developments.

This second criterion distinguishes mixed-use developments from other real estate projects that may include three or more significant revenue-producing uses but do not fully integrate them. Some examples of such lower-intensity, more-spread-out developments include master-planned communities and business parks, in which densities and physical integration tend to be significantly less than in mixed-use developments, resulting in less-regular interaction among uses and more reliance on automobiles for movement within the project.

Large-scale business parks often include light industrial uses, office buildings, retail and restaurant space, hotels, health clubs, golf courses, daycare centers, and a host of other uses. Usually, however, they are configured in a low-density environment that is primarily auto-oriented and does not provide for good pedestrian circulation. Many master-planned communities also exhibit multiuse characteristics, incorporating shopping centers, office buildings, and hotels, as well as a variety of residential and recreational uses. Those projects are generally large scale—often reaching several thousand acres—and tend to be low density; they typically require automobiles for internal movement.

Development in Conformance with a Coherent Plan

Mixed-use developments are usually developed from the outset in conformance with a coherent development strategy and plan. Master planning for a mixed-use development, compared to a single-purpose project, demands a much greater diversity of specialized participation from developers, market analysts, architects and land planners, property managers, and capital/financing sources. The planning process—including the market analysis—is therefore far more complex than for most other real estate projects.

From a marketing perspective, the point of mixed-use is that the diversity of activities can enhance the economic viability of the project. Because each use can be marketed and absorbed simultaneously, a larger scale can be achieved in a shorter amount of time—if the project is well-planned and in tune with the market.

Analyzing Market Potential of Mixed-Use Projects

Mixed-use development projects present certain unique challenges as well as opportunities for the market analyst. The opportunity for the analyst is to help the project's developer and investors capitalize on synergies among complementary uses and create an overall cumulative market attraction that exceeds what the individual project components would generate independently. The challenge for the analyst is to identify and measure these market premiums. The market analyst should begin with the caveat that each element of the project must be able to stand on its own in terms of marketability.

The basic real estate theory of mixed-use development is that people will take advantage of colocated land uses to concentrate their trips for commuting, shopping, and entertainment plus other activities within the project or location. This phenomenon can have the advantage of creating certain captive-market advantages for the various project components. It can also create economic advantages from a shared investment in supporting infrastructure, such as off-site road improvements, and on-site parking and open space, as well as common services ranging from trash collection and disposal to marketing and advertising.

Interactions among uses are not always positive. Critics often cite the noise and odors from street-level restaurants as a negative factor in locating residences above them. Nighttime activity from theaters or other entertainment facilities may be a detriment to marketing a hotel. In some cases negative effects can be minimized or eliminated through careful planning and design. In assessing the market potential for a new project, the analyst must answer the following questions.

- Are certain kinds of locations more suitable? The site should have good access and exposure, often within a larger multiuse context like a downtown or edge city. It should be in a jurisdiction that favors such projects. Sometimes an emerging or reemerging locale is good. Also, proximity to transit, convention facilities, historic districts, and other advantages may produce a superior site.
- How should each element be phased? Proper timing and phasing of project components are crucial. Each phase must be able to work independently of future phases, because there might be a considerable lag between each. The project should begin with the uses that have the strongest current market potential, creating cash flow that can be funneled into later phases of the project.
- How should the uses be configured in the project to take advantage of market forces? Visibility is important for retail and entertainment uses; hotels must have pedestrian and vehicular access, convenient parking, and security; privacy and security

should be maximized for any residential component. A site plan for a large mixed-use project usually places offices in the interior locations, with hotel, retail, and entertainment uses at the edges for the best visibility and access.

Notwithstanding the presumed advantages of mixed-use developments, the market analyst must start with the basics described in previous chapters: the analysis of market demand, an assessment of effective competition, and a determination of potential market capture. These key steps are performed for each separate use as if each were to be independently located and built. The research can then be refined to reflect cross sales between colocated uses and to estimate any cumulative attraction in terms of greater market penetration and higher rates of capture of available outside patrons.

The matrix in Figure 7-1 identifies the interrelationships between markets for different types of development that are typically found in a mixed-use project. Where strong market synergy exists among uses, there are opportunities to realize market premiums from these combinations. Naturally, every mixed-use development is different in design and configuration as well as in relation to its sources of market support. So there can be no hard-and-fast rules. Nevertheless, the relationships suggested by the matrix hold true in most instances. They are discussed briefly in the following paragraphs.

Residential

Clearly a powerful relationship can exist between residential development and office employment. Hence, the popularity of downtown housing is growing where there is a tradition of urban living supported by good services and public transportation, such as in San Francisco, Chicago, New York, and Boston; or where there has been a successful concerted effort to create needed urban amenities, such as in Cleveland, Kansas City, and Minneapolis. Likewise, a natural affinity exists between residential development and convenience retail activity, although there can be a conflict between the image and scale of price-competitive convenience retail uses and that of image-conscious resident owners and renters.

Two key questions the market analyst must answer are (1) whether people will be attracted to living in the mixed-use development by the option of office employment in the same complex, and vice versa, and (2) whether they will concentrate their convenience-retail expenditures within the complex when

Figure 7-1

Market Grid for Mixed-Use Developments

Primary Use Components	Health Care	Marina	Entertainment: Sports	Entertainment: Theaters	Entertainment: Bars & Restaurants	Retail: Comparison	Retail: Specialty	Retail: Convenience	Hotel	Offices	Residential
Residential	□	●	×	×	□	□	□	●	×	●	
Offices	□	–	□	–	●	□	□	□	●		●
Hotel	□	□	●	□	●	□	●	□		●	×
Retail: Convenience	–	●	□	□	□	□	×		□	□	●
Retail: Specialty Stores	–	●	□	●	●	●		×	●	□	□
Retail: Comparison	–	□	□	●	●		●	□	□	□	□
Entertainment: Bars & Restaurants	–	●	●	●		●	●	□	●	●	□
Entertainment: Theaters	–	–	□		●	●	●	□	□	–	×
Entertainment: Sports	□	□		□	●	□	□	□	●	□	×
Marina	–		□	–	●	□	●	●	□	–	●
Health Care		–	□	–	–	□	–	–	□	□	□

Level of Market Synergy in MXD

●   Strong
□   Weak or Uncertain
–   Neutral, Absence of Synergy
×   Potential Market Conflict

---

they are likely to pay higher prices because merchants will probably lack broad market patronage from a large residential community. These questions can best be answered by careful attitudinal research—surveys and focus groups—involving a sample of prospective residents and office employees.

Office

More than any other use, office development has been the driving force behind mixed-use development, with nearly all mixed-use projects including an office component. The office component often does not achieve the strong identity that a freestanding building does, which can mean the project will not appeal to tenants who want to create a strong image in a distinct building. Projects in which office space is a secondary use often have a different look and feel, and the office space is positioned and marketed differently. The demand for such space tends to rely on the sense of place created by the project's other elements. Analysts should not assume that a high percentage of people who work in a mixed-use development will want to live there, or vice versa.

Office development has clear market synergy with hotels, bars, and restaurants, and, to a lesser extent, with most types of retail activity. Most offices have occasional, if not frequent, out-of-town visitors and find it desirable to refer them to a nearby lodging facility. The extra boost to hotel patronage from a companion office facility can be readily estimated, especially if the major tenants are known and can be interviewed. Such research will indicate the frequency at which these firms attract visitors from out of town and the types of accommodations the visitors prefer. Likewise, bars and restaurants are natural amenities expected by office employees and employers alike.

Hotel

Hotels can be a vital component in mixed-use developments for several reasons. Hotels can be the most profitable component of the project where the market is strong. They can be important for market synergy, thereby improving the overall marketability of the project. A good hotel can enhance the project's image and provide name recognition. Hotels attract visitor patronage that would otherwise not be drawn to the development. Thinking that the office component will generate enough demand for rooms to support the hotel, however, is a major mistake. Such demand is rarely the case.

In addition to the strong positive relationship of hotels to office users, hotels tend to provide patrons for most types of retail activity, especially unique specialty shops and boutiques, bars and restaurants, and sports entertainment. The type of hotel, however, can have a big influence on the amount of retail patronage that is generated. Most business travelers do not take the time to shop, but conference attendees, tourists, and vacationers do. Failure to know and consider the nature of the hotel patrons can lead to serious misjudgments of hotel-generated demand for retail goods and services in a mixed-use project.

Retail

Because of the market support that can be gained from on-site uses, the potential for retail uses often cannot be determined until the size and character of the other uses are determined, and market potential for each of the other uses is assessed. Most mixed-use developments include a retail component, which can range from a small amount of convenience- and service-retail space ancillary to the project's major components to a super-regional shopping center that offers a full array of shopping goods and services.

The analysis proceeds differently depending on the nature of the retail component. For example, a major shopping destination relies on a regional market, whereas a service- and convenience-retail component would focus on local and on-site markets.

- Convenience Retail. When the single head or both heads of a household work, the tendency is to shop for convenience items just once or twice a week. Thus, a car is required to conveniently transport several days' or a week's provisions. The exception would be an intensely pedestrian- and transit-dependent urban environment such as New York City or San Francisco. Thus, the most significant market synergy in a mixed-use development would be for convenience-retail uses scaled to the needs of the project's resident households. This demand can be readily measured by conventional market analysis.
- Specialty Retail. In addition to the strong affinity between unusual specialty shops and convention travelers and tourists, specialty-retail use is otherwise primarily drawn to cluster with other types of shopping and entertainment. The niche nature of most such specialty merchants requires a large, fairly affluent base of residential market support. Thus, although specialty-retail uses may enliven and enrich the mixed-use development, they will fail unless combined with other comparison shopping, entertainment, and dining uses that together achieve a critical mass capable of attracting patrons from a large area.
- Comparison Retail. Like specialty-retail projects, comparison-retail developments achieve market synergy primarily with other types of retail activity that create a critical mass to attract broad residential patronage.

Specialized Uses

In addition to office, retail, and residential uses, several special categories of uses can be part of mixed-use developments. Specialized analysis is required for each use. As indicated earlier, the standard techniques discussed in previous chapters would be used to analyze the sources and scale of demand for each component of a mixed-use development. Then, it is necessary to estimate cross sales between colocated uses: How many hotel nights will be generated by office users that are part of the complex? How many office employees will rent or buy an apartment or condominium in the complex? What percentage of lunchtime expenditures by office employees for meals or comparison goods can be captured within the complex?

Entertainment

Often the key factors affecting the success of a mixed-use development are related to the sense of place that the project can create and the project's activity cycle. Usually, a primary objective of commercial mixed-use projects is to create an environment that generates activity throughout the day and the week, including evenings and weekends. Entertainment facilities—theaters, concert halls, cinemas, restaurants, and clubs—serve this objective well, and they have become key ingredients in many mixed-use developments. The kinds of entertainment uses that may be included vary considerably depending on the location and nature of the development. The most common are multiplex cinemas, but this product has become overbuilt in many regions, as have certain types of theme restaurants.

Sometimes a cultural facility like a museum or performing arts center is part of a mixed-use development. Such institutions add two elements that other entertainment cannot. They expand the mix of audience, often adding a well-educated and affluent component. Cultural facilities give the development a strong identity, marketing focus, and image of quality. However, including these uses generally requires forging a public/private partnership involving private developers, public agencies, and arts organizations.

Within the entertainment category, bars and restaurants tend to have the greatest market synergy with both retail and nonretail uses. Theaters tend to be destinations in themselves without much interdependence with hotels, offices, or residential uses located in the mixed-use project.

Marina

Because many urban waterfronts are shifting away from industrial uses to mixed uses, cities are looking to commercial and recreational uses to fill these remaining underused areas. Pleasure boaters can be a key demand segment, making marinas a focal point of many redevelopment projects. Although marinas are a very specialized use, an appropriately located marina can contribute to a wide range of market synergies with other uses in a mixed-use

Yokohama Bayside Marina, Yokohama, Japan.

development. Analysts should study comparable marinas and learn about marina patrons for an indication of how extensive the market potential might be. As with other market sectors, it is crucial not to overstate potential and to understand that a new development cannot create a market, but can only capitalize on an untapped existing market.

Health Care

Considerable market synergy can be gained from the location of physicians' offices and associated health care practitioners within a mixed-use complex that includes both residential and office components. But like various forms of retail goods and services, health care businesses need an independent marketing image or identity to enable them to attract patronage from beyond the project's boundaries.

Non-Revenue-Generating Uses

The development potential for public, non-revenue-generating, and other ancillary uses should also be studied. The addition of a cultural facility to the project must be assessed to determine whether the facility would attract patrons, as well as what its impact would be on the remaining uses. A public library does not generate revenue, but generates activity, and therefore may enhance the revenue of the overall project.

Data and Analysis

Much data can best be derived from careful attitudinal research involving each of the key constituencies to be represented in the mixed-use development. This research would ideally involve some combination of focus-group interviews, intercept surveys of potential shoppers, and interviews of key representatives of potential retail and office tenants as well as homebuyers or renters. Although each survey technique has certain strengths and weaknesses, an optimum approach combines a set of professionally administered focus-group sessions with a broader survey program, whether by mail, hand delivery, telephone, or direct respondent interviews, that will allow for statistical inference to the larger market universe represented by the respondents. The overall question to be answered is whether the users, occupants, and visitors who are associated with one project component will concentrate and increase their patronage, as well as pay higher prices, to avail themselves of the convenience of the colocated uses and facilities. In other words, will they in fact generate market premiums?

After market demand has been measured for the individual and the combined components, the effectiveness of competing projects must be determined. Large-scale mixed-use projects usually have few, if any, directly comparable projects in the same market area with a similar combination of uses. (One notable exception would be North Michigan Avenue in Chicago, where at least three large mixed-use developments are situated within a few blocks of each other.) If such analogs do exist in the same market, their relative success or failure must be analyzed in detail. At the same time, it is necessary to document and analyze the inventory of competitive space for each use component.

Marketability

The final step in the market analysis for mixed-use development is to estimate its overall marketability on the basis of the known demand for and supply of effective competition. As in all market studies, this last step requires the application of informed judgment regarding the likely response to the new product in the marketplace. To what extent will people shift their patronage from existing competition because it fails to meet their standards for convenience, quality, and value? Will the proposed development embody the physical and locational qualities that result in a landmark attraction in the marketplace? What increment of market capture for each use component can be attributed to the cumulative attraction of the mixture of uses? To what degree will the project be self-supporting based on cross sales among users, occupants, and patrons of the colocated uses? Ideally, final answers to these questions will be used to refine the design and the marketing strategy for the mixed-use project, thereby avoiding unrealistic expectations while taking advantage of the potential benefits of market synergies.

In conclusion, it is useful to review some of the lessons learned and reasons for market failure or underperformance of mixed-use developments. First, the mixed-use development too often has been assumed to be self-supporting to an unrealistic degree. In most instances, each project component requires a majority of its market support from outside the mixed-use development, with cross sales accounting for a smaller but marginally significant share of the economic benefits. Therefore, the design of the mixed-use development needs to present a marketable image for each of its major components to attract patrons from well beyond the project. It is unrealistic to believe that the market premium for the colocation and interdependence of complementary uses will be generous.

Another major pitfall encountered by mixed-use developments is the sin of hubris—that is, the assumption that the project will, because of its design, anchor tenants, or other key attribute, establish such a dominant position in the marketplace that further competition will be precluded from entering. Such market domination is rarely the case in a highly competitive, open economy where success breeds competition and copycats.

Some of the most celebrated and successful mixed-use developments are shown in Table 7-1. In each example, the various project components contribute patrons to the other components, thereby achieving superior levels of occupancy, rents, and overall project value.

Case Study

Case study 7.1 illustrates a market analysis to formulate a plan for a military base reuse in Orange County, California. The objective was to use the 4,700-acre suburban site to stimulate growth, attract good jobs, and create synergies among uses. Economic drivers were identified and three alternative scenarios were laid out for mixed-use developments.

Table 7-1

Selected Mixed-Use Developments

Project/Location	Description	Land Uses	Size
Phillips Place, suburban Charlotte, North Carolina	Pedestrian-oriented street grid with low-rise buildings	Retail Rental apartments Hotel Multiplex cinema	130,000 sq. ft. 402 units 124 rooms 10 screens
Heritage on the Garden, Boston, Massachusetts	12-story building with underground garage	Retail Office Condominium Garage parking	50,000 sq. ft. 125,000 sq. ft. 87 units 180 spaces
Pine Square, downtown Long Beach, California	Six-story complex with structured parking	Retail Multiplex cinema Rental apartments	37,000 sq. ft. 16 screens 142 units
Pioneer Place, downtown Portland, Oregon	Three city blocks: office tower with two-level department store, retail pavilion, structured parking	Retail Office Garage parking	215,000 sq. ft. 284,000 sq. ft. 630 spaces
Tower City, downtown Cleveland, Ohio	34-acre transit-oriented urban conversion, rehab and new construction	Retail Office Hotel Garage parking Multiplex cinema Transit station	360,000 sq. ft. 1,000,000 sq. ft. 208 rooms 3,150 spaces 11 screens 123,000 sq. ft.
Reston Town Center, suburban Reston, Virginia	85-acre pedestrian-oriented street grid; high-rise with street-level retail/entertainment	Retail/entertainment Office Hotel Parking Ice rink	240,000 sq. ft. 530,000 sq. ft. 514 rooms 3,000 spaces

Mixed-Use Development:
El Toro Military Base Reuse (1998)

Emma Tyaransen

The sharp scaling back of the defense industry initiated by the Base Realignment and Closure (BRAC) Act in 1988 has created opportunities for reusing a large number of military bases across the country. Although these closures significantly affect many communities, with potentially thousands of military-serving and military-dependent jobs lost, the strategic redevelopment of the former bases can provide strong opportunities for the long term by creating more jobs than the former base supported while providing substantial tax revenues to the communities.

The Department of Defense (DoD) has been using the BRAC process to reduce the number of military facilities and to transfer properties to civilian control. As part of that process, DoD requires that a reuse plan guide the conversion of each base from military to civilian use. The reuse plan demands a significant effort on the part of the benefiting local redevelopment authority (LRA). The LRA typically has a broad-based membership, including, but not limited to, representatives from jurisdictions with zoning authority over the property. Generally, only one LRA is recognized per military installation.

Typically, a team of consultants is hired by the LRA to assemble the reuse plan. The team generally includes market and economic experts, transportation planners, land planners, infrastructure engineers, environmental planners, and public relations and marketing specialists.

The initial step in base property disposal is called "screening." Screening gives other military departments the first opportunity to apply for base property. After the screening process is completed, that portion of the base not identified for military use is considered "excess." Other federal agencies may then apply to use the excess property. Property identified for use for military or other federal agencies through the screening process can be conveyed directly to the requesting agency from the authorizing military department at no cost. After screening for federal uses is completed, any remaining base property is considered surplus.

Before it becomes available for general public acquisition, surplus property on the base is made available to state and local agencies, as well as to federally recognized Native American tribes. All of these groups are accorded equal status. Applications are examined for compatibility with the LRA's reuse plan and the goals and objectives for the redevelopment of the base. Property recommended by the LRA for conveyance is conveyed either to the benefiting entities directly or to the LRA itself for sublease to those entities.

Background

This study addresses the economics-based market analyses that are required as inputs to the reuse plan of a military facility. This analysis includes (1) setting goals and objectives; (2) researching potential uses proposed for the property; (3) performing market, economic, fiscal, and financial impact analyses of alternative scenarios combining the proposed land uses; (4) refining alternative scenarios to create a market-driven strategic plan; and (5) generating a marketing and implementation plan for the program.

Such an analysis was recently completed for the reuse of Marine Corps Air Force Station (MCAS) El Toro, a military base located in Orange County, California, that has been slated for conversion by July 1999. MCAS El Toro, a 4,700-acre property, is one of the largest remaining areas of developable land in the county. Infill in character, it is surrounded by residential and commercial uses and open space.

Like many military facilities preparing for conversion, MCAS El Toro is the subject of a heated public debate regarding its future use. But unique to MCAS El Toro is the prospect of the conversion of the majority of the site to a commercial airport. Orange County, and the cities of Irvine and Lake Forest, formed El Toro Reuse Planning Authority (ETRPA) as a joint-powers agency in 1994 to plan for civilian reuse of MCAS El Toro. DoD then designated ETRPA as the LRA to prepare the required reuse planning documents. In November 1994, a county ballot initiative was passed that called for commercial aviation reuse of the base.

Orange County withdrew from ETRPA in 1995, and subsequently the county was designated as the LRA by DoD. In July 1997, the county began preparing an aviation reuse plan. ETRPA, now composed of seven Orange County cities, requested county acceptance of its MCAS El Toro Reuse Plan as the nonaviation alternative to be addressed in the county-prepared Environmental Impact Report. The Orange County Board of Supervisors agreed to ETRPA's preparation of a nonaviation reuse plan, and ETRPA selected a consulting team to prepare the plan.

Establishing Objectives

According to DoD, the LRA's objectives are to develop "a comprehensive redevelopment plan based upon local needs. The plan should recommend land uses based upon an exploration of feasible reuse alternatives.... [and] is enforceable under state and local land use laws." The overall objectives of the reuse plan process for a military facility are established by the LRA with input from the consulting team. Those objectives are subjected to the scrutiny of the public at large. Specifically, the objectives of the economic and market analyses that are components of the study are to develop scenarios that maximize the market opportunity of the property, balanced with the community's needs and respect for the environment.

The preferred reuse scenario serves as a guideline through the property's buildout. The time frame established for the buildout is the likely length of time necessary to achieve absorption of all proposed land uses. The time frame for buildout is based on the projected health of the economy, both national and in the region affected by the base closure, as well as on the needs of the surrounding communities. The buildout estimate is generated by the market consultant, reviewed by the other members of the consulting team, and approved by the LRA.

Definition of the Scope of Work

The scope of work for the economic and market analyses is designed by the market consultant, then refined in a group setting by the entire consulting team, and finally approved by the LRA. Members of the consulting team provide input relating to their areas of expertise, conferring to test the validity of the assumptions used. Typically, the economic and market analysis portion of the effort involves the following:

1. Generating a menu of potential uses for the site. The process requires vision, starting with as broad-

based a set of choices as possible, then narrowing the options down to the most likely set.

2. Performing a physical inspection of the subject property and making an analysis by potential land use with respect to locational factors, visibility, access, topography, and effect of surrounding land uses, with specific focus on the market potential for the proposed land uses identified in the previous step.

3. Defining the primary market area (PMA) for each land use under consideration. The PMA is used as a framework for demographic and demand potential analyses.

4. Making a macro-level study of the economy. This step involves analysis of historical and projected employment trends by Standard Industrial Classification (SIC) to determine industrial sectors that are projected to grow over the lifetime of the redevelopment.

5. Identifying industries that drive both the local and global economy. The focus is to determine the land use and other requirements of each driver industry, and to determine the ability of the base property to respond to those needs.

6. Collecting and analyzing demographic data for the PMAs for each land use under consideration, including population and household trends, age and income distributions, household size, owner/renter preferences, and so forth.

7. Identifying the competitive market area (CMA), which is the area in which each project is expected to compete on a more or less equal basis. CMAs can vary greatly in size from one potential land use to the next.

8. Investigating and analyzing the supply conditions in the CMAs of the land uses under consideration. Existing supply is examined relative to defining characteristics, such as location, positioning, densities, tenant/owner types, marketing, and rates of absorption. Planned and proposed projects are analyzed relative to projected product type, timing of introduction, absorption, and sellout.

9. Preparing statistical analyses of potential demand and capture for land uses under consideration. The

analyses identify the depth of potential opportunity from the PMAs of the land uses under consideration and the annualized capture potential of the base facility.

10. On the basis of the research and analysis outlined in the previous steps, producing multiple land use scenarios to provide the framework of the reuse plan.

11. Performing quantitative analysis of the economic impacts of the scenarios. This step examines the effect that each land use scenario would have on employment (both on and off site), income, output, and land sales revenue. The results indicate the scenario(s) that best maximize the economic opportunities offered by the redevelopment of the property.

12. Making a fiscal analysis of the proposed land uses, which is used to determine the public sector revenues or costs that can be anticipated from the development, occupancy, and servicing of a new project. The analysis evaluates project-generated revenues and costs in terms of their net effect on a specific jurisdiction relative to particular land uses on a per acre basis.

13. Based on the economic and fiscal analyses of each land use scenario, refining the proposed mix of uses to maximize economic return to the communities surrounding the base.

14. Conducting a financial analysis of the implementation of the selected scenario(s). The analysis quantifies the cash flow generated by a particular scenario, overall through buildout, and by development phase, after accounting for all revenues and costs.

15. Creating an implementation plan for the preferred economic scenario (i.e., how and to which target audiences the property should be marketed relative to land sales, etc.).

Market Analysis
Identification of a Product Menu
As discussed, one objective of the economic and market component of a reuse plan is to identify the array of land uses that maximizes the economic opportunity of the site.

The identification of a product/land use menu should be undertaken with as broad a vision as possible, with the ultimate goal of creating a plan with a synergistic array of land uses. The menu of potential opportunities is compiled by the consulting team. Public input from individuals and various interest groups is expected and accepted.

Through the analysis that follows, the range of potential land uses is narrowed down to those that are most feasible and most likely to succeed at the subject site. One of the most important issues to consider regarding the identification of land uses appropriate for the redevelopment of any large property, including brownfield parcels, is that the land plan must always remain *flexible*. Major shifts in the global, national, or regional economy will almost certainly occur during the lengthy buildout period. Such shifts will influence the mix of land uses at the redeveloped base and could potentially influence the needs and priorities of the affected communities and the LRA.

To identify the initial product menu at MCAS EL Toro, the LRA and the consulting team met in a brainstorming session. In addition, the LRA was inundated with suggestions from the public, all of which were considered when generating the list of potential land uses for the property. Proposals from the public included development of the site for a World's Fair, a national cemetery, a film studio, a national sports complex, and as a campus for a religious organization. The list that was generated included an arena/stadium, a convention center, a mixed-use entertainment center, an auto center, and various types of residential, retail, office, and industrial uses.

Site Analysis
The site analysis involves conducting a physical study of the base property and evaluating it from a market perspective. Site characteristics examined are regional location, regional and local access, size, topography, visibility, and surrounding land uses. The property is ranked according to its appropriateness for the land uses under consideration. This process serves to confirm the suitability of proposed land uses and to eliminate less-suitable ones.

The property is typically evaluated in its entirety. Particular attention is paid to existing conditions, such as areas formerly used to store hazardous materials, and to existing structures that may have interim utility. Most important is how the site's characteristics relate to or affect development of the land uses being considered.

The El Toro site offers an outstanding development opportunity. A predominantly flat, infill site supported by a strong regional infrastructure network, the property is surrounded by clean residential, commercial, industrial, and open space uses, in an area (Orange County) recognized nationally for its high quality of living.

The reuse plan for MCAS El Toro was designed to incorporate as many of the existing facilities as possible. Existing uses that were designated for inclusion are

- The Marine Memorial golf course, which will be expanded and linked to residential uses and the planned Sports and Entertainment Village;
- Aviation hangars, which have been designated for industrial purposes such as warehousing, manufacturing, or sound stage uses;
- Recently constructed former barracks facilities, which can be reused as student dormitory housing or as a hotel;
- An equestrian center, which will be adapted for civilian use and linked to residential areas and to a regional riding and hiking trail.

As of January 1998, 85 percent of the MCAS El Toro site was "clean" and suitable for any land use. By the time of acquisition by the LRA, all of the site will be developable for urban uses. Thus, the land planning efforts considered no environmental constraints and assumed a clean property.

Definition of the Primary Market Area

The PMA for each land use under consideration is identified through interviews with representatives of relevant businesses already operating in the area and with operators of new and innovative uses that could be attracted to the redeveloped property. Depending on the product type, PMAs can range greatly in size—from a radius of a few miles in diameter, to a regional or even national level.

Macro-level Economic Analysis

Historic and projected employment trends provide data for the analysis of a region's growth potential and how that will influence development at the reused property. Analysis by SIC identifies industrial sectors that show the strongest expansion potential and, therefore, that should be addressed during the buildout of the base facility. Additionally, this analysis helps in further refining the selection of uses that are most likely to succeed at the base property.

In the often politically charged environment of military base reuse, the use of growth projections that have been adopted by a number of major local and regional governing entities is strongly recommended. Such projections are typically published by a well-recognized university research center or governmental entity located in the region.

The Center for Demographic Research at California State University at Fullerton and the California State Economic Development Department provided the projections used for the analysis of MCAS El Toro. The study examined employment growth projections overall and by SIC in Orange County, comparisons to a national index, and the current and projected jobs/housing balance in the county. Strong employment growth is projected for the buildout period of the base, with the county maintaining concentrations in high-skill, high-income sectors. For instance, in the high-tech manufacturing sector, which includes biotechnology, computer software and hardware, and aerospace, Orange County has 2.4 times the national average concentration.

Identification of Economic Drivers

Important to the future economic growth of the region is the targeting of economic drivers for location or expansion at the former base. Economic drivers are industries that stimulate growth, create synergy, bring high-wage and high-skill jobs to the area, create spin-off jobs, and foster economic growth in the region. Typically, economic drivers are "export industries," that is, those that sell the majority of their goods and services outside of the region. For instance, an airport can be an economic driver, potentially generating strong demand for related uses and thus creating jobs. (The analysis of the market potential of development with aviation uses is typically done by specialty firms with expertise in aviation planning.)

Research into the most appropriate economic driver industries for the base redevelopment plan provides a framework for the uses to be included in the plan. The application of a widely accepted methodology and economic model is extremely useful in this process. Typically, the model calculates for a given study area the economic multiplier of a given industry. The economic multiplier is the cumulative effect of new jobs introduced (direct), inter-industry jobs created as a byproduct (indirect), and jobs created by household expenditures increased by the addition of income from new jobs (induced). An impact, or output, analysis combines these factors to assess change in overall economic activity, and yields data in dollars or number of employees for economic comparison.

Targeting Economic Drivers

The likelihood of an economic driver industry locating or expanding at the base depends on creating a magnet site to attract the most sought-after sectors. Creating a magnet site is addressed using the following research and analysis:

1. Identifying emerging industries in the region that have strong positive economic effects.
2. Interviewing representatives of those industries to determine their space and location needs and preferences. Specifically, identifying needs and preferences in terms of building type (low-rise, mid-rise, or high-rise office; research and development space; multitenant industrial; warehouse; or manufacturing space) and proximity to suppliers, labor force, educational facilities, other related firms, clients, and retail services.
3. Identifying industries that drive economies elsewhere, but that have only a limited local presence, and that would have a positive economic effect if attracted.
4. Interviewing representatives of those industries to determine their level of interest in locating at the former base and to identify features that might attract them.
5. Investigating the possibilities of attracting special uses to the site that would benefit the area's economy and/or quality of life. These uses may include

educational institutions, sports arenas, museums, entertainment complexes, and tourist attractions.
6. Interviewing representatives of such uses to determine their site-selection criteria, their level of interest in the site, and what features might attract them.
7. Analyzing case studies of areas elsewhere in the region, nation, and world where clusters of such uses have developed to identify features and conditions that are important to those industries that can be incorporated into the specific plan.
8. Analyzing in case study format successful redevelopment of former military bases and large brownfield sites throughout the country, identifying mistakes made and lessons learned with respect to land use synergy.

This type of research provides valuable input for determining criteria to create a magnet site at the former base. It is also useful for identifying a preliminary focus or theme for the land use plan.

Using factors from the widely recognized and accepted Minnesota Implan Group model that can be applied to Orange County, the analysis yielded key findings with regard to local economic drivers and resulted in the following three-part answer:

1. Those industry sectors with the highest employment multipliers (most spin-off jobs from each base industry job) are finance, insurance, and real estate (FIRE) (2.5 spin-off jobs); transportation and public utilities (2.4); high-tech manufacturing (2.3); wholesale trade (2.1); and standard manufacturing (2.0).
2. Industries that produce the greatest output per employee are transportation and public utilities ($350,000), high-tech manufacturing ($291,000), FIRE ($287,000), standard manufacturing ($266,000), and wholesale trade ($200,000).
3. Industries with the highest total income per employee are FIRE ($94,000), transportation and public utilities ($93,000), high-tech manufacturing ($91,000), and wholesale trade ($80,700).

The analysis served to identify on a preliminary basis the industries that should be targeted for the MCAS El Toro property. Interviews with regional economists confirmed that these sectors are feasible at the site and validated the economic effects suggested by their multipliers. Interviews with representatives of these sectors helped to define the requirements of those industries and how the site could be developed to accommodate them.

Demographic Analysis

The demographic portion of the market analysis analyzes population and household growth for the local area and region. Strong demographic growth trends are an important engine of a growing economy.

The recognized academic or government source used for employment projections most likely publishes population and household forecasts as well. These should be used for consistency and to reduce any potential objections about source. The demographic projections are used to forecast growth in the PMA for each of the land uses proposed.

Definition of the Competitive Market Area

The CMA, or trade area (TA) in the case of retail land uses, is the area in which the planned product is expected to compete on a more or less equal basis. It is determined through surveys and interviews with users, brokers, and representatives of the various uses under consideration. Depending on the use in question, the CMA can be as small as the five- to ten-mile radius surrounding the property (e.g., for residential product) or can encompass the entire nation (e.g., in the case of a major theme park or convention center).

Existing and projected competitive supply for the various land uses under consideration for MCAS El Toro were analyzed not only in Orange County, but also for worldwide case-study analogues. This extended analysis was found to be particularly useful for special land uses such as stadiums, convention centers, and mixed-use entertainment centers because these destination locations compete on a large geographic scale, and few comparables existed in the immediate market area.

Competitive Market Analysis

A survey of the competitive market for the proposed product types is an essential component of the market analysis.

Given the long-range plans typically associated with base closure and reuse, most important with regard to the competitive market is a macro-level market analysis for each of the major land uses under consideration. An examination of historical trends (e.g., home sales and prices; rents and vacancies; and industrial, commercial, and retail occupancies and lease rates) can serve as a guide for the future. An examination of the existing supply of competitors in the given CMA provides the following information:

1. Indicates what has been successful for the various product types under consideration in the local area, and why;
2. Identifies product gaps that have occurred in the CMA and examines the potential of their being filled by redevelopment at the base facility;
3. Analyzes effective demand for each product type in its CMA, for use in the statistical analyses of future demand and capture potential for the site.

Analysis of existing supply is also necessary to determine achievable per acre land sale prices by product type in the CMA, which will be applied in the economic evaluation of one land use scenario against another (described in detail later in this study). Identification of future supply, or planned and proposed projects in the CMA, is important in projecting future competition for proposed product types and in pinpointing future opportunities. Key factors in the analysis of proposed product include projected product type, location, timing, and projections for absorption and buildout.

If no local comparables exist, analogous situations can be useful as case studies. Analyzing successful military base and large brownfield developments from around the country, and indeed the world, is a useful tool in determining the competitive benefits and drawbacks associated with large-scale redevelopment. Of particular importance to the study of a large-scale development are the mistakes made and lessons learned with regard to (1) land use distribution, (2) synergy of uses, (3) economic driver tenants and other employment generators, (4) satisfaction of the needs of the surrounding communities, and (5) harmony with surrounding land uses.

Comparable projects for many of the land uses under consideration for MCAS El Toro, such as residential, retail, office, and industrial, were found in Orange County. Analysis of analogous military base and brownfield projects elsewhere were useful as well. Case study analyses included Lowry Air Force Base in Denver, Colorado; Research Triangle Park in Raleigh, North Carolina; Sophia Antipolis Science Park in Nice, France; Chiba Industrial Triangle in Tokyo, Japan; and the Multimedia Super Corridor in Kuala Lumpur, Malaysia. The analyses provided examples of successful land use distributions; high-income, high-output job generation; and maximizing the opportunities offered by existing infrastructure and amenities.

Analysis of Demand and Capture Potential

Statistical demand potential and absorption forecasts are necessary for the majority of primary land uses. They identify supportable absorption on site that fits in with buildout in the local market area. Demand potential is generated by population and employment growth, as well as by turnover in the existing product supply.

Analyses of demand and capture potential for residential land uses are based on both quantitative and qualitative methodologies, including projected household growth in the PMA, affordability indices, and historical data such as sales trends in the CMA. The analysis yields an estimate of the total number of dwelling units that can be absorbed in a given time frame, by price or rent range, and by ownership versus rental.

Analyses of demand potential for industrial and office uses are based on employment projections by SIC for the appropriate CMAs. Incorporating factors such as (1) typical capture of a particular industrial sector by product type, (2) average square footage per employee by product type, and (3) existing and projected land use patterns by type of space, the analyses estimate annual absorption potential by square foot and type of space.

Demand potential analyses for retail land uses are based on population growth in a given TA. The analysis includes factors such as per capita spending by product type, sales potential per square foot by product type, floor area ratio, and additional demand from outside the

TA. Demand potential analysis for retail uses yields annual absorption potential figures in supportable square footage.

Estimates of demand and absorption potential using standard methodologies may yield conservative results. Analyses should be adjusted to include a qualitative factor to reflect the full effect of the on-site synergy among various uses, such as technology and educational space, residential and employment centers, and cultural resources, which cannot be quantified.

As discussed earlier, flexibility of product mix is essential for the success of a long-range reuse plan. Opportunities should remain open to intensify land uses as well as to reorganize the uses when market conditions change during the buildout period.

Creation of Land Use Scenarios

When the objectives of the economic and market analyses are applied to create a plan that maximizes economic return to the region in harmony with the needs of the surrounding communities and the environment, the proposed land uses are assigned an acreage amount. This process results in alternative land use scenarios that are tested using the following analytical tools. The mix is subject to revision and refinement.

Economic Impact Assessment of Land Use Scenarios

An economic model is used to evaluate the relative benefits of each scenario over a 20-year period, or to buildout; the model typically presents five-year development phases. It is based on assumptions generated by the market analysis and yields the following outputs by land use: total units or square feet, on-site employment, total employment generated, land sale revenue, total output, and total income.

The model allows the team to refine the land use scenarios by adjusting the jobs-to-housing balance, the concentrations of industrial and commercial uses, the inclusion of special uses, and the amount of open space. The goal of such refinements is to create a reuse plan that works in accordance with the study objectives.

At this point, the land planners apply the acreage mixes of each scenario to a map of the property. The evolving land plans are closely scrutinized by the transportation and environmental team members to ensure that the scenarios are feasible from the perspective of their disciplines. Throughout the process, the consulting team meets regularly with the LRA to discuss evolving land plans, verifying that plans are in accordance with the agreed upon goals and objectives.

Fiscal Impact Analysis

The fiscal impact analysis projects the public sector revenues that can be expected from development, occupancy, and servicing of the project. The analysis evaluates project-generated revenues and costs in terms of their net effect on a specific jurisdiction relative to particular land uses on a per acre basis. Certain recognized guidelines, assumptions, and factors from the locality may be required for the fiscal impact analysis.

Revenue to local agencies generated by the new development (fiscal revenue) includes a portion of the basic property tax, sales taxes (in some cases), transient occupancy taxes, taxes from the transfer of real property, subventions from other agencies, business license revenues, and other taxes and fees. Costs incurred by a local government to provide public services to a new project (fiscal expense) typically include the cost of general government, public safety, public works, parks and recreation, and in some cases, education and social programs.

Financial Analysis

The financial analysis portion of the market study quantifies the cash flow generated by a particular scenario, overall and by development phase, after accounting for all revenues and costs through buildout. Advantageous mechanisms specific to the military base closure process (such as Public Benefit and Economic Development Conveyances) are incorporated into the analysis. Using these tools, the objective of the analysis is to provide a preliminary assessment of the plan's ability to pay for itself without the infusion of local public funding.

Revenues to the LRA are generated through land sales to third parties (private or public/private ventures) and interim leases of buildings before they are demolished or converted to the final plan use. Land sales and lease

values are determined in the survey portion of the market analysis.

Implementation of the Reuse Plan

As the reuse proceeds to implementation, an effective organizational framework to guide the redevelopment, marketing, and management of property disposition is needed. Implementing a long-range reuse plan requires ongoing management by the LRA. It is the task of the LRA to review the feasibility of certain options such as

■ Creating an operating company to direct the implementation process, including issues of staffing and financing;
■ Working with a master developer to oversee development of the site, either as an active developer or by hiring subdevelopers or subcontractors to complete specialized phases of the project;
■ Employing a development manager who is responsible for contracting out the development and construction management of the entire base or portions of the base;
■ Using other alternatives that may be deemed appropriate.

Agencies that may administer the plan include a reuse agency, a department of the local jurisdiction, a redevelopment agency formed specifically for the base reuse, or a joint-powers authority.

Public Participation in the Development of the Reuse Plan

Given the often contentious environment associated with the proposed closure and reuse of a military facility, public participation is extremely important. Local residents, whose futures will be affected by the base redevelopment, have a strong and valid interest in proposed reuse plans. The public's perception of the LRA should be as a "people's entity" working to create a "people's plan" with the good of the economy, the community, and the environment as its prime concerns. Public participation should be strongly emphasized and interwoven into the planning process. The public participation process, and any media attention, are typically handled by the public relations team member and can be addressed in the following ways:

1. Public meetings and community outreach programs. These efforts are conducted throughout the planning process and when the proposed scenario is taken on a "road show," presented to the public, and discussed in an open forum.
2. Community volunteer programs. Members of the affected communities have the opportunity to provide input throughout the planning process by serving on subcommittees. These subcommittees, which meet on a regular basis, help identify the goals and objectives of the reuse effort, provide critical input to the constantly evolving scenarios, and recommend the scenarios to be submitted to the review committee.

Results of the MCAS El Toro Reuse Planning Effort

The ETRPA team developed three alternative scenarios for the nonaviation reuse of MCAS El Toro. Each alternative was reviewed by members of the public who served on sub-committees. The alternatives addressed three opportunities for the reuse of the base: (1) high economic output, (2) focus on open space, and (3) a balance of jobs and housing.

HIGH-ECONOMIC-OUTPUT ALTERNATIVE

The first alternative concentrated on uses that generate high economic output while maintaining acceptable traffic generation. It focused on a central mixed-use area of community commercial, museums, convention center, hotels, low- and mid-rise offices, and medium- to high-density residential development.

With 12,000 to 13,000 residential units, the plan would achieve a 50 percent jobs/housing balance. It includes more than 40 acres of commercial uses and 500 acres of industrial uses. Special uses include a stadium, an outdoor sports complex, a convention center, and a museum complex. This alternative also includes a major educational facility adjacent to industrial areas, encouraging synergies between teaching and technology facilities.

Nonresidential uses create 70,000 to 80,000 jobs on and off site, with a total county output of $7.0 billion to $7.5 billion by the year 2020, and a positive fiscal impact of $11.5 million to $12.5 million. Preliminary calculations estimate that this alternative would generate traffic of 335,000 to 375,000 daily trips.

OPEN-SPACE-PRESERVATION ALTERNATIVE

This scenario optimizes the natural open spaces with a 300-acre regional park as its focus. Other uses include residential and many of the same nonresidential uses as the previous alternative: a stadium, an outdoor sports complex, a convention center, a university, and a museum complex.

Almost 200 acres are dedicated to office uses, and 400 acres to industrial uses. In addition, the plan calls for a 300-acre theme park/mixed-use entertainment facility. In an effort to create open space while maintaining an acceptable economic output, acreage was transferred from residential to open-space uses, reducing the jobs/housing balance to 25 percent.

Nonresidential uses result in a total economic output of $6.0 billion to $7.0 billion by the year 2020, with a positive fiscal impact of $10 million to $11 million, and the creation of 60,000 to 70,000 jobs. Daily traffic generation is estimated at 270,000 to 305,000 trips.

BALANCE-OF-JOBS-AND-HOUSING ALTERNATIVE

This alternative maintains a jobs/housing balance of 100 percent on the site. Uses include a 330-acre college campus, a stadium, an outdoor sports complex, a convention center, an entertainment center, and automobile commercial uses, as well as residential and other nonresidential. Although large portions of acreage go to residential uses, the plan calls for 40 acres of neighborhood and community commercial, 200 acres of office, and 300 acres of industrial uses.

The nonresidential uses create an estimated 50,000 to 60,000 jobs and result in a total output of $4.5 billion to $5.5 billion by the year 2020. Fiscal benefit to the county is estimated at $5.5 million to $6.5 million. Daily traffic is estimated at 275,000 to 315,000 trips, similar to the previous alternative.

The Final Proposal

In response to the subcommittees' recommendations, the primary element of Alternative 3, the research and technology campus, was incorporated into Alternative 1, and Alternative 3 was eliminated from consideration. After further revision to Alternatives 1 and 2 in accordance with the subcommittees' recommendations, the proposals were sent to the ETRPA Coordinating Review Committee (CRC), whose members were a group of Orange County leaders and representatives of various interest groups. The CRC reviewed Alternatives 1 and 2, then recommended development of a third plan that would fully achieve the objectives of ETRPA. All three plans are outlined below.

CRC-1: Education/Research/Technology (ERT) focus

- Urban village image including a large central park and major residential and retail areas within the 700-acre ERT campus
- Total job creation: 85,000 to 95,000
- Total economic output: $8.5 billion to $9.5 billion
- Total annual income at buildout: $2.5 billion to $3.5 billion
- Net fiscal benefit: $10 million to $11 million

CRC-2: Arts/Culture/Education/Sports focus

- Two urban village centers with museums, entertainment centers, hotels, a convention center, an outdoor sports complex, and a 200-acre ERT campus, plus a 700-acre central park
- Total job creation: 55,000 to 65,000
- Total economic output: $5.0 billion to $6.0 billion
- Total annual income at buildout: $1.5 billion to $2.5 billion
- Net fiscal benefit: $13.5 million to $14.5 million

CRC-3: Economic and Open Space dual focus

- Four districts, each with its own focus—(1) education, research, and technology, (2) arts and culture, (3) sports

and entertainment, and (4) habitat preservation—and a mixed-use village as its activity core, containing approximately 2,300 acres of active and passive open space (more than 50% of the total acreage)
- Total job creation: 80,000 to 90,000
- Total economic output: $8.0 billion to $9.0 billion
- Total annual income at buildout: $2.5 billion to $3.5 billion
- Net fiscal benefit: $11.0 million to $12.0 million
- Financial analysis: positive net cash flow of ±$398 million by 2020

The CRC recommended some refinement of the CRC-3 plan, which resulted in the final land use program. Millennium, as the plan was called, was presented by the consulting team to the ETRPA board.

Final CRC-3: Millennium

- Total job creation: 100,000 to 112,000
- Total economic output: $10.4 billion to $12.9 billion
- Total annual income at buildout: $3.7 billion to $4.4 billion
- Net fiscal benefit: $7.5 million to $8.5 million
- Financial analysis: positive net cash flow of ±$397 million by 2020

The ETRPA board authorized the consulting team to use the recommended alternative to prepare the ETRPA MCAS El Toro Reuse Plan. The ETRPA planning team completed the Millennium plan in March 1998. The plan fulfills the economic, social, and environmental goals that reflect the quality of life ETRPA seeks to provide.

The next phase in the process involves submitting the Millennium plan to the county and the Department of the Navy. Should Millennium be selected as the preferred alternative, the reuse plan would serve as a specific plan for the property.

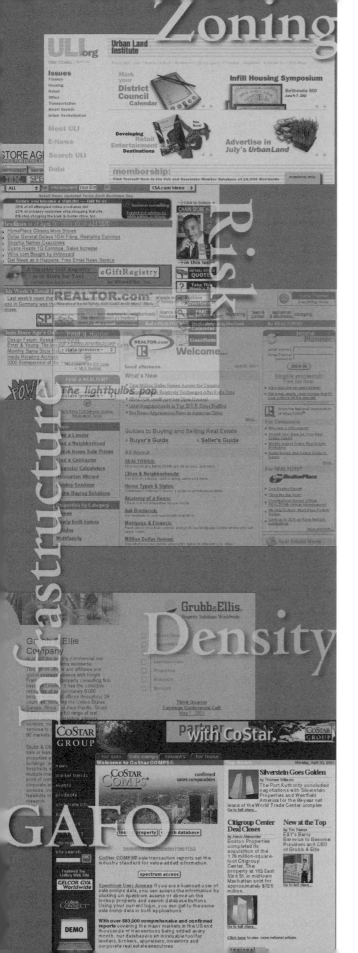

Appendices

Sources of Data

Market Forecast Sources

Apts.com
apartment comparables
www.apts.com
Market Coverage: U.S. markets
Property Types: multifamily rental
Types of Data: comparables

CB Richard Ellis
Pacific Corporate Towers
200 North Sepulveda Boulevard, Suite 300
El Segundo, CA 90245
310.563.8600
www.cbrichardellis.com
Market Coverage: U.S. and international major
   markets
Property Types: office; industrial; retail
Types of Data: vacancy rates; absorption rates;
   construction activity; rental rates

Colliers International
4 State Street, Third Floor
Boston, MA 02109
617.772.0221
www.colliers.com
Market Coverage: U.S. and international major
   markets
Property Types: office; industrial; residential; retail
Types of Data: vacancy rates; absorption rates;
   construction activity; sale and lease comparables

Corporate Real Estate Service Advisors (CRESA)
14785 Preston Road, Suite 475
Dallas, TX 75240
972.866.6800
www.cresa.com or www.globest.com
Market Coverage: U.S. major markets
Property Types: industrial
Types of Data: vacancy rates; rental rates; sale
   comparables

CoStar Group
2 Bethesda Metro Center, Tenth Floor
Bethesda, MD 20814
301.215.8300
www.costargroup.com
Market Coverage: U.S. major markets
Property Types: office; industrial
Types of Data: vacancy rates; absorption rates;
   construction activity; sale and lease comparables

Cushman & Wakefield, Inc.
51 West 52nd Street
New York, NY 10019
212.841.7500
www.cushmanwakefield.com
Market Coverage: U.S. and international major
   markets
Property Types: office; industrial
Types of Data: vacancy rates; absorption rates;
   construction activity; rental rates

Delta Associates
320 King Street, Suite 250
Alexandria, VA 22314
703.836.5700
www.deltaassociates.com
Market Coverage: Baltimore/Washington, DC;
   Houston; Los Angeles; Phoenix
Property Types: office; industrial; lodging;
   multifamily; retail
Types of Data: market overview; vacancy rates;
   absorption rates; construction activity; rental
   rates; custom research

Entertainment Data Solutions, Inc.
3688 Research Way
Carson City, NV 89706
775.885.2522
www.ent-data-solutions.com
Market Coverage: U.S. markets
Property Types: entertainment venues
Types of Data: ticketing and admission sales; food
   and beverage sales; merchandise and other sales
   at entertainment facilities

EY Kenneth Leventhal

787 Seventh Avenue
New York, NY 10019
212.773.4900
www.ey.com
Market Coverage: U.S. major markets
Property Types: lodging
Types of Data: regional occupancy; supply and
    demand; revPAR; average daily rates; revenues
Publications: National Lodging Forecast

F.W. Dodge Market Forecasts

F.W. Dodge Market Analysis Group / The McGraw-
    Hill Companies
24 Hartwell Avenue
Lexington, MA 02173
800.591.4462
www.mag.fwdodge.com
Market Coverage: U.S. major markets
Property Types: office; industrial; lodging; retail
Types of Data: construction activity; vacancy;
    absorption; supply and demand; general
    economic indicators; custom research
Publications: Construction Outlook

Grubb & Ellis

2215 Sanders Road
Northbrook, IL 60062
847.753.7500
www.grubb-ellis.com
Market Coverage: U.S. major markets
Property Types: office; industrial; retail
Types of Data: vacancy rates; absorption rates;
    construction activity; rental rates; custom
    research
Publications: The National Real Estate Market Forecast

Insignia/ESG Commercial Market Report

Insignia/ESG
Liberty Plaza, 45th Floor
New York, NY 10006
212.618.7000
www.insigniaesg.com
Market Coverage: U.S. major markets
Property Types: office; industrial; lodging
Types of Data: market overviews; properties for sale
    and lease; construction activity

Jones Lang LaSalle

200 East Randolph Drive
Chicago, IL 60601
312.782.5800
www.joneslanglasalle.com
Market Coverage: international major markets
Property Types: office; industrial; lodging;
    multifamily; retail
Types of Data: market overviews; property listings;
    construction activity
Publications: Investment Strategy Annual

Landauer Realty Group

55 East 59th Street, Fourth Floor
New York, NY 10022
212.621.9500
www.landauer.com
Market Coverage: Atlanta; Boston; Dallas; Los
    Angeles; New York; south Florida
Property Types: office; multifamily; industrial; retail;
    lodging
Types of Data: custom research; general economic
    indicators

Lend Lease Real Estate Investments

787 Seventh Avenue, 46th Floor
New York, NY 10019
212.554.1600
www.lendleaserei.com
Market Coverage: U.S. major markets
Property Types: office; industrial; lodging; senior
    living; retail
Types of Data: vacancy rates; absorption rates;
    construction activity; rent; investment returns
Publications: Emerging Trends in Real Estate (in
    conjunction with PricewaterhouseCoopers)

Marcus and Millichap

16830 Ventura Boulevard
Encino, CA 91436
818.907.0600
www.mmreibc.com
Market Coverage: U.S. major markets
Property Types: office; retail; multifamily; seniors'
housing; lodging; self-storage
Types of Data: national and regional trends; property
listings; custom research
*Publications: National Real Estate Investment Report;
Senior Housing Report*

Meyers Group

The Meyers Group
1920 Main Street, Suite 200
Irvine, CA 92614
949.263.8755
www.meyersgroup.com
Market Coverage: U.S. major markets
Property Types: residential
Types of Data: construction activity; economic and
housing statistics; mortgage rates; demographics;
psychographics; comparables

M/PF Research

4000 International Parkway
Carrollton, TX 75007
972.820.3100
www.mpfresearch.com
Market Coverage: U.S. major markets
Property Types: multifamily residential
Types of Data: occupancy rates; vacancy rates; rent;
supply and demand; employment growth;
inventory; custom research
Publications: MarketSmart

Mr. Office Space.Com

Yale Robbins, Inc.
31 East 28th Street
New York, NY 10016
212.683.5700
www.yrinc.com
Market Coverage: northeast U.S. markets
Property Types: office
Types of Data: market statistics; comparables

NAI Direct

572 US Route 130
Hightstown, NJ 08520
609.448.4700
www.naidirect.com
Market Coverage: international markets
Property Types: office; industrial; retail; hotel;
multifamily
Types of Data: vacancy rates; land prices;
demographics; comparables

National Association of Home Builders

1201 15th Street, NW
Washington, DC 20005
800.368.5242 or 202.822.0200 within the Washington,
D.C., metropolitan area
www.nahb.org
Market Coverage: U.S. markets
Property Types: residential
Types of Data: affordability index; construction data;
home prices and characteristics; sales data;
mortgage rates
*Publications: Housing Economics; Housing Market
Statistics*

National Association of Realtors

700 11th Street, NW
Washington, DC 20005
www.realtor.com
Market Coverage: U.S. markets
Property Types: residential
Types of Data: listings and sales by zip code;
mortgage data

Oncor International

1747 Pennsylvania Avenue, NW, Suite 350
Washington, DC 20006
202.452.1852
www.oncorintl.com
Market Coverage: international markets
Property Types: office
Types of Data: inventory; leasing data; transaction
costs; property taxes; vacancy rates; absorption
rates; construction activity

PikeNet

Box 1177
Ross, CA 94957
www.pikenet.com
Market Coverage: U.S. markets
Property Types: office; retail; multifamily; industrial;
 hotel; land
Types of Data: links to sites on demographics,
 listings, consultants, news, and other data
*Publications: PikeNet Directory of Commercial Real
 Estate; PikeNet Dispatch*

PKF Consulting

425 California Street, Suite 1650
San Francisco, CA 94104
415.421.5378
www.pkfonline.com
Market Coverage: U.S. markets
Property Types: lodging
Types of Data: revenue; expenses; investment
 returns; occupancy rates; custom research

PricewaterhouseCoopers

1301 Avenue of the Americas
New York, NY 10019
212.520.2666
www.pw.com
Market Coverage: U.S. regional
Property Types: office; industrial; lodging; residential;
 retail
Types of Data: vacancy rates; absorption rates;
 construction activity; rent; investment returns
Publications: Emerging Trends in Real Estate (in
 conjunction with Lend Lease Real Estate
 Investments)

Real Estate Report

Real Estate Research Corporation (RERC)
980 North Michigan Avenue, Suite 1675
Chicago, IL 60611
312.587.1800
www.rerc.com
Market Coverage: U.S. markets
Property Types: office; industrial; lodging; residential;
 retail
Types of Data: general economic indicators;
 demographics; custom research
Publications: RERC Real Estate Report; Metro e-Trends

REIS

5 West 37th Street, 12th Floor
New York, NY 10018
212.921.1122
www.reis.com
Market Coverage: U.S. markets
Property Types: office; industrial; multifamily; retail
Types of Data: vacancy rates; absorption rates; rents;
 inventory; construction activity; maps;
 comparables

Smith Travel Research

105 Music Village Boulevard
Hendersonville, TN 37075
615.824.8664
www.str-online.com
Market Coverage: U.S. markets
Property Types: lodging
Types of Data: occupancy rates; room rates; revPAR;
 inventory
Publications: Lodging Outlook; HOST Study

Society of Industrial and Office Realtors (SIOR)

The Comparative Statistics of Industrial and Office
 Real Estate Markets
700 11th Street, NW, Suite 510
Washington, DC 20001
202.737.1150
www.sior.com
Market Coverage: U.S. markets
Property Types: office; industrial
Types of Data: inventory; vacancy rates; absorption
 rates; construction activity; sales prices; rents

Springstreet.com

www.springstreet.com
Market Coverage: U.S. markets
Property Types: multifamily rental
Types of Data: apartment comparables

The Staubach Company

15601 Dallas Parkway, Suite 400
Addison, TX 75001
800.944.0012
www.staubach.com
Market Coverage: international; U.S. markets
Property Types: office; industrial; retail
Types of Data: rents; costs; demographics and
  psychographics; competitor market share; drive-
  time analysis; custom research

TCN Real Estate

2419 Coit Road, Suite A
Plano, TX 75075
972.769.8701
www.tcnre.com
TCN Real Estate has 13 member companies that
  provide real estate market data.
Market Coverage: international; U.S. markets
Property Types: varies by market and by member
  company
Types of Data: varies by market and by member
  company

Torto Wheaton Research

200 High Street
Boston, MA 02110
617.912.5200
www.tortowheatonresearch.com
Market Coverage: international; U.S. major markets
Property Types: office; industrial; retail; multifamily
Types of Data: vacancy rates; rents; investment risk
  and returns; inventory; construction; comparables
Publications: TWR Outlook

Urban Land Institute

1025 Thomas Jefferson Street, NW
Washington, DC 20007
202.624.7000
www.uli.org
Market Coverage: international; U.S. markets
Property Types: office; industrial; lodging; residential;
  retail
Types of Data: income and expense data; rents;
  trends
*Publications: ULI Real Estate Forecast; MetroPackets;
  Dollars & Cents of Multifamily Housing®; Dollars &
  Cents of Shopping Centers®*

Economic and Demographic Data Providers

CACI

1100 North Glebe Road
Arlington, VA 22201
800.292.2224
www.demographics.caci.com

Claritas

5375 Mira Sorrento Place, Suite 400
San Diego, CA 92121
800.866.6510
www.claritas.com

Demographics USA

45 Danbury Road
Wilton, CT 06897
203.563.3100
www.tradedimensions.com

Economy.com, Inc.

600 Willowbrook Lane, Suite 600
West Chester, PA 19382
610.696.8700
www.economy.com/rfa

NPA Data

1413 South 20th Street
Arlington, VA 22202
703.979.8400
www.npadata.com

U.S. Census Bureau

Washington, DC 20233
301.457.4608
www.census.gov

Wharton Econometric Forecasting Associates (WEFA)

800 Baldwin Tower
Eddystone, PA 19022
610.490.4000
www.wefa.com

Woods & Poole Economics
1794 Columbia Road, NW, Suite 4
Washington, DC 20009
800.786.1915
www.woodsandpoole.com

Directories

Black's Guide, Inc.
444 North Frederick Avenue, Suite 240
Gaithersburg, MD 20877
301.948.0995
www.blacksguide.com
Property data for more than 75,000 office and
industrial properties; coverage spans 19 major
U.S. markets

Chain Store Guides
3922 Coconut Palm Drive
Tampa, FL 33619
813.627.6800
www.csgis.com
Data on more than 300,000 retailers, distributors,
and wholesalers in North America

Commercial Property News, Goldbook
Miller Freeman, Inc.
1515 Broadway
New York, NY 10036
212.869.1300
www.cpnrenet.com
Information on major real estate firms and
executives nationwide

National Real Estate Investor (NREI) Sourcebook
Intertec Publishing Group
6151 Powers Ferry Road, NW
Atlanta, GA 30339
770.955.2500
www.nreionline.com
Major players in commercial real estate

Retail Tenant Directory
Trade Dimensions
45 Danbury Road
Wilton, CT 06897
203.563.3100
www.tradedimensions.com
Annual directory of more than 5,000 actively
expanding retail chains in North America

Shopping Center Directory
National Research Bureau (NRB)
Trade Dimensions
45 Danbury Road
Wilton, CT 06897
203.563.3100
www.tradedimensions.com
Listings for 38,000 shopping centers, 4,600
headquarter contacts, and property list
information for more than 1,300 major real estate
companies

Periodicals

American City Business Journals
120 West Morehead Street
Charlotte, NC 28202
704.973.1000
www.bizjournals.com

American Demographics
Intertec Publishing
11 River Bend Drive South
Box 4274
Stamford, CT 06907
203.358.9900
www.americandemographics.com

Builder
Hanley-Wood, Inc.
One Thomas Circle, NW
Washington, DC 20005
800.829.9127
www.builderonline.com

Building Design & Construction
Cahners Business Information
Cahners Plaza
1350 East Touhy Avenue
Des Plaines, IL 60018
847.635.8800
www.bdcmag.com

Buildings
Stamats Building Group
615 5th Street SE
P.O. Box 1888
Cedar Rapids, IA 52406
319.364.6167
www.buildings.com

Chain Store Age
Lebhar-Friedman
425 Park Avenue
New York, NY 10022
800.216.7117
www.chainstoreage.com

Commercial Investment Real Estate
Commercial Investment Real Estate Institute
430 North Michigan Avenue
Chicago, IL 60611-4092
312.321.4460
www.ccim.com

Commercial Property News
Miller Freeman, Inc.
1515 Broadway
New York, NY 10036
212.869.1300
www.cpnrenet.com

Expansion Management
9500 Nall Avenue, Suite 400
Overland Park, KS 66207
913.381.4800
www.expandman.com

Lodging Outlook
Smith Travel Research
105 Music Village Boulevard
Hendersonville, TN 37075
615.824.8664
www.str-online.com

National Real Estate Investor
Intertec Publishing Group
6151 Powers Ferry Road, NW
Atlanta, GA 30339
770.955.2500
www.nreionline.com

Plants, Sites & Parks
Cahners Business Information
49 Music Square West
Nashville, TN 37203
615.321.1500
www.bizsites.com

Professional Builder
Cahners Publishing Company
8773 South Ridgeline Boulevard
Highlands Ranch, CO 80126
303.470.4000
www.probuilder.com

Real Estate Forum
Real Estate Media, Inc.
520 Eighth Avenue
New York, NY 10018
212.929.6900
www.globest.com

Sales & Marketing Management
Bill Communications, Inc.
770 Broadway
New York, NY 10003
646.654.7259
www.salesandmarketing.com

Shopping Center Business
France Publications, Inc.
3500 Piedmont Road, Suite 415
Atlanta, GA 30305
770.952.4300
www.shoppingcenterbusiness.com

Appendix A: Sources of Data *(continued)*

Shopping Center World
Intertec Publishing
6151 Powers Ferry Road, NW
Atlanta, GA 30339
770.955.2500
www.scwonline.com

Shopping Centers Today
International Council of Shopping Centers
1221 Avenue of the Americas
New York, NY 10020
646.728.3800
www.icsc.org

Site Selection
Conway Data
35 Technology Parkway, Suite 150
Norcross, GA 30092
770.446.6996
www.siteselection.com

Value Retail News
International Council of Shopping Centers
1221 Avenue of the Americas
New York, NY 10020
646.728.3800
www.icsc.org

Absorption rate: The amount of real estate that will be leased or sold in a given time period.

Amenity: Nonmonetary tangible or intangible benefit derived from real property (often offered to a lessee), typically recreational facilities, concierge services, or planned activities.

Anchor tenant: The major chain(s) or department store(s) in a shopping center, which are positioned to produce traffic for the smaller stores in the facility.

Appraisal: An opinion or estimate of value substantiated by various analyses.

Asset manager: A person who balances risk and reward in managing investment portfolios, including, but not limited to, real property and improvements. Asset managers either oversee property management or manage the property themselves.

Attached housing: Two or more dwelling units constructed with party walls (for example, townhouses or stacked flats).

Bottom-up approach: An approach to developing an analysis based on the most disaggregated data available.

Broker: A person who, for a commission, acts as the agent of another in the process of buying, selling, leasing, or managing property rights.

Brokerage: The business of a broker that includes all the functions necessary to market a seller's property and to represent the seller's (principal's) best interests.

Build to suit: Construction of land improvements according to a tenant's or purchaser's specifications.

Building Owners and Managers Association International (BOMA): A trade association of owners and managers of apartment and office buildings.

Buildout: Construction of specific interior finishes to a tenant's specifications.

Capital: Money or property invested in an asset for the creation of wealth; alternatively, the surplus of production over consumption.

Capitalization: The process of estimating value by discounting stabilized net operating income at an appropriate rate.

Capitalization rate (cap rate): The rate, expressed as a percentage, at which a future flow of income is converted into a present value figure.

Capture rate: Percentage of total demand within a targeted market segment that a project can attract.

Cash flow analysis: The analysis of income and expenditures, usually on a year-by-year basis from the project's inception to its completion.

Central business district (CBD): The center of commercial activity within a town or city; usually the largest and oldest concentration of such activity.

Commercial real estate: Improved real estate held for the production of income through leases for commercial or business use (for example, office buildings, retail shops, and shopping centers).

Community development corporations (CDCs): Entrepreneurial institutions combining public and private resources to aid in the development of socioeconomically disadvantaged areas.

Comparable or **comparable property:** Another property to which a subject property can be compared to reach an estimate of the subject property's market value.

Comprehensive planning: Long-range planning by a local or regional government encompassing the entire area of a community and integrating all elements related to its physical development, such as housing, recreation, open space, and economic development.

Concentric zone theory: Urban development theory holding that because mobility is paramount to community growth, land uses tend to be arranged in a series of concentric, circular zones around a city's central business district.

Concession: Discount given to a prospective tenant to induce it to sign a lease, typically in the form of free rent or cash for tenant improvements.

Condominium: A form of joint ownership and control of property in which specified volumes of air space (for example, apartments) are owned individually while the common elements of the building (for example, outside walls) are jointly owned.

Construction loan: A loan made, usually by a commercial bank to a builder, for the construction of improvements on real estate with a term usually running six months to two years.

Convenience goods: Items typically purchased at the most convenient locations. They are usually not very expensive or long lasting, and their purchase involves little deliberation. Convenience goods are distinguished from shoppers' goods in retail market studies.

Credit tenant: Strong national retailers with solid credit ratings that are needed as tenants to acquire financing for a shopping center.

Demographics: Information on population characteristics by location, including such aspects as age, employment, earnings, and expenditures.

Density: The level of concentration (high or low) of buildings, including their total volume, within a given area. Density often is expressed as a ratio, for example, dwelling units per acre or floor/area ratio.

Detached housing: A freestanding dwelling unit, normally single-family, situated on its own lot.

Developer: One who prepares raw land for improvement by installing roads, utilities, and so on; also a builder (one who actually constructs improvements on real estate).

Development fee: Compensation paid to a developer in return for managing a development project on behalf of a client such as a corporation or public sector agency.

Development process: The process of preparing raw land so that it becomes suitable for the erection of buildings; generally involves clearing and grading land and installing roads and utility services.

Development team: The range of participants engaged by a developer, both public and private, to assist in the planning, design, construction, marketing, and management of a development project.

Discounted cash flow: Present value of monies to be received in the future; determined by multiplying projected cash flows by the discount factor.

Due diligence: The analytical evaluation, in a timely manner, of all reasonable considerations, including environmental, financial, legal, and other aspects, that relate to developing the property.

Econometrics: The application of statistical methods to the study of economic data and problems.

Economic driver: Industry that stimulates growth and creates spin-off jobs in a region. Economic drivers sometimes are called export industries because their products or services are exported beyond the local region.

Effective rent: Rental income after deductions for financial concessions such as no-rent periods during a lease term.

Eminent domain: The power of a public authority to condemn and take private property for public use on payment of just compensation.

Equity: That portion of an ownership interest in real property or other securities that is owned outright, that is, the value in excess of amounts financed.

Escalation clause: A provision in a lease that permits a landlord to pass through to the tenant increases in real estate taxes and operating expenses, with the tenant paying its proportional share. Also, a mortgage clause that allows the lender to increase the interest rate pursuant to the terms of the note.

Estoppel letter: A written statement made by a tenant, lender, or other party establishing certain facts and conditions with regard to a piece of real estate.

FAR (floor/area ratio): The ratio of floor area to land area, expressed as a percentage or decimal fraction, that is determined by dividing the total floor area of the building by the area of the lot. FAR typically is used as a formula to regulate building volume.

Feasibility study: A combination of a market study and an economic study that provides the investor with knowledge of both the environment in which the product exists and the expected returns from investment in it.

Fee simple absolute: The most extensive interest in land recognized by law, which is absolute ownership subject only to the limitations of police power, taxation, eminent domain, escheat, and private restrictions of record.

Fee simple determinable: Fee simple ownership that terminates on the happening (or failure to happen) of a stated condition. Also referred to as a "defeasible fee."

FIRE (finance, insurance, real estate): An employment classification used by the Department of Labor when analyzing the service industry.

Focus group: Market analysis tool in which a moderator presents a set of carefully prepared questions to a group, usually eight to 12 people, in order to collect detailed and specific information on consumer attitudes and preferences.

GAFO: In retailing, general merchandise, apparel, furniture, and other merchandise.

Garden apartments: Two- or three-story multifamily housing development that features low density, ample open space around buildings, and on-site parking.

Gravity model: Reilly's Law of Retail Gravitation states that shoppers will travel to the largest retail center that is most easily reached.

Gross income multiplier: Rule-of-thumb calculation to estimate the value of residential rental property, derived by dividing the sale price of comparable properties by their gross annual or monthly rent. It is used most often by appraisers.

Gross leasing activity: The sum of all leases signed during a given time period in a specific geopgraphic location, including renewals and leases signed in new buildings.

Ground lease: A long-term lease on a parcel of land, separate from and exclusive of the improvements on the land.

High rise: A tall building, usually more than 16 stories for office buildings or ten stories for apartment buildings.

Highest and best use: The property use that, at a given time, is deemed likely to produce the greatest net return in the forseeable future, whether or not such use is the current use of the property.

Hypermarket: A large store, generally 50,000 square feet or more, with ample parking, that sells a broad range of retail merchandise including groceries, apparel, home furnishings, and more.

Improved property: Land that has been developed.

Industrial park: A large tract of improved land used for a variety of light industrial and manufacturing uses. Users either purchase or lease individual sites.

Inflow: Retail spending from outside the trade area (see "leakage").

Infrastructure: Services and facilities including roads, highways, water, sewerage, emergency services, parks and recreation, and so on. Infrastructure can include public and private facilities.

Intelligent building: A building that incorporates technologically advanced features to facilitate communications, information processing, energy conservation, and tenant services.

International Council of Shopping Centers (ICSC): A trade association for owners, developers, and managers of shopping centers.

Joint venture: An association of two or more firms or individuals to carry on a single business enterprise for profit.

Land development: The process of preparing raw land for the construction of improvements by clearing, grading, installing utilities, and so forth.

Leakage: The portion of aggregate spendable income that is unsatisfied by existing retail offerings and escapes to retailers beyond the local trade area.

Lease: A contract that gives the lessee (the tenant) the right of possession for a period of time in return for paying rent to the lessor (the landlord).

Lease concession: A benefit given to induce a tenant to enter into a lease; usually takes the form of one month or more of free rent.

Lease-up: Period during which a real estate rental property is marketed, leasing agreements are signed, and tenants begin to move in.

Lien: The right to hold property as security until the debt that it secures is paid. A mortgage is one type of lien.

Limited partnership: A partnership that restricts the personal liability of the partners to the amount of their investment.

Loan-to-value (LTV) ratio: The relationship between the amount of a mortgage loan and the value of the real estate securing it; the loan amount divided by market value.

Location quotient: Market analysis tool used to compare local workforce estimates with national averages, derived by taking the percentages of the workforce employed in each major industry locally and dividing them by the percentages of the workforce employed in the industry groups nationally.

Low rise: A building, usually in outlying areas, with one to three stories.

Market analysis: The synthesis of supply and demand analysis in a particular market.

Market area: The geographical region from which the majority of demand and the majority of competitors are drawn.

Market niche: A subgroup within a market segment distinguishable from the rest of the segment by certain characteristics.

Market penetration: The percentage of total demand in a market area that a project captures.

Market research: A study of the needs of groups of people used to develop a product appropriate for an identifiable market segment.

Market screening: A broad overview analysis of the economics and demographics of a region.

Marquee tenants: Major tenants in an office building.

Metropolitan Statistical Area (MSA): An urban area containing multiple political jurisdictions grouped together for purposes of tabulating statistics by the U.S. Census Bureau.

Mid rise: A building with four to 15 stories.

Mixed-use development: A development, in one building or several buildings, that combines at least three significant revenue-producing uses that are physically and functionally integrated and developed in conformance with a coherent plan.

Mortgage: An instrument used in some states (rather than a deed of trust) to make real estate security for a debt. It is a two-party instrument between a mortgagor (a borrower) and a mortgagee (a lender).

Move-up housing: Typically, larger, more expensive homes that homeowners buy as their incomes increase. First homes, or "starter homes," are generally more modest in size and price.

Multifamily housing: Structures that contain more than one housing unit. The U.S. Census Bureau considers multifamily housing to be buildings with five or more housing units.

Neighborhood: A segment of a city or town with common features that distinguish it from adjoining areas.

Net absorption: The change in square feet of occupied inventory over a specified period of time, including the addition or deletion of building stock during that period of time.

Net operating income (NOI): Cash flow from rental income on a property that remains after operating expenses are deducted from gross income.

Operating budget: A budget, usually prepared a year in advance, listing projected costs of maintenance and repair for a building.

Option: The right given by the owner of property (the optionor) to another (the optionee) to purchase or lease the property at a specific price within a set time.

Pass-through: Lease provision whereby certain costs flow through directly to the tenant rather than to the owner (for example, property tax increases on a long-term lease).

Permanent loan: A long-term loan on real estate used to finance a completed development (as opposed to a construction loan).

Planned unit development (PUD): A zoning classification created to accommodate master-planned developments that include mixed uses, varied housing types, and/or unconventional subdivision designs.

Present value: The current value of an income-producing asset estimated by discounting all expected future cash flows over the holding period.

Pro forma: A financial statement that projects gross income, operating expenses, and net operating income for a future period on the basis of a set of specific assumptions.

Property life cycle: The three periods in the life of a building—the development period, the stabilization period, and the decline period.

Property manager: An individual or firm responsible for the operation of improved real estate. Management functions include leasing and supervising maintenance.

Psychographics: The study of a group's characteristics that goes beyond personal data, such as place of residence, and includes more psychological aspects, such as interests and levels of aspiration.

Purchasing power: The financial means that people possess to purchase durable and nondurable goods.

Rack rate: In hotels, the published or highest room rate charged.

Raw land: Undeveloped land without any infrastructure or other improvements.

Real estate investment trust (REIT): An ownership entity that provides limited liability and liquidity and that is exempt from U.S. income tax. Ownership is evidenced by shares of beneficial interest similar to shares of common stock.

Real estate mortgage investment conduit (REMIC): An issue of publicly traded debt securities backed by a fixed pool of mortgages that can be used as a pass-through entity for federal income tax purposes.

Realtor: A member of the National Association of Realtors®. "Realtor" is also a generic term used to describe professionals involved in selling property.

Redevelopment: The redesign or rehabilitation of existing properties.

Rent control: Limitations imposed by state or local authorities on the amount of rent a landlord can charge in certain jurisdictions.

RevPAR: A hotel's revenue per available room, calculated by multiplying annual occupancy by average room rate.

Risk: The possibility that returns on an investment or loan will not be as high as expected.

Segmentation: The classification of a population group into segments for the purpose of identifying marketing subgroups.

Shoppers' goods: Items purchased after some degree of deliberation or shopping around. Generally, they are differentiated through brand identification, the retailer's image, or the ambience of the shopping area. Purchases of shoppers' goods are made less often, and the product is typically more durable and more expensive than convenience goods.

Shopping center: Integrated and self-contained shopping area, usually in the suburbs.

Single-family housing: A dwelling unit, either attached or detached, designed for use by one household and with direct access to a street. It does not share heating facilities or other essential building facilities with any other dwelling.

Stabilization: In appraisal, the use of one year's typical property income and expenses plus annualized capital reserve expenditures to represent each year's income stream.

Subdivision: Division of a parcel of land into building lots. A subdivision can also include streets, parks, schools, utilities, and other public facilities.

Submarket: A geographic area usually surrounding a site that will provide a substantial portion of the customers for a real estate project.

Tenant: One who rents from another.

Tenant allowance: A cash payment made by the developer to a tenant (usually of income-producing property) to enable the tenant, rather than the developer, to complete the interior construction finish and/or fixturing work for the leased premises.

Tenant improvements: Improvements made to the property at the tenant's expense.

Tenant mix: The combination of various types of tenants in a leased building.

Title: Evidence of ownership of real property to indicate a person's right to possess, use, and dispose of property.

Top-down approach: An approach to developing an analysis based on first using aggregated data.

Total-marketing concept: The process of determining consumer desires, producing a product to match those desires, and persuading the consumer to purchase or rent that product.

Townhouse: Single-family attached residence separated from another by party walls, usually on a narrow lot offering small front- and backyards; also called a rowhouse.

Trade area: Geographic area from which a retail facility consistently draws most of its customers; also called market area.

Warehouse: A building that is used for the storage of goods or merchandise and that can be occupied by the owner or leased to one or more tenants.

Zoning: Classification and regulation of land by local governments according to use categories (zones); often includes density designations as well.